FUTURE WARS

FUTURE WARS

THE WORLD'S MOST DANGEROUS FLASHPOINTS

**Col. Trevor N. Dupuy,
U.S. Army (Ret.)**

WARNER BOOKS

A Time Warner Company

COLLABORATORS

Four of my colleagues have collaborated with me in the preparation of this book, and are truly co-authors. They are:

C. Curtiss Johnson, Vice President for Research, HERO-TNDA, Publishers and Researchers, Inc. Curt helped me to organize and co-ordinate the work on this book. He devoted particular attention to the chapter on South Africa, as well as carefully reviewing each chapter.

David L. Bongard, Research Associate at HERO-TNDA. Dave worked on the chapters on Hungary–Romania, Nicaragua–Honduras, Korea and China–USSR/CIS.

Richard C. Anderson, Jr., Research Associate at HERO-TNDA. Rich worked on the chapters on Libya–Egypt and Iran–Iraq.

L. Jay Karamales, Jr., Research Associate at HERO-TNDA. Jay worked on the chapters on India–Pakistan and on the Soviet Union/CIS.

I am greatly indebted to the contributions each of these colleagues made to this book.

First published in 1992 by Sidgwick & Jackson Limited, Cavaye Place, London.

Warner Books, Inc., 1271 Avenue of the Americas, New York, NY 10020

 A Time Warner Company

Printed in the United States of America
First U.S. Printing: January 1993
10 9 8 7 6 5 4 3 2 1

Library of Congress Cataloging-in-Publication Data

Dupuy, Trevor Nevit.
    Future wars : the world's most dangerous flashpoints / T.N. Dupuy.
      p.   cm.
    ISBN 0-446-51670-8
    1. Imaginary wars and battles. I. Title.
  U313.D85   1993
  355.4'8—dc20   91-51167
                                            CIP

CONTENTS

LIST OF MAPS

EGYPT'S WAR WITH LIBYA AND SUDAN

THE SINO–RUSSIAN CONFLICT

LIST OF TABLES

THE SINO–RUSSIAN CONFLICT

TNDM statistics

INTRODUCTION

ABOUT THIS BOOK

The world does not seem to have become less dangerous with the end of the Cold War. When, some months ago, in company with my colleagues at HERO-TNDA, Publishers and Researchers, Inc., I surveyed the dramatically evolving world scene in order to try to predict where war might break out in the next five years, more than twenty possible candidate situations emerged.

We decided to examine ten of these situations in some detail in order to see not only why such a war would break out, but also how it would be likely to be fought in each instance. To assist us in our evaluation of the results of these ten wars, we decided to analyze some of the battles with the assistance of an analytical tool I developed a few years ago. This tool is the Tactical Numerical Deterministic Model (TNDM), a computerized combat simulation which is used in several defense ministries around the world. It is described in general terms below, and in more technical terms in the Appendix B to this book.

During the course of our survey of the possibilities of future wars, our candidate list grew and then contracted. Of course, at different times during the process, it looked as though first one, and then another, of our candidate situations would break out into actual war before we had a chance to finish and publish our predictive analyses. And, of course, this could still happen between completion of the analysis, which has now become a book manuscript, and the publication of that book.

In writing each chapter, I calculated when the war described in that chapter would be likely to break out. Having selected the date, I then wrote each chapter from the standpoint of a historian writing retrospectively about this hypothetical war as though it had occurred a year or two earlier. Thus, each chapter starts as true history and at some point (around late 1991) becomes hypothetical history, or fiction.

Some of the individuals mentioned in these pseudo-historical chapters are real people. Others, particularly those appearing on the scene during the transition from historical fact to fiction, are purely imaginary. However, the words, thoughts, and actions attributed to these individuals, be they real or fictional, particularly after 1991, are completely imaginary. No one should think that the real people would necessarily have spoken, thought, or acted as here portrayed should the fictional circumstances ever be approximated in reality.

I make no claim to clairvoyance. Thus, this book is not intended as a prediction. Rather, it is speculation, presenting what *might* happen under certain circumstances in ten of the possible 'flashpoints' or trouble spots around a troubled world. I hope the reader enjoys the results of my speculation as much as I have enjoyed speculating.

One question that bothered me, as we approached the end of the process, was how to determine the sequence of chapters, each of which, with one minor exception, is self-contained. I finally decided that the simplest way was to ignore chronological sequence and to put them in the order of the sequence in which they were prepared.

THE MODERN BATTLEFIELD

The reader will look in vain for descriptions of employment of modern weapons in the high-technology fashion employed by US forces in the Kuwait (or Gulf) war in January and February 1991. Where are the 'smart bombs', the 'stealth' intruders, laser-guided cruise missiles, stand-off air attacks, night vision devices, and the like? Rather, the battlefield activities will seem more like those of the 1973 Arab–Israeli war, or the 1982 Falkland war. There is a reason for this perception.

I have not ignored either of the effects of the new weapons, or the experience of the Gulf war. In fact, the chapters in this book assume that many ultra-modern weapons and techniques are being used on both sides, but have not had the same kind of effect as they did in the Gulf war. One reason is that no two wars are alike, and all of those in this book are very different from that of the UN coalition against Iraq. In that war most of Iraq's sophisticated weapons were knocked out by the allies in the first few hours of the conflict, and the US and its allies were able at relative leisure both to test and to demonstrate the virtuosity of their amazing new weapons.

In these wars I have assumed that neither side has weapons as exotic as some of those used by the US Air Force in January and February 1991. For instance, only the US has 'stealth fighters'. Most of the contestants in these wars are assumed to have a few – but very few – 'smart bombs', and it can be further assumed that they will not waste such scarce and costly weapons. None of the contestants in these wars will (for a variety of reasons) fire long-range surface-to-surface missiles at their enemy's cities, and thus there is no reason for any of them to demonstrate that they have anything comparable to the famous 'Patriot' anti-missile missile. All contestants will unquestionably use night vision devices, but this is nothing new; earlier versions of these were used by both sides in 1973.

Except in the two instances in which US forces are involved in a small way, all the contestants will be equipped with quite modern – but not ultra-modern – armed forces, and they appear to be relatively equally matched. Therefore, it is not surprising that most of these wars are in many ways reminiscent of 1973. But none of them is a re-run of that war.

ACKNOWLEDGMENTS

As the author of this book, I am responsible for all of its contents, and each of the chapter situations is based upon my own assessments – assisted in each instance by one or more of four colleagues. In some chapters this assistance has included the preparation of extensive drafts, based upon my outlines. In each such case I have adapted the materials prepared by my collaborators to fit into my concept of the book. In other instances, I am responsible from the beginning to the end of the chapter, although I have of course profited from colleagues' advice and comments.

Thus, while I am unequivocally the author of the book, and bear full responsibility for it, it is a truly collaborative effort, and – as acknowledged elsewhere – I am deeply indebted to all of my colleagues.

I wish also to express my appreciation for assistance from old friends in the preparation of two of the chapters: that on the sixth Arab–Israeli War, and the one on the Soviet Civil War.

Those who contributed to Chapter One are: Maj. Gen. M.D. Zohdy, retired, of the Egyptian Army, one of the most respected military analysts of the Arab world; Dr. Meir Pa'il, a retired colonel of the Israeli Army, a noted military historian and analyst, and former member of the Knesset; and Dr. Mordechai Gichon, one of Israel's leading archaeologists, a professor of history at Tel Aviv University, and a reserve colonel of the Israeli Army. All of them responded most helpfully to a series of questions that I posed to them. But none of them has seen the chapter in its final form, and none bears the slightest responsibility for either the concept or the specifics of the chapter.

Four people assisted me by providing advice about the chapter on the Soviet Civil War. These were Harriet F. Scott; her husband, Col. William F. Scott, USAF, Retired, PhD.; Col. Graham Vernon, USA, Retired, PhD.; and Lt. Col. John Sloan, USA, Retired. Harriet Scott is perhaps the most knowledgeable person in the US regarding military personalities in the USSR. She began to acquire this knowledge while living in Moscow with her husband, who was twice the US Air Attache there. They are now both consultants to the US Government on Soviet military affairs. I met Graham Vernon, now a professor at the Defense Intelligence College, in Moscow, when he was the Army Attache there. John Sloan, a specialist on Russian history, has been an intelligence analyst and official both in uniform and since he retired. All four have travelled around the US with me, lecturing on the Soviet armed forces. I am indebted to them for their comments on the chapter.

T. N. Dupuy
McLean, Virginia
August 1991

FUTURE WARS

CHAPTER ONE

A WAR FOR PEACE:
The Sixth Arab–Israeli War

BACKGROUND

On 29 September 1993 the Jerusalem *Post*, Israel's highly respected English-language newspaper, carried an unusual front page editorial, entitled 'Back to 1973?'. After noting that the twentieth anniversary of the beginning of the Yom Kippur War – as the Israelis call the October war of 1973 – was exactly one month away, the editorial drew attention to how similar the regional situation was, on that date, to what it had been on the same date in 1973. Threatening concentrations of Syrian forces were carrying out manoeuvres south-west of Damascus, so disposed that they could easily turn to strike Israel's north-eastern frontier with overwhelming force. Equally threatening concentrations of Egyptian troops were involved in similar manoeuvres just west of the Suez Canal, capable of a sudden thrust eastward across the Canal and across Sinai toward the heart of Israel.

'At that time,' began the concluding paragraph of the editorial, 'our leaders were convinced that this was all bluff and bluster, and that the Arabs would not attack. But they did attack, and they came close to winning the war in the first seventy-two hours. Today our leaders tell us that an attack this time is not likely, because the situation is better for Israel, and the Arab governments cannot survive another defeat. Yes, the situation is better for Israel today in some respects. But it is worse in others, and in one respect far worse. At that time we could count on the support of the United States. And we received that support when we needed it. But today the Arab threat is even more dangerous, and US support is very much in doubt. How could our government allow this to happen?'

How, indeed, many Israelis were asking one another; how had this happened?

A little more than forty-five years earlier – 14 May 1948 – Israel had declared its independence, even as it was mobilising its small population to meet five Arab armies invading from the north (Lebanon), the north-east (Syria), the east (Iraq and Transjordan) and the south (Egypt). Almost miraculously, it had seemed, the remarkably well-prepared, even if hastily mobilised, Israeli forces repelled four of these invasions, and fought the fifth (from Transjordan) to a stalemate. An uneasy truce followed this successful defensive war, and Israel gained its independence. But the state of war continued. While active hostilities were suspended, there was no peace, and in the ensuing forty-five years the violence of war had smouldered beneath a surface of relative calm and tranquillity. But over that time there had been four more episodes of full-scale armed conflict – in 1956, 1967, 1973 and 1982 – and countless other brief but violent eruptions.

Despite the seemingly overwhelming numerical superiority of the Arab world that nearly encircled their country, the Israelis had been successful in each of these conflicts. Although this was due largely to the legendary military prowess of the Jewish state, not a little of the Israeli success – as the Jerusalem *Post* editorial hinted – had been a consequence of firm support from the US.

The state of Israel had emerged from the 1948 War of Independence with a very vulnerable land frontier, and the implacable enmity of the defeated neighbour (or near-neighbour) states of Lebanon, Syria, Iraq, Jordan and Egypt. These Arab nations had recognised that their humiliation by the tiny Jewish republic was due mainly to their own prior unpreparedness, and had been determined to rectify this failure as soon as possible, so that they could 'drive the Jews into the sea'. They refused to recognise the independence of Israel, and even tried to deny the very existence of 'the Jewish entity', as they called Israel when it could not be ignored. Egypt's defeat in the 1956 war did not really change this state of affairs since that was – with considerable reason – attributed by the Arabs to the Suez Canal intervention against Egypt by Great Britain and France.

In 1967, however, after the Arab 'confrontation states' had substantially strengthened their armed forces, came the remarkable and overwhelming Israeli victory over Egypt, Jordan and Syria in the 'Six-Day War'. Suddenly it was realised by the Arabs – and the rest of the world – that Israel was a power of significance far exceeding its tiny size, and was, in fact, militarily the most powerful nation in the Middle East. Israel had conquered from Egypt the sizeable desert region of Sinai, and the populous Palestinian enclave of the Gaza Strip; Israeli troops had seized from Jordan the remainder of Arab Palestine, the so-called West Bank of the Jordan River; and they had overrun Syria's Golan Heights, a small but strategically significant region south-west of the Syrian capital of Damascus.

Although chastened by their defeat, the Arabs' enmity toward Israel was in no way diminished by the results of the Six-Day War. They redoubled their efforts to build up military strength that would enable them to defeat Israel and recover their lost territories. (There was less rhetoric about 'driving the Jews into the sea', however, although that thought remained on most Arab minds.)

On 22 November 1967 the United Nations Security Council passed its Resolution 242, an effort to resolve the Arab–Israeli conflict. In summary, its even-handed provisions were:

1   acquisition of territory by war was 'inadmissible' (favours the Arabs);
2   a just and lasting Middle-East peace should include:
    (a) withdrawal of Israeli forces from territories occupied (favours the Arabs);
    (b) termination of belligerency (favours Israel);
    (c) acknowledgement of sovereignty, territorial integrity and political independence of states within secure and recognised boundaries (slightly favours Israel);
3   affirmation of the necessity for:
    (a) freedom of navigation through international waterways (slightly favours Israel);
    (b) just settlement of 'the refugee problem' (slightly favours the Arabs; this is the only mention of the 'Palestinian problem' in the resolution);
    (c) territorial inviolability and independence of every state through measures including demilitarised zones (slightly favours Israel).

From this resolution emerged the concept, still debated in Israel, of 'trading land for peace'. In other words, if the Arabs were to agree to 'a just and lasting peace', to include an end to belligerency, and recognition of Israel, in turn Israel should be willing to return occupied territories to the Arab nations from which they had been seized, subject to some modification of the pre-war frontiers to give Israel 'secure and recognised boundaries'. However, a large proportion of Israelis, probably a majority, were convinced that to have secure frontiers Israel must retain all of the West Bank and the Golan Heights.

Arabs were also ambivalent about Resolution 242. They liked the provisions for Israeli withdrawal from 'territories occupied' but were not yet ready to terminate belligerency or to recognise Israeli sovereignty. Significantly, despite lip-service, few Arabs (other than the Palestinians) were concerned by the scant attention the resolution gave to the 'Palestinian problem'.

Palestinian refugees, however, did their best to keep this problem constantly on the mind of other Arabs. They established, under the leadership of Yasser Arafat, the Palestine Liberation Organisation (PL), an association of a number of groups of militant Palestinian refugees. The PLO was dedicated to regaining some or all of the lands lost to Israel in 1948 and 1967, by a combination of terrorism, propaganda and anti-Israeli diplomatic activity. In 1970 and 1971 the PLO actually tried to seize control of Jordan, but this attempt was firmly suppressed militarily by Jordanian King Hussein, and most of the defeated PLO militants fled to Lebanon.

Two years (1968–70) of low-level hostilities between Egypt and Israel (called the War of Attrition), mostly involving the exchange of artillery and missile fire across the Suez Canal, did not change the situation. It did change somewhat, however, as a result of the October 1973 war (called the War of Ramadan by the Arabs, the Yom Kippur War by the Israelis). In surprise attacks that precipitated the war, the Egyptians and Syrians inflicted initial defeats upon the Israelis, regaining some of the pride lost in ignominious defeat in 1967. The Israelis recovered with remarkable rapidity from those defeats, and had the better of the last half of that war, but it was far from an overwhelming victory. Israeli confidence had been badly shaken by the apparent imminence of defeat in the opening days of the war, and it was never fully recovered.

One result of that loss of confidence was a growing debate in Israel about 'trading land for peace'. However, the right-wing Likkud government, which has controlled Israel during most of the period since the 1973 war, was strongly opposed to making any territorial concessions. It was particularly adamant about retaining the West Bank (referred to by the Likkud leaders as Judaea and Samaria, the ancient names of the region) which, despite its large Arab population, government leaders saw as an area for future Jewish population expansion. In the West Bank and in the Gaza Strip, as well as on the Golan Heights, the government initiated a policy of setting up Israeli settlements, in part to make it more difficult for any future government to give up any of this territory.

The Likkud government did, however, make one positive 'land for peace' deal: with Egypt, following the dramatic visit of Egyptian President Anwar Sadat to Jerusalem in 1977. With the active negotiating involvement of American President Jimmy Carter, the Camp David Accord was agreed between President Sadat and Israeli Prime Minister Menachim Begin. This was ratified on 26 March 1979 by a treaty in which, in return for peace and recognition, Israel restored Sinai to Egypt.

Syrian hostility towards Israel remained implacable, however, and was reciprocated by Israel. Syrian President Hafez el Assad gave covert (and not so covert) support and assistance to Palestinian refugees who had strongly established themselves in southern Lebanon in the mid-1970s. From these bases the PLO undertook a campaign of terrorism and long-range artillery and missile harassment against northern Israel. An Israeli invasion of southern Lebanon in 1978, intended to drive the Palestinians from these positions, achieved little except to arouse anti-Israeli sentiment around the world. Under pressure from the UN, the Israelis soon withdrew. The PLO took advantage of a civil war in Lebanon (which it had, in fact, precipitated) to strengthen its hold on southern Lebanon, from which the PLO had eliminated the authority of the Lebanese government. Syria also took advantage of the chaos to occupy much of east-central Lebanon. Despite Israeli air retaliation, the PLO intensified raids and missile firings against Israel from south Lebanon bases.

In June 1982, in a much larger and more carefully planned operation, the Israelis again invaded southern Lebanon. Israeli Defence Minister Ariel ('Arik') Sharon, a noted Israeli general in the 1967 and 1973 wars, in apparent defiance of Prime Minister Begin and the rest of the Cabinet, seems to have deliberately enticed Syrian intervention. The Israeli Army then inflicted a crushing defeat upon Syrian forces in Lebanon's Bekaa Valley. With Beirut – and in it, the PLO leader Yasser Arafat – within his grasp, Sharon (who was under great pressure from an indignant Cabinet, and a largely indignant Israeli population) seems to have lost his nerve, and agreed to a cease-fire.

The Israelis had initially been greeted by the Lebanese as liberators from their Palestinian oppressors. However, they soon wore out their welcome, and the next year again withdrew from most of southern Lebanon. The bad press reaction the Israelis had received around the world as a result of their 1982 invasion of Lebanon was not improved as the Likkud government – now under the leadership of Yitzhak Shamir – continued to establish Israeli settlements in the occupied West Bank, with the clear intent of impeding any implementation of UN Resolution 242. Israeli popularity around the world declined further when, beginning in late 1987, a low-intensity Palestinian revolt – called 'the Intifada' (or resistance) – spread throughout the West Bank and the Gaza Strip. Stern Israeli measures kept the uprising under control, but the result was to spread across the world an image of a militaristic Israel suppressing a popular uprising by use of excessive force. The founding of Israel had been in large part due to worldwide sympathy for the suffering of the Jews at the hands of German Nazis during the Holocaust of World War II.

Although the comparison was wildly overdrawn, nonetheless the Israelis were now being compared to the Nazis in their treatment of the Palestinians.

PEACE CONFERENCE AND WAR CLOUDS

The Israelis, nevertheless, had largely suppressed the Intifada before the Middle East Peace Conference was held, in Geneva, in November 1991. That conference had been convened on 28 October under the joint chairmanship of US President Bush and President Gorbachev of the USSR. After the opening ceremonies were over, the two presidents left conduct of the conference to their foreign ministers: American Secretary of State James Baker and Soviet Foreign Minister Boris Pankin. The Arab confrontation states – Syria, Lebanon and Jordan – were represented by their foreign ministers; the Jordanian delegation included a highly articulate sub-delegation of Palestinians from the West Bank. Prime Minister Yitzhak Shamir represented Israel, apparently because he feared that Foreign Minister David Levy might be too willing to compromise.

Despite the efforts of Baker, Pankin and their assistants, the conference soon bogged down, since the Arabs and the Israelis merely talked at each other. However, subsequent meetings were held in Washington – despite objections by the Israelis, who wanted the follow-up meetings to take place in the capitals of the conferees in the Middle East, which would have meant at least a de facto recognition of Israel by the three Arab governments.

At the second of these meetings, in mid-January 1992, procedural wrangling seemed to give way to tentative substantive discussions. This led to a political upheaval in Israel. On 19 January two small right-wing parties, Tehiya and Moledet – with a total representation of four in the Knesset – withdrew from Shamir's government, to protest this tiny advance in the peace process. Resigning Science Minister Yuval Neeman of Tehiya said this could only lead to Palestinian autonomy, which he called 'a mortal danger to the state of Israel'. This right-wing defection reduced the Likkud strength in the 120-member Knesset to 59 votes, virtually assuring the early collapse of the government. Shamir bore this blow to his government with remarkable equanimity. He prepared for new elections, and went on television to tell the Israeli people that the peace process would continue despite the election campaign. However, his principal opponent, Shimon Perez, leader of the Labour Party, demanded that the peace process be suspended, since, as he said, 'no serious negotiations would be possible since [Shamir's government] would simply use the negotiation sessions to posture before the electorate'.

Not known at the time was the convoluted conspiracy that was behind these political events in Israel. It has since been revealed that Shamir and the leaders of the two tiny right-wing parties had secretly agreed in advance that they would resign. Despite the apparent setback, the political advantages of this to Shamir were tremendous. It meant that – for all practical purposes – the peace process would indeed be halted until after the Israeli elections. This was to the mutual benefit of Shamir and the right-wingers; both were counting on the possibility that this turn of events would cause the Arabs to break off the negotiations. It also helped Shamir in his pre-election campaign. He could appeal to the centrists of the Israeli electorate as the man who had initiated, and who was determined to continue, the peace negotiations with the Arabs. He could also remind his normal, right-wing, constituency of his staunch and consistent refusal to give up Judea and Samaria to the Palestinians, or to give up the Golan Heights to Syria. At worst the peace process would be delayed for six months to a year. At best the Arabs would be so frustrated that they would break off negotiations. And the leaders of the Tehiya and Moledet parties agreed that after the elections they would rejoin Shamir's party to form a government, if their support were needed.

But what Shamir did not know, at the time, was that the leaders of the two right-wing parties were also meeting secretly with his greatest rival in the Likkud: Housing Minister Ariel Sharon. They assured Sharon that, if again the election should result in a virtually even split between the Likkud Party and the Labour Party, they would support Sharon as the leader of Likkud, rather than Shamir, if he would agree in advance to abandon the peace process. Sharon agreed.

The election in June 1992 gave the Labor and Likkud parties (and their splinter party allies) each fifty-eight Knesset seats. Sharon was able to show the leaders of the Likkud Party that, with the assistance of the four Tehiya and Moledet seats, he could form a majority government, whereas Shamir could not. As a result, control of the Likkud shifted from Shamir to Sharon, who thereupon became the Prime Minister of Israel.

Sharon had for years been one of the strongest proponents of Jewish settlements in the West Bank and Gaza Strip. He now used the influx of Jewish immigrants from the former Soviet Union as an excuse for expanding and expediting the settlement programme. This had two principal results. First there was an intensification of the Intifada, as violence spread throughout the West Bank and Gaza Strip, despite the efforts of the Israeli Army to restore order. Second, the Palestinians received worldwide sympathy, and the Israelis equally intense opprobrium. Anti-Israeli feeling was particularly outspoken in the US, where newspapers traditionally supportive of Israel roundly criticised the Israeli government in general, and Sharon in particular, for the settlement policy and the brutal suppression of Palestinians.

More ominous, in March 1993, Egypt broke diplomatic relations with Israel, and called an emergency meeting of the Arab League in Cairo. The press noted that the Arab heads of state attending the meeting all brought their senior military officials with them. Significantly, while the political leaders were meeting in the Arab League headquarters near the Nile River, the military were conferring in the massive Egyptian Ministry of Defence building (the 'Cairo Pentagon') near the outskirts of the city. Meanwhile, the newspapers of the world were full of photographs of warm greetings being exchanged among Assad of Syria, Saddam Hussein of Iraq, King Hussein of Jordan, King Fahd of Saudi Arabia and Mubarak of Egypt.

On 20 April 1993 the Arab League published a remarkable document, called 'the Cairo Proclamation of Ramadan' (the meeting was being held during the Muslim holy season of Ramadan). The provisions of the Proclamation as issued to the press were as follows:

> The Arab League – aware that Arab brethren in the historic region of Palestine are being denied their normal rights by brutal suppressive actions of the Israeli government – nonetheless is aware of fears among the people of Israel that can at least explain, if not justify, such actions. Accordingly, the Arab League has unanimously agreed that the League, and all of its members, are prepared to carry out the provisions of United Nations Resolution 242 of 1967, and unconditionally to recognise the State of Israel, subject to the acceptance by Israel of all of the provisions of said Resolution 242, in accordance with the following terms which we believe are consistent with that Resolution:
>
> 1   Withdrawal of Israeli occupying forces from the following territories:
>   (a) The West Bank of the Jordan River, as it existed on 4 June 1967, subject to the provisions regarding boundaries, demilitarised and extraterritorial areas, and withdrawal procedures in paras 6, 7, 8 and 9, below.
>   (b) The Gaza Strip, as it existed on 4 June 1967, subject to the provisions regarding boundaries, demilitarised and extraterritorial areas, and withdrawal procedures in paras 6, 7, 8 and 9, below.

(c) The Golan Heights region of south-western Syria subject to the provisions regarding boundaries, demilitarised and extra-territorial areas, and withdrawal procedures in paras 6, 7, 8 and 9, below.

2 Recognition by all members of the Arab League of the sovereignty of the State of Israel.

3 Recognition by Israel of the sovereignty of the State of Palestine, to consist of the areas now known as the West Bank and the Gaza Strip.

4 Negotiation and signature of peace treaties between:
(a) Israel and Syria
(b) Israel and Jordan
(c) Israel and Lebanon
(d) Israel and Iraq.

5 All members of the Arab League are prepared to recognise, by declaration or by treaty, the following:
(a) West Jerusalem as the capital of Israel;
(b) the boundaries established pursuant to the provisions of para. 6, below;
(c) the demilitarised areas established pursuant to para. 7, below.

6 Boundary adjustments, to be established at a conference under the auspices of the United Nations, in accordance with the following general guidelines:
(a) For the West Bank:
    (i) movement of boundaries by as much as 10 kilometres in either direction;
    (ii) area of the West Bank with adjusted boundaries to be between 99 and 101 per cent of the area on 4 June 1967.
(b) For the Gaza Strip:
    (i) movement of boundaries by as much as 5 kilometres in either direction;
    (ii) area of the Gaza Strip with adjusted boundaries to be between 99 and 101 per cent of the area on 4 June 1967.

7 Demilitarised areas or zones will be established as indicated below. Specific provisions with respect to limitations on equipment, size and deployment of specific forces will be established in negotiations between representatives of Israel and the Arab League, under the auspices of the United Nations.
(a) Palestine, general. The armed forces of the State of Palestine will consist only of lightly armed ground forces; they will have no armoured vehicles over 10 tons gross weight; cannon and mortars will not exceed 110 mm in calibre; they may

have only unarmed observation aircraft, and unarmed patrol vessels.

(b) West Bank. Except for border guards of agreed composition at agreed border crossing points, no Palestinian military forces will be permitted within 10 kilometres of the boundary with Israel.

(c) Gaza Strip. Except for border guards of agreed composition at agreed crossing points, no Palestinian military forces will be permitted within 5 kilometres of the boundary with Israel.

(d) Golan Heights. Except for border guards of agreed composition at agreed crossing points, no military forces of Syria will be permitted in the region now known as the Golan Heights.

8   Extraterritorial areas will be established as shown below. Specific provisions, such as size of areas, limitations in equipment size and on deployment of specific forces in those areas, and provisions as to access, will be established in negotiations between representatives of Israel and the Arab League, under the auspices of the United Nations.

(a) West Bank. Three Israeli observation posts, with a total area no greater than 150 square kilometres, may be established by Israel in the area now known as the West Bank.

(b) Gaza Strip. One Israeli observation post, with a total area of no more than 10 square kilometres, may be established by Israel in the area now known as the Gaza Strip.

(c) Golan Heights. One Israeli observation post, with a total area of no more than 50 square kilometres, may be established by Israel in the area now known as the Golan Heights.

(d) Holy Places in Jerusalem. One or more enclaves, under United Nations control, will be established in or near Jerusalem to assure protection of, and unhindered access to, places or shrines considered holy to the Hebrew, Islamic and Christian religions.

(e) Land route from West Bank to Gaza Strip. A route for unfettered travel of Palestinians between the West Bank and the Gaza Strip will be established under provisions which ensure that there will be no military threat to Israel.

9   Israeli withdrawals from occupied territories will be scheduled in such a fashion as to cause the least possible disruption of Israeli civilians living in those areas. Such civilians will be permitted to remain in those areas, if they wish, with dual citizenship.

10 The Arab League is prepared to modify, amend or expand the provisions of this proclamation as may seem appropriate on the basis of a Preliminary Conference between representatives of the Arab League and the State of Israel, under the auspices of the United Nations.

11 If Israel refuses either to accept the provisions of this proclamation, or to meet at the proposed Preliminary Conference, within 90 days, the Arab League and its members reserve the right to take such action as may appear appropriate to help establish peace and tranquillity in the West Bank and Gaza Strip.

Reaction in Israel to the Ramadan Proclamation was varied, both in immediacy and in nature. Prime Minister Sharon responded to questions in the Knesset and from the press with an unvarying statement: 'The Government of Israel will study the proclamation. Until such study is complete, neither I nor any member of the Government will have any comment whatsoever.' All members of the Cabinet gave the same, or a similar, response to questions from media reporters.

Yitzakh Rabin, the new leader of the Labour Party, was somewhat more forthcoming than the Prime Minister, but not much. 'It is an interesting proposal,' he said. 'It is remarkably even-handed, given its source. That the Arabs were able to agree on this unanimously is in itself worthy of notice. It seems to contain some provisions that Israel would have great difficulty in accepting. My colleagues and I shall study the Proclamation very carefully, and will present our views privately to the Government as soon as possible.'

Uri Dan, formerly a close associate of the Prime Minister, and believed to represent the point of view of the Likkud, was less restrained. 'This is an Arab trap,' he said. 'They demand concessions from Israel that would throw away the security we gained in the Six-Day War, and confirmed in the Yom Kippur War, at the cost of much Israeli blood and treasure. No Israeli worthy of his religion or his national heritage could dream of accepting these terms. But it is a trap, I say, because it has been presented in an apparently conciliatory fashion, to gain support from liberals in America and Europe who are ready to join the United Nations in demands that will irreparably threaten the security of Israel. Furthermore,' Dan added derisively, 'Paragraph 11 of the so-called Cairo Proclamation means that it is really the "Cairo Ultimatum". How can we negotiate with a gun held at our head?'

A very different point of view was presented by Meier Pa'il, former member of the Knesset, prolific author, and spokesman for the 'Peace

Now' movement. 'The Arab League has produced a remarkable document,' he said. 'I cannot endorse every provision, and I doubt if any member of our "Peace Now" group could or would offer such blanket endorsement. But this is a serious move toward peace. I agree with the former Defence Minister [Rabin] that the fact that the Arabs were able to agree upon this unanimously is worthy of our attention. In any event, it is a splendid basis for negotiation, and offers promise that – if we Israelis remain open-minded – negotiations can be fruitful.'

Ze'ev Schiff, one of Israeli's most respected journalists, took a position between Dan and Pa'il. He said: 'I agree with Meierky [Pa'il] that the Cairo Proclamation of Ramadan is a serious move toward peace. It is not merely a propaganda document. Nor do I agree with Uri Dan that it is an ultimatum. On the other hand, it contains provisions that must be unacceptable to Israel, and which ignore the security we won at such heavy cost in past wars. Nevertheless, it is doubtful if we can ever get a less biased document as the basis for starting serious negotiations.'

As the Arabs had undoubtedly hoped, and as the Israelis obviously feared, world reaction to the Cairo Proclamation was generally favourable. The US government publicly and privately urged the Israeli government to agree at the very least to the Preliminary Conference which had been suggested in the two final paragraphs of the Proclamation.

The Israeli government remained quiet for nearly two months, while vigorous debate swirled in Israel, in newspapers, on radio and television, and at almost every social gathering of two or more Israelis. Finally, Sharon broke his silence. In a radio and television address to his fellow countrymen on 29 June, he rejected the Arab League initiative. He closed his brief announcement with the following words:

We are asked to meet with the Arab League under the auspices of the United Nations. For nearly half a century the Arab League has been trying to destroy our nation. From bitter experience we know that we cannot trust the United Nations, with its rampant anti-Semitism. This is like asking the lamb to meet with the tiger in the lair of the lion.

But, most important, Israel can never abandon Samaria and Judaea [the West Bank]. This is the heart of our homeland, integral to the ancient land of Israel, which we have inherited, and which we have consolidated through the sacrifices of thousands of Israeli fighting men over the past forty-four years. To give up the land that has always been ours, and for which we paid so heavily in recent wars, would be a betrayal of our brave martyrs, would be a betrayal of our forefathers, would be a betrayal of the Zionist heritage of our nation, and would be a betrayal of those who follow behind us! The Palestinians have a homeland on the other side of the River Jordan. Let those of them remaining on our soil move away and join their brethren in a Palestinian nation on the East Bank. We have fought for what is rightly ours, and if we must, we can and will fight again. Even if – God forbid – we should be defeated in battle, it would be better to follow the example of the brave men and women of Masada than to allow ourselves once more to be led meekly to the slaughterhouse in a new Holocaust!

It is not unlikely that a number of the Arab leaders who had reluctantly agreed to the Ramadan Proclamation were greatly relieved by Sharon's rejection. Yasser Arafat, in a fiery speech to his followers in Tunis, assured them and all Arabs that Sharon would soon get the new Masada for which he was asking. There were similar speeches throughout the Arab world.

The Arab League officially denounced Israel for having rejected its peace offer. The Intifada continued unabated; if anything violence increased throughout the West Bank, and more Israeli reservists were called to active duty to contain the increasingly bloody insurrection. Heads of state in most Arab countries deplored Israel's 'brutal' treatment of the Palestinian people.

More ominous, however, was evidence of renewed meetings of senior military personnel from several Arab countries, which soon came to the attention of the intelligence services of Israel and other nations. It was duly noted that representatives from Egypt, Syria, Jordan and Saudi Arabia were always present at these meetings, with less regular attendance by military men from Morocco, Algeria and Oman. The absence of Libyans and Iraqis was also noted.

On 17 and 18 July there was a summit meeting at the small desert palace of Jordan's King Hussein at the Azraq oasis. Attending were Presidents Mubarak of Egypt and Assad of Syria. Among uniformed men in attendance two Saudi Arabian generals were noted. Both before and after the summit Hussein visited Riyadh to meet with King Fadh. There was no announcement or press release after the meeting.

BUILD-UP OF FORCES

By early August it was evident that reserves had been called up in Syria, Jordan and Egypt. Syrian units in eastern Lebanon were reinforced. There was apparently a build-up of other Syrian forces south and west of

Damascus. Meanwhile, the Egyptian Army had begun large-scale manoeuvres just west of the Suez Canal. Saudi Arabian aircraft were concentrating at north-western airfields at Tabuk, Ha'il, Jawf, Turayf and Ar'ar. Three of Saudi Arabia's five E-3A electronic surveillance aircraft were believed to have been moved to the Ha'il air base in the north central part of the country.

Because of the rupture of diplomatic relations with Egypt, Israel no longer had a channel to demand information from, or issue warnings to, any of the nations exhibiting this increasing evidence of military hostility. The Israeli government therefore requested the US to ask the four Arab nations for explanations of their activities. The only responses to this initiative were public demands from the Arab League and from several Arab states – including Egypt, Syria, Jordan and Saudi Arabia – that Israel accept the principle of the Ramadan Proclamation and agree to attend the Preliminary Conference suggested by it. At the very least, the Arab leaders asserted, in statements that had obviously been co-ordinated, if Israel truly wanted peace it should respond positively with an alternative peace proposal.

Prime Minister Sharon took note of the Arab statements at a press conference in early September. He reminded the Arabs of what happened to them in their five previous military confrontations with Israel. 'We do not want war,' he said, 'but if they ask for it, we shall smash them again!' He ordered a partial mobilisation of the Israeli Army.

In late September American Secretary of State James Baker made a flying visit to the Middle East. He stopped first at Cairo, then went on to Jerusalem, Damascus, Amman and Riyadh. He then returned to Israel, and a long meeting with Prime Minister Sharon. A scheduled joint press conference following the meeting was cancelled without explanation, and an obviously furious Secretary Baker stalked out of the Prime Minister's residence, climbed into his limousine and returned to his plane. Baker refused to speak to reporters or to answer their shouted questions. But on the return trip to Washington 'a high, unidentified official accompanying Secretary Baker's party' spoke informally to reporters. Bitter statements by this 'high official' appeared in newspapers the next morning, 29 September. 'Sharon is intransigent and a boor. The Arabs have offered him a real opportunity for peace. If he thinks the United States will save Israel, as we did in 1973, he's got another think coming. If this goes to war, the United States will stay completely on the sidelines.'

Israeli newspapers reported that the 'high official' had been Secretary Baker himself. And so it was that on 30 September Israelis were more concerned about the Arab military build-up, and the attitude of the

American Secretary of State toward that build-up, than they were with the planned celebration of the twentieth anniversary of the Yom Kippur War. Late that day Prime Minister Sharon ordered full mobilisation of the Israeli armed forces. In a statement to the Israeli people he said that he was ordering this action because Egyptian forces had for twenty-four hours been crossing the Suez Canal in large numbers, in violation of the Treaty of Washington of 1979. He also announced that he had sent a message to Egypt, through the US government, to the effect that if all Egyptian forces that had crossed to the east bank of the Suez Canal had not returned to the west bank by 7.00 a.m. on 1 October, Israel would consider that it was at war with Egypt.

A press release from the Prime Minister's office disclosed that identical messages had also been sent, through the US, to the governments of Syria and Jordan, informing them that Israel had no quarrel with them, but that if any major Syrian or Jordanian forces were sighted by Israeli reconnaissance aircraft within ten kilometres of their frontiers with Israel at 7.00 a.m. on 1 October, Israel would assume that this was evidence of hostile intentions, and thus an act of war.

THE FORCES

The mobilised military strength of the four Arab nations – Egypt, Syria, Jordan and Saudi Arabia – was about double that of Israel. A summary comparison is shown in Table 1.1. The deployment of these forces, following completion of the Israeli mobilisation at 7.00 a.m. on 1 October, is shown on Map 1.1.

ISRAELI PLAN AND DEPLOYMENTS

As early as mid-July Lieutenant General Ehud Barak, Chief of Staff of Israeli Defence Forces (IDF), had asked his staff to update the standard war plan for a three-front war against Syria, Jordan and Egypt. At that time he had remarked to them that the current situation was not dissimilar to that which had existed before the Six-Day War in 1967. He felt sure that this similarity would be noted also by Arab planners, and they would most probably be looking for an Israeli repeat of the strategy of that war. For that reason, he said, he would like a plan that was quite different from the 1967 plan.

TABLE 1.1

COMPARISON OF COMBAT FORCES

ARMY	Total Israel	Arab	Egypt	Syria	Jordan	Saudi Arabia
Manpower (thousands)	598	1,500	800	500	100	100
Field divisions	17	40	20	12	4	4
Main battle tanks	4,100	8,900	3,200	4,050	1,100	550
APCs and IFVs	10,000	11,260	3,600	4,100	1,360	2,200
Artillery pieces/rockets	1,400	5,600	2,000	2,800	400	400
AIR FORCE						
Manpower (thousands)	45	175	90	60	10	15
Combat aircraft	650	1,335	475	560	100	200
Armed helicopters	75	200	75	100	25	–
AIR DEFENCE						
Manpower (thousands)	20	150	100	40	5	5
AAA guns	850	4,850	2,500	1,700	400	250
SA missiles	160	1,700	900	500	100	200
NAVY						
Manpower (thousands)	10	40	30	5	–	5
Submarines	3	13	10	3	–	–
Destroyers/frigates	–	15	5	2	–	8
Fast missile craft	26	42	21	12	–	9

Barak pointed out to his planner – Major General Shimon Gal – that the situation in 1993 differed from that of 1967 in two significant respects. In the first place, of course, Israel – not Jordan – held the West Bank. Second, if the Egyptians entered the war, they would not be deployed in pre-war fortifications close to Israel's frontiers. They would have to displace eastward from the Suez Canal, and so they were not likely to pose any immediate threat to Israeli territory, particularly since any movement to a threatening position would be bombarded by the Israeli Air Force. Barak said he would not try to give more detailed guidance, and would await Gal's plan.

That plan, code-named Operation Arrow, was delivered to Barak in early August. As he had expected, Operation Arrow provided for an

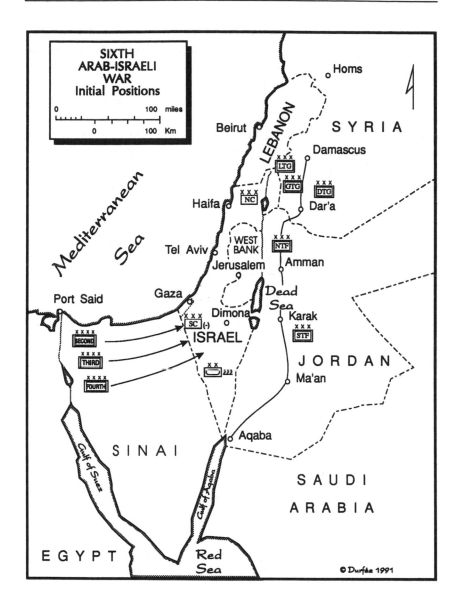

initial Israeli concentration in the north, against Syria. If possible, it would be preceded by a pre-emptive air strike against Syrian, Jordanian and Egyptian air bases. Then, more than half of the Israeli Army – nine of its seventeen divisions – would mount a two-pronged offensive against Syrian forces in Lebanon, and in the region between the Golan Heights and Damascus. Commanding this operation would be Major General Mordechai Goren, commanding general of Northern Command. The left prong, a corps-sized task force of four divisions, was to drive north up the

Bekaa Valley, very much as had been done in 1982, to the Beirut–Damascus Road. Leaving one division to hold open the line of communications, the other three divisions of the task force would turn east toward Damascus.

Meanwhile Northern Command's right prong – a task force of five divisions – would envelop Damascus from the south. While one division, deployed north and south of Kuneitra, conducted a holding attack in the general direction of Damascus, two divisions would strike due east from the southern Golan, toward the town of Shaykh Miskin, on the Amman–Damascus highway. The remaining two divisions would follow behind the enveloping wing, prepared to deal with any Syrian forces that might try to operate against the left flank of the spearhead.

Major General Yitzhak Mir, commanding Southern Command, and responsible for the defence of Israel's frontier with Sinai, was to be given five field divisions, in addition to his local security division deployed in field fortifications along the frontier south of Gaza. Four of these divisions were to be deployed initially in the area between Gaza and Beersheba, their further deployment depending on the development of the Egyptian threat. The remaining division was deployed in widely dispersed locations in the central Negev. General Mir was authorised to initiate limited offensive operations as soon as Egyptian dispositions were clear.

Central Command, under Major General Karmel Yoffe, had a completely defensive mission. He had three field divisions, in addition to his frontier defence division. One of these divisions was deployed generally between Hebron and Jericho, another to the north, in the Nablus–Jenin area. The third division, in reserve, was west of Ramallah.

THE ARAB PLAN AND DEPLOYMENTS

The Arab High Command consisted of the commanders in chief of the armed forces of Egypt, Syria, Jordan and Saudi Arabia (see Table 1.2). In frank discussions among these four Arab military chiefs in early July 1993, it was agreed that the senior member of the group – General Mustafa el T'lass, Defence Minister and Commander in Chief of the Syrian Army – would be Supreme Commander. It was also agreed that T'lass was to be a true commander and that the other three military leaders would loyally follow his orders. A secret Combined Planning Staff of 120 officers – 30 from each of the four allied Arab nations – had promptly been set up near T'lass's office, in the Syrian Ministry of Defence in Damascus. The four heads of state agreed that they would accept the military primacy of T'lass, who was thereupon promoted to field marshal by President Assad of Syria, so that he was at least the equal in rank to Field Marshal Mohammed el Kasseb, Commander in Chief and Minister of Defence of Egypt. Kasseb pledged his wholehearted loyalty and support to T'lass, as did General Fathi Abu Taleb, commander in chief of Jordan's army, and General Nabil Shoubeily, commander in chief of the Saudi Arabian armed forces.

TABLE 1.2

THE HIGH COMMANDS

SYRIA
President: Hafez al Assad
Commander in Chief: F M Mustafa el T'lass (Arab Supreme Allied Commander)

EGYPT
President: Hosni el Mubarak
Commander in Chief: F M Mohamed el Kasseb

JORDAN
King: Hussein
Commander in Chief: General Fathi Abu Taleb

SAUDI ARABIA
King: Fahd
Commander in Chief: General Nabil Shoubeily

ISRAEL
Prime Minister: Ariel Sharon
Commander in Chief: Lieutenant General Ehud Barak

The Arabs were determined not to allow the Israelis to initiate the war with a pre-emptive air strike. They had no illusions about the possibility that they might compete on even terms with the Israeli Air Force. They realistically recognised that, plane for plane and pilot for pilot, the Israelis were better than they were, by a margin of at least three to one. It was their intention, therefore, to degrade that initial Israeli superiority to some extent by a co-ordinated surprise air attack on Israeli air bases by all four Arab air forces, and then to use their formidable air defence capabilities to protect their own air bases, while avoiding air-to-air combat with the Israelis. At the same time air defences with the Arab ground armies should prevent the Israelis from securing a major advantage from their possession of air superiority.

On the ground the Arabs calculated – rightly, as it turned out – that the Israelis would make their main effort against Syria. (Their plan was flexible enough, however, to be adjusted to take advantage of an Israeli concentration against Egypt.) Thus, while retaining readiness to advance toward northern Israel if the opportunity offered, the Syrians prepared themselves to defend against an Israeli offensive, whether directly from the Golan Heights or through Lebanon.

The Arab main effort would be made by Egypt. The Egyptian plan was to cross the Suez Canal and to advance eastward across Sinai as rapidly as possible, using the three main roads in northern Sinai. The principal objective of this advance was to be Dimona, in central Negev, known to be the location of Israel's nuclear weapons manufacturing plant, and the stockpile of its unacknowledged nuclear weapons.

Jordan's four excellent divisions – two armoured and two mechanised – were to be deployed defensively to protect the heights above the Jordan River and Dead Sea valleys, and to be prepared to reinforce either the Egyptians in the Negev or the Syrians in southern Syria. The Israelis were not expected to make a serious effort against Jordan, and the Arabs had no intention of becoming unnecessarily involved in major operations in the oppressive, below-sea-level heat of the Jordan–Dead Sea valley. Jordan's small air force was to participate in the initial major air assault against Israeli Air Force bases, and then to shift to bases in Saudi Arabia. This would permit the whole of Jordan's air defence capability to be allocated to the ground forces.

Saudi Arabia was to make a major contribution to the initial air strike against the Israeli Air Force. The Saudi Air Force was then to operate as three support task forces, one to augment the Syrian Air Force, one to work with the Jordanian Air Force in support of the Jordanian Army, and one to be prepared to work in co-ordination with the Egyptian Air Force in support of the Egyptian ground invasion of the Negev. A provisional corps of two division-size task forces under the command of General Nabil Shoubeily, the Saudi Arabian commander in chief, was to advance overland to assist Jordan. This force was to be in reserve. It would join the Jordanians in defensive combat, if the Israelis were to attack Jordan. Otherwise, its components could move into static defensive positions, relieving Jordanian divisions for offensive action either in Syria or the Negev.

This was the first time an Arab coalition had prepared a truly co-ordinated plan for combat against Israel, and thus the first time the Arabs had seriously attempted to take advantage of their numerical superiority to offset the Israeli advantage of interior lines.

EGYPTIAN DEPLOYMENT AND DISPOSITIONS

The Egyptian Expeditionary Army Group consisted of thirteen divisions, organised in three armies of four divisions each, with one division in army group reserve. At dawn on 1 October the Second Army, in column along the coast road, had just reached El Arish, with the 21st Armoured Division in the lead, followed by the 23rd Armoured and the 16th and 18th Mechanised Divisions.

On the Ismailia–El Auja road the head of the Third Army was passing the historic, deserted Abu Agheila road junction, and advance guard scout cars were approaching El Auja. The 4th Armoured Division was followed in column by the 6th Armoured and the 7th and 19th Mechanised Divisions. Further south the 1st Armoured Division of the Fourth Army was midway between Bir Hassna and Kusseima. Following were the 2nd Armoured Division and the 3rd and 5th Mechanised Divisions. In GHQ Reserve, following behind the Third Army, was the 10th Mechanised Division.

In addition to its organic air defence units, each of these thirteen divisions had a powerful Air Defence Force brigade attached, equipped with both AAA guns and Hawk or SA-7 missiles.

The Egyptian plan was simple. Moving as rapidly as possible, the Fourth Army was to strike for Dimona. To facilitate this main effort, the Second Army was to drive toward Gaza and the Third Army toward Beersheba, attracting the attention of the bulk of Israel's Southern Command, known to be concentrated in this region. The rear divisions in both the Second and Third Armies' columns were to be held in reserve, and not to be committed without the express approval of the Egyptian commander in chief, Field Marshal Kasseb. (There was no such restriction on the commander of the Fourth Army.) In this way Kasseb was prepared to use these reserve divisions, plus the 10th Mechanised in GHQ Reserve, as a task force to deal with any unexpected threat to the Fourth Army in the accomplishment of its mission. That mission was to occupy and secure Dimona and the immediate vicinity, and to destroy both the nuclear weapons factory and the stockpiled weapons. A special engineer task force was attached to the Fourth Army for this purpose.

SYRIAN DEPLOYMENTS AND DISPOSITIONS

Three of Syria's twelve divisions were deployed in northern and eastern Syria in purely defensive roles, the remaining nine being organised into three task groups. In the Lebanon Task Group, deployed in the Bekaa Valley, were the 1st Armoured Division and the 7th and 9th Mechanised

Divisions. The Golan Task Group, deployed between Damascus and the Israeli-held Golan Heights, consisted of the 3rd Armoured Division, and the 10th and 11th Mechanised Divisions. The Dar'a Task Group, deployed generally along the road from Damascus to Dar'a, near the Jordanian border, consisted of the 5th Armoured Division and the 4th and 8th Mechanised Divisions.

All three task groups had been assigned primarily defensive missions, but were to be prepared to attack if the opportunity offered. Field Marshal T'lass authorised each of the task group commanders to exercise this offensive option on their individual initiative. He considered the mission of the Dar'a Task Group to be particularly important, since Arab intelligence anticipated that an Israeli offensive from the Golan would endeavour to envelop the south flank of the Syrian Army. The task of the Dar'a Task Group was to prevent such envelopment.

If the Israelis did not attack, the Syrians planned to move quickly to the offensive. The Lebanon Task Group would advance south down the Bekaa Valley, toward Metulla, the northernmost town of Galilee, in northern Israel. While the Golan Task Group undertook a holding attack north and south of Kuneitra, the Dar'a Task Group would strike through the southern Golan Heights towards the Sea of Galilee and the southern Hula Valley, to threaten all of Galilee.

JORDANIAN DEPLOYMENTS AND DISPOSITIONS

General Abu Taleb deployed his mobilised four-division army in two task forces. The Northern Task Force consisted of the 1st Armoured and the 3rd Mechanised Divisions, and was deployed in the Irbid–Zarqa–Mafraq area. The Southern Task Force, the 2nd Armoured and 4th Mechanised Divisions, was deployed between Ma'an and Karak. Both task forces initially had defensive missions, in the event of an Israeli invasion. If such an attack did not come – and the Arabs did not expect it – the task forces were to be prepared to move to join the Syrians in the north, or the Egyptians in the south. Abu Taleb – a cautious man – did not expect to exercise both of these offensive options, although he was prepared to do so. And he had made clear to both Field Marshal T'lass and General Shoubeily of Saudi Arabia that he would not exercise either option unless he received sufficient Saudi Arabian forces, under his command, to occupy the defensive positions now held by the Jordanian troops. Both T'lass and Shoubeily assured him that this would happen.

The Jordanian Air Force was prepared to participate in the initial allied Arab air offensive against Israeli air bases in the Negev. Returning from that mission the Jordanian planes would fly directly to the Saudi Arabian

Air Force base at Turayf. Ground crews and maintenance equipment were already deployed to Turayf.

SAUDI ARABIAN DEPLOYMENTS AND DISPOSITIONS

General Shoubeily established a Saudi Arabian Expeditionary Force under his personal command, consisting of the 1st Provisional Armoured Division and the 1st Provisional Mechanised Division. The provisional armoured division consisted of the 1st and 2nd Armoured Brigades, and the 1st and 5th Mechanised Infantry Brigades. The provisional mechanised division consisted of the 2nd, 3rd and 4th Mechanised Infantry Brigades and the 3rd Armoured Brigade. At dawn on 1 October the head of the 1st Provisional Armoured Division was approaching the Jordanian frontier, travelling on the Amman–Hail highway. Close behind was the 1st Provisional Mechanised Division.

The Saudi Arabian Air Force had been reorganised for its combat missions into four air wings. The headquarters of the Northern Air Wing was at Ar'ar, and consisted of three squadrons of F-15C aircraft. Following the initial air strike at Israel, the principal mission of this wing was to reinforce the Syrian Air Force in support of Syrian ground forces. A subsidiary mission was to support the Central Air Wing in the air defence of the country. The headquarters of the Western Wing was at Turayf, and consisted of two squadrons of Tornados. The Jordanian Air Force was to be attached under the command of this wing. Its principal mission, after the initial air strike against Israel, was to support Jordanian and Saudi Arabian ground forces in the defence of Jordan. A subsidiary mission was to support the Central Air Wing in the air defence of Saudi Arabia. Headquarters of the Hejaz Air Wing was at Tabuk. It consisted of three squadrons of F-5Es and two of Tornados. After the initial air strike, this wing was to reinforce the Egyptian Air Force in support of Egyptian ground forces in Sinai and Negev. Like the other two advanced air wings, it also had a subsidiary mission to assist in the air defence of the country. The Central Air Wing, with headquarters at Riyadh, was to provide air defence for sensitive government, military command and infrastructure facilities in the heart of Saudi Arabia. This wing had three squadrons of F-15C fighters, and controlled the five EC-3A electronic surveillance and warning aircraft which had proved so valuable in the allied air operations against Iraq in the Kuwait war.

PRE-EMPTING PRE-EMPTION

Arab intelligence anticipated that the Israeli Air Force would plan to carry out a pre-emptive air strike against Arab air bases sometime before the 7.00 a.m. deadline set by Prime Minister Sharon in his ultimatum of 30 September. Accordingly, Field Marshal T'lass's planning group set 5.00 a.m. (about half an hour before dawn) as the time for an Arab air strike intended to pre-empt the Israeli pre-emption.

The possibility of such an Arab air pre-emption had been considered by the Israeli Air Staff, and alert measures had been taken accordingly. However, the Israelis did not really expect such a strike because previous experience suggested that this would require a level of Arab co-operation and co-ordination which they had never previously been able to achieve. Thus, when their EC-2 early warning aircraft discovered massive concentrations of aircraft over Syria, Jordan and Sinai at about 4.50 a.m. on Friday 1 October, the Israelis were prepared but not really ready.

Hurriedly they halted the arming of their aircraft for their own planned strike, as their air defence planes scrambled and climbed for altitude. More than 100 Israeli air defence fighters were airborne when the leading Arab planes approached Israeli airspace shortly before 5.00 a.m. Thus almost 100 spectacular dogfights took place in the lightening skies all over Israel as air-raid sirens screamed on the ground. The formidable array of Israeli air defence missiles deployed at the air bases were unable to fire, since they could not distinguish friend from foe.

The second wave of Arab planes came in relatively low over their assigned targets as the high-altitude struggle was taking place. They were attacked from above by some of the Israeli planes, which had been able to avoid the dogfights. But by this time the Israeli air defence – consisting solely of aircraft, without support of SAM missiles – was saturated. While many of the attacking aircraft were shot down, most of them reached their targets and dropped their bombs.

By 6.30 a.m. the opening air battle was over. More than 250 Israeli aircraft had been involved in this battle, most of which survived: only 17 were lost, and some of these losses were due to collisions or to friendly air or ground fire. More than 800 Arab aircraft had participated in the carefully planned attack, and they had suffered heavily, losing 196 aircraft. The exchange ratio was – as the Arabs themselves had expected – unfavourable: more than 11 Arab planes shot down for every Israeli plane lost.

But the Arabs had accomplished their purpose. On the ground 210 Israeli planes had been hit, and at least half of these were beyond repair. For the first time in history, the Israelis lost more aircraft in an air battle than did their Arab opponents. Furthermore, the planned Israeli opening strike was thwarted, and for several hours the Israeli Air Force was unable to provide significant support to its now heavily engaged ground forces.

DETERRENCE OF MASS DESTRUCTION

At 11.00 p.m. on 30 September the Secretary General of the United Nations, at home in New York reading a book in his living room, received a telephone call from his office. (It was 6.00 a.m. in the heart of the Middle East.) An aide read the following message to him:

> Your Excellency:
>
> It is with regret that we inform you that since 5.00 a.m. on 1 October in our capitals of Riyadh, Amman, Damascus and Cairo, a state of war and active hostilities exists between Saudi Arabia, Jordan, Syria and Egypt, on the one hand, and Israel, on the other. This is the direct result of the refusal of Israel to accept the peace offer made by our nations and the other members of the Arab League, and by the hostile Israeli actions which have accompanied that refusal.
>
> We attach to this letter an open communication to the Government of Israel, which we request that Your Excellency both note and transmit officially to that Government.
>
> We are authorising immediate release to the world's press of this letter and the attachment.
>
> With sentiments of the highest esteem, we remain:
>
> > Fahd, Saudi Arabia
> > Hussein, Jordan
> > Assad, Syria
> > Mubarak, Egypt

The Secretary General sighed. 'Please read me the attachment,' he said. He listened as his aide continued reading:

> To the Government of Israel:
>
> Your refusal to accept the recent peace offer of the Arab League, and your obvious preparations for offensive military action against our nations, force us to declare that a state of war and active hostilities now exists between Israel, on the one hand, and the Arab Coalition of Saudi Arabia, Jordan, Syria and Egypt, on the other.

As you are aware, our nations have at their disposal long-range missiles capable of striking any point in Israel with high-explosive or mass-destruction weapons, including chemical and biological weapons. We are aware that Israel has the capability to strike civilian targets in our nations with conventional high-explosive weapons and weapons of mass destruction, including nuclear weapons.

We solemnly declare that in this current war the forces of the Arab Coalition will not strike any civilian targets in Israel with either conventional or mass-destruction weapons of any kind, save in response to provocation by Israeli attacks against civilian targets.

We call upon the Government of Israel to match this declaration by similarly forswearing any use of weapons of any kind against civilian targets in the course of this current war.

> Fahd, Riyadh
> Hussein, Amman
> Assad, Damascus
> Mubarak, Cairo

The Secretary General asked: 'Is that all?'

'Yes sir.'

'All right, prepare an immediate cable to Prime Minister Sharon, forwarding both those messages to him. I'll be in my office in half an hour to sign the covering transmission.'

The Secretary General replaced the telephone and buttoned his shirt collar. He wondered if his Arab origins would permit him to remain objective in this crisis.

OPENING MOVES IN THE SOUTH

(The force deployments in this theatre are shown in Table 1.3.)

By mid-morning Egyptian spearheads were crossing the frontier into Israel, where most of them immediately encountered fierce opposition. The Second Army's 21st Armoured Division ran head-on into the Israeli 262nd Armoured Division between Rafah and Khan Yunis. As the Egyptian 23rd Armoured Division came up on the right of the 21st Division, the Israeli 246th Armoured Division was hurrying up from the vicinity of Ashkelon on roads passing east of Gaza.

At about the same time reconnaissance elements of the Israeli 144th Armoured Division were establishing a thin, hasty defensive line east of El Auja, to slow down the advance of the Egyptian Third Army's 4th

TABLE 1.3

FORCES IN THE SOUTHERN ARAB–ISRAELI THEATRE

EGYPTIAN EXPEDITIONARY FORCE: General Mohamed el Hafiz

Second Army (Lieutenant General Saad Mohneim)

21st Armoured Division

23rd Armoured Division

16th Mechanised Infantry Division

18th Mechanised Infantry Division

Third Army (Lieutenant General Ibrahim Azmy)

4th Armoured Division

6th Armoured Division

7th Mechanised Infantry Division

19th Mechanised Infantry Division

Fourth Army (Lieutenant General Ismail Bader)

1st Armoured Division

2nd Armoured Division

3rd Mechanised Infantry Division

5th Mechanised Infantry Division

GHQ Reserve

10th Mechanised Infantry Division (Major General Nabil Zekry)

JORDANIAN ARMY, SOUTHERN TASK FORCE: Lieutenant General
Fakhri Mahmoud

2nd Armoured Division

4th Mechanised Infantry Division

ISRAELI SOUTHERN COMMAND: Major General Yitzhak Mir

144th Armoured Division (Major General Menachim Erez)

222nd Armoured Division (Major General Dovic Pinchas)

246th Armoured Division (Major General Amnon Tamir)

248th Armoured Division (Major General Israel Levi)

262nd Armoured Division (Major General Dani Zamir)

Armoured Division, while the remainder of Major General Menachim Erez's 144th Division was deploying to the north, preparing to attack the left flank of the Egyptian 4th Division. Erez had to call off that attack, however, when he learned from aerial reconnaissance that the Egyptian 6th Armoured Division was deploying to the left of the 4th Division, threatening the vulnerable right flank of the 144th.

Leading elements of the Fourth Army's 1st Armoured Division were beyond Bir Hafir, when they encountered their first resistance from elements of the Israeli 222nd Armoured Division, hurrying from south-central Negev. By this time the leading Egyptian troops were less than sixty kilometres from Dimona. Major General Youssef Moneim, com-manding the 1st Armoured Division, deployed his 1st Brigade to deal with these Israelis, and continued north, only to run into more tanks of the 222nd Division mid-way between Bir Hafir and Sede Boqer, near the ruins of ancient Eboda. Major General Dovic Pinchas, commanding the 222nd Division, was able to establish a hasty defensive line there, forcing the Egyptians to halt at least momentarily. However, the Egyptian 2nd Armoured Division was advancing on the left of the 1st, and the 3rd Mechanised Division on its right. By mid-afternoon General Pinchas realised that he was opposed by a far larger force than his division could handle, and he appealed for help to General Mir, now at Beersheba.

It was now evident to General Mir that the situation was serious along his entire front. It was also becoming obvious to him that Dimona, with its nuclear facilities and its nearby air base, was the immediate objective of the Egyptian offensive. He had originally ordered the 248th Division, under Major General Israel Levi, to join General Erez in blocking the Egyptian Third Army east of El Auja. Mir changed those orders, and directed Levi to move to Dimona to establish defensive positions protect-ing the town, nuclear facilities and air base. He ordered Pinchas to delay the Egyptian Fourth Army's offensive as well as he could, and to fall back slowly toward Dimona. He ordered Major General Dani Zamir, commanding the 262nd Division, engaged against the Second Army near Khan Yunis, to take command of the three-division task force, consis-ting of the 262nd, 246th and 144th Divisions, to cover Gaza and Beersheba.

Mir then telephoned a report of his actions to General Barak in Tel Aviv. He suggested that the Dimona air base be evacuated. Shortly after dark Mir arrived by helicopter at Dimona to take personal command of the defence of that threatened point.

OPENING MOVES IN THE NORTH

(The force deployments in this theatre are outlined in Table 1.4.)

Meanwhile, the Israeli offensive against Syria had begun shortly after dawn. The Bekaa Valley Task Force, commanded by Major General David Baram, drove quickly into southern Lebanon. No resistance was encountered until Israeli spearheads approached Lake Karaoun. There they were halted by Syrian infantry in prepared defensive positions,

TABLE 1.4

FORCES IN THE NORTHERN ARAB–ISRAELI THEATRE

SYRIAN FIELD FORCE ARMY: Lieutenant General Mohamed Heyal

Lebanon Task Group (Major General Shafiq Aslan)
- 1st Armoured Division
- 7th Mechanised Infantry Division
- 9th Mechanised Infantry Division

Golan Task Group (Major General Youssef Abrash)
- 3rd Armoured Division
- 10th Mechanised Infantry Division
- 11th Mechanised Infantry Division

Dar'a Task Group (Major General Ali Sharba)
- 5th Armoured Division
- 4th Mechanised Infantry Division
- 8th Mechanised Infantry Division

JORDANIAN ARMY, NORTHERN TASK FORCE: Lieutenant General Mohamed Kawass
- 1st Armoured Division
- 3rd Mechanised Infantry Division

ISRAELI NORTHERN COMMAND: Major General Mordechai Goren

Bekaa Valley Task Force (Major General David Baram)
- 163rd Armoured Division (Major General Avraham Shalev)
- 175th Armoured Division (Major General Eliahu Amir)
- 233rd Armoured Division (Major General Avraham Magen)
- 241st Armoured Division (Major General Haim Raviv)

Golan Heights Task Force (Major General Reuven Matt)
- 138th Armoured Division (Major General Granit Shapiro)
- 147th Armoured Division (Major General Mordechai Govam)
- 168th Armoured Division (Major General Moshe Peled)
- 214th Armoured Division (Major General Jacob Ysrael)
- 227th Armoured Division (Major General Yitzhak Even)

covered by small arms fire from the steep mountains on both sides of the lake, and supported massively by artillery and tank guns. All afternoon Major General Avraham Shalev's 163rd Armoured Division tried vainly to penetrate the Syrian defences. The 175th Armoured Division, advancing up the east corridor of the Bekaa Valley, encountered similar resistance and was also unable to reach its immediate objective of Rachiya.

The Israeli Bekaa Valley Task Force had encountered the ready and waiting 7th and 9th Mechanised Division of Syrian Lieutenant General Shafiq Aslan's Lebanon Task Group. The 7th Division was in field fortifications near Karaoun, the 9th in similar strong defences near Rachiya. The Syrian 1st Armoured Division was deployed in reserve near Joub Janine, where General Aslan had his command post. General Baram reported his situation to Northern Command's General Goren; he said that it would take several days of hard fighting before he could break through the Syrian defences.

Major General Reuven Matt's Golan Heights Task Force had not been much more successful. His 147th Armoured Division (under Major General Mordechai Govam), deployed north and south of Kuneitra, had encountered very strong resistance in the Syrian fortified zone, but was making a holding attack, so lack of progress there was anticipated. Further south the 138th Armoured Division, under Major General Granit Shapiro, attacked eastward, abreast of Major General Moshe Peled's 16th Armoured Division. In tandem, behind these two leading divisions, were the 214th Armoured Division of Major General Jacob Ysrael and the 227th Armoured Division of Major General Yitzhak Even. The 138th and 168th Armoured Divisions were halted in their tracks in front of the fortified positions held by the 4th and 8th Mechanised Divisions of Syrian Major General Ali Sharba's Dar'a Task Group. By evening, however, enough progress had been made that General Matt felt confident that he would break through the next day. His 425th Paratroop Brigade was working its way up the Yarmuk River valley gorge, and would attack the left flank of the 8th Mechanised Division, in coordination with a renewed frontal attack by the 168th.

COMMAND POSTS IN AMMAN AND TEL AVIV

Things were very quiet along the entire Israel–Jordan frontier. By nightfall on 1 October the Saudi Arabian Expeditionary Force was bivouacking east of Amman. After greeting General Shoubeily, General Abu Taleb returned to his command bunker under the Kayadah (Jordanian Army headquarters) in Amman.

On his desk Abu Taleb found a press report with a copy of a letter from Prime Minister Sharon of Israel to the Secretary General of the United Nations. He read it.

Your Excellency:

I wish to inform you that Israeli military installations were attacked without provocation or warning at 5.00 a.m., Jerusalem time, this morning, by combat aircraft from the so-called Arab Coalition of Egypt, Syria, Jordan and Saudi Arabia. The Knesset has declared that a state of war now exists between Israel and those four states.

Israel will respond energetically with all the conventional military means at our disposal, to this unprovoked aggression. I wish to inform you, however, that Israel will scrupulously avoid attacking any non-military or civilian targets in any of the four nations with which we are now at war, so long as none of those nations attacks any civilian targets in Israel. In the event, however, that any of those nations attacks civilian targets in Israel, or uses any weapons of mass destruction against Israeli civilians or military forces, Israel reserves the right to respond by whatever means, and against whatever targets, are suitable under the circumstances.

Sharon
Prime Minister

Abu Taleb tossed the paper to his chief of staff, sitting in a chair beside his desk.

'Sharon has got the message,' he said. 'I don't trust him, but I believe that most of his officers are honourable men, and that they will abide by the terms of our declaration, and his.'

Abu Taleb then telephoned his liaison officer in Cairo. The report from Cairo was good. He then called his liaison officer in Damascus: another encouraging report. He and his staff then prepared an estimate of the situation. Shortly after midnight he told his staff to start preparing plans for the commitment of his Southern Task Force into the Negev east of Dimona. One of the two Saudi Arabian divisions was to take over the positions now held by the Southern Task Force.

Abu Taleb next called Field Marshal T'lass and reported his plans. T'lass approved, and then reminded Abu Taleb that he might also need Jordan's Northern Task Force north of Dar'a. When Abu Taleb seemed non-committal, T'lass mentioned that earlier that evening he had been with President Assad when the President had a telephone conference with King Hussein. The King had promised full support if there should be an Israeli breakthrough south of Damascus. Abu Taleb promised to talk to the King about this the first thing in the morning.

In his Tel Aviv command post, General Barak had also been through an estimate of the situation with his staff. He first asked for a report on how the air force had recovered from its surprise attack in the morning. Major General Levi Marron, Air Chief of Staff, reported candidly that his service had been badly hurt. 'Almost a quarter of the air force was wiped out in an hour. Nevertheless,' he continued, 'we have established unchallenged air superiority over the two major fronts, and over Jordan. However, we have not been very successful in providing help to the ground forces. The Arabs are making good use of their air defence resources, and we cannot fly low enough to deliver effective support.'

Barak next received reports on the ground situation on the Egyptian and Syrian fronts. He then remarked that in the early hours of the 1973 Yom Kippur War, when he had been a junior staff officer in that very war room, all the news had been bad. Just at this moment the burly, white-haired Prime Minister entered the war room and quietly sat down beside Barak. Sharon agreed with the Chief of Staff that the situation was similar to that in 1973. He was reminded, he said, of the meeting he had attended at Southern Command Headquarters with the then Chief of Staff, General Eleazar, on the evening of 7 October 1973. He then added, looking around the room at the young officers: 'Things were bad that night. But, as I told Dado [Eleazar], "We are better than they are; we shall beat them!"' His voice rose, as he pounded the table. 'We did beat them. We are still better than they are, and we shall beat them again!' Suddenly he realised that he was interrupting the business of the war room. He stood up, and said to Barak: 'Ehud, you have my confidence. I don't expect victory tomorrow, but I am sure you will give it to me and the nation within a week.' He then left.

APPROACHING SHOWDOWN IN SYRIA

Northern Command's Bekaa Valley Task Force was making little progress. Efforts aimed at enveloping the strong Syrian Bekaa Valley positions through the neighbouring mountain ranges had been disappointing, blocked at every point by Syrian infantry. Air support had little effect upon the Syrian defenders, well supported by AAA guns and surface-to-air missiles. By the evening of 4 October the situation in the Bekaa Valley had settled into a stalemate, and General Goren was considering withdrawing the task force for commitment in the plain south of Damascus.

As Generals Goren and Matt had expected, the co-ordinated attack of the 168th Division and the 425th Brigade was successful early on 2 October. The Syrian 8th Mechanised Division was driven from its positions, and by evening had fallen back about ten kilometres, toward

Shaykh Miskin, on the Dar'a–Damascus highway. To the north the 4th Mechanised Division had also been driven from its main positions by General Shapiro's 138th Division. Early on 3 October General Matt, the task force commander, committed General Even's 227th Division on the right of the 168th, intending to envelop the southern Syrian flank. He had hoped the 227th would reach the highway between Dar'a and Shaykh Miskin that day, but the hope was thwarted when General Sharba threw in his reserve, the Syrian 5th Armoured Division.

On 4 October, however, Matt's task force reached the highway, just north of Dar'a, after he committed General Ysrael's 214th Armoured Division on the right of the 227th. The 214th continued east past the highway to reach the abandoned narrow-gauge railway (famous from T E Lawrence's *Seven Pillars of Wisdom*). On 5 October Matt ordered a general advance and, by evening, despite fierce resistance, the Syrians were falling back to Shaykh Miskin.

That night President Assad spoke to King Hussein and asked that the Jordan Northern Task Force enter the battle now raging between Dar'a and Shaykh Miskin. Hussein, encouraged by the news from the Negev front, assured him that the Northern Task Force would start moving into Syria the next day. The King then called General Abu Taleb and ordered the movement. The Jordanian Commander in Chief, also encouraged by the news from the south, did not object. He told the King that he would issue orders immediately. When he received a call from Field Marshal T'lass later that evening, Abu Taleb was able to assure him that the Northern Task Force had already begun to move toward Dar'a.

APPROACHING SHOWDOWN IN THE NEGEV

In the Gaza–Beersheba area the Egyptian Second Army had been stopped near Khan Yunis, but the Third Army was still advancing slowly toward Beersheba. The drive of the Fourth Army had been slowed by Israeli General Pinchas's 222nd Division. But the 222nd was stretched thin on a thirty-kilometre front, being slowly driven back toward Dimona by the 1st and 2nd Egyptian Armoured and 5th Mechanised Divisions, while its southern flank was being threatened by the Egyptian 3rd Mechanised Division.

On 4 October Egyptian General el Hafiz decided that the time had come to force a decision in the Negev. He established a Reserve Task Force, under the command of Major General Nabil Zekry, commander of the 10th Mechanised Division, and attached to it the reserve divisions of the Second and Third Armies: the 18th and 19th Mechanised Divisions. Zekry was to move his task force to the east of the Fourth Army, and be prepared to attack northward from the vicinity of Oron toward Dimona at dawn on 6 October. By the time this attack was ready to begin, the fifty-kilometre front of the Fourth Army was a shallow concave arc, which was within ten kilometres of Dimona in the south.

By this time, also, the Israelis realised that Dimona was being threatened by the Jordanian Southern Task Force approaching from the east. The Jordanian 2nd Armoured Division, which had crossed the newly dry bed of the southern Dead Sea, was deployed just south of Masada, having established contact with the 4th Mechanised Division near Sodom. At dawn on 6 October the two Jordanian divisions were to begin an advance on Dimona, co-ordinated with that of the nearby Egyptian Reserve Task Force.

Israeli Chief of Staff Barak was now well aware of the threat to Dimona. Two Israeli divisions – the 222nd and 248th – were being encircled by seven Egyptian and two Jordanian divisions. It was not possible to withdraw any of the three divisions east of Gaza from their fierce struggle with the six Egyptian divisions of the Second and Third Armies, without possibly opening the road to Tel Aviv and Jerusalem. On 4 October the 211th Division, in the Jerusalem–Jericho area, was ordered to rush south to the vicinity of Dimona to join General Mir's Dimona Task Force. However, the division had great difficulty in moving, hampered at every step by Intifada insurrectionists. Despite the slaughter of hundreds of Palestinian civilians, the division had not cleared Hebron by evening of 5 October, and was facing countless road blocks to the south.

Earlier that day (5 October) Barak also ordered the 173rd Armoured Division, deployed just east of Tel Aviv, to move to Dimona as rapidly as possible. By midnight the head of the 173rd column had passed Beersheba, and was continuing east, with headlights blazing.

INTERNATIONAL REACTION

Despite the ominous threats and warnings that had pervaded the Middle East since the Cairo Proclamation, most of the world was surprised by the sudden outbreak of hostilities. The Chairman of the Security Council, M. René Duchamps of France, called the Council into emergency session. But the debate was surprisingly inconclusive, as most governments – particularly those of the five permanent members of the Council – had not yet decided upon their positions with regard to the conflict and the opponents. The Chinese representative denounced both sides. The representative of Libya, the only Arab League country represented on the Council at the time, vehemently accused Israel of provoking the war, and predicted an overwhelming Arab victory. The US representative said nothing.

The silence of the American representative was not due to any lack of interest in the war in Washington. Many members of Congress – senators and representatives alike – accused Secretary of State Baker of having given the Arabs a 'green light'. There were similar accusations in the press, either in reports of consternation and outrage in the American Jewish community, or in editorial opinions. There were widespread demands for a presidential statement, but all that emanated from the White House Press Office, on the afternoon of Sunday 3 October, was a simple two-sentence release: 'The President deplores the outbreak of hostilities in the Middle East. He has directed the Secretary of State and his National Security Advisor to study the situation urgently, and to submit recommendations to him promptly.'

Press demands for an elaboration of this statement, and for an explanation of what was meant by 'promptly', were ignored. Neither Secretary of State Baker nor General Brent Scowcroft would speak with reporters.

Perhaps most interesting was the reaction of US military 'experts', particularly those of the newspapers, radio and television. This reaction was summed up on Tuesday 5 October by CNN's hastily recruited military specialist, retired Air Force Major General Hanson Drew:

Many of my colleagues have been surprised at how different the first five days of this war have been from the Kuwait war of a little less than three years ago, and by the fact that the operations have been much more reminiscent of 1973 than of 1991. Where are the 'smart bombs', the 'stealth' intruders, laser-guided cruise missiles, stand-off air attacks, night vision devices, and the like?

The truth is that many ultra-modern weapons and techniques are being used on both sides, but have not had the same kind of effect as they did in the last Gulf war. The reason is that no two wars are alike, and this one is very different from that of the UN coalition against Iraq. In that war most of Iraq's sophisticated weapons were knocked out by the allies in the first few hours of the conflict, and the United States and its allies were able at relative leisure both to test and to demonstrate the virtuosity of their amazing new weapons.

In this war, neither side has weapons as exotic as some of those used by the United States Air Force in January and February 1991. Neither side has 'stealth fighters'. Both sides seem to have a few – but very few – 'smart bombs', and they are not going to waste them. Neither side is firing long-range surface-to-surface missiles at their enemy's cities, and thus neither can demonstrate that they have anything comparable to the famous 'Patriot' anti-missile missile. Both sides are unquestionably using night vision devices, but this is nothing new; they were using earlier versions of these in 1973.

The truth is that we have two opponents with quite modern – but not ultra-modern – armed forces, and they appear to be relatively equally matched. In the light of the way in which the war broke out, it is not surprising that it is in many ways reminiscent of 1973. But it is far from a rerun of that war. When it is over, it will have provided many lessons, some reinforcing those of 1973, as well as those of 1991. But there will also be many new lessons, to be studied by general staffs in the future.

THE BATTLE OF SHAYKH MISKIN

At dawn on 6 October General Matt's Golan Heights Task Force attacked in a co-ordinated offensive against General Sharba's badly battered Dar'a Task Group. The front extended about fifty kilometres from near Kuneitra, in the west, to beyond the railroad east of Shaykh Miskin. Three Israeli divisions were in line: the 138th, 214th and 227th. The 168th – with the 425th Paratroop Brigade attached – had been pinched out near Dar'a, and was now in reserve. Defending were the Syrian 4th and 8th Mechanised Divisions and the 5th Armoured Division astride the highway and railroad. In reserve was the 3rd Armoured Division, attached that morning from the Golan Task Group. The other two divisions of the Task group – the 10th and 11th Mechanised – were heavily engaged against the Israeli 147th Division in the fortified area just north of Kuneitra and south of Jebel Sheikh (Mount Hermon).

All that day the three attacking Israeli divisions forged slowly but steadily ahead. Advancing past Shaykh Miskin, at nightfall the Israeli 214th Division had achieved a clear breakthrough between the Syrian 8th Mechanised and 5th Armoured Divisions. However, the line was re-established early the next day when General Sharba committed the 3rd Armoured Division. At around noon General Matt was informed by the air force that an enemy force was approaching from the rear. It was the Jordanian Northern Task Force, commanded by Lieutenant General

Mohamed Kawass. The Jordanian general had deployed his 3rd Mechanised Division on his left, west of the main highway, with the 1st Armoured Division on the right, astride the railroad line. By noon on 7 October the Jordanians were advancing steadily northward, past Dar'a.

General Matt called off the attack of the Golan Heights Task Force and hastily deployed his 168th Division facing south in defensive positions across the highway and railroad about ten kilometres south of Shaykh Miskin. Beginning at about 3.00 p.m. the Jordanian 1st Armoured Division launched a fierce attack on the left flank of the 168th Division, while the 3rd Mechanised Division pinned down the Israelis in a frontal attack. It was soon evident to General Peled, commander of the 168th, that his exhausted troops, disrupted by the shock of the surprise Jordanian attack, would not be able to hold their positions. He so informed Matt, and began to pull his left flank back toward the highway. This, of course, exposed the right rear of the Israeli 214th Division, which also began to fall back to the highway, linking up with the left of the 168th.

Around 4.00 p.m. General Sharba ordered the divisions of his Dar'a Task Group to counterattack. He pulled back the 3rd Armoured Division into reserve, to be ready to attempt a penetration early the following morning. He reported his situation to Field Marshal T'lass.

T'lass recognised that, for the first time in nearly half a century of intermittent warfare, there was an opportunity for a decisive Syrian victory over Israeli forces. He received President Assad's permission to commit the Presidential Guard Brigade, and two independent armoured brigades that were protecting Damascus. He organised these into a provisional armoured division under Brigadier General Hassan el Rashid, commander of the Presidential Guard. Assad insisted, however, that the 1st Armoured Division must be withdrawn from Lebanon to take the place of these three brigades in and around Damascus. T'lass agreed, and issued the necessary orders.

Thus, at dawn on 8 October seven Arab divisions – three battered but four fresh or nearly fresh – were facing four tired and somewhat demoralised Israeli divisions in the region between Shaykh Miskin and Kuneitra. Sharba committed the 3rd Armoured and the provisional armoured division abreast on a fifteen-kilometre front west of Shaykh Miskin, between the 4th and 8th Mechanised Divisions. They were faced by the right wing of the Israeli 138th Division, and the left wing of the 227th. Israeli resistance was fierce, but the defenders were forced to give way. At the same time the Jordanian Northern Task Force was hammering with comparable vigour at the Israeli 168th Division, which was also forced to pull back.

It was now evident to General Matt that the battle was lost, and he so

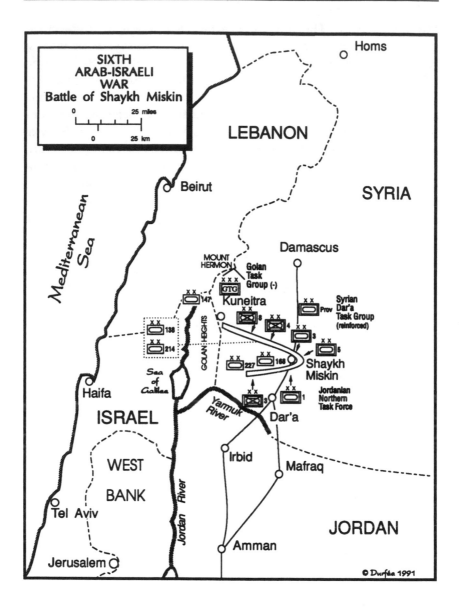

SIXTH
ARAB-ISRAELI
WAR
Battle of Shaykh Miskin

informed General Goren, who gave Matt permission to withdraw to the
old Golan Heights fortified line. Despite continuing Arab pressure, and
with considerable assistance from the Israeli Air Force, the Israelis withdrew in good order. By the early morning of 9 October they were back
in the positions from which they had started their offensive eight days
before.

THE BATTLE OF DIMONA

Just before dawn on 6 October the Israeli 173rd Armoured Division, after marching all day and all night, took up defensive positions north and east of Dimona, awaiting attack by the Jordanian Southern Task Force. The Israelis did not have long to wait. By dawn a full-scale battle was raging along a line extending from about ten kilometres west of Masada to a similar distance west of Sodom.

At the same time the Egyptian Reserve Task Force struck north from the vicinity of Oron. The right flank of the Egyptian 10th Mechanised Division quickly made contact with the left flank of the Jordanian 4th Mechanised Division. This completed a continuous front, nearly eighty kilometres long, around three sides of Dimona, now defended by three Israeli divisions: the 222nd, 248th and 173rd. Attacking were nine Arab divisions: seven Egyptian and two Jordanian.

It was soon obvious to General Mir that a successful defence of Dimona was impossible, unless he were promptly to receive substantial reinforcements. He radioed General Barak to ask what had happened to the 211th, which he had expected to join him the previous day. Barak told him that the 211th was bogged down in the West Bank by Intafada insurrectionists, and would probably not be able to break loose in time to reach Dimona before 8 or 9 October. The only other possible source of reinforcement was divisions from the Bekaa Valley Task Force, which could not possibly arrive before 9 or 10 October. Barak ordered Mir to begin destroying the nuclear weapons plant, and to destroy the nuclear weapons stockpile, in accordance with contingency plans to be followed by the special nuclear personnel stationed there. As soon as the destruction was complete, Mir was to withdraw his task force northward, to link up with the remainder of Southern Command and establish a new defensive line from the Mediterranean to the Dead Sea, roughly from Gaza to Masada.

Barak next ordered Northern Command to withdraw the Bekaa Valley Task Force from Lebanon, and to send three of its divisions south to the vicinity of Afula to await further orders. This would give him a reserve, should there be any further disasters. The Chief of Staff then telephoned the Prime Minister to inform him of the situation, and of the measures he (Barak) had just taken.

As Barak expected, there was an eruption at the other end of the telephone line. Sharon accused the general of being weak-willed, and of paying too much heed to his fears. Barak calmly replied: 'Mr Prime Minister, I hereby tender my resignation, to be effective as soon as you have appointed a replacement for me.' There was a brief silence, then

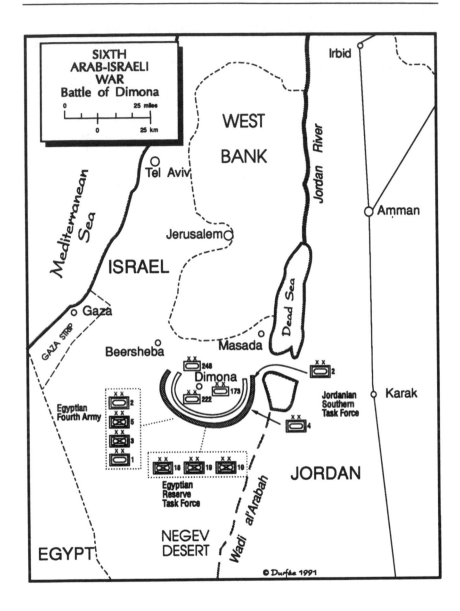

Sharon apologised. 'I will not accept your resignation. You have done as well as anyone could. But what should we do now?'

'Mr Prime Minister, my respectful response to that question is the same as that of Field Marshal von Rundstedt to a similar question from Hitler after the disaster at Stalingrad.' Another long silence. (Sharon knew that Rundstedt's reply had been: 'Make peace, you fool!')

'All right,' the Prime Minister finally said. 'I wish you to attend a

Cabinet meeting in my Tel Aviv office at eight o'clock tomorrow morning.'

At the Cabinet meeting Barak reported that Mir believed that he could complete the destruction of all the critical facilities, equipment and weapons at Dimona within another twenty-four hours, and that he could hold his positions around Dimona until then. He expected to start his withdrawal from Dimona at about midday on 8 October, and to have completed the establishment of a new Southern Command defensive line by noon two days later.

Barak also reported on the hitherto favourable course of the battle of Shaykh Miskin, but then added the ominous news of the advance of the Jordanian Northern Task Force through Dar'a. 'Matt may be able to hold his position,' the Chief of Staff concluded, 'but I greatly fear he will have to withdraw, perhaps as far as the original Golan Heights defensive line.'

Again the Prime Minister exploded in anger. 'We are better than they are,' he shouted. 'How can this happen?' 'Yes,' responded the Chief of Staff, 'we are better than they are. An American analyst named Dupuy has calculated that we are twice as good as they are. But they outnumber us by more than two to one. And, I must reluctantly admit, this time they had a better plan than we did, and they have outmanoeuvred us. They can never seriously threaten the existence of the state of Israel – at least not in this war. With the reserves I now have in hand, we can stop both their offensives. But we no longer have the capability to defeat them, in *this* war, because we cannot fight much longer without massive resupply from the United States.'

The Cabinet then discussed the various peace overtures that Israel had received from the UN, the US and elsewhere around the world. It was agreed that diplomacy must be initiated to bring the war to as early a conclusion as possible. They also agreed that they could accept the Arab League's Cairo Proclamation of Ramadan as a reasonable basis for post-war negotiations.

Mir kept his promise to the Chief of Staff, despite terrible pressure from the attacking Arab forces all along the line. Shortly after noon on 8 October, the Israeli defenders of Dimona began to pull out from the smoking ruins. As he had planned, Mir had his force back in a continuous defensive line from the Mediterranean to the Dead Sea well before noon on 10 October.

CEASE-FIRE

At 6.00 p.m. that evening a cease-fire was agreed at the United Nations in New York, to be effective four hours later – 5.00 a.m., Jerusalem time, on 11 October. The Ten-Day War, as the Arabs now called it, had come to an end.

A major provision of the cease-fire agreement was for the implementation of the Arab League's Proclamation of Ramadan, with the proposed Preliminary Conference to begin in Geneva between representatives of Israel, the Arab League and the United Nations on 11 November, one month after the conclusion of hostilities.

TABLE 1.5

HUMAN COST OF THE WAR

Nation/regime	Killed	Wounded	Total casualties
Israel	1,572	6,257	7,829
Syria	1,004	3,719	4,723
Egypt	1,588	5,853	7,441
Jordan	435	1,709	2,144

TNDM ADDENDUM: SIXTH ARAB–ISRAELI WAR

THE BATTLE OF SHAYKH MISKIN

On 6 October 1993 the Israeli Golan Heights Task Force, commanded by Major General Reuven Matt, undertaking a major envelopment from the south of Syrian forces east of the Golan Heights, attacked north-eastward toward Damascus. The Israelis were opposed by the Syrian Dar'a Task Group, under Major General Ali Sharba, which had been severely battered in four previous days of combat. The attacking force, which had not gone unscathed, consisted of four Israeli armoured divisions (138th, 214th, 227th and 168th) and the 425th Paratroop Brigade. The Syrian defenders were the 4th and 5th Mechanised Infantry Divisions, and the 3rd and 5th Armoured Divisions.

On that day the Israeli attack was generally successful, and advanced nearly four kilometres, despite strong Syrian resistance. An Israeli breakthrough near Shaykh Miskin was prevented, and the Israeli advance slowed, when General Sharba committed the 3rd Armoured Division, which had been in reserve.

Early on 7 October, however, as the Israelis continued to advance, the hard-pressed Syrians were reinforced by a provisional armoured division rushed from the garrison of Damascus. Even more serious for the Israelis, however, was the appearance to their right rear of the Jordanian Northern Task Force, under Lieutenant General Mohammed Kawass, consisting of the 1st Armoured and 3rd Mechanised Infantry Divisions. The Jordanians were advancing northward, through Dar'a, astride the Damascus–Amman highway. The surprised Israelis hastily pulled back their right-flank division – the 168th – to meet the Jordanian threat, while the other three Israeli divisions were struck by a Syrian counterattack.

By the end of 7 October the Israelis had been forced to pull back from the highway toward the Golan heights and, on 8 October, the battle ended as they withdrew to their starting positions.

Table TNDM 1.1 summarises the statistics of the battle.

TABLE TNDM 1.1

TNDM STATISTICS: BATTLE OF SHAYKH MISKIN

ISRAEL	Strength	Losses	Daily losses (%)
Men	54,530	2,759	2.53
Armour	1,282	466	18.17
Artillery	369	10	1.36
SYRIA			
Men	95,010	3,675	1.93
Armour	2,920	610	10.45
Artillery	704	16	1.14
JORDAN			
Men	32,500	488	1.50
Armour	740	28	3.78
Artillery	180	1	0.56

THE BATTLE OF DIMONA

On 6 October 1993 a combined-arms Arab force of a reinforced Egyptian Army and a Jordanian corps-sized task force attacked the Dimona Task Force of Israel's Southern Command, defending the secret industrial facility at Dimona, in the Negev. The Egyptian contingent was the Fourth Army, commanded by Lieutenant General Ismail Bader, and consisting of the 1st and 2nd Armoured Divisions and the 3rd and 5th Mechanised Infantry Divisions, to which a three-division reserve task force had been attached: the 10th, 18th and 19th Mechanised Infantry Divisions. The Jordanian contingent was the Southern Task Force, commanded by Lieutenant General Fakhri Mahmoud, consisting of the 2nd Armoured Division and the 4th Mechanised Infantry Division. The Israeli force consisted of the 173rd, 222nd and 248th Armoured Divisions, under the immediate command of Major General Yitzhak Mir, commander of Southern Command.

A rapid, surprise offensive of the three-army Egyptian Expeditionary Force had in four days of combat brought the right-wing Fourth Army deep into the Negev, to threaten Dimona, site of Israel's secret nuclear weapons production factory, from the south. The Reserve Task Force, committed late on 5 October on the Fourth Army's right, threatened Dimona from the south-east. These Egyptian forces were opposed by the Israeli 222nd and 248th Divisions.

The Jordanian task force, approaching Dimona from the north-east, was opposed by the Israeli 173rd Armoured Division, which had arrived from central Israel during the night of 5–6 October. Thus the Israelis were deployed in a defensive semi-circle around Dimona, and were threatened with encirclement.

While troops under his command were destroying the industrial facilities and nuclear weapons stockpile in Dimona, General Mir and his three divisions held off the attacking Arabs, who outnumbered him by more than three to one. After sustaining heavy casualties, and only with difficulty keeping open a withdrawal route to the north-west, Mir completed his destruction mission on the morning of 8 October, and began a fighting withdrawal. By that evening he had been able to break contact with the attacking Arabs and had linked up with the remainder of Southern Command, to form a defensive line from just south of Ashkelon on the Mediterranean to just north of Masada on the Dead Sea.

Table TNDM 1.2 summarises the battle statistics.

TABLE TNDM 1.2

TNDM STATISTICS: BATTLE OF DIMONA

ISRAEL	Strength	Losses	Daily losses (%)
Men	39,540	3,084	2.59
Armour	1,080	486	15.00
Artillery	288	13	1.50
EGYPT			
Men	108,500	5,841	1.79
Armour	1,743	481	9.20
Artillery	845	22	0.87
JORDAN			
Men	32,500	1,657	1.50
Armour	740	99	3.78
Artillery	180	3	0.56

CHAPTER TWO

THE FOURTH INDIA–PAKISTAN WAR

There is a history of twelve centuries of hostility and warfare between Hindus and Muslims in the Indian subcontinent. There was a lull in that hostility when they lived side by side relatively peacefully during a century and a half of British colonial rule over a united India. But when the British granted freedom to India in 1947, revival of the ancient Hindu–Muslim hostility resulted in a divided subcontinent, shared by two sovereign states: India, with more than two-thirds of the people, mostly Hindu; and Pakistan, with the remainder of the population, mostly Muslim. Pakistan existed in two widely separated parts, one in the west along the Indus River and one in the east in Bengal.

Independence Day, 14 August 1947, was also moving day for 10–15 million refugees. Muslims in the territories of the new Indian state moved to new areas in Pakistan and Hindus in Pakistan moved to India. Those who refused to leave were often forced out or killed. Violence also flared as Muslim and Hindu militias fought for control of the border provinces. Most of the fighting, known later as the First India–Pakistan War, centred around the provinces of Punjab and Kashmir, and resulted in the deaths of more than half a million people, most of them civilians. It also resulted in an unofficial boundary line being established in those two provinces, along the line occupied by the two armies at the time a UN-sponsored cease-fire was imposed on 1 January 1949.

The next decade and a half saw continued tension between India and Pakistan, and occasional skirmishes along their borders. In 1962 India was badly defeated by China in a border dispute and lost large tracts of land to China in northern Kashmir and in the North-East Frontier province. The defeat was the catalyst for a massive reform and modernisation of the Indian armed forces, financed and facilitated mainly by the Soviet Union, which was happy to have India as an ally in its rivalry with China.

Pakistan had looked to the West for support in the 1950s and early 1960s, joining SEATO and forging close ties with the US, from whom it obtained military support. Pakistan had the chance to use its new military hardware in 1965 when it invaded India on the pretext of liberating the rest of Kashmir. The Indians reacted more quickly and effectively than the Pakistanis had expected, launching counterattacks all along the front. Casualties were heavy on both sides. Each performed better in defence than in attack, and this Second India-Pakistan War, which lasted just three weeks, was a draw.

Failure to prosecute the war successfully caused political problems for Pakistan's leaders, problems complicated by beginnings of secessionist rumbles from East Pakistan. Heavy-handed pacification efforts by the government (located in West Pakistan) only exacerbated the tension, and in 1971 East Pakistan revolted, adopting the name of Bangladesh. The rebels were aided by an Indian invasion to dislodge the Pakistani garrison. This began the Third India–Pakistan War. The Indians swiftly gained control of the new country, while successfully defending against Pakistani attacks in the west. In two weeks India was completely victorious, and the loss of Bangladesh and its 70 million people severely weakened Pakistan and secured India's place as the dominant military power in South Asia.

THE DEVELOPING SITUATION 1971–92

Its swift victory in the 1971 war restored India's prestige, which had suffered badly in the 1960s. The uneasy peace which was maintained between India and Pakistan for the next twenty years was possible largely because of Pakistan's weakness, resulting from the loss of Bangladesh, and the steady economic growth and parallel military build-up in India. Considerable potential for conflict remained, however, primarily because of unrest in India among Sikh separatists in the Punjab, and among Muslims in Kashmir who wished to join Pakistan. The political temperature remained barely below boiling point.

KASHMIR

Six months after the third war, in July 1972, the new Pakistani President, Zulfiqar Ali Bhutto, and the Indian Prime Minister, Indira Gandhi, met in the Indian town of Simla to discuss, among other issues, the *de facto* Kashmir boundary lines, known as 'lines of actual control'. Relations between the two antagonists seemed to improve throughout the late

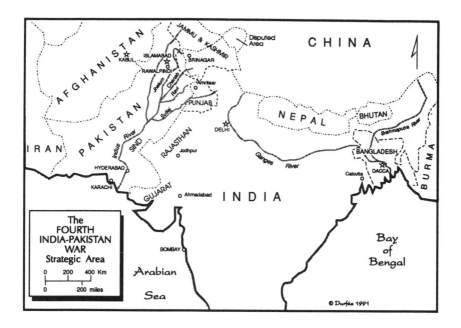

1970s and early 1980s, and official diplomatic relations were restored in 1976. Several points of contention remained, however, among them control of the remote (and intrinsically useless) Siachin Glacier in northern Kashmir. Tension eased slightly when Rajiv Gandhi replaced his assassinated mother as prime minister in 1984, and meetings to resolve the Siachin Glacier issue were begun in early 1986. However, Kashmir remained the only Indian state with a Muslim majority, and no degree of autonomy granted by Delhi could satisfy the longings of most Kashmiris to be free from Hindu rule, and to join Pakistan.

Unrest in the province grew in the mid- and late-1980s, partly as a result of Muslim uprisings in other parts of the world, notably Iran and the Soviet Union. The unpopular (Hindu) state government in Kashmir was forced to resign by public (Muslim) outcry in January 1990. On 25 January India flew additional troops into the area in a vain attempt to control widespread rioting. Meanwhile, skirmishes along the 1971 cease-fire line continued to flare between Indian and Pakistani troops. In May both countries put their troops on full alert and war seemed inevitable and imminent.

However, leaders on both sides reassessed the situation, although both continued to posture and threaten each other. By the end of September the death toll in the Kashmir uprising had climbed to 1,645 civilians. Twice during October Indian troops rampaged through

Srinagar, burning Muslim shops and homes.

Even the worldwide reaction to Iraq's occupation of Kuwait did not distract the two countries from their posturing – indeed, on 15 August Pakistani Army Chief General Asif Nowaz boasted that the contingent of 5,000 Pakistani troops which was being sent to Saudi Arabia would not detract from Pakistan's border defences, as he could mobilise 700,000 reserves in only a week!

The crisis subsided a little during late October and November 1990. The two countries held another round of inconclusive peace talks in mid-December to discuss the crises in Kashmir and Punjab. Tensions rose again at the end of the year as the death toll in Kashmir reached 2,500. India rushed new reinforcements to the border on 7 January 1991 and placed all its armed forces on maximum alert. Indian troops continued to sweep the Vale of Kashmir periodically for Muslim insurgents; cross-border artillery duels continued. Both sides deployed even more troops along the border in late March 1991 and fired on each other's border patrols. By April India had 600,000 men stationed in Punjab and Kashmir; Pakistan had fewer, perhaps 350,000, across the border. Firefights and artillery exchanges continued throughout May and June.

PUNJAB

Tensions between India and Pakistan in the Punjab region were complicated by unrest among the Sikh inhabitants of Indian Punjab. The Sikhs came to prominence in the late eighteenth century when they became dominant in Punjab. Their religion, which has been described as being descended from both Hinduism and Islam, has been the major factor setting them apart from their neighbours. Since the annexation of Punjab by the British in the mid-nineteenth century, and its incorporation into modern India in 1947, the Sikhs (comprising about 2 per cent of the Indian population) have yearned to re-establish their state as a separate nation, known as Khalistan.

Commencing around 1981, increasingly violent Sikh demands for independence, coupled with increasingly heavy-handed Indian government responses, drove a deep wedge between Sikhs and Hindus and posed a serious threat to India's stability. Unrest led to a series of clashes between Sikh militants and Indian armed forces throughout the early 1980s, culminating in a massive Indian Army assault on the Golden Temple in Amritsar in June 1984. This sacred shrine is central to Sikh religious life, and its 'violation' served to polarise the two camps even further. In retaliation, Sikh bodyguards assassinated Indian Prime Minister Indira Gandhi in October of that year. This act quenched any residual feelings of warmth between Hindus and Sikhs, and mobs of angry Hindus descended on Sikh communities to seek vengeance.

The next eight years saw little success for efforts to reconcile the Hindus and Sikhs. Indian troops again raided the Golden Temple in May 1988, and yet again in August 1990. Unlike the Muslim infiltrators in Kashmir, the Sikhs appeared to have had little, if any, support from the Pakistani government, which saw them as a convenient nuisance to India but not one worth going to war for. The fact that Sikh efforts for autonomy or independence coincided with the ongoing crisis in Kashmir led the Indian government to take sometimes draconian measures in order to quell the violence in its north-western provinces.

THE INDIAN ARMED FORCES: ARMY

In 1993 India possessed the fourth largest armed force in the world, with some 1.26 million active duty personnel. Of these, 1.1 million were in the Indian Army, which could draw upon an additional 300,000 Territorial Reserves when needed. The ground forces were divided into five regional commands, each roughly corresponding to a field army: Northern, Western, Southern, Eastern and Central. Subordinate to the area commands were ten corps headquarters, whose compositions and deployments varied according to circumstances and missions.

Comprising the army's line units were two armoured divisions, one mechanised division, nineteen infantry divisions and eleven mountain divisions. In addition, there were five independent armoured brigades, seven infantry brigades, one airborne/commando brigade, one mountain brigade and three artillery brigades. For support there were six air defence and four engineer brigades. Two-thirds of this force, including nine of the eleven mountain divisions, was already deployed along the troubled border with Pakistan, most of it in Kashmir and Punjab; the remainder faced the Chinese in northern Kashmir or north-eastern India, or was scattered throughout the country.

The Indian Army underwent a major reorganisation and modernisation programme after the successful conclusion of the 1971 war. This included securing contracts with various Western countries, especially West Germany, to provide modern weapons and equipment. However, the bulk of that Indian equipment which is not produced domestically came from the Soviet Union, which was gladly willing to arm a fellow adversary of China.

In October 1993 the Indians possessed about 3,150 main battle tanks, including 800 Soviet T-55s and 650 T-72s; the remaining 1,700 or so tanks were Indian Vijayantas. There were also 100 amphibious PT–76 light tanks, and 50 BRDM-2 APCs used for reconnaissance. The Indians employed some 700 Soviet-built BMP-1 armoured personnel carriers, along with a few BMP-2s (known locally as Saraths), as well as 400 OT-62s and OT-64s, and 50 BTR-60s. India was building the T-72 under licence from the Soviet Union, and had just begun full-scale production of its own Arjun main battle tank.

Towed artillery in the Indian Army consisted primarily of 75 mm/ 76 mm mountain howitzers, old British 25-pounder (88 mm) guns (which were being retired), 105 mm howitzers, and M-46 130 mm pieces. It also had around 80 Abbott 105 mm self-propelled howitzers and 100 M-46 130 mm SP gun variants, as well as 80 Soviet BM-21 122 mm rocket launchers, a thousand or so Soviet M-43 120 mm mortars, and a variety of other mortar calibres, including 81 mm, 82 mm and 160 mm.

The Indians employed the Soviet AT-3 Sagger and AT-4 Spigot missiles for anti-tank defence, as well as the French SS-11-B1 and European Milan; over a thousand old US M-40 106 mm recoilless rifles were also still in service. India first tested its own third-generation anti-tank missile, the Nag (Snake), on 29 November 1990 at the Chandipur test range.

Air defence was provided by an array of Soviet-made anti-aircraft guns, including the ZU 23–2 and ZSU 23–4 SP, but came primarily from 40 mm and 94 mm AD gun platforms. The Indians made extensive use of the Soviet-made SA-7 anti-aircraft missile, and also used a number of SA-6, SA-8A, SA-8B, SA-9 and British Tigercat missile launchers.

The Indian Army had thirteen ground support helicopter squadrons, nine of them armed with 20 Chetak helicopters each (although some of these squadrons also contained AS-11s) and four with 25 Chetaks each.

India had a number of paramilitary organisations on which it was able to draw for additional manpower when needed, including the National Security Guards anti-terrorist force (5,000 men); the Central Reserve Police Force (120,000 men with 250,000 more in reserve); the Border Security Force (130,000 by the end of 1991); the Assam Rifles (40,000); the Ladakh Scouts (5,000); the Indo–Tibetan Border Police (14,000); the Special Frontier Force (8,000); the Central Industrial Security Force (70,000); the Defence Security Force (30,000); the Railway Protection Forces (70,000); and the Provincial Armed Constabulary (250,000).

THE INDIAN ARMED FORCES: AIR FORCE

The Indian Air Force (IAF) consisted of five regional air commands controlling 110,000 people, fifty-two fixed-wing combat squadrons, one helicopter attack squadron, three reconnaissance helicopter squadrons, thirteen fixed-wing transport squadrons and eleven transport helicopter squadrons. The IAF relied heavily on Soviet-built aircraft, especially MIG-21, -23, and -27 variants, although it also employed some French Mirage-2000s, Anglo–French Jaguars, and domestically produced Ajeets and Maruts. Soviet helicopters, such as the Mi-8, Mi-17, and Mi-26 were also in extensive use. Combat units were broken down as shown in Table 2.1.

TABLE 2.1

INDIAN AIR FORCE: COMBAT UNITS

Mission	Aircraft type	Squadrons	Aircraft
Bomber	Canberra	1	10
Ground attack	MiG-23	4	60
Ground attack	MiG-21	13	190
Ground attack	Jaguar	5	70
Ground attack	Ajeet	5	80
Ground attack	Marut	1	20
Fighter	MiG-29	3	48
Fighter	Mirage-2000	3	51
Fighter	MiG-23	4	64
Fighter	MiG-21	12	204
Maritime attack	Jaguar	1	8
Attack helicopter	Mi-25	1	8

Indian fighter planes were armed with Soviet AA-2 Atoll or AA-7 Apex missiles, or with R-550 Magic or Matra Super 530-D air-to-air missiles. For air-to-surface attacks they carried French AM-39 Exocets, Soviet AS-7 Kerrys, AS-118 ATGWs, AS-30s or Sea Eagles.

The IAF also controlled some thirty battalions of surface-to-air missile launchers, which used Soviet SA-3s and Divina V75SM/VKs (about nine per battalion).

India, in co-operation with the German company MBB, was

developing an advanced light helicopter (ALH), for military and commercial purposes, but it was not in production in time for use in the war. India was considering the development of an indigenous cruise missile to enhance its strategic capability and improve deterrence against its nuclear-armed neighbours, Pakistan and China, but this programme had barely begun when the war broke out.

THE INDIAN ARMED FORCES: NAVY

Since 1971 India had put much money and effort into developing a powerful navy. Naval personnel strength in 1993 was 41,000, plus 1,000 marines and 5,000 naval aviators who operated from India's aircraft carriers as well as from land bases. Many of the navy's vessels were bought or leased from the Soviets.

There were three naval commands: Western, based in Bombay; Eastern, with its headquarters at Visakhapatnam; and Southern, centred at Cochin. Visakhapatnam also housed the headquarters of the country's submarine command.

India had a respectable submarine fleet, including 1 *Charlie-I* nuclear-powered guided missile submarine (which may have had Soviet SS-N-7 missiles with it), 8 *Kilo*-class diesel submarines, 8 older *Foxtrots* and 2 West German-built *T-209*s. On 30 September 1989 India launched the *Shakli*, its first locally produced submarine, but its domestic submarine programme advanced only by fits and starts. *Shakli* was considerably overbudget by the time it was completed, and was preceded by another craft whose hull was so poorly welded that it had to be scrapped.

India's surface naval expansion programme, the only one of its kind in Southern Asia, proceeded well. The navy hoped to produce domestically three aircraft carriers (based on French designs), with the first to be deployed by 1998. Each carrier was to be the nucleus of a surface naval task force and would be accompanied by eight escorting destroyers or frigates and a replenishment ship. India clearly planned to be the dominant naval power in the Indian Ocean in the twenty-first century.

In 1993 the Indian surface fleet consisted of 28 major combatants, the most significant of which were the two aircraft carriers, *Viraat* (formerly the British HMS *Hermes*) and *Vikrant* (ex-HMS *Glory*). Each of these vessels carried British Sea Harrier attack planes and Sea King helicopters armed with Sea Eagle anti-shipping missiles. The Indians had purchased 5 Soviet *Kashin*-class guided missile destroyers, each of which fired SA-N-1 Goa and powerful SS-N-26 Styx anti-ship missiles, in addition to having 5 torpedo tubes and a single Ka-25 Hormone or Ka-27 Helix ASW helicopter. The fleet was rounded out by a variety of frigates: three domestically produced *Godavari* FFH, which fired Styx missiles and carried 2 Sea King helicopters each; 6 British *Leander*-class (renamed *Nilgiri*-class); 1 ex-British *Whitby*-class (renamed *Talwar*), with Styx missiles and Chetak helicopter; 8 *Kamorta* (ex-Soviet *Petya*-class), 1 indigenous *Khukri* with Styx, and 2 British *Leopard*-class vessels which were used for training. India was trying to expand its 'in-house' naval construction capability, as evidenced by the launching of the guided missile destroyer *Delhi* in March 1991. At 6,500 tons, it was the largest warship ever built in India, but was not ready for service until 1995, well after the Fourth War.

The Indians used a variety of smaller craft (most of them Soviet-made) for coastal patrol duties, including 3 *Nanuchka II*s, 5 *Tarantul*s, 15 *Osa*s, 12 *Natya* minesweepers, 6 *Yevgenya* minesweepers, 9 *Polnocny* landing ships, 2 British *Ham* minesweepers, 1 domestic *Magar* tank landing ship, and 9 *Vasco da Gama* utility landing craft. Finally, the navy owned several tankers, tugs and support vessels.

The combat elements of the Indian naval air force comprised three attack squadrons of 8 British Sea Harriers each; one land-based fixed-wing ASW squadron with 4 Alize 1050s, and five rotary-wing ASW squadrons with a mix of Chetaks, Ka-25 Hormones, Ka-27 Helixes and Sea King MK 42As and Bs; and two maritime reconnaissance squadrons which employed BN-2, Il-38 and Tu-142 Bear-F planes.

India also had a small coastguard of about 2,500 men and women, with 1 British-built Type 14 frigate (the *Kuthar*), 31 various locally built patrol craft, and three air squadrons of various fixed- and rotary-wing aircraft.

The Indian Navy had one regiment of marines and had just finished forming and training a second regiment when the war broke out.

INDIAN NUCLEAR CAPABILITY

Although India had maintained an intentionally ambiguous public stand on its nuclear policy since 1974, when it exploded a 12-kiloton atomic device in the Pokhran Desert, it had clearly worked steadily for the past two decades to develop a strong nuclear weapons capability.

By 1993 India boasted two 220-Mw power reactors at Madras, a 100-Mw research reactor at Dhruva, and reprocessing plants for spent fuel at Tarapur and in the Babha Atomic Research Centre at Trombay. It has been estimated that the plutonium derived in 1990 alone from the

Madras and Dhruva reactors would have been enough to construct 35 to 115 (conservative and liberal estimates) 20-kiloton devices, and that by 1995 India's plutonium production would have been sufficient for 215 to 632 devices. By 2000 these figures would be 410 and 1,257.

The Indian Air Force had over 220 aircraft able to carry nuclear bombs (64 MiG-23BN/UMs, 80 Jaguars and 80 MiG-27s). The IAF had dedicated four squadrons, or approximately 100 planes, prepared to perform nuclear airstrikes if ordered. It had also been training pilots to conduct 'flip bombing', or 'toss bombing', attacks since 1984, and possibly earlier; this is a standard technique used for aerial nuclear weapon delivery.

In addition to its nuclear-capable aircraft, India had been aggressively pursuing a programme of indigenous ballistic missile development, focusing on two models: the Prithvi and the Agni. The Prithvi was a single-stage liquid-fuel rocket with a range of 250 kilometres and a payload of 1,000 kg. Its first successful test flight was in 1988. The payload capacity was sufficient for a nuclear weapon, but only bomblet, minelet, incendiary bomblet and prefragmented munitions warheads were being officially considered. The Prithvi completed its final testing stages in early 1992, with plans for full-scale production for the Indian Army. It gained effective battlefield mobility through the use of an eight-wheeled Kolos Tatra truck which served as a transporter–erector–launcher (TEL).

The Agni was a medium-range ballistic missile that consisted of the solid-fuel rocket booster of the Indian SLV-3 space launch vehicle (a derivation of the US Scout, used to place an Indian satellite into orbit) topped by a shortened Prithvi rocket. It completed its first successful test flight in May 1989. The Agni retained the Prithvi's 1,000-kg payload capacity, but with a 2,500-kilometre range it was a much more potent weapon, capable of use against targets anywhere in Pakistan or in China as far north as Beijing. The Indian Army had fielded the weapon by mid-1991. The Agni was capable of carrying either fission or thermonuclear warheads, and could be used with a mobile launcher.

THE PAKISTANI ARMED FORCES: ARMY

With 480,000 men on active duty, the Pakistani Army in 1993 was not quite half as large as that of India. There were seven corps headquarters, which between them commanded two armoured divisions, fourteen infantry divisions, five armoured brigades, four infantry brigades, eight artillery brigades (or brigade equivalents), three air defence artillery brigades, six armoured reconnaissance regiments and three special services battalions joined into one special services group. The army had one flight of fixed-wing observation aircraft (35 0-1Es and 50 Mashshaqs), one squadron of liaison aircraft (including 80 Mashshaqs), one attack helicopter squadron armed with AH-1s (with TOW) and three transport helicopter squadrons with a variety of models.

The Pakistani Army had a mix of tanks in its armoured units: 500 old US M-47s and M-48s, 51 Soviet T-54s and T-55s and, as its main model, 1,200 Chinese Type-59 tanks (which were themselves variants of the Soviet T-55). The Chinese Type-63 amphibious tank, derived from the Soviet PT-76, was used in the light tank role. It also had about 800 APCs, mostly old US M-113s but some Chinese Type-531s. Pakistan completed the prototype of its new domestic main battle tank, the P-90 (which was based on the Chinese T-85, which is basically a T-69 with a 125 mm gun), but it did not go into full production until 1994. Meanwhile, in June 1990 China agreed to let Pakistan begin licensed production of T-69 and T-85-II tanks (which used NATO-standard 105 mm guns), and to assist in the development of the P-90. In July 1990 Pakistan started constructing a new defence plant, which included three factories for building tanks, cannon and armoured vehicles; the complex cost $1.15 billion.

The Pakistani Army had more than 500 towed artillery pieces in its inventory, including the US M-101 105 mm and M-198 155 mm, and Chinese Type-54-1 122 mm and Type-59-1 130 mm pieces. Its self-propelled artillery consisted primarily of 95 US-made M-109A2 155 mm, plus 48 M-7 105 mm and M-110A2 203 mm guns as well. Like the Indians, the Pakistanis had a number of Soviet-made BM-21 122 mm MRLs, and they had deployed the Haft-1 surface-to-surface missile. Tests of the Haft-2 (built with Chinese assistance) were completed in 1991; it had a range of 300 kilometres (185 miles).

The Pakistanis relied on Cobra and TOW missiles for anti-tank defence, although they also employed the Chinese-made Red Arrow, of which they were building copies under the name Green Arrow; it had a 2,000-metre range. They still used the M-20 3.5-inch rocket launcher (successor to the American bazooka of World War II), the Chinese Type-52 75 mm recoilless rifle, and the venerable US M-40A 106 mm recoilless rifle, for which local factories produced new ammunition that gave the weapon a range of 1,500 metres and a penetration of 600 mm.

Air defence weapons in the Pakistani Army consisted mostly of small-calibre automatic weapons, such as 14.5 mm heavy machine guns, Chinese Type-55/-65 37 mm and Type-59 57 mm autocannons, and US M1 40 mm guns. There were only a few modern surface-to-air missiles

(SAMs) in the Pakistani arsenal, among them about 144 RBS–70s and 100 Stingers bought from the US.

In addition to the army, Pakistan had a 75,000-strong National Guard; the Frontier Corps (65,000); the Pakistan Rangers (15,000); and the Northern Light Infantry (7,000).

THE PAKISTANI ARMED FORCES: NAVY

The diminutive Pakistani Navy (15,000 men, including air, 6 submarines, 17 surface combatants) was nothing like the blue-water navy India had built. Its only base was at Karachi, and most of its vessels were useful only for operations near the coast.

Pakistan's submarines were all of French manufacture: 2 former *Agosta*-class (renamed *Hashmat*) and four *Hangor*-class (ex-*Daphne*). Its surface ships, in contrast, were either American or British in origin. Of its 7 destroyers, 6 were US *Gearing*-class (renamed *Alamgir*), while one, the *Babur*, was formerly the HMS *Devonshire*. The *Alamgir*s had the Harpoon missile as their primary weapon; the *Babur* relied on 4 Sea King helicopters and 4 114 mm guns. Pakistan also had 4 American *Brooke*-class guided missile frigates (renamed *Khyber*-class) on a five-year lease (and in November 1989 it purchased Vulcan-Phalanx anti-missile cannon for use on them), 2 US *Garcia*-class (renamed *Badr*-class) and 2 British *Leander*-class frigates (called *Shamsher*).

Pakistan also owned an array of Chinese-built coastal craft: 4 *Huangfeng* and four *Hegu* missile boats, all with Hai Ying 2 SSMs; 4 *Huchuan* torpedo boats, 4 *Hainan* (renamed *Baluchistan*) coastal patrol craft, and 12 *Quetta* (formerly *Shanghai*) and *Rajshahi* inshore patrol boats. Additionally, there were 3 former US minesweepers, a tanker, a survey boat and an ocean tug.

The Pakistani Navy was augmented by a small aviation contingent, consisting of one squadron of 4 Atlantics with Exocet missiles and two squadrons of ASW helicopters, armed with Exocets and SA-316B ASW torpedoes. All these aircraft were land-based, as Pakistan had no aircraft carriers.

Pakistan also had a small coastguard, with 2,000 personnel and some small craft.

THE PAKISTANI ARMED FORCES: AIR FORCE

The Pakistani Air Force (PAF) was primarily a defensive force, with no bombers or attack helicopters (the latter were attached directly to the army). The force's 450–odd aircraft were split almost evenly between fighters and ground attack planes bought from the US, France and China, disposed as shown in Table 2.2.

TABLE 2.2

PAKISTANI AIR FORCE: COMBAT UNITS

Mission	Aircraft type	Squadrons	Planes
Fighter/ground attack	Mirage-IIIEP/ Mirage-IIIDP	1	15
Fighter/ground attack	Mirage 5	4	64
Fighter/ground attack	Q-5	9	135
Fighter	J-6/JJ-6	9	153
Fighter	F-16	3	20
Fighter	J-7	1	20

The PAF also had two fixed-wing transport squadrons, equipped primarily with US-built C-130s, and a single rotary-wing transport squadron with only 6 helicopters. Pakistani combat planes were armed with US AIM-7 Sparrow or AIM-9 Sidewinder missiles, or French R-530 or R-550 Magic missiles. For anti-shipping missions the Mirage-IIIs carried the French Am-39 Exocet missile.

Air defence was provided by six batteries each armed with 6 French Crotale launchers, and one battery with 6 Soviet SA-2s.

In 1993 Pakistan and China were co-operating in the joint production of some aircraft, including the L-8 single-engine jet trainer being built in Nanchang in China.

In May 1990 Australia agreed to sell 50 old Mirage-III fighters to Pakistan, despite protests from India (the Mirage is capable of carrying nuclear weapons). Pakistan took delivery of 32 of them in late November, a welcome addition to the PAF since the cut-off of US military aid earlier in the year meant the suspension of the delivery of 71 more F-16s.

PAKISTANI NUCLEAR CAPABILITY

The development of nuclear weapons was a key priority to Pakistan, primarily because of its perceived vulnerability to India's conventional and nuclear superiority. Pakistan hoped to establish a credible deterrent to prevent Indian nuclear attacks in a future crisis. The Pakistanis also believed (rightly) that being the first Muslim nation to possess nuclear weapons would catapult them to the leadership of the Muslim world, including the vital Arab nations of the Middle East.

One nuclear facility, completed in the mid-1980s, was able to produce 10–20 kg of processed plutonium a year. Pakistan had also started building a 50-Mw reactor, but it was not yet operational. There was one 125-Mw nuclear power plant in the country and one enrichment plant at Kahuta. Another enrichment plant was under construction at Golra when the war began.

Pakistan had some experience with uranium as well as plutonium processing. Using natural uranium fuel, the Kahuta plant could produce 21 kg of weapons-grade uranium each year, sufficient for one atomic device; however, Pakistan had been stockpiling low-enriched uranium for several years, so Kahuta was actually able to generate up to 156 kg a year, enough for six crude atomic devices. Pakistan built its atomic weapons according to Chinese designs so they simply relied on data from Chinese tests, which were conducted periodically.

Until about 1990 the F-16s and Mirages of the Pakistan Air Force were the country's only delivery methods for any nuclear devices, and not very effective ones at that. There were only sixty F-16s, the plane best suited for the mission, but they were also the best escort and air defence suppression weapon in the PAF inventory and diverting some to perform a risky nuclear attack would have caused a noticeable deficiency elsewhere on the battlefield. They also did not possess the software to perform 'toss bombing', although that software could have been added easily. At the start of the war, not all of Pakistan's F-16s had yet been fitted with bomb racks strong enough to carry nuclear weapons, which are heavier than conventional bombs of comparable size.

In February 1989 Pakistan announced the successful test of its own surface-to-surface ballistic missile, the Haft-1, with a range of 80 kilometres and a payload capacity of 500 kg, sufficient for a small, crude atomic weapon. The Haft-2, with the same payload but a 300-kilometre range, was also under development. In addition to the Haft series, China sold two of its ballistic missile models, the M9 and M11, to Pakistan. The M11 has a range of 300 kilometres, the M9 about 600, and either missile could be configured to carry a chemical, biological or nuclear warhead and could be fired from fixed-site or mobile launchers. Deployment of these weapons drastically increased both Pakistan's strategic capability and tensions in the region.

A comparison of the military forces available to the belligerents is shown in Table 2.3.

TABLE 2.3

COMPARISON OF COMBAT FORCES

ARMY	India	Pakistan
Manpower* (total mobilisable)	2,486,000	1,063,000
MBTs	3,150	1,750
IFVs	800	600
ACs	150	80
APCs	450	845
Artillery pieces	4,100	1,445
MRLs	80	20
AIR FORCE		
Combat aircraft	805	450
Armed helicopters	288*	20†
AIR DEFENCE		
AAA guns	2,750	1,500
SAMs*	691	786
NAVY		
Submarines	19	6
DDs/FFGs	28	15
Fast missile craft	12	8

  * Includes army and air force elements.
  † One squadron in the army.

THE ROAD TO WAR

Between 1991 and 1993, revolutions and strikes in the Soviet republics tore that superpower apart, and a consequent general upsurge in Muslim awareness sparked a similar insurgency in the Vale of Kashmir. As so often in the past, Pakistan covertly aided the agitators, allowing them to train and gather supplies inside Pakistan, but this time there was a new twist to the situation. Other Muslim nations, notably Libya, Iran, Iraq and Afghanistan, let it be known that they would support Pakistan in any future conflict with India, even hinting that they might send ground troops as a show of 'Muslim solidarity'. One reason for this hitherto unexpected support from far-off Muslim quarters was the fact that, early in 1993, information was leaked that a Chinese nuclear test in the Sinkiang desert was actually a Chinese-supervised test of Pakistan's first fusion device. News of this breakthrough greatly increased Pakistan's prestige in the Muslim world; even to the point that Libyan leader Qaddafi made veiled references to the Kashmir crisis as the beginning of the restoration of the Mogul Empire.

This latest crisis was a serious threat to India. Its relations with China were already deteriorating due to Indian ballistic missile deployments in Assam. At the same time, uprisings in Tamil Nadu and Punjab were diverting a large number of troops and resources. As the rhetoric intensified and several Arab countries appeared to be preparing forces for deployment to Pakistan, the Indian Prime Minister called a secret emergency meeting of top government officials and military leaders. They decided to launch an all-out pre-emptive strike on Pakistan before troops could arrive from other nations, hoping to eliminate the Pakistani threat to the western border once and for all.

To strike as quickly as possible and with the least warning to Pakistan, the Indians decided to launch the assault with the ground forces already in place: two corps in Kashmir, two in Punjab and one in Rajasthan. No other forces could be brought into play during the opening attacks because moving them up to the border would alert the Pakistanis and give the other Muslim allies time to deploy small tripwire forces, which if attacked could escalate the war into one against a Muslim coalition rather than just Pakistan. As soon as the war began, however, one mountain corps was scheduled to be brought west from the Eastern Region, along with the infantry/armour corps from the Central Region; meanwhile, the Southern Region command would retain its corps of four infantry divisions to suppress the Tamil riots, while the other elements of the Eastern Region would guard the border of Bangladesh in case the Bengali Muslims tried to support their former countrymen with diversionary attacks (an event deemed unlikely considering the bad blood between the two groups). This Eastern force also had the responsibility of keeping an eye on China, although Indian leaders realised that if the Chinese staged a massive ground intervention there would be little they could do, short of nuclear attack, to stop them. Meanwhile, the

Central Region retained two infantry divisions and one mountain division as a strategic reserve.

Unlike the ground forces, it was easy to redeploy the Indian air units to the western theatre in a short time, and orders were quickly issued to concentrate 80 per cent of the IAF's squadrons in the west (two-thirds were already there). The final tally of squadrons flying against Pakistan on the first day was:

1   Canberra bomber squadron (10 planes)
2   6 MiG-23 ground attack squadrons (90 planes)
4   Jaguar ground attack squadrons (56 planes)
4   MiG-21 ground attack squadrons (56 planes)
4   Ajeet ground attack squadrons (64 planes)
1   Marut ground attack squadron (20 planes)
3   MiG-29 fighter squadrons (48 planes)
3   Mirage-2000 fighter squadrons (51 planes)
4   MiG-23 fighter squadrons (64 planes)
8   MiG-21 fighter squadrons (136 planes)
1   Jaguar maritime attack squadron (8 planes)
1   Canberra reconnaissance squadron (8 planes)
1   MiG-25 reconnaissance squadron (8 planes)
1   Mi-25 attack helicopter squadron (12 helicopters)

This provided a total of 619 planes (603 of them combat aircraft) to support the Indian attacks.

OUTBREAK OF WAR

The war began shortly after midnight on 18 October 1993, with Indian airstrikes on Pakistani forward airfields and civilian airports at Islamabad/Rawalpindi, Lahore and Karachi. These raids knocked out some of the PAF on the ground, suppressed Pakistani air defences and established Indian air superiority. More importantly, they prevented the Muslim allies from flying in any troops to aid the Pakistanis.

At the same time, naval aircraft (one squadron of Sea Harriers) from the carrier *Vikrant* struck the Pakistan naval base at Karachi (the *Viraat* carrier group remained in the Bay of Bengal for the first week of the war). A series of brief naval clashes sank most of the outmatched Pakistani Navy; the few surviving craft fled to Iran. From that point on, India instituted an airtight blockade of Pakistan's only major port, Karachi, preventing the arrival of troops transports from the Muslim allies. Indian naval aircraft also interdicted the two highways running through Baluchistan, stopping the flow of supplies and troops from Iran. As a result, what little aid Pakistan did receive from the Muslim allies trickled through Afghanistan.

India had considered using its nuclear weapons as part of the opening attacks on 18 October. An Indian first strike against Pakistani military targets would have virtually eliminated Pakistan's ability to retaliate and might also have caused enough 'collateral damage' to force Pakistan's collapse. However, the Indian leaders decided against the nuclear option for three reasons. First, India had enough bombs, delivery systems and bases beyond Pakistan's reach to survive a Pakistani first strike and still deliver a crippling retaliatory strike. Second, they believed they could defeat Pakistan without resorting to nuclear weapons. Finally, India wanted to avoid the censure of being the second country in the world's history to use nuclear weapons in war.

As planned by the Indian leaders, the opening ground attacks occurred simultaneously along the western front at dawn on 18 October. The I Corps, advancing from Srinagar (with some elements at Poonch) drove toward Islamabad and Rawalpindi from the east, running into the Pakistani I Corps (reinforced later in the fighting by elements of the V Corps). The II Corps' objective was to seize Sialkot from positions around Jammu, then drive north through Gujrat and Jhelum to meet the I Corps at Islamabad. This was the only facet of the Indian ground offensive that went more or less as planned. The III Corps and the IV Corps at Amritsar, supplemented by the V Corps at Firozpur, were to drive on Lahore against the Pakistani II Corps. Meanwhile, the Indian Navy landed its two marine regiments to seize Karachi. As the war began, contingency plans were also being considered for an air assault to capture Hyderabad.

The thrust with which India hoped to conclude the war speedily, that of the I Corps toward Islamabad and Rawalpindi, ground to a halt against strong forward Pakistani defences on the east side of the Jhelum River. Despite a two-to-one superiority in combat aircraft and over three to one in personnel, the I Corps suffered over 1,500 casualties on 18 October alone, partly a result of the lack of effective preparation time before the attack. The Indians regrouped and renewed the attack on 19 October, but with the same results. Even the arrival of an armoured division from the Central Region did little to dislodge the Pakistanis, and forty-two Indian tanks were lost on 20 October in ambushes near Kitli and Uri. Two infantry divisions from the strategic reserve were thrown into the line on 22 October to try to crack the line near Muree, but they were matched on the Pakistani side by the arrival

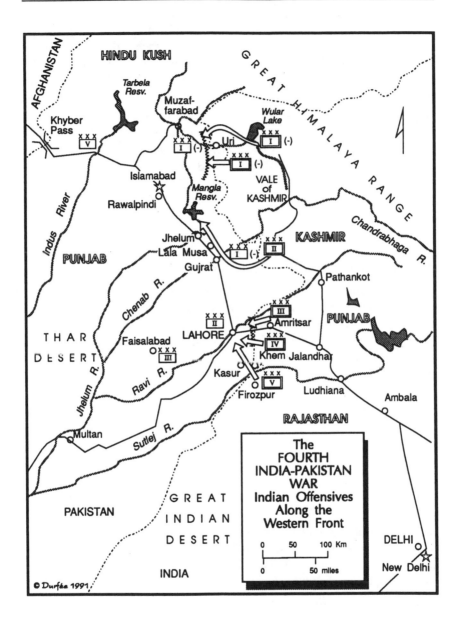

The
FOURTH
INDIA-PAKISTAN
WAR
Indian Offensives
Along the
Western Front

of one infantry brigade and one artillery brigade, hurriedly brought down from the V Corps at Peshawar. The Indians continued to funnel reinforcements into the offensive as they arrived from the Central and Eastern Regions, never despairing of breaking through, but, after the first week, aiming more toward tying down Pakistani reserves so they could not interfere with the II Corps' drive in southern Kashmir, which was gaining momentum.

That drive had commenced late on 18 October with a six-to-one Indian superiority in men and tanks. Exploiting the weakness that resulted from Pakistani reserves shifting north earlier in the day to meet the I Corps attack, the II Corps had advanced halfway to Sialkot by the next morning. The advance picked up steam the next day, fifty Pakistani tanks being destroyed in an enormous armour battle, and by evening the hard-driving Indians were pushing into the outskirts of Sialkot, though at a frightful cost. On 20 October the II Corps penetrated into and through the city and reached Wazirabad. The axis of advance turned north on 21 October to drive on Rawalpindi from the south. At Gujrat the Indians engaged a fresh Pakistani infantry division. The Indians were hardly slowed, and seized Gujrat near the end of 22 October. After regrouping and being reinforced by a mountain division the next day, on 24 October the Indians overran the Pakistani line at Kharian and reached the suburbs of Jhelum on 25 October. There the advance became bogged down in costly urban fighting that destroyed much of the city.

The Indians now recognised that the Pakistani line protecting Islamabad, their capital, was strengthening as it contracted, despite the dreadful toll exacted by incessant Indian fighter-bomber attacks. For four days a costly war of attrition raged; both sides suffered severe losses, but the Pakistanis, their reserves exhausted, gave way first. Late on 29 October a portion of their line on the south side of the Mangla Reservoir collapsed, and reinforcements had to be rushed from the northern sector to plug the gap. This gave the Indian I Corps the opening it had awaited for nearly two weeks. It pushed the Pakistani line in the north back about a kilometre towards Muzaffarabad that afternoon, and another two kilometres the next day. By 31 October the Pakistanis were in retreat north and south of Islamabad, losing five kilometres in the north while in the south their line was ruptured in several places. The Indians pushed forward fifteen kilometres on 30 October and almost twenty the next day. Late that night the Indians reached Gujar Khan, the last major town south of Rawalpindi, with only scattered elements of Pakistani units between them and the city's airport.

The other main Indian thrust was intended to seize Lahore, push to Faisalabad, and (depending on results elsewhere) perhaps even continue to Multan. The objective was to split Pakistan almost in two, bringing the heavily populated area east of the Indus River under Indian control. This proved to be too ambitious a goal. The Indian III and IV Corps, based along the border west of Amritsar, made little progress in the Atari–Wagah corridor along the Amritsar–Lahore highway on 18 October, primarily because the bulk of Pakistan's armoured units were based near there. A savage Pakistani counterattack cost the Indians

55 tanks and 1,021 casualties, compared to 24 tanks and less than 300 men lost by the Pakistanis. Heavy fighting the next day brought similar losses but no Indian advance.

Meanwhile, the Indian V Corps, advancing from Firozpur, staged a brilliant flanking manoeuvre against the Pakistani line at Ganda Singhwala and raced ten kilometres up the highway toward Kasur on the first day and seized that town on 19 October. The V Corps had been scheduled to turn west at that point and proceed toward Jaranwala and Faisalabad, but was instead directed to continue pressing north to help the III and IV Corps achieve their breakthrough. After regrouping for a day at Kasur, the V Corps joined in a combined assault with the III and IV Corps on 21 October, but the pause had allowed a Pakistani artillery brigade from the III Corps (at Faisalabad) and an independent armoured brigade to reach the area and bolster the defences. Consequently, neither Indian attack gained ground despite heavy losses. The same was true for the fifth day, and the sixth and seventh, and it appeared that the southern offensive had completely failed. Then, late on 24 October, one mountain and two infantry divisions from the Eastern and Central Regions reached Amritsar. They were the last available Indian reserves. Coincidentally, the last immediately available Pakistani reserve, an infantry brigade from the III Corps, went into the line near Raja that same day. The scales now tipped in favour of the Indians, who pushed to Luliani Jang and to a point halfway between Atari and Lahore on 25 October. On 26 October the V Corps overran Lahore airport, and two days later the three Indian corps linked up in and around Lahore as the dazed Pakistanis withdrew toward Jaranwala, Shekhupura and Kamoke, establishing a new line behind the Degh River. The Indians pressed on, regardless of losses, breaching the Degh line on 30 October and advancing to Sharqpur and the outskirts of Shekhupura on 31 October.

As its defences were being overrun, Pakistan's leaders hurriedly conferred to consider playing their trump card: a nuclear strike against India. However, using the F-16s, only a few bases were within reach, and Pakistan did not have enough bombs on hand even to hit all of those, so India's second strike capability would remain devastatingly intact. In addition, Pakistani leaders knew that the Indian air defence system was very sophisticated, and that not many of the precious F-16s would get through to their targets. Those bombs that were dropped might still cause heavy civilian casualties (the term in vogue at the time was 'collateral damage'), which would provoke massive Indian retaliation. For these reasons, the Pakistani leadership decided against using their nuclear weapons.

After two weeks of very bloody fighting, diplomatic pressure and threats of sanctions by the US, UN and China forced a cease-fire. The Pakistanis, exhausted and on the verge of collapse, were all too eager to accept: their nuclear plants at Kahuta and Golra, outside Islamabad, had been bombed into rubble, as had their only major port, Karachi. All their roads, bridges and industrial facilities east of the Indus River had been terribly damaged by Indian fighter-bombers and missiles. The Indians, with complete victory almost in their grasp, had been harder to convince, but reported Chinese troop movements in Tibet finally forced them to agree.

Two weeks had been sufficient time to cripple the Pakistani defence force and economic infrastructure and at the same time severely to damage the Indian forces' offensive capabilities. Indian personnel casualties, at 48,036 killed and wounded, were almost double Pakistan's figure of about 25,000, largely due to ill-prepared and clumsy Indian frontal assaults and tenacious Pakistani defensive actions. But Pakistani casualties were mounting rapidly. These figures represented about 4.6 per cent of the Indian Army and 5.2 per cent of Pakistan's, seemingly not devastating percentages until it is realised that most of these casualties were from front-line combat units. Tank losses were remarkably similar: 788 for India (25 per cent of its entire tank force) and 785 for Pakistan (43.6 per cent). Air attacks by Indian fighter-bombers played a major role in knocking out Pakistani tanks, which were often hidden in dug-in, concealed positions from which to launch ambushes.

Aircraft on both sides paid a heavy price: 124 Indian planes had been destroyed or damaged (15 per cent of the IAF) as opposed to 125 Pakistani (28 per cent). India was able to make up its air losses within a short time after the war (most of its losses were older MiG-21s and Canberras); Pakistan, with its economy in ruins, has still not fully recovered. Of the non-tank vehicles (trucks, jeeps, APCs, etc.) associated with modern mechanised armies, India lost 7,032 in the short war and Pakistan 4,426 – a staggering figure indicative of the carnage strewn about the entire 500-kilometre border area.

The Pakistani Navy was obliterated, the port of Karachi occupied and sacked by Indian marines, and countless bridges in the Indus, Sutlej, Chenab, Ravi and Jhelum River valleys destroyed. Although at a higher cost than most analysts predicted, India achieved its goal of removing the Pakistani armed forces as a threat while avoiding hostilities with other Muslim nations, and (albeit perhaps narrowly) averting a war with China.

SUPERPOWER RELATIONS AND THE WAR

The war between India and Pakistan did not take place in a political vacuum; however, it was over before any of the major powers could become deeply involved in the conflict.

Of the three principal powers (China, the Commonwealth of Independent States (CIS, formerly USSR) and the US), the CIS was the least directly concerned. Although the USSR had sold much military hardware to India in the previous decade and had participated in other projects that improved relations between the two countries, the CIS had no treaty obligation to India which would have compelled them to intervene. In any case, the former Soviet republics had enough internal problems to occupy their attention, and had no inclination to support India against Pakistan.

The relationship of the US with Pakistan was different. For many years Pakistan had been a staunch US ally in the region, alongside Turkey and pre-revolutionary Iran. Pakistan was traditionally one of the top five or ten recipients of American foreign aid each year, receiving over half a billion dollars in financial year 1990 alone ($239 million of which was for military supplies, the rest for economic and food aid; an increase of $15 million over 1989, in spite of US budget cuts). However, the warm relations between the two countries which had developed during their joint opposition of the eight-year Soviet adventure in Afghanistan had recently cooled because of Pakistan's determined pursuit of nuclear technology and America's equal determination to prevent the spread of nuclear weapons. By law, each year the US President had to certify to Congress that Pakistan did not possess nuclear weapons in order to allow the aid money to Pakistan to be appropriated.

The Pakistanis, who resented this intrusion but who were also heavily dependent on the aid to maintain their defence establishment, were reluctant to provide the necessary proof to the President. In 1990 the Pakistani government refused altogether, and this was possibly a factor in the fall of the Bhutto government. President Bush asked Congress to delay suspending the aid in order to give the new government of Prime Minister Sharif time to comply, but Sharif declined to do so, citing his country's need 'to develop self-reliance above all else'. He did, however, announce the implementation of the International Nuclear Events Scale accident reporting system on a one-year trial basis. Bush tried to tempt Pakistan into signing the Nuclear Non-Proliferation Treaty (NPT) with offers to sell it a new reactor in return, but Pakistan, which had consistently refused to sign the treaty unless India also did so, bought a reactor from China instead. By the beginning of 1991 it was clear that Pakistan's rulers had no intention of altering their nuclear research goals or comp-lying with US demands, with the result that military aid was suspended and non-military aid fell to only $208 million.

The US had strong economic ties to both India and Pakistan (it was the principal trading partner, in dollar terms, of both countries). There-fore, rather than taking sides in the Fourth India-Pakistan War, the US used its influence to back a UN cease-fire plan as quickly as possible, and used the incident to push through more international regulations pro-hibiting the spread (and punishing the use) of nuclear weapons.

The 'wild card' power with respect to the war was China, which had strong ties to Pakistan and bore considerable animosity toward India. They were natural rivals, since they were not only neighbours but were the world's two most populous countries, and both sought a dominant share of regional power. The fact that China was a permanent member of the UN Security Council while India was not was particularly galling to India. Their rivalry had been fuelled by India's development of its own nuclear capability and rocket technology, which China saw as a very real threat. (Ironically, India's quest for nuclear power really began in earnest after China exploded its own first device in 1964; to India, that event was ominously close on the heels of India's defeat by China in the 1962 war.)

TABLE 2.4

HUMAN COST OF THE WAR

Nation	Killed	Wounded	Total casualties
India	9,607	38,429	48,036
Pakistan	c.5,000	c.20,000	c.25,000

China had refrained from intervening militarily in the earlier India–Pakistan wars, however, even when Pakistan was being badly beaten as in the 1971 war. It again chose not to intervene in the fourth war. China instead joined the US and the UN in trying to stop the war before it started, and was active in the diplomacy which eventually resulted in a cease-fire. Chinese leaders had earlier considered that providing full nuclear capability to Pakistan would be the only way to offset India's growing power in South Asia. However, belatedly recognising that this could have led to nuclear catastrophe in the war, China tried not only to avoid direct involvement, but also to bring the war as quickly as possible to a non-nuclear conclusion.

TNDM ADDENDUM: FOURTH INDIA–PAKISTAN WAR

THE BATTLE OF LAHORE

The capture of Lahore was a major objective of the initial Indian offensives of the war. The Indian III Corps, commanded by Lieutenant General Ashok Gupta, and the IV Corps, under Lieutenant General Harpal Singh, attacked westward along the axes of the Amritsar–Lahore highway, and the parallel railroad, on 18 October 1993. (The III Corps consisted of the 6th Armoured and 6th Infantry Divisions; the IV Corps comprised the 4th Mechanised Infantry and 15th Infantry Divisions.) This drive was quickly halted near the border towns of Atari and Wagah by the Pakistani II Corps, commanded by Lieutenant General Omar Kandahari.

After several days of stalemate near the border, on 25 October Major General Satinder Kapoor's Indian V Corps swung northward to make a massive assault at Luliana Jang against the right of the II Pakistani Corps. This corps, which had been recently reinforced, consisted of the 10th, 11th, 12th and 35th Infantry Divisions and the 20th Mountain Division. The Indian attack drove back the right flank of the Pakistani corps, and forced General Kandahari to commit his reserves, and then to shift forces from his left flank, to prevent a collapse of his right. This permitted the Indian III and IV Corps to capture Wagah, and to continue slowly advancing westward.

Pounded by Indian air attacks, Kandahari's corps began to crumble on 26 October, and an Indian tank brigade seized Lahore airport, south-east of the city. Heavy fighting raged in southern and eastern Lahore throughout 27 October. Next day the two Indian forces linked up in the centre of the city, then continued west and north in pursuit of the battered Pakistanis.

TABLE TNDM 2.1

TNDM STATISTICS: BATTLE OF LAHORE

INDIA	Strength	Losses	Daily losses (%)
Men	101,343	8,181	2.02
Armour	893	503	14.08
Artillery	654	31	1.19
PAKISTAN			
Men	29,530	4,763	4.03
Armour	634	411	16.21
Artillery	524	28	1.34

CHAPTER THREE

CIVIL WAR IN RUSSIA

INTRODUCTION

The Soviet Union was a vast patchwork empire that was held together for seventy years by the iron will of the Communist Party of the Soviet Union and its right arm, the Soviet Army. The largest nation on the planet, it was simply too large and too diverse to be ruled effectively by a centralised government. The measures and policies which allowed the Communist Party to maintain control as long as it did also caused the Soviet economy to fall behind the West technologically and to become riddled with corruption, as capitalist tendencies won over those in a position to gain money or power by abusing the system. The reforms introduced by President Mikhail Gorbachev in the years 1985–91 were intended to redress these abuses and deficiencies in the Soviet system. Although they met with some success they did not do so quickly enough. They did, however, allow the fifteen constituent republics of the USSR to experience just enough freedom to make them want more.

The event that began in the Soviet Union in 1989 had much in common with an era in Russian history called 'The Time of Troubles'. During a tumultuous eight-year period, from the death of Tsar Boris Godunov in 1605 to the accession of Michael Romanov in 1613, Russia had five tsars, was wracked by internal turmoil and numerous attempted *coups d'état*, and was invaded by two foreign countries (Sweden and Poland) attempting to take advantage of the chaotic situation in Russia.

THE NEW TIME OF TROUBLES

The internal stresses and strains within the Soviet Union, and within its constituent republics, had become evident to the rest of the world even before the collapse of the Eastern European empire which Soviet dictator

Joseph Stalin had created during and just after World War II. While the USSR remained without question one of the two most powerful countries in the world – in terms of armed forces and armaments – the political and economic bankruptcy of Marxist–Leninist communism made that military might almost irrelevant when moderate non-communist regimes in Hungary, Poland, Czechoslovakia, East Germany, Romania and Bulgaria pulled away from the Eastern Bloc military alliance, the so-called Warsaw Pact, in 1989 and 1990.

Furthermore, the internal problems of the Soviet Union absorbed much more of the attention of the people of the USSR than did the collapse of the external empire. In 1989 internal strife and disorder spread through various portions of the Soviet Union. Particularly disrupting were the strenuous efforts by the peoples of the three Baltic republics – Estonia, Latvia and Lithuania – to secede completely from the Soviet Union, and to regain the independent status they had enjoyed before they were absorbed by Stalin's aggression in 1940. These efforts at secession were at least partly successful, although they did not at first gain full sovereignty. There followed other – less strident – demands for independence from other republics, most notably the Ukraine.

At the same time, virtual civil war was going on in the Transcaucasian republics, between Azerbaijan and Armenia, and within Georgia. Only with difficulty, and considerable bloodshed, were Soviet troops able to maintain a semblance of law and order in these three republics. Internal violence was also rampant in much of Soviet Central Asia, and in the Moldavian Republic. By mid-1991 the USSR appeared close to dissolution.

Hard-line communists in the government blamed this state of affairs upon the liberal policies of President Gorbachev. On 9 August a group of senior Soviet officials – hard-line communists, led by Vice-President Gennady Yanayev – seized control of the government, and announced Gorbachev's ousting as president. They sent troops to Gorbachev's vacation home in the Crimea to place the defiant President under house arrest. They also sent troops into central Moscow to seize the President of the Russian Republic, Boris Yeltsin, and members of his government. However, Yeltsin exercised charismatic leadership; he courageously denounced the coup leaders, and inspired his followers and thousands of ordinary citizens of Moscow to erect barricades around the 'White House' (the building containing the offices of the Russian Republic). The troops and tanks sent by the coup leaders surrounded the White House barricades, but refused to storm them, or to open fire upon the defenders.

In the face of popular resistance from the people of Moscow, the top leaders were unable to exercise control over the army, and on 21 August they lost their nerve. One committed suicide; the others were soon arrested, and Gorbachev came back from the Crimea to join Yeltsin in triumphant celebration of the survival of the new but apparently sturdy democracy of the USSR. The three Baltic republics took advantage of the turmoil in Moscow to reassert sovereignty, and under pressure from the US and other European countries Gorbachev recognised their independence.

The hero of the democratic victory was undoubtedly Yeltsin, who probably could have seized power with popular support, but who had demanded the restoration of the constitutional government under Gorbachev. Although for a while Gorbachev seemed to be dominated by Yeltsin by fall he apparently emerged from the shadow of the Russian President. The triumph of democracy was less complete, however, than the euphoric press accounts of the affair and its aftermath suggested. The basic economic troubles of the USSR remained unsolved. Conservative communists were still numerous, powerful, and totally opposed to Gorbachev and his reforms. The army (still the largest in the world) was dissatisfied with the decline of Soviet power. And unrest and violence continued unabated in the Transcaucasus and parts of Central Asia.

To appreciate fully the turmoil that occurred in and around Russia during the early years of its 'New Time of Troubles', it is essential to understand something of the diversity of the people and the problems in the twelve republics remaining in the USSR after the coup, and the central significance of the Russian Republic in relation to the other eleven, and in relation to the central government of the Union (see Map 3.1 for the geography).

RUSSIA: THE RUSSIAN SFSR

The Russian Soviet Federated Socialist Republic was some 6.6 million square miles in area, almost twice that of the US – and 77 per cent of the area of the entire Soviet Union. The Russian SFSR extended from the Black and Baltic Seas in the west, to the Pacific Ocean in the east, and from well north of the Arctic Circle to the mountains and deserts of Mongolia. One hundred and forty-nine million of the USSR's 290 million people lived in Russia, most of them west of the Urals, in European Russia, and could be divided into sixty distinct nationalities and hundreds of ethnic groups. The largest of the groups was the Russians, a Slavic people dating back to the third century AD, with a

political history beginning in the ninth century. Among the numerous other ethnic groups in the Russian SFSR were many that most Westerners (and, one suspects, many Russians) had never heard of, such as Chuvash, Bashkirs, Udmurts, Chechens and Cheremis. Russia was no less of a melting pot of cultures than was the US.

Geographically, Russia was divided into nine zones, including the East European Plain, the Ural Mountains, the Far East, and several Siberian areas. Politically it was divided into sixteen ASSRs (autonomous soviet socialist republics), ten autonomous *okruga* (districts), six *kraya*, forty-nine *oblasti* (regions), and five autonomous oblasti.

The economy can be summarised by saying that Russia, like the US, made almost everything; only quantities and qualities varied. The Russian economy was neither as service– nor as information–orientated as America's, tended to be more industrial, and was technologically backward in comparison with the US and Western Europe.

Before the New Time of Troubles, Westerners, particularly Americans, tended to use the terms 'Russia' and 'Soviet Union' interchangeably. While the Soviet Union was nearly identical in area to the tsarist Russian Empire, and was essentially a continuation of that empire in the sense that its ruling class was composed primarily of Russians, the

Russian Republic and the Soviet Union (of which it was a component) had been distinct political entities since the conclusion of the Russian Civil War in 1922.

The liberal era in Soviet politics that ended the Cold War and freed Eastern Europe from almost fifty years of communist domination began in 1985 with the accession of Mikhail Gorbachev to the post of General Secretary of the Communist Party of the Soviet Union (CPSU) and his introduction of *glasnost* (openness) and *perestroika* (restructuring). He brought a new youthful dynamism and flexibility to Soviet politics and worked to improve relations with the West; he also gradually initiated programmes to reintroduce free trade and private ownership into the ailing Soviet economy. His reforms, welcomed enthusiastically by a majority of the Soviet people, were viewed with a jaundiced eye by more conservative elements, particularly the professional military and hard-line communist politicians. They felt threatened by Gorbachev's plans to cut military spending and to divorce the CPSU from the country's economic affairs. Moreover, these conservatives had been raised under the leadership of Stalin, Khruschev and Brezhnev, and were uncomfortable with the uncertainty that accompanied innovation and openness. Gorbachev rode a wave of popularity, especially abroad, as a result of his reforms, but those reforms had acted to loosen the lid tightly clamped on the boiling Soviet political pot.

In 1990, as several republics along the southern and western edges of the USSR took advantage of their new freedoms to try to break from the Union, Gorbachev seemed to retrench, taking conservative stands against the calls for autonomy from those republics and using the armed forces to restore stability. He doubtless feared that the pace of his reforms would lead the hard-liners to oust him before his plans for total reform could bear fruit. His new conservatism angered some of his radical allies, particularly Boris Yeltsin, the earthy, popular Moscow Communist Party Secretary who had accompanied Gorbachev on his political rise. In early 1991 Yeltsin was elected President of the Russian SFSR by an overwhelming majority in the first popular election ever held in Russia. He began to criticise Gorbachev's backsliding from liberalism, and called for accelerated reforms. This erosion of liberal support was both frustrating and dangerous to Gorbachev, plagued as he was with crippling strikes by coalminers and rebellious republics, while his position, if not his head, was also being threatened by conservatives. Given Yeltsin's growing popularity in Russia, Gorbachev was eventually forced to reach accommodation with Yeltsin, who then praised Gorbachev for regaining the liberal track. The result of Gorbachev's move back toward liberalism was increased opportunity for several of the republics to break away from the Soviet Union. There were also prophetic whispers that the military and conservative communist bureaucrats might engineer a coup to replace Gorbachev to prevent the USSR's disintegration and to restore a centralised dictatorial regime.

THE SOUTH-WESTERN REPUBLICS

The three republics on the south-western edge of the Soviet Union – the Ukraine, Belorussia and Moldavia – were all, at one time, either independent countries or provinces of other countries that the Russian Empire had absorbed over past centuries. This early expansion of the Russian Empire had been largely to form a buffer between the *Rodina* (motherland) and invaders from Central Europe. The people of the Ukraine and Belorussia were Slavs, related to the Russians; the Moldavians were essentially Romanians, descended from Roman-Dacians, with some admixture of Walachs (or Vlachs). All three harboured a long-standing desire for independence. Indeed two of them had a relatively recent legal basis for claiming it: Belorussia and the Ukraine were founding members of the United Nations. This was engineered by the Soviets at the San Francisco Conference at the end of World War II in order to offset to some degree what they felt would be the numerical advantage of an opposing bloc of Western countries. For the Ukraine they could make the case with some sincerity, since it had twice been a sovereign nation, if only briefly. For Belorussia, however, it was historically pure fiction. Nonetheless, these two republics, which in the 1980s had been anything but sovereign, could in 1990 use this legal anomaly as a lever with which to pry themselves away from the Soviet Union.

Apart from the damage to the Soviet economy and population base which the potential loss of these republics posed, Soviet leadership was particularly concerned about the military and psychological effects: removal of the buffer the Russians had set up to protect themselves from their traditional Western enemies, specifically Poland and (most important) newly reunified Germany. For this reason alone, the Russian leadership of the USSR fought to retain its grip on the Western republics.

UKRAINIAN SSR

The Ukraine is often referred to as 'the breadbasket of Europe'. The collective and state farms of this Texas-sized republic produced more than a fifth of the USSR's annual agricultural harvest, most of it grain, and also potatoes, vegetables, fruits, sunflower seeds (grown for their oil) and sugar beets. There were also herds of many types of domestic animals, and fishing along the Black Sea coast was rewarding. In addition to agricultural wealth, the Ukraine had rich iron and manganese deposits and a plethora of other minerals, including coal, petroleum, bauxite, titanium and sulphur. Because of this abundance of resources, the Ukraine had been a main objective of the German invasion of the Soviet Union in 1941. The fighting that raged there in World War II had utterly destroyed the republic's economy, but massive Soviet reconstruction efforts after the war restored the Ukraine to its pre-war prosperity within ten years.

The Ukraine was the second most heavily populated Soviet republic, home to over 52 million people, mostly Ukrainians, but also including more than a hundred separate ethnic groups, most of them Slavic (such as Russians, Poles, White Russians and Bulgarians) as well as Greeks, Romanians, Armenians, Gypsies, Hungarians, Tatars, Lithuanians and Kazakhs. The Ukrainian language, also called Ruthenian, was a dialect of Russian and Belorussian that had split from the mainstream of the language in the twelfth and thirteenth centuries.

The Ukraine – or at least part of it – was an independent nation in the mid-seventeenth century, when the Cossack rulers appealed to the Russian state of Muscovy for aid against Poland. The Muscovites took this as an invitation to absorb the Ukraine into their state, which they accomplished by the end of the eighteenth century. They ruled the Ukraine until the 1917 Revolution, when a succession of Ukrainian governments struggled to maintain it as a free state against communists who were just as determined to keep it in the new Soviet Union. The communists won, and set about reshaping the Ukrainian culture. They seized all private lands and forced all farmers to move to collective and state farms. Peasant resistance led to widespread famine in which more than 5 million peasants died.

When the Germans invaded the Soviet Union in 1941, the Ukrainians saw them as liberators from the Stalinist reign of terror, but xenophobic Nazis lumped them with other despised Slavic 'non-Aryans' and treated them with contempt. Nazi atrocities turned the Ukrainians against the conquerors, many becoming effective partisans fighting for the Soviet Union. These same partisans often operated against the Soviets after they reconquered the region. Anti-communist resistance continued in the Ukraine into the early 1950s, and the intellectual vestiges of resistance continued through the 1980s. One result was that, on 16 July 1990, the Ukraine declared independence from the USSR.

At first Moscow appeared willing to acquiesce, and the central government even signed a mutual co-operation treaty on 19 November

1990, referring to the Soviet Union and the Ukraine as 'sovereign states'. One result of Moscow's lenience was Ukrainian agreement to vote in the referendum on a new Union Treaty on 17 March 1991. The measure passed with a 52 per cent majority (although 60 per cent of the voters would have preferred an alternative choice that allowed autonomy for all the republics). On 21 March Britain took the unusual step of opening a consulate in Kiev, the Ukrainian capital, which the Soviets uneasily (and Ukrainians joyfully) saw as a first step toward international recognition of an independent Ukraine.

There were, however, internal tensions in the Ukraine. Chief among these was the pro-Soviet tendency of the Crimeans, who were predominantly Russian. In a 20 January 1991 referendum Crimea voted to break away from the Ukraine and join the Russian SFSR. Native Tatars and Ukrainians boycotted the vote, and no immediate steps were taken to implement it. Possibly encouraged by this, Moscow's attitude toward the Ukraine changed abruptly. On 19 April 1991 Soviet troops seized a Ukrainian border post and banned all strikes in order to keep Ukrainians from supporting a massive strike by Russian coalminers. Relations between Kiev and Moscow were severely strained, but in subsequent months both sides avoided significant violence.

BELORUSSIAN SSR

Also known as Byelorussia or White Russia, Belorussia was a republic on the USSR's western border, adjoining Poland, and the size of England and Scotland. It was a land of contrasts, heavily industrialised and thickly populated but containing vast areas of forest and marsh that sheltered perhaps the densest concentrations of wildlife remaining in Europe. The capital, Minsk, was the largest industrial centre in the western Soviet Union. The republic had made an amazing recovery from World War II, when virtually all industry and agriculture were destroyed by the German invasion and subsequent Soviet counteroffensives. In 1992 over 60 per cent of Belorussia's economy was based on industry, semi-manufactured goods being the major product. Recent discoveries of oil in southern Belorussia sparked a growing oil industry. In addition, the republic's moderate climate favoured large crops of rye, oats, flax, potatoes and sugar beet.

Four-fifths of the population were Belorussians, descendants of a Slavic people that settled in the region between the sixth and eighth centuries AD and who were later conquered by the Lithuanians and Poles. The remaining people were Russians, Ukrainians, Poles, Jews, Tatars, Lithuanians, Gypsies and Latvians.

Russia acquired Belorussia in a series of three partitions of Poland (carried out in concert with Prussia and Austria–Hungary) in 1772, 1793 and 1795. After signing the Treaty of Brest-Litovsk with the Germans in March 1918, Soviet revolutionaries proclaimed the Belorussian SSR on 1 January 1919. After a war with a revived Poland, by 1921 the Soviet Union owned half Belorussia. Stalin gained the remainder from Poland after World War II.

In 1990 a wave of separatism swept over the USSR, largely influenced by the dramatic revolutions in the former Soviet satellites of Poland, Hungary, Czechoslovakia, Romania and East Germany. Without a prior national identity, Belorussians at first appeared unsure how to chart their future. In March 1990 Minsk warned Lithuania that if the Baltic republic seceded, Belorussia would demand the return of large areas that had been ceded to Lithuania in 1940. Yet on 27 June 1990 the Belorussian parliament declared nominal independence. In response to popular pressure, on 11 April 1991 the Belorussian government ended communist control of industry. Later that month thousands of Belorussian citizens blocked rail lines to prevent Soviet troops from entering Lithuania. Only the deployment of MVD units around key rail junctions kept the trains moving.

MOLDAVIAN SSR

Soviet Moldavia – formerly known as Bessarabia – was a hilly strip of land between the Prut and Dnestr Rivers. Bessarabia became part of Russia in 1812. After World War I and the Russian Revolution it became a part of Romania. Pressured by Stalin, in 1944 the newly communist government of Romania "gave" the area to the Soviet Union. The Moldavian Soviet Socialist Republic was highly industrialised, specialising in food processing, machinery construction, consumer goods and building materials. Dairy products, pork, sunflower seeds, wheat and corn were its most important agricultural products.

Just under 4.5 million people lived in Moldavia. While it was the second smallest in size, it had the highest population density of any of the Soviet republics. Two-thirds of the people were ethnic Moldavians (virtually identical to Romanians); the rest were Russians, Ukrainians, Gagauzis (a people of Turkic stock), Jews and Bulgarians.

Although possession of Moldavia had been a bone of contention between Romania and the Soviet Union since World War II, for seven decades the Romanians were unable to force the issue because of the Soviet domination of their country. Moldavia was thus spared the devastating ethnic and anti-Soviet violence experienced in some of the other republics before 1989. That year, however, there were signs of growing discontent with Soviet rule, and unrest in Moldavia was one of the many manifestations that the Soviet Union was entering a New Time of Troubles.

Demonstrations, particularly by the Gagauzi minority (which had no use for either Russians or Moldavians), grew in frequency until, on 1 February 1990, the Moldavian government banned all political protests. In violation of this edict, on 24 October 1990 the Gagauzis formed their own parliament and declared independence from the USSR. This annoyed most other Moldavians and they called on Moscow to send troops to suppress the Gagauzis. When these MVD troops arrived, however, they were attacked by Moldavian nationalists.

Amid all the confusion the Russian minority in Moldavia declared the independence of the Russian-speaking 'Republic of the Dnestr'. This declaration was promptly nullified by the Moldavian Parliament, which refused to meet President Gorbachev to discuss the situation. It also refused to take part in the Union Treaty referendum, scheduled for the spring of 1991. On 31 December 1990 the parliament had proclaimed Romanian to be the national language of Moldavia (replacing Russian). Gorbachev promptly declared this change to be illegal. Soviet consternation over this small republic increased on 20 March 1991 when the US declared that it still recognised the 1933 Soviet borders, implying that it still considered Moldavia to be part of Romania. Although tensions remained high, Romania made no move to reclaim Moldavia, preoccupied as it was with its own internal problems and (understandably) still intimidated by Soviet might.

THE TRANSCAUCASIAN REPUBLICS

Three small republics in the southern USSR were wedged between the Black and Caspian seas and separated from the rest of the Soviet Union by the Caucasus Mountains. The strategic and economic importance of this Transcaucasian region was out of all proportion to its small size and population. It was rich in petroleum and other natural resources, and warm in climate. It was heavily industrialised and produced a significant array of goods both for domestic consumption and for export, generating much-needed hard currency to prop up the Soviet economy.

The area was populated by several ethnic groups, all with long and proud histories and traditions of independence, and all mutually hostile. Considerable violence had shaken this area in recent years, presaging the choas which would sweep the area during the New Time of Troubles.

GEORGIAN SSR

Georgia, just south of the Caucasus Mountains, bordered Turkey and the Black Sea. It was a little smaller than Scotland, and was similarly mountainous, with a central east–west valley through which the Kura River flowed into the Caspian Sea. It had a population of about 5.5 million.

The Caucasus Mountains sheltered Georgia from cold northern winds and allowed it to enjoy the warm, moist breezes of the Black Sea. Its climate was conducive to growing tea (95 per cent of the Soviet domestic crop) and citrus crops. Georgia had a number of hydroelectric plants, many mines, and was industrially developed, producing heavy machinery. Georgia also produced wine, tobacco and canned foods.

Georgia had been inhabited since the Palaeolithic era. By 65 BC the Romans had incorporated the area into their empire, and over succeeding centuries it fell under the suzerainty of Byzantines, Persians, Arabs, Mongols and Turks, with intermittent periods of independence. To defend against renewed Persian invasions, in 1783 the independent Georgian government signed a treaty of protection with Russia. By 1864 Russia had annexed all of Georgia. In the wake of World War I and the Revolution, Georgia was again briefly independent, protected first by Germany in 1917–18, then by Britain until early 1921. But the Red Army reconquered the province in February 1921 and proclaimed it part of the Transcaucasian SFSR. In 1936 the Georgian SSR was formed and made a constituent republic of the USSR.

Despite, or because of, centuries of rule by others (and despite the fact that the Soviet Union's most brutal dictator, Josef Stalin, was a Georgian), the Georgians remained fiercely independent and committed to winning self-rule. In fact, in November 1989 Georgia was granted permission by a newly lenient Moscow to hold a referendum on independence. This led to an upsurge of hope among Georgian nationalists, and by mid-January 1990 thousands of people were holding pro-independence rallies in the capital, Tbilisi. Moscow treated the Georgian independence movement with alternate leniency and ferocious repression.

Elections were held on 28 October 1990 and drew a heavy voter turnout. The communists garnered only 25 per cent of the vote; the pro-secession Round Table party won with 57 per cent. Two weeks later, former dissident and strident anti-communist Zviad Gamsakhurdia was elected president by 86.5 per cent of the voters on a platform of independence.

Complicating affairs in Georgia, in December 1990, the Georgian province of South Ossetia declared itself 'sovereign and independent'. The government of Georgia, with no worries about a double standard, sent in newly created militia units (which Moscow had declared illegal) to crush the Ossetian separatist elements. When Moscow sent troops to keep the peace, Georgia demanded that they be placed under Georgian control or withdraw. Moscow refused.

Meanwhile, fighting between the Georgian militia and Ossetian nationalists continued. On 30 January the Georgian Parliament resolved to establish its own national army, an action strictly forbidden by the Soviet Constitution. On 18 February 1991 the first direct conflict between Soviet and Georgian troops occurred as MVD and army troops forcibly disarmed a militia unit in Tbilisi after a short skirmish. In mid–March, just prior to a nationwide referendum on whether the USSR should remain united (in which Georgia and five other republics had refused to vote), the Soviets sent extra troops into those republics to man the polling stations, increasing Georgian resentment of the Soviet presence.

On 24 March 1991 Georgia held a referendum on independence. Not surprisingly, 98.93 per cent of the voters (according to the Georgian government) favoured secession. Violence in South Ossetia flared again on 29 March as Georgian militia torched several Ossetian villages, leading Moscow to declare a state of emergency in Ossetia on 1 April.

On 9 April Georgia declared independence from the USSR. President Gamsakhurdia called on President Gorbachev to recognise Georgia's independence even as the Georgian militia was trying to force South Ossetia to rescind its secession from Georgia. Inconclusive and frequently bloody three-way violence raged sporadically in Georgia for the remainder of 1991.

ARMENIAN SSR

Landlocked Armenia lay on the southern frontier of the Soviet Union, meeting the borders of Turkey and Iran. The Armenians were an ancient people, strong enough at their zenith to pose a threat to the Roman Empire, but struggling through most of their history to maintain independence against foreign conquerors. Armenia had, by turns, been a province of the Median Empire, the Achaemenian (Persian) Empire, Alexander the Great's Empire, the Seleucid Empire, the Roman Empire (under which most Armenians converted to Christianity around AD 300) and the Byzantine Empire. Then it was ruled by the Seljuq Turks, the Mongols, the Mamelukes, the Ottomans and, finally, in the nineteenth century, the Russians. Since then ancient Armenia has been divided between Russia and Turkey. During its long history Armenia has enjoyed brief periods of independence, remembered proudly by contemporary Armenians.

In relatively modern times Armenians had suffered from both Russian and Turkish pogroms, the worst of which was the Turkish massacre of about 600,000 Armenians in 1915 and forcible relocation of the survivors to desert areas of Turkey. In 1920, after the collapse of the Tsar's government, Russian Armenia was again briefly free, but with Azerbaijan and Georgia it was swiftly reconquered by the Soviets and incorporated into the USSR as part of the Transcaucasian SFSR in 1922. It was made a constituent republic in 1936. Today 90 per cent of the population is Armenian; the rest includes Russians, Azeris (Azerbaijanis), Ukrainians, Kurds and others. The total population is 3.3 million.

Armenia was the smallest of the Soviet republics, slightly smaller than Belgium, and very mountainous. Its economy was a diverse and healthy mix of agriculture and industry, and its recent industrial growth had been the greatest of any Soviet republic. It produced chemicals, metals and metal ores, machines, precision instruments, and textiles, as well as brandy, wines, fruits, nuts and canned foods.

AZERBAIJAN SSR

Lying between Armenia and the Caspian Sea was the republic of Azerbaijan, which included the Nakhichevan ASSR and Nagorno-Karabakh Autonomous Oblast. Much of Azerbaijan was hilly or mountainous, yet the republic produced about 10 per cent of the Soviet Union's agricultural output (including cotton, tobacco and grapes) thanks to its pleasant climate. It was also an industrial region, with particular emphasis on food processing, machinery manufacturing, and oil and natural gas production. In fact, Azerbaijan was one of the first places to have an oil industry and, early in the twentieth century, was the world's leading petroleum producer. The oilfields of the Caucasus were one of Hitler's major objectives when he invaded the USSR in 1941. Among Azerbaijan's other mineral resources were mineral waters, lead, zinc, iron, copper and salt.

The Azeris themselves were a Turkic people descended from an intermixture of invading Seljuq Turks in the eleventh century and native tribes living in the area. About half of the Azeris lived in the Iranian (or Persian) province of Azerbaijan, the remainder in the Soviet Union. Just over 7 million people inhabited the republic, which is rather larger than Scotland. About 85 per cent of these are Azeri, 10 per cent Russian and the rest Armenians (most of whom lived in Nagorno-Karabakh or Baku) and other groups.

HOSTILITY OF ARMENIANS AND AZERBAIJANIS

The modern trouble between the two republics goes back to the 1920s and 1930s, when Armenian workers were recruited to help work the burgeoning oil fields in Azerbaijan. To keep their culture intact, the Soviets allowed the Armenians to establish the Nagorno-Karabakh enclave (under Soviet control). This only exacerbated long-standing historical tensions between the Christian Armenians and Muslim Azeris.

The tension boiled over in February 1988 when Azeris in Sumgait (north-west of the Azerbaijan capital of Baku) rioted against the local dominance of Armenians. The riots quickly spread throughout the republic, leaving many dead, mostly Armenians. Armenian leaders began clamouring for transfer of the Nagorno-Karabakh enclave to control of the Armenian republic, a move strongly opposed by the Azeris. On 1 December 1989 Armenia voted to absorb the territory; Azerbaijan responded by unilaterally rejecting Soviet control of the enclave and putting it under direct Azerbaijani control.

The unrest took a decidedly anti-Soviet turn in early 1990 when Azeris rampaged along the Soviet–Iranian border, tearing down signs, border fences, fortifications and guard posts, and demanding the right to cross the border freely to visit relatives in Iranian Azerbaijan. They also demanded the return of farmlands confiscated by the Soviets for military use. MVD troops hurried to pacify the region.

Confused, vicious and bloody three-way fighting among Soviet troops and Azeri and Armenian militias flared through the region for months. No sooner would the Soviet forces restore an uneasy peace than fighting would break out elsewhere.

Economic considerations made this situation grave for the Soviets. Not the oil production centre it once was, Azerbaijan produced only 5 per cent of the USSR's total petroleum output; but it manufactured 60 per cent of the country's oilfield equipment, the remaining 40 per cent being imported from abroad using precious hard currency. For a Soviet economy already in severe difficulty, retention of a peaceful and productive Azerbaijan in the national family was imperative.

In the following year sporadic clashes between Armenians and Azeris continued to flare, with Soviet troops often being caught in the middle or finding themselves the target of one side or the other. President Gorbachev met the presidents of both republics in early May 1991 in an effort to retain them in the Union without excessive use of force and bloodshed. By late 1991 relative calm prevailed in the region, but after the collapse of the Soviet government, the violence intensified in 1992.

THE ISLAMIC REPUBLICS

The Islamic, or Central Asian, republics of the Soviet Union represented cultures and peoples very different from the 'European' populations west of the Urals and in Siberia. The predominantly Muslim inhabitants, usually of Turkish or Persian descent, had lived under Russian rule for about 150 years. In the last half of the twentieth century these republics became industrialised through Soviet development plans and contributed significantly to the overall Soviet economy. But with the global upsurge in Muslim awareness they also felt the stirrings of nationalism and the desire for self-determination.

Particularly affecting the role of these republics in the USSR was birth rate. The results of the Soviet 1989 census were so startling that they were not publicly revealed, but a copy smuggled out of the country showed that the population of ethnic Russians (the *de facto* 'ruling class' in most of the republics) increased by only 5.6 per cent in the decade 1979–89, while that of Muslims in the Central Asian republics climbed precipitously: 33 per cent in Turkmenistan and Uzbekistan, 42 per cent in Tadzhikistan. These figures, as well as the knowledge that Soviet attention was focused on other troublesome areas like the Baltics and Transcaucasus, gave the Soviet Muslims hope of throwing off the Russian yoke in the not too distant future. This hope, long harboured in secret, began to come into the open shortly before the New Time of Troubles.

KIRGHIZ SSR

Kirghizistan, about three-quarters the size of the UK, was located high in the Tien Shan mountains along the Soviet border with China. At its lowest altitudes it was hot desert plains; at its highest, cold windswept desert plateaux. In between is a narrow habitable belt where its 4.3 million citizens resided.

Only about 48 per cent of the population were Kirghizis, a Turkic people. The rest of the population was composed of Russians and Ukrainians (26 per cent), Uzbeks (12 per cent) and the descendants of Germans who were deported to the area from the western Soviet Union in 1941.

Clans of ancient Kirghizi nomads settled in this inhospitable region over a thousand years ago, and their way of life was largely undisturbed until the nineteenth century. They were originally brought under Russian control during the tsarist colonisation period in 1864–81, which resulted in Russian annexation of the entire Trans-Caspian region. Even though they had been conquered, the Russian occupation at first had little impact on Kirghizi lifestyles except that most of the scarce good land in the province was taken from the clans and given to ethnic Russian landowners.

Russian supremacy rankled the proud Kirghizis, and they rebelled against the Tsar's government in 1916 in reaction to wartime conscription of non-Russians for forced labour. The revolt was savagely suppressed by the Russian Army, and about a third of the Kirghizis fled into China. Resistance continued against the Bolsheviks for several years after World War I before they were finally beaten.

Under the communists the Kirghizis faced more changes to their way of life. Their province was incorporated into the Russian SFSR in 1924, was made an autonomous SSR in 1926, and became one of the fifteen constituent republics in 1936. Most Kirghizis were forced to move into agricultural collectives, although in 1991 about 15 per cent of them held positions (usually menial) in industrial facilities. Between 1926 and 1959 large numbers of ethnic Russians and Ukrainians moved to Kirghizistan, taking over managerial and government positions and effectively colonising the area. Before the New Time of Troubles, Kirghizis (like most non-Russians) were frequently treated as second-class citizens in their own homeland; relatively few were even allowed to join the Communist Party, which was virtually the only route to success in the USSR.

Kirghizistan was a largely agricultural province; sheep and cattle raising was the principal occupation. Mining of metals and minerals was also a major economic enterprise.

In the late 1980s Kirghizistan had been moving toward independence from the Soviet Union (and enmity with some of its neighbouring republics). In February 1990 anti-Soviet rioting spread to Kirghizistan from Tadzhikistan, and recurred periodically for several months. Making matters worse, in June other riots broke out between Shiite Kirghizis and Sunni Uzbeks over which group would be allowed to build a new housing project on a desirable piece of land in the city of Osh. The rioting spread to the Kirghizi capital of Frunze (so named in 1926 in honour of a Bolshevik leader who was also a military theorist). Despite the arrival of MVD troops, the rioting continued for more than a month, and spread to Uzbekistan. Not until August did Soviet troops restore order, but ethnic and religious tensions continued to simmer below the surface.

In February 1991 the government of Kirghizistan changed the name of its capital city from Frunze back to its original name of Bishek, one of many indications of the Kirghizis' desire to distance themselves from Moscow.

TADZHIK SSR

Just south of Kirghizistan lay Tadzhikistan, which bordered on China and on Afghanistan. It too was very mountainous, encompassing much of the Pamir range, a spur of the great Tien Shan range. Tadzhikistan was a little larger than England and was home to about 5.1 million people of many different ethnic groups, mostly Muslim. The two major Tadzhik subgroups were the Pamir Tadzhiks and the Yaghnabis (descended from the ancient Bogdians). Together they comprised about 59 per cent of the population. Tadzhiks, who were Sunni Muslims, were closely related ethnically to their neighbours, the Uzbeks. They spoke an Iranian dialect. Other populations represented in Tadzhikistan included Uzbeks (23 per cent), Russians and Ukrainians (together about 10 per cent), Tatars, Germans, Kirghizis and a few Jews. Most Russians and Ukrainians lived in the cities, particularly in Dushanbe (the capital, once known as Stalinabad) and Leninabad. The majority of the Tadzhiks lived as they had for centuries in *qishlaqs*, collections of several hundred small houses constructed along river banks or canals.

The Tadzhiks were descendants of Persian-speaking Iranian peoples who were subjugated first by the Arabs in the eighth century, then by Muslim Turks in the tenth. Eventually they became Turkicised and their Persian language was replaced by Turkish. They remained under Turkish rule (the Emirate of Bokhara) until the mid-seventeenth century, when the Turks were briefly replaced by Afghan invaders who ruled until driven out by tsarist Russians in the 1860s and 1870s. When news of the Russian Revolution reached the area, many Tadzhiks hoped to establish an autonomous nation, but the Red Army captured Dushanbe and Kulyab in 1922 and put down the Basmachi Revolt the next year. Tadzhikistan was established as an autonomous province within the Uzbek SSR in 1924, and became a separate constituent republic in 1929. Soviet attempts to collectivise agriculture in the area in 1928–9 met stiff opposition, which the communists ruthlessly crushed. The Tadzhiks continued to suffer occasional purges of their ruling structure by Russian communists, the most recent being in 1961.

Tadzhikistan was heavily dependent on agriculture; half of all workers were farmers. Cotton was the staple crop supporting the Tadzhik economy, made possible only by massive irrigation projects begun by the Soviets in the 1930s. Many of the rest of the Tadzhiks were miners or textile workers. Tadzhikistan was home to the USSR's largest carpet factory, and was the country's largest producer of some chemical compounds.

Industrialisation and the subsequent rise in the standard of living

resulted in a very high birth rate and an influx of immigrants from other
Soviet republics. The Tadzhik growth rate was three times the Soviet
average, and half the republic's population in 1992 was under the age of
twenty-one. Somehow, despite these demographic changes, the
Tadzhiks managed to keep their traditions and culture mainly intact.

Perhaps this youthfulness of population, combined with pride in
Tadzhik history and increasing contact with the world outside Soviet
borders allowed by *glasnost*, helps explain the unrest that swept through
the republic in 1990. Also, apparently, outside Islamic fundamentalists
from Afghanistan and Iran crossed the border from Afghanistan to incite
Islamic revivals and revolution.

In February 1990, during the height of unrest in the Transcaucasus,
the Soviets evacuated some Christian Armenians from the Azerbaijani
city of Baku and brought them to Tadzhikistan for safety. Riots broke
out when the rumour spread in Dushanbe that hundreds of newcomers
would be given priority for scarce housing in the area. (In fact, the Soviet
authorities had brought only about forty Armenians to the city, and they
all had relations in Dushanbe with whom they were housed.) The rioting
spread to Kirghizistan and turned into anti-Soviet protests when MVD
troops arrived to quell the violence. Thousands of Tadzhiks took to the
streets demanding secession from the Soviet Union. Snipers shot at
Soviet soldiers while rioters looted and burned the local Communist
Party headquarters.

As violence continued, Soviet President Gorbachev vowed to stop the
riots once and for all and dispatched a Soviet parachute division to
Dushanbe. Order was soon restored, but unrest seethed beneath the
surface.

UZBEK SSR

Uzbekistan, in the middle of Soviet Central Asia, contained the ancient
cities of Tashkent, Samarkand and Bokhara. It was largely desert, with
some high mountains of the Pamir range in the south-east. About the
size of Sweden its population was 19.9 million. It was the most populous
of the Soviet Islamic republics.

Early empires such as those of Bactria and Sogdiana existed in the
region hundreds of years before Christ. Successive Persian, Macedonian,
Mongol, Turkish and Iranian conquerors held the area over the next
2,000 years. Finally, the Russian campaign of conquest in Central Asia
reached Uzbekistan in 1855 and was complete by 1876. Communists and
nationalist Muslim–Turkmen factions vied for control of Uzbekistan
during the Russian Revolution, with the communists gaining the upper

hand by suppressing the Basmachi Revolt in 1923. Uzbekistan was established as one of the fifteen constituent republics of the USSR in 1924.

Uzbekistan – particularly the Bokhara–Samarkand corridor – remained a Sunni Muslim cultural centre, as it had been for centuries. In 1992 some sixty ethnic groups lived in the republic; 69 per cent of the population were Uzbeks, and most of the rest were Russians (11 per cent), Tatars and Kazakhs. About three out of four Uzbeks still led rural lives despite the increasing industrialisation of the region. As in other Soviet Islamic republics, the urban populations of Uzbekistan were composed primarily of Russians, as well as Tatars, Ukrainians, Jews and Armenians, while Uzbeks and other groups remained scattered throughout the arid countryside.

The primary product of Uzbekistan was cotton; the republic was responsible for two-thirds of the USSR's output, and it was the third largest producer in the world. The economy also depended heavily on raising sheep and silkworms. Uzbekistan boasted large natural gas, oil and coal deposits, and was the largest producer of machinery and heavy equipment in Central Asia.

Uzbekistan had its share of ethnic troubles in the years preceding the Second Revolution. In 1989 rioting broke out between Uzbeks and Meskhetian Turks. In mid-1990 ethnic and religious rioting in neighbouring republics spread to Uzbekistan, leading to clashes between Sunni Uzbeks and local Armenian Christians. Soon afterward ethno-religious strife broke out with neighbouring Kirghizistan.

In the midst of this turmoil, anti-Soviet sentiment ran high. On 9 July 1990 the Uzbek government declared independence from the Soviet Union and declared that Uzbek would replace Russian as the national language.

TURKMEN SSR

Turkmenistan also lay along the southern edge of the Soviet Union, bordering Iran and Afghanistan to the south and the Caspian Sea to the west. It was slightly smaller than Spain, but nine-tenths of its area was covered by the Kara Kum desert, so most of the republic's 3.5 million people lived either on the shores of the Caspian or along the Amu Darya, Murgab and Tedzen rivers. The major exception was the capital of Ashkabad, located in the mountainous (and earthquake-prone) Kopet Dag region that formed the border with Iran.

The Kara Kum desert was not a complete wasteland but was studded with oases and dotted with mines, chemical refineries and heavy industrial sites. There were a number of fisheries along the Caspian coast.

About 68 per cent of the republic's population were ethnic Turkmen. Russians comprised another 13 per cent and Uzbeks 9 per cent; the remainder was made up of Kazakhs, Tatars, Ukrainians, Armenians, Azerbiajanis and Kara-Kalpaks. The Turkmen population growth in the late twentieth century far outstripped that of the politically dominant Russians. There were comparable increases among Turkmen living in Iran, Afghanistan, northern Iraq, Syria and central Turkey.

The Turkmen enjoyed a nomadic pastoral existence until their conquest by Russia in the mid-nineteenth century. They were then forced into a more sedentary lifestyle and began to develop a concept of nationality. During the Russian Revolution there were scattered skirmishes between the provisional Turkmen socialist government (supported by a small contingent of British troops) and Bolsheviks advancing from Tashkent in Uzbekistan. The communists seized Ashkabad in 1919 and by early 1920 had cleared the final pocket of Turkmen resistance at Krasnovodsk on the Caspian Sea. The area was proclaimed as the Turkistan ASSR, then changed to the Turkmen SSR in 1924.

Due to its isolation enforced by its forbidding terrain, Turkmenistan remained largely free of the ethnic and anti-Soviet violence that wracked the other Central Asian republics in the 1980s and 1990s.

KAZAKH SSR

Kazakhstan was the second largest of the fifteen Soviet Republics, smaller only than the Russian SFSR, comprising 12 per cent of the Soviet Union's vast area. It was predominantly a flat tableland, much of which was either steppe or covered by the Kara Kum desert, but it rose to mountain ranges on the southern and south-eastern borders with Kirghizistan and China. It was the second most populous of the Islamic republics, with almost 17 million inhabitants.

Kazakhs are a Mongoloid people. Their culture and religion are Shiite Muslims while their language is Turkic. Since antiquity they had been pastoral nomads, living in tents and moving their herds from pasture to pasture. This lifestyle began to change in the mid-1800s as some Kazakh tribes began to establish permanent farming communities. This transformation was accelerated after the Russian conquest, which began in the early 1700s and was completed by the late 1850s. By the turn of this century, many Kazakhs yearned for the return of self-rule. During the 1917 Revolution the Kazakhs, backed by White Russian forces, declared an autonomous state. By 1920, however, Bolshevik troops had completely defeated the Kazakhs and their allies and established the Kazakh ASSR, which became an SSR in 1936.

In the 1990s the Soviets' main spaceport was located at Baikonur in central Kazakhstan, and nuclear tests were conducted at Semipalatinsk until they were banned by the Kazakh government in October 1990. The republic was an important centre for mining and quarrying due to rich mineral deposits in its mountains and deserts. Many Soviet factories were relocated to Kazakhstan during World War II to keep them from falling to the Germans, and that marked the beginning of the republic's industrialisation. Kazakhstan also produced a third of Soviet wheat on farms run by Russians but worked by Kazakhs and other ethnic groups. Many Kazakhs lived on these farms or on collective cattle-breeding ranches, where they were forcibly resettled after the first revolution.

Ethnic Kazakhs constituted only about 36 per cent of the republic's population, due to extensive colonisation of the area by Russians (41 per cent) in the late nineteenth and early twentieth centuries. There were also small populations of Ukrainians (6 per cent), Germans, Tatars, Belorussians, Uighurs, Dungans and even Koreans (relocated by Stalin's orders from the Soviet Far East). In addition, numbers of Poles, Bulgarians, Jews and Mordvins settled in the area between the two world wars, adding to the flavour of this central Asian melting pot. Half the republic's population (most non-Kazakhs and about half the Kazakhs) lived in urban centres. Like other Islamic republics, Kazakhstan enjoyed one of the highest birth rates in the USSR, especially among the Kazakhs and other non-Russian populations.

Like Turkmenistan, Kazakhstan, with its vast area and relatively low population density, by and large escaped the tension and violence troubling its Muslim neighbours to the south in the late 1980s and early 1990s. There was some rioting in Alma-Ata in 1986 when a Russian replaced a Kazakh as head of the Kazakh Communist Party, but he was removed the following year and that seemed to mollify the Kazakhs.

DISSOLUTION OF THE SOVIET UNION

In the light of all of the political, social, economic, and ethnic unrest seething within the Soviet Union in 1991, it is not surprising that a major result of the failed *coup d'état* in August 1991 was a serious weakening of the strength and authority of the central government in the Kremlin. In fact, it is almost surprising that there were not more immediate defections to independence than those of the three Baltic states. However, all

of the other twelve republics had longer histories of subservience to
Moscow, and – given those histories, and despite the long-standing
antipathy of several of the republics to central Russian authority – their
hesitation to take a final step to irrevocable and truly sovereign independence is understandable.

But, as the short Russian summer progressed into fall, and as the
inability of President Gorbachev's government to deal with the growing
economic crisis became more and more evident, the centrifugal process
continued. It reached the critical point of dissolution during a weekend in
December.

On 7 December 1991 the presidents of Russia, the Ukraine and
Belorussia met at a country estate near the Belorussian city of Brest.
Yeltsin, of course, represented Russia. Representing the Ukraine was
recently-elected Leonid M. Kravchuk. The third conferee was the parliamentary chairman (or president) of Belorussia, Stanislav S. Shushkevich.
As reported at their press conference in Minsk, late the following day,
the three presidents came to the conclusion that 'the USSR is ceasing its
existence'. Since their three republics (plus the former Transcaucasus
Republic) had created the Soviet Union on 30 December 1922, and since
they represented 80 per cent of the land area of the USSR, and 73 per cent
of its population, they decided that it was their historic right, nearly 69
years later, to dissolve that union. In its place they established a Commonwealth of Independent States, inviting the nine remaining former
Soviet states to join. The seat of central authority – they did not call it a
capital – of this Commonwealth of Independent States, or CIS, would be
Minsk. This assured a break from the tradition of central government in
Moscow, which would remain, of course, the capital of Russia. (The
published agreements revealed that the name 'Ukraine' had replaced 'the
Ukraine', and that 'Belarus' had become the official name of what had
been 'Belorussia'.)

On 21 December the presidents of eleven of the fifteen former Soviet
states met at Alma-Ata, capital of Kazakhstan, formally to confirm the
establishment of the Commonwealth of Independent States. Absent, of
course, were the Baltics, whose independence and departure from the
USSR had long been accepted both within and without the Soviet
Union. Also not represented was Georgia, whose president, Zviad Gamsakhurdia, was besieged in Tbilisi in an ongoing civil war.

The eleven presidents agreed in principle that the Commonwealth
would be a loose confederation, and established some procedures for
continuing to function as a single sovereign state. They agreed that the
Commonwealth would honour all the international commitments of the
USSR. However, they could not agree on the future of the Soviet armed

forces. So they decided that temporarily the Soviet Defence Minister, Marshal Yevgeny I. Shaposhnikov, would remain in command of conventional and nuclear forces, and promised to decide this issue in a later meeting.

On 9 December Soviet President Gorbachev had denounced as illegal and unconstitutional the actions of Yeltsin, Kravchuk and Shushkevich in establishing the Commonwealth of Independent States. But the Alma-Ata meeting made it obvious that the authority and power of the central government had eroded to the point of extinction. Gorbachev resigned on Christmas Day 1991, when the blood-red Soviet flag, with its golden hammer and sickle emblem, was for the last time hauled down the flagpole over the Kremlin. This, in effect, legalised the Commonwealth of Independent States. Next day Yeltsin moved into Gorbachev's former Kremlin office, over which the blue, white and red banner of Russia was now waving.

In a meeting at Minsk on 30 December, the eleven presidents again tackled the thorny issue of the future of the Soviet armed forces. Again they could not agree. So they decided that each of the individual republics should be free to establish its own armed forces, vaguely implying that the existing Soviet forces would be divided up among the eleven independent republics. They made an exception for strategic nuclear forces, however, which they declared would remain under centralised control, to be exercised by Shaposhnikov, under the authority of the Commonwealth.

However, the presidents did not specify what was included in 'strategic forces'. It was soon evident, furthermore, that the four republics which had former Soviet strategic nuclear weapons within their boundaries (Russia, Ukraine, Belarus and Kazakhstan) did not agree about this. The issue was particularly serious for Ukraine and Russia. Ukraine insisted that the provision for centralised control applied only to the former Soviet Strategic Rocket Forces. A Russian spokesman stated, however, that strategic forces also included most of the navy, as well as elements of the air force, air defence force, and army.

Following the Minsk meeting President Kravchuk of Ukraine demanded that all Soviet forces stationed in his country swear an oath of allegiance to his government. Most army units stationed in Ukraine agreed, although a number of individual officers and soldiers refused. Admiral Igor Kasatonov, commander of the Black Sea Fleet, based at Sevastapol, also refused, in the name of the entire fleet. In this he was supported by Russian President Yeltsin, who declared that that fleet was, always had been, and always would be, Russian.

DISSENSION IN THE ARMED FORCES AND THE KGB

On 17 January 1992, with the future of the former Soviet armed forces thus in doubt, 5,000 senior officers – mostly colonels and general officers, elected representatives of units scattered throughout the former USSR – met in the Kremlin. Presiding over the meeting was the former Soviet Defence Minister, and still the Commonwealth military commander in chief, Marshal Yevgeny Shaposhnikov. It was obvious that the vast majority of these officers, including Shaposhnikov, were strongly opposed to the division of the armed forces among the republics of the CIS. Many of them insisted that the dissolution of the Soviet Union in December had been unconstitutional. They adopted a resolution, warning of 'tragic consequences' if the army were to be divided. During the debate on this resolution, one officer stood up and pointed to Shaposhnikov and shouted: 'You are not on our side,' and demanded his resignation. In fury the marshal stood up, declared his resignation, put on his coat, and stormed out of the Great Hall of the Kremlin. (He was later persuaded to withdraw his resignation, and to return to the presiding chair.) The officers then elected a permanent council to represent the armed forces in relations with the eleven republics of the Commonwealth. The armed forces had virtually proclaimed themselves the twelfth republic of the CIS.

While the armed forces were thus publicly registering their unhappiness about the recent course of events in the former USSR, a similar movement was afoot among members and former members of the KGB. For all practical purposes the KGB had been taken over by the Russian Republic, and many of its elements had been disbanded. But its status was unclear. In late January 200 senior KGB officials met secretly for a week at the Hotel Metropole in Ostankino, a northern suburb of Moscow. The Metropole was adjacent to an old mansion which had been for many years a KGB 'safe house', and which had remained under KGB control. The self-appointed chairman of the Metropole meeting was Anatoly Strelenko, a senior KGB official.

Staunch communists all, these KGBers – past and present – were not ideologues. They recognised that it would be unrealistic to try to put together the old Soviet Union. To do so, furthermore, would demand expressing loyalty to former President Gorbachev, and those present were as unanimous in their condemnation of Gorbachev as they were of Yeltsin. The former, they were convinced, had set the stage for destroying his own government by his policies of *glasnost* and *perestroika*, while the latter had completed the destruction of that government by his populist espousal of democracy. Over some objections from non-Russian participants, the group declared themselves 'the shadow government of Greater Russia'. They elected Strelenko as the President of Greater Russia, and established an Executive Council under his leadership. Strelenko then appointed eighteen 'Regional Governors', one for each of the twelve Commonwealth states, plus six regions within the Russian Republic.

The Regional Governors, each with a small 'Regional Council', were given three missions. First, they were to establish a true shadow government for each region, capable and ready to seize control when Strelenko gave the order. The secret KGB telephone and radio network, which had never been dismantled, was to be used to maintain communications between the central Executive Council and the regional shadow governments. The Executive Council would install itself in the old 'safe house' near the Metropole.

Second, the Regional Governors and their councils were to establish cells of supporters – mostly former communist officials – to recruit supporters among the many people dissatisfied with the course of events in the Commonwealth. Third, they were cautiously to establish relationships with the armed forces units in their regions, and particularly with the representatives who had attended the Kremlin meeting in mid-January.

In a speech concluding the meeting, Strelenko urged his colleagues to be cautious and discreet – 'as becomes members of the KGB' – and predicted that they should be ready for action in about a year. He warned them, however, that they must be prepared to move sooner, if necessary, as a result of civil unrest resulting from the economic disintegration of the nation.

THE TROUBLES INTENSIFY

With considerable financial and food assistance from the European Community, Japan and the United States, the Commonwealth struggled through the winter of 1992. However, it soon became obvious that the economic reforms which Yeltsin introduced in Russia early in the year were not taking hold. Inflation soared. Unemployment spread. And the collapse of the Russian economy directly affected all of the eleven other republics of the Commonwealth – Georgia had joined in mid-1992. Least disrupted of the republics was Ukraine, which at least was able to feed itself.

The dispute over the future of the armed forces also remained mostly unresolved. With great difficulty and severe financial pain Yeltsin and

Shaposhnikov were able to hold most of the old Soviet Army, Air Force, and Air Defence Forces together within Russian territory. The Strategic Rocket Forces remained under centralised control from Moscow, with its newly appointed chief, General Stefan Bogramovich, operating under the direction of Shaposhnikov.

The crisis over control of the Black Sea Fleet, however, had been resolved by an unexpected political development. In May 1992 the oblast of Crimea again held an election to choose between remaining federated with Ukraine or rejoining Russia. As in the abortive vote in 1991, a substantial majority voted to join the Russian Republic, a move accepted reluctantly by the Ukrainian government, and with pleasure in Moscow. This automatically put the Black Sea Fleet main base at Sevastapol under Russian authority. Yeltsin thereupon struck a deal with President Kravchuk of Ukraine, as a result of which a small portion of the Black Sea Fleet, with vessels manned by Ukrainians, moved to Odessa, and became the Ukrainian Fleet.

Meanwhile, the long-standing dispute between Armenia and Azerbaijan over the Nagorno-Karbakh region erupted into open warfare in January 1992. There ensued two months of very bloody fighting, which destroyed most of the Armenian militia in the enclave. Severe casualties were also suffered by the civilian Armenian population. With the world appalled at the prospect of a new Armenian massacre, Yeltsin was able to persuade the two republics to negotiate a cease-fire. This included an agreement that Armenian survivors in the enclave would be allowed to emigrate to Armenia, and the enclave would remain under the control of Azerbaijan.

The winter of 1992-3 was fully as disastrous in Russia and most of the Commonwealth as the earlier winter had been. Nevertheless, with increasingly grudging financial and nutritional aid from the United States, Japan and the European Community, the Commonwealth survived, with no serious internal disorders. But by late summer of 1993 it became obvious that a severe drought would ensure a poor grain crop not only in Russia, but also in Ukraine and the other Commonwealth states. When the dimension of the catastrophic shortfall in the 1993 grain harvest became known in early September, food riots broke out in a score of major cities. The rioters demanded that the central government take steps to make food more available, having seen Western supermarkets on television and being exasperated with their own poor production and distribution systems. Russian troops, easily visible targets representing Moscow to the frustrated and hungry people, were coming under attack throughout Russia. This created severe tensions between soldiers and civilians in a number of regions.

In a strange shifting of sentiments, President Yeltsin became extremely unpopular, and there were many calls throughout the country for Gorbachev's return to power. Yeltsin, his back figuratively up against the wall, and also faced with mounting opposition from the restless, frustrated armed forces, decided to offer Gorbachev the post of Prime Minister. To the surprise of many, Gorbachev accepted the position, subject to a vote of approval by the Parliament, which was rapidly forthcoming. After conferring with each other, with the Cabinet, and with a number of foreign ministers and the US Secretary of State, Yeltsin and Gorbachev jointly decided that a desperate situation required desperate measures. In late September 1993, Russia concluded an agreement with the European Community, which was a virtual declaration of Soviet bankruptcy. In return for massive Western aid, mainly in food, Russia surrendered control of its Treasury to a panel of three EC High Commissioners, who were authorised to approve all major expenditures of Soviet Treasury funds. The agreement, endorsed by the United States and Japan, provided for aid which included airlifts of food and medical supplies, as well as other necessities, on an unprecedented scale. The principle contributors and guarantors were the United States, Canada, Great Britain, France, Germany and Japan. This agreement pleased many people, particularly since it meant food on their tables again.

There were many Russians, however, who were furious with Yeltsin and Gorbachev for making such a deal. The hard-line communists, the KGB and some senior military officers, were outraged to see their government so casually allowing Russian sovereignty to be subject to Western economic veto, thus prostrating the *Rodina* before the decadent Western democracies like a poor relation come begging its bread. What was needed, to their thinking, was not handouts from the West, but rather more firmness and commitment to the socialist principles of the former Soviet government.

BLOODY MONDAY

Prime Minister Gorbachev called a special session of the Soviet Parliament on Monday 4 October 1993 to ratify the agreement with the EC. As he rose to address the body, in the Great Hall of the Kremlin, automatic gunfire erupted from several points in the chamber. Gorbachev was riddled with bullets, as were more than a dozen other senior officials. President Yeltsin, sitting on the dais behind the speaker, had his arm shattered by a bullet. Marshal Shaposhnikov, sitting to the right of the speaker, died instantly from a bullet in the brain.

In the ensuing confusion the murderers fled; they were never apprehended, and their exact identity was never ascertained, although speculation was rife. The entire nation was electrified and horrified at this, the first overt assassination of a Russian government leader since Alexander II was killed by a terrorist bomb in 1881.

Early on the morning of October 5 Anatoly Strelenko, recently appointed head of the Russian KGB, announced that he was assuming control of the government until President Yeltsin recovered from his wound. He proclaimed himself Acting President of Russia. The speed with which the KGB reacted to the events suggested that it was at least in part responsible for the outrage. The efficiency with which Strelenko and his hastily appointed Cabinet acted also showed that the lessons of the Three-Day Coup had been well learned, and that the plans initiated at the Metropole Conference had been well prepared. Strelenko declared martial law, and announced that he had appointed General Vladimir Basilev, commander-in-chief of the Russian Army, as Minister of Defence to replace Shaposhnikov.

Basilev immediately issued orders for Russian troops to seize most of the key facilities and factories in Moscow, St Petersburg and Nizhni Novgorod (formerly Gorky). He also sent troops to Yeltsin's residence with orders to place the President under 'protective custody'. However Yeltsin was nowhere to be found. To the frustration of Strelenko and Basilev, the President and most of Gorbachev's cabinet had disappeared. The mystery was solved the next day, 6 October, when Yeltsin, pale, and with his left arm in a bandaged sling, made a TV broadcast from an army base at Stavropol, in south Russia. He bitterly denounced Strelenko and Basilev as traitors, and appealed to the people and the armed forces to support him, the constitutional leader of Russia. He also called upon forces loyal to him to concentrate in south Russia and the northern Caucasus, but to avoid hostilities, if possible, with any forces loyal to Strelenko and Basilev.

It soon became evident that Basilev actually had the support of less than half of the army and of an even smaller proportion of the air force. Many units declared allegiance to Yeltsin. Others refused to be drawn into taking sides in an incipient civil war.

The most senior of those adopting a posture of neutrality was Fleet Admiral Constantin Alexandrov, Commander in Chief of the Russian Navy. In late 1992 he had heard rumours of the activities of Strelenko's KGB 'shadow government'. He saw that there was likelihood of a repeat of the Three-Day Coup, but much better organised. He discussed this possibility with the commanders of the four major fleets: Black Sea, Baltic, Arctic and Pacific. They agreed that in any such event the navy should avoid involvement, and remain neutral. The five admirals and a few trusted staff officers then prepared plans for carrying out such a policy.

Alexandrov was particularly concerned about safeguarding the arsenal of nuclear weapons – shared by Russia and the Commonwealth – should there be another coup, and should it lead to a civil war. He quietly discussed this matter with General Stefan Bogramovich, Commander in Chief of the Strategic Rocket Forces, whom he trusted as a serious and responsible professional officer. Bogramovich promptly committed the strategic rocket forces to join the navy in a posture of neutrality, should this be necessary. The two commanders in chief then co-ordinated joint plans for such a contingency.

Thus it was that within two hours of Strelenko's announcement that he was assuming the position of Acting President, Alexandrov and Bogramovich sent the following joint letter to the Secretary General of the United Nations by radio:

Dear Mr Secretary General:

In the light of recent exceptional events within Russia and the Commonwealth of Independent States, the Commanders in Chief of the Russian Navy and the CIS Strategic Rocket Forces wish to assure Your Excellency, and all members of the United Nations, that they have taken measures to secure and safeguard all strategic nuclear weapons of the armed forces of the Commonwealth. These weapons will not be used in any circumstances other than in response to a nuclear attack upon the Commonwealth or one of its constituent states by a hostile power, in which case they will be used vigorously. In particular, these weapons will not be used in any fashion within the boundaries of the Commonwealth in the unlikely event of hostilities between component elements of the Commonwealth armed forces, with one important exception.

That exception is that in the event there should be hostilities between components of the Commonwealth armed forces, or those of any of its constituent states, and if any such component should employ tactical nuclear weapons in such hostilities, the two commanders in chief undersigned pledge that they will employ the forces at their disposal to obliterate the headquarters of such components using tactical nuclear weapons.

With expressions of the highest respect and esteem, we are:

Constantin Alexandrov, Commander in Chief, Russian Navy
Stefan Bogramovich, Commander in Chief, Commonwealth
Strategic Rocket Forces

Having provided copies to representatives of the foreign press, the two commanders in chief sent a two-sentence message to each of their major subordinate commanders:

'Implement neutrality plan. I am proceeding at once to Headquarters Black Sea Fleet.'

Alexandrov and Bogramovich, accompanied by their senior aides, then flew off in Bogramovich's private plane to Sevastapol. As a result of their order, all major bases of the strategic rocket forces were placed on alert, and wartime security measures initiated. At the same time all Russian naval vessels were concentrated at Archangelsk, Murmansk, Sevastapol and Vladivostok, with naval infantry deployed to protect the four naval bases.

Despite the obvious mutual hostility of two major groups of powerful military forces – the Strelenko–Basilev forces and the Yeltsin forces – there were no armed clashes for several days. Meanwhile, Strelenko and Yeltsin were cautiously attempting to find out who were their friends and who were their foes. In a televised speech to his troops, Basilev referred to them as 'the Red Army', invoking the traditions of the Soviet armed forces, who had been victors in the 1918–20 Civil War and in World War II. In response, Yeltsin promptly began to refer to his soldiers as the 'Blues', a major colour in the Russian flag. He specifically disassociated himself and his army from the 'Whites', who had been the losers in the earlier Civil War.

OUTBREAK OF CIVIL WAR

The first battles of the Second Russian Civil War broke out on Sunday 10 and Monday 11 October 1993, as mutinies erupted in army and air force barracks throughout Russia. Most Red units gravitated towards those cities in the north which had been occupied early in the crisis by KGB and army units loyal to Strelenko and Basilev. Yeltsin's new Republican, or Blue, Army sought to concentrate in southern Russia, particularly around Volgograd, Rostov and the northern Caucasus.

On 18 February, Basilev dispatched two reinforced divisions to retake the city of Tula and its defence factories, which had been seized by Blue forces. It took five days and 10,000 casualties before the 35,000 Blue defenders were rooted out, but not before most of the city had been burned to ashes.

Heavy fighting swept the north Caucasus and the area between the southern Don and Volga rivers almost from the beginning of the war, as Blue forces struggled to secure the region as a staging area for drives north and east against the Strelenko–Basilev Reds. The largest battle of this early campaign was at Rostov-na-Donu on 21–22 November 1993, when a Blue force of two motorised rifle divisions, four tank divisions, and one independent motorised rifle regiment attacked into the city to drive out a Red force of four depleted divisions: one tank, one paratroop, and two motorised rifle. Losses were heavy on both sides. But the Blues had considerable air superiority and defeated the Reds in two days of tough city fighting. Other Blue forces cleared an area up to a line extending roughly from Voronezh to Saratov. South of this line was the area that Yeltsin proclaimed as the Free Russian Republic on 18 November 1993.

COMMONWEALTH NEUTRALITY AND UNREST

Although all the other eleven Commonwealth republics declared neutrality, none of them was able completely to escape the effects of the turmoil in their giant neighbour. Ukraine, as we shall see, was most directly affected, but all of the republics suffered violence in one form or another. In all of the Islamic Central Asian republics, with their large Russian minorities, there was widespread military unrest. In some instances entire units, under officers still loyal at heart to the old Soviet armed forces, declared support for the Red cause of Strelenko and Basilev, and attempted to compel their republics to join the Red cause. All such efforts were suppressed by troops loyal to the local regimes, but in some instances bloodshed was severe.

During this military unrest and violence, there came about a major political shake-up. In November Kazakhstan and Kirghizistan joined to create the new Shi'ite Islamic Republic of Kokanistan. A few days later the Sunni Moslems of Uzbekistan and Tadzhikistan proclaimed their unity in the Islamic Republic of Khivastan, reviving a name that had been used briefly in 1919, before the communists took over. Turkmenistan, which suffered less violence than its neighbours, stayed aloof from both of these new Islamic unions.

The Transcaucasian republics were too busy with their own wars to pay much attention to what was going on in Russia. In Georgia the opponents of Gamsakhurdia slowly established their control over most of the country, forcing the ex-president to flee to Bulgaria. Then, in a show of reasonableness unusual in that part of the world, the new ruling junta of Georgia opened negotiations with the South Ossetians, and were able to reach an agreement whereby the Ossetians, with considerable local autonomy, remained in the Georgian republic.

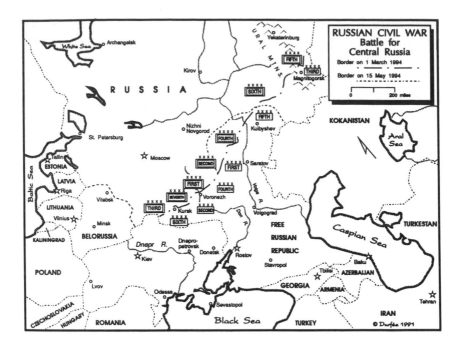

There was no such reasonableness in Georgia's neighbours to the
south: Azerbaijan and Armenia. There had been a lull in their hostilities
after the Azeri conquest of the Armenian enclave of Nagorno-Karabakh
in mid-1992. However, both sides had been preparing themselves for a
showdown.

In mid-April 1994, Azerbaijan, with just under 100,000 men under
arms, launched a series of attacks against Armenia, which was able to
field only about half as many troops. From their mountain strongholds
near Berd, Vardens and Goris, the Armenians were able to keep the
Azeris at bay for almost a month of vicious fighting. However, on
14 May a renewed Azeri three-division offensive broke the Armenian
line. The Azeris drove ahead, north of Lake Sevan, to the Armenian
capital of Yerevan. As Turkish troops massed on their side of the border
to prevent Armenian refugees from entering Turkish Armenia, the
Azeris began wholesale massacres, while annexing Armenia into Azerbaijan. Full casualty counts are still unavailable, as the Republic of
Azerbaijan has clamped a tight lid on all news of internal events since
June 1994. However, some accounts indicate that there were pogroms to
equal or surpass those by the Turks in 1915. Some rumours also indicate
that the Turks helped the Azeris set up their new political infrastructure,
and that Turkish troops aided in 'pacifying' Armenia and Nakhichevan,

which briefly declared itself independent before being reconquered by the Azeris on 11–13 June 1994.

During this time of turmoil, another republic disappeared from the Commonwealth of Independent States. On 8 November 1993 Moldova declared itself part of Romania. Romanian troops rushed in the next day to consummate the union.

Meanwhile, on 7 November 1993, Poland annexed the small Kalinigrad *oblast* practically unnoticed. In the light of what the Poles had suffered at the hands of the Russians over the previous two and a half centuries, no other nation was willing to contest the move. Strelenko denounced the Polish annexation as 'aggression', and vowed revenge 'in due course'. Yeltsin sent a conciliatory message to President Walesa of Poland, recognising the annexation, but suggesting that there should be post-war negotiations 'to regularise the affair'.

UKRAINIAN CAMPAIGN

Meanwhile, Strelenko thought there was an opportunity to reincorporate Ukraine into his modern 'Greater Russia'. He ordered Red forces to advance southward and westward into Ukraine, with Kiev and Lvov the principal objectives. However, the Reds soon discovered that the Ukrainian Army, some 720,000 strong and equipped with many tanks and armoured vehicles seized in 1992 from Soviet armouries, was a formidable opponent. The Ukrainians counterattacked the Red invaders. The Reds suffered a series of humiliating defeats, at Krivoi Rog (11 November), Doneck (29 November), Dnepropetrovsk (22 December), Zhitomir (24 December) and Lvov (28 December).

The Ukrainian Army then turned its attention to a Red armoured column which had penetrated to the vicinity of Kiev in November, before having bogged down. In two weeks of tough fighting the Red invaders were overwhelmed, 45,000 survivors surrendering on 14 January. The Ukrainians then dealt with the final Red units on Ukrainian soil, two divisions in north-east Ukraine, near Kharkov. Three corps of the now battle-hardened Ukrainian Army fell upon these Red divisions and ejected them from Ukrainian soil in the two battles of Kharkov on 27 and 30 January 1994.

THE STRUGGLE FOR RUSSIA

The Red effort to annex Ukraine had proven a boon to Yeltsin and his Blues, who took advantage of the opportunity to assemble large forces in the region south and east of the Don River.

By the beginning of March 1994 Yeltsin had solidified his hold on the south-western portion of the Russian republic and had even extended his holdings to Kuibeshev and Magnitogorsk. Now he was preparing to launch offensives to recapture Moscow and the industrial city of Nizhny Novgorod. Similarly, Basilev, at least temporarily accepting his failure in Ukraine, was marshalling his forces in the region south of Moscow.

By this time Basilev had assembled a force of twenty-seven divisions (six of them understrength) organised into seven armies. To oppose them Yeltsin mustered twenty divisions (two at half-strength) in five armies. Yeltsin, however, commanded more air power than Basilev, and also controlled a sizeable (up to 2 million men) and increasingly well armed and organised Russian partisan militia inside the Red–dominated areas. Both sides were still plagued by roving bands of bandits, but these were militarily insignificant. The greatest problem faced by both sides was supplying the troops and displaced civilian populations with the necessities of life; the entire Soviet economic infrastructure was wrecked, and finding enough gasoline and food even for limited campaigns was becoming difficult. It was clear to all that the coming confrontation would by necessity be the final one to determine the fate of what was left of Russia.

Yeltsin had at first exercised personal command over the Blue forces; he obviously enjoyed wearing a uniform. He was smart enough to realise, however, that he lacked the professional competence to direct a military campaign. Early in February, therefore, he had selected Colonel General Anatoli Kuropatkin as the Commander in Chief of the Russian Republican Army. Kuropatkin, descended from a long line of Russian soldiers, proved himself to be a more capable leader than his great-grandfather had been in Manchuria in the Russo-Japanese War.

Basilev struck first on 5 March, sending his Third and Seventh Armies in a pincer movement against Kuropatkin's Sixth Army near Kursk. The seven Red divisions bogged down against the Blues' deep defensive positions. This gave time for Kuropatkin's Russian Republican Air Force to work over the attackers. The Reds were repulsed with about 5,000 casualties and many vehicles destroyed. Particularly devastating was the loss of most of the Red 39th Parachute Division, which was ambushed and nearly annihilated by ground-attack planes while crossing the Seim

River. Republican airmen also destroyed a large ammunition depot in the rear of the Red forces.

On 9 March Kuropatkin launched a counterstroke, sending his Blue First Army (with two tank and two motorised rifle divisions) against a weak portion of Basilev's line near Penza, north-west of Saratov. The defenders were thrown back to Saransk, and Kuropatkin transferred most of his Fifth Army to the breakthrough area on 12 March to exploit the success. The Fifth Army mission was to drive all the way to Nizhni Novgorod if possible. This attack was aided by partisan attacks in the Red rear areas and by demonstrations along the western portions of the line which pinned most of Basilev's Third, Seventh, First and Second Armies in place. The Blues drove hard, reaching Arzamas, about sixty miles south of Nizhny Novgorod, before reinforcements from the Red Sixth Army arrived to halt the penetration by 20 March.

On the extreme right (far-eastern portion) of the Blue line, Kuropatkin attacked on 12 March with his Third Army toward Yekaterinburg (formerly Sverdlovsk) to support his main attack in the centre. However, this effort, hampered by rain and limited fuel and ammunition, was stopped by the four divisions of Basilev's Fifth Army. The Reds counterattacked on 14 March but were unable to make any headway.

Intent on reaching Nizhny Novgorod and Moscow, and seeing his drive faltering, on 20 March Kuropatkin, after consulting Yeltsin, took the bold step of abandoning Magnitogorsk and most of the area east to Kuibeshev, pulling his Third Army to new positions west of the Orenburg–Ufa highway. This allowed him to shorten his line and concentrate his forces for another drive on Nizhny Novgorod. This drive jumped off on 25 March 1993 on a three-army front: the Fifth Army in the east, the First Army in the centre, and the Fourth Army in the west. The Fifth Army suffered heavy losses and made virtually no gain, running into dense Loyalist minefields at Alatyr on the Sura River. The heavy fighting and attrition virtually wrecked the Blue Fifth Army as a combat force, with almost 12,000 casualties compared to Basilev's 5,000. The attack by the Fourth Army was also stopped with losses of about 10,000 men by strong defences and a vast forest fire at Lipeck and Tambov. The Red defenders suffered about 7,000 casualties. The centre attack by the First Army made better progress, advancing to within thirty kilometres of Nizhny Novgorod before running out of steam. This drive marked the high point of the Blue advance. Kuropatkin's three best armies were exhausted by the hard fighting which had netted them little but ruined towns and burned fields and forests. Furthermore, he was so low on ammunition, especially artillery, that his ability to fight even a defensive battle appeared in doubt. A series of Red counterattacks in April and May pushed the Blues back to their original line by 15 May.

The war entered a static phase, as both sides were too weak and too poorly supplied to resume the offensive. In June the UN mounted a massive relief operation to provide food and housing to the millions of Russians left homeless and starving by the fighting and earlier rioting, and to counteract the famine that was sweeping the entire area west of the Urals.

FROM SIDELINES TO CENTRE STAGE

Sitting on the sidelines through this half-year of bloodshed and destruction were Russian forces east to the Urals, in what had been three military districts: Siberian, Transbaykal and Far Eastern. This region stretched from the Urals to the Pacific Ocean and included most of Siberia. General Valentin Vasilyev, who had been the commander of the Far Eastern Military District, had assumed command of all Soviet troops in this area when the fighting broke out in European Russia in October. He had declared strict neutrality and refused to let any troops of the warring contestants cross the line of the Irtysh and Ob rivers. After suppressing several mutinies in his own ranks, General Vasilyev assured Chinese leaders that the war would not affect them. To confirm this assurance he began withdrawing troops from the Chinese frontier. By late spring of 1994, when it was clear that there was a stalemate west of the Urals, Vasilyev declared the independence of the Republic of Siberia, with himself as 'Interim Military Governor'. He established his new capital at his headquarters at Omsk.

On 20 May Vasilyev received a message from Admiral Alexandrov and General Bogramovich, suggesting a conference 'to discuss the fate of the Motherland'. Alexandrov and Bogramovich invited Vasilyev to meet at Archangelsk, but offered the alternative of going to Omsk to confer with him. 'We, of course, on our military honour, guarantee your protection and safe passage coming and on the return if you meet us at Archangelsk. We are certain that we can count on your military honour to provide us with the same guarantees if we go to Omsk.'

Vasilyev responded that same day. 'I cordially invite both of you to Omsk, where you will be received with the respect, security and full guarantees of safe passage warranted by your distinction. You are welcome at any time. Please allow twenty-four hours' notice to make the necessary arrangements. Please have the commander of your bodyguard arrange your flight plan and other details with my chief of staff.'

Early on 23 May Admiral Alexandrov and General Bogramovich,

escorted by interceptor planes of the strategic rocket forces, flew into Omsk airport. They were met there by General Vasilyev, and accorded full military honours. The three flag officers then withdrew to Vasilyev's office, where they met all day, without any aides being present. Some day the full story of that meeting will probably be told in the memoirs of one or more of the three participants. All we know today is the result of the meeting.

Late in the afternoon identical letters went by radio from Omsk to Moscow and Stavropol, addressed to Acting President Strelenko and President Yeltsin. The letters read as follows:

Your Excellency:

You are hereby informed of the unanimous agreement of the commanders in chief of the Russian Navy, of the Commonwealth Strategic Rocket Forces and of the Russian Far East Military District with respect to the catastrophic civil war which is now tearing apart our beloved Motherland.

We recognise the legitimate presidency of the Republic of Russia of the Honourable Boris Yeltsin. Accordingly, we reject all claims to senior authority in Russia by Acting President Anatoly Strelenko.

We call upon the aforesaid Anatoly Strelenko and to his Defence Minister, General Vladimir Basilev, to issue orders to the forces under their command on or before noon, 26 August 1993, to lay down their arms, and to recognise the authority of the aforesaid Boris Yeltsin as President of the Russian Republic. If Messrs Strelenko and/or Basilev comply with this non-negotiable demand, we guarantee him or them safe conduct, through Archangelsk, to any foreign country or countries he or they may choose.

If this demand is rejected, we call upon the forces now under their command to arrest Messrs Strelenko and Basilev as enemies of the state, to deliver them to the forces of the Russian Republic and to lay down their arms.

If this demand is also rejected, Messrs Strelenko and Basilev, and the forces under their command, are warned that, as of noon, 26 May 1993, the forces of the Soviet Navy, of the Strategic Rocket Forces, and of the Far East Military District, will be placed at the disposal of President Yeltsin, to be employed as he sees fit in restoring peace to Russia.

Constantin Alexandrov
Stefan Bogramovich
Valentin Vasilyev

Another message, signed with the same three names, was sent to Stavropol:

> The Honourable Boris Yeltsin:
> Your Excellency:
>   We request permission to report to you at noon on 26 May 1993, to place at your disposal the forces under our commands.

Late on May 24 a KGB plane from St Petersburg requested permission to land at the airfield of the Arctic Fleet headquarters at Archangelsk. Anatoly Strelenko was on his way to exile. Early the next morning an air force plane from Moscow made a similar request. Vladimir Basilev was also accepting the inevitable.

The Second Great Russian Civil War had come to an end. The human cost of the war is shown in table 3.1.

TABLE 3.1

HUMAN COST OF THE WAR

Nation/regime	Killed	Wounded	Total casualties
'Red' Russian forces (President Strelenko)	64,000	179,000	243,000
'Blue' Russian forces (President Yeltsin)	47,000	142,000	189,000

NEW COMMONWEALTH OF INDEPENDENT STATES

On 27 May President Yeltsin sent messages from the Kremlin to the presidents of the other eleven pre-civil war republics of the Commonwealth of Independent States, inviting them to meet with him in Moscow on Monday 27 June to discuss the future of the Commonwealth. Within forty-eight hours he had received replies from ten of them. The presidents (or, in two cases, former presidents) of Ukraine, Belarus and all five Central Asian republics agreed to attend the 27 June conference. The presidents of Georgia and Azerbaijan sent similar responses, congratulating Yeltsin for his victory, but informing him that the decisions of their peoples to remain independent were irrevocable. The former President of the Moldavian SSR also congratulated Yeltsin, but informed him that Moldova was now a province of Romania. There was no message from Armenia.

On 28 June 1994, at the conclusion of a two-day conference, the presidents of Russia, Ukraine, Belarus, Kokanistan, Khivastan and Turkestan held a news conference. President Yeltsin of Russia was the spokesman. He said that the six republics had agreed to remain members of the Commonwealth of Independent States, as a loose confederation of sovereign states. He said that they had agreed to hold a constitutional convention that would meet in Minsk later that year to draw up a new constitution for the Commonwealth. Meanwhile, Yeltsin said, they had agreed that the agencies of the Commonwealth, as set up in early 1992, would continue to operate, consulting as necessary with the governments of the constituent republics, and that he had been elected by the others as the chairman of the Council of Heads of State, which would meet as necessary to deal with any constitutional issues that might arise before the new constitution was ratified and promulgated. He said that the presidents were agreed that Minsk should remain the seat of the central administration of the Commonwealth.

INTERNATIONAL IMPLICATIONS

In July 1994 the United Nations received applications for membership from the republics of Georgia, Azerbaijan, Kokastan, Khivastan and Turkestan. (Russia – as successor to the USSR – Ukraine and Belarus, of course, were already members.) These applications were speedily processed, all were approved by the General Assembly, and the five new delegations were seated when the General Assembly next convened in September 1994.

That meeting of the General Assembly was addressed by the political leaders of the five Permanent Members of the Security Council. The longest and most sustained applause was given to the first speaker, President Yeltsin of Russia. He began his address as follows:

'Thank you for your overwhelming welcome. I know that your applause is meant less for me personally than for the patriots of Russia who so gloriously defended democracy in our recent civil war, and whom I here represent. But before I go further I must pay specific tribute to four of those patriots. I would not be standing here before you if our martyred president and prime minister, Mikhail Gorbachev, had not courageously and steadfastly as president taken the initial steps which permitted freedom to return to my country, and then attempted to consolidate those gains as prime minister. Nor would I be standing here before you if three professional military men had not remained faithful to their oaths of allegiance to the constitution, and put the rule of law ahead of their personal well-being: Fleet Admiral Constantin Alexandrov, General Stefan Bogramovich and General Vasily Vasiliyev.'

After less memorable addresses by the Presidents of the United States and France and the Prime Minister of China, the session was closed by Prime Minister John Major of the United Kingdom. He concluded his address as follows:

'It is fitting that the highlight of this session has been today's address by the President of the Republic of Russia. He deserves the honour we have paid him, and the respect of all of us, for the dramatic role that he has played in the recent history of his nation. I predict that future historians will remember him as the man who successfully led his nation through its Second Time of Troubles and, in so doing, inaugurated, we hope, a period of prolonged and deserved peace for that great nation.'

TNDM ADDENDUM: CIVIL WAR IN RUSSIA

THE BATTLE OF ROSTOV

One of the early objectives of Yeltsin's Free Russian Republicans (known as the Blue Army), commanded by General Kuropatkin, was to clear the area of southern Russia of Red Army forces loyal to the hard-line communists in Moscow. The largest concentration of these forces in that area was located in and around the city of Rostov, at the mouth of the Don River. This Red force, commanded by General Valeri Demyanov, consisted of elements of the 1st and 34th Guards Tank Divisions and of the 9th, 19th and 24th Guards, and the 73rd and 266th Motorised Rifle Divisions, totalling nearly 50,000 men and about 1,800 tanks and other armoured fighting vehicles.

General Kuropatkin assembled his Army of the Black Sea, comprising the 1st and 7th Tank Divisions, and the 1st, 4th and 7th Guards, and the 11th and 14th Motorised Rifle Divisions. Kuropatkin attacked on 20 November from the vicinity of Novocherkassk, Sachty and Zernograd.

The Blue Army, with substantial air support, made slow but steady progress of about one kilometre a day for six days in an operation that Kuropatkin had expected to be completed in two. The Reds, pushed back behind the Don and Aksai Rivers, and the Azov Canal, now stopped the Blues. Kuropatkin then secretly pulled from the Volga–Saratov region elements of the 4th Tank Division and the 10th and 12th Motorised Rifle

Divisions. Advancing rapidly westward, north of the Don, this Blue force struck the left rear of the Reds late in the afternoon on 1 December, before Demyanov was aware of their approach. This initiated the four-day Battle of Rostov.

Demyanov quickly committed his reserve of one tank and three motorised rifle regiments to counter this unexpected threat, but the movement was hammered by Blue ground-attack planes, and suffered heavy losses. The Reds, already suffering from lack of food and ammunition, soon crumbled. The two Blue drives met in the eastern suburbs of Rostov on 4 December. Demyanov surrendered the next evening.

TABLE TNDM 3.1

TNDM STATISTICS: BATTLE OF ROSTOV

BLUE ARMY	Strength	Losses	Daily losses (%)
Men	110,175	6,011	1.36
Armour	4,102	556	3.39
Artillery	837	22	0.66
RED ARMY			
Men	47,370	8,355	4.41
Armour	1,897	630	8.72
Artillery	338	24	1.78

CHAPTER FOUR

THE SECOND WAR FOR AFRICA

BACKGROUND

As 1993 drew to a close the prospect of racial civil war in South Africa, or racial strife in South Africa accompanied by regional war in southern Africa, seemed remote, a remarkable turnabout from the tinderbox-like situation (and occasional serious flare-ups) that had characterised the closing years of the troubled 1980s.

In the late 1980s and early 1990s two decades of internal conflict, brought about by the seething unrest of the black majority under apartheid, peaked at about the same time serious tribal and political divisions within the black population surfaced. This resulted in bloody clashes between the two principal black 'political' organisations: the African National Congress (ANC), led by Nelson Mandela, and the Inkatha Freedom Party of Zulu chieftain Mangosuthu Buthelezi.

These South African internal problems were set against a background of unresolved regional conflicts, particularly ongoing civil warfare in Angola and Namibia (South-West Africa), and in Mozambique. Because of the strategic importance of the region, including its location astride vital east–west sea lines of communications (see Map. 4.1) and its rich mineral resources, the great powers were hardly uninterested in the outcomes of these various conflicts, and their agents and surrogates were at work everywhere. Thus it was that between August 1987 and July 1988 South African and Cuban troops, the former supporting Angolan opposition forces and the latter stiffening Angolan government troops, clashed in the greatest war in the history of black Africa. The South Africans called this the 'First War for Africa'.

While these several conflicts proceeded simultaneously, South Africa's white minority debated the abandonment of apartheid, the noxious system of racial separation and oppression that had made South Africa a pariah among nations. An important consideration in the debate was the

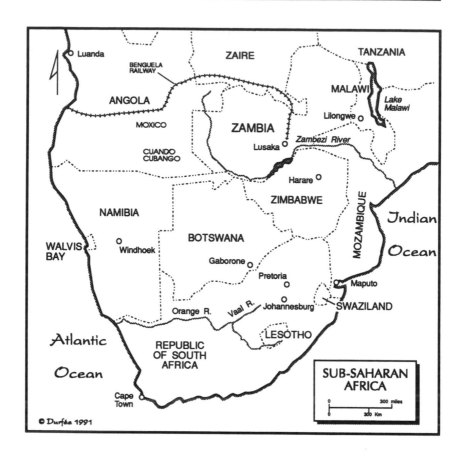

post–minority rule status of the 'white tribe', if it were to surrender power, and particularly its future political and economic security: always factors of principal importance to the white minority.

This debate led to the bold decision by the government of State President Frederik W. de Klerk to abandon apartheid and initiate a transition to a system of 'power-sharing', in which blacks and other disenfranchised sectors of the population would gradually attain an ill-defined measure of presumably equitable participation in the politico-economic life of the nation. De Klerk's initiative had a rocky start, and there were the inevitable scandals as both sides 'came clean' – the pervasive influence of the South Africa Communist Party (SACP) within the ANC and the cosy, occasionally criminal, relationship of the South African government's security apparatus and Inkatha. Nevertheless, progress, if halting, was steady, largely peaceful, and, it seemed, irreversible.

At about the same time the government's decision to jettison apartheid was made, the endemic, long-term regional security problems of South Africa were seemingly solved, one by one. From Namibia and Angola in the west to Mozambique in the east, the guns fell silent and 'jaw, jaw' replaced 'war, war'. For the first time in over two decades the prospect of regional peace *looked* very real indeed.

But the calm that had settled on the region was more apparent than real. In fact, many of the several 'solutions' to the myriad problems of the region were little more than Band-Aids – temporary accommodations to palliate the economic distress and general war-weariness of nations and peoples that had not known real peace since the early 1970s. Although to many it appeared that the cup was 'half full' and that there was genuine hope for a lasting peace, others recognised that much hard work was yet to be done, that the underlying contradictions and tensions remained, and that the cup was perhaps 'half empty' at best. True statesmanship (and there were many true statesmen in the region) would be necessary to overcome the drag of the past, but the overall situation was fraught with difficulty.

HISTORY OF PRIOR RELATIONS OF CONTESTANTS

Although Bartolomeu Dias discovered the Cape of Good Hope in 1487, and Vasco da Gama rounded Cape Agulhas, South Africa's southernmost point, in 1497, the Portuguese explorers were seeking the riches of the Indies and were little interested in the African land mass they negotiated on their difficult voyages. Over a century and a half would pass until a permanent European presence was established in southern Africa. That occurred when the Dutch founded a colony at Table Bay in 1652.

The Dutch Cape Colony soon attracted other settlers, including persecuted co-religionists like French Huguenots and German Calvinists. The original settlers were a unique ethnic and cultural mix, hardy and xenophobic. They spoke Afrikaans – a derivative of seventeenth-century Dutch that is still one of two official languages in South Africa – and styled themselves Afrikaners or Boers (Afrikaans for peasant, or farmer).

The Cape Colony remained Dutch until 1795, when it was seized by Britain as a consequence of Holland's alliance with revolutionary, later Napoleonic, France. The British occupation lasted until 1802, when it was briefly ended by terms of the Treaty of Amiens. The British returned for good in 1806, and in 1815 the Cape Colony was ceded to them (the Act of the Congress of Vienna, 8 June).

Until the advent of the British the Afrikaners were largely unchallenged in their pastoral homeland. By the mid-eighteenth century the aboriginal inhabitants, whether Bushmen or Hottentots, had been destroyed, absorbed as indentured servants or driven off, and the Boers had yet to encounter serious native resistance. And the Cape government – whether Company, Dutch or British – was considered a moribund irrelevance by the hardy Boers, who were adept at putting space between themselves and the authorities in the Castle at Cape Town. Primarily stock-farmers, the free burghers established enormous farms and gradually overspread the country to the north and east, reaching the line of the Great Fish River in the eastern Cape by about 1750.

It was at the Fish River during the next several decades that the frontier separating the great white migration northward from the vanguard of a simultaneous massive black migration southward was established when the Boers encountered the Bantus of the Nguni tribe, one of several tribal groups migrating southward from Central Africa. Like the Boers, the Nguni were cattlemen and, as semi-nomadic herdsmen, they required land in order to grow and flourish. Also like Boers, they had destroyed or driven off the indigenous blacks they had encountered on their migration.

The two great migrations (some might say imperialisms) confronting each other along the Fish River frontier were soon engaged in intermittent fighting to establish dominance in the suddenly delimited land area available. Moreover, in both cases there was no going back – each great migration was pressed against the other by irresistible forces in its rear.

In the case of the Boers, the pressure was from the British. Although insignificant numerically at first, the British attempted to impose their language, laws and values on the Boers and backed their regime by the implicit threat of military force.

The Boers inevitably were not successful in perpetuating their isolation. They pushed deep into the interior in great treks (similar to the westward migration of the wagon trains in the US). They defeated the Matabele (1837) and the Zulus (1838) and established a Boer republic in Natal, only to come into conflict again with the British, who annexed Natal in 1843. The majority of the Boers then moved on to the northwest, over the Drakensberg Mountains, and founded two landlocked Boer republics in the Orange Free State and the Transvaal.

Although the British recognised the independence of these republics (in 1852 and 1854), the two were subsequently swallowed up by the burgeoning British empire in southern Africa after bitter wars in 1881 (First Anglo–Boer War) and 1899–1902 (Second, or Great Anglo–Boer War). Meanwhile, the persistent problem of black opposition to white imperialism was solved in a series of conflicts, the most important and decisive of which was the Anglo–Zulu War of 1879. (A possibly more significant event in the destruction of black power in southern Africa was the purposeful slaughter of all the Xhosa's cattle in 1856 in response to the 'prophecy' of a witch-doctor. This catastrophe resulted in the virtual self-annihilation of the powerful Xhosa.)

Although the conduct of the British during the Second Boer War had been harsh in some instances, they behaved with generosity once the war was ended, and by 1909 the former Boer republics and the Cape Colony and Natal were united in the Union of South Africa, which had a Boer majority and a Boer prime minister: General Louis Botha, who had led Boer forces against the British less than ten years earlier. The new Union was a self-governing dominion within the empire, with its foreign relations managed by London.

The wisdom of the British settlement with the Boers was borne out subsequently, as shown particularly by the loyalty of the Union in two world wars and the Korean War. The Union achieved full independence in 1931 (Statute of Westminster) and became a member of the British Commonwealth of Nations. However, in May 1961 the Boer government withdrew from membership in the commonwealth partnership, becoming the Republic of South Africa.

The enormous resources, wealth and military potential of the Republic had made it one of the most powerful nations in Africa, despite its many political problems. In the post-colonial turmoil of sub-Saharan Africa, it was without doubt the single most important player on a rather crowded stage and has been involved one way or another in every neighbouring conflict of recent times.

In 1975, in response to unrest in Angola and Portugal's precipitate grant of independence to its troubled former colony, South Africa became involved in the ongoing conflict there. South Africa sided with Dr Jonas Savimbi's UNITA (Union for the Total Independence of Angola) against the communist-dominated, Eastern Bloc-supported MPLA (Popular Movement for the Liberation of Angola), which gained control of the government apparatus. The Angolan regional conflict had international implications as well, since Soviet and Eastern Bloc advisers and Cuban troops fought alongside the MPLA, and the US and other Western nations supplied UNITA with advanced weapons.

The MPLA was never able to defeat UNITA and its Boer ally, despite mounting a series of massive and costly offensives during the civil war begun in 1975 (and lasting a decade and a half), and despite South African disengagement from Angola (begun in February 1984 and completed in 1989). The civil war continued, but at a much reduced level of intensity, due to the exhaustion of both sides. Cuban troops were withdrawn from Angola (August 1991), and the warring parties made tentative efforts to settle the conflict.

The failure of the MPLA government's last weak offensives in 1991 brought both sides to the conference table in the now notorious Lisbon Conference, which met intermittently under UN auspices (March 1992 to February 1994) before its final breakdown. Analysts viewing retrospectively the tortuous history of the peace talks in Lisbon were surprised at their failure, since the belligerents appeared to have entered the conference seriously intending to reach a comprehensive settlement. As time passed, however, it became clear that little real progress was being made, and some began to suspect that the talks were a screen masking the military resuscitation of one, or both, of the warring parties. When the conference recessed finally in February 1994, most in the region expected that it would meet again, once the latest petty squabble was ironed out by diplomacy, at arm's length. Few suspected that the recess was a harbinger of renewed regional war.

SOUTH AFRICAN DEFENCE FORCE (SADF)

Remarkably, considering the array of external and internal threats, South Africa's armed forces – the most powerful, experienced and efficient in sub-Saharan Africa – are relatively small in relation to the nation's population. Until recently, the total personnel of the active armed forces (Permanent Force and National Service) was about 80,000, just 0.23 per cent of the population, including the 'independent homelands'. (The figures were further reduced after disengagement from Angola and withdrawal from Namibia, when total personnel was reduced to about 60,000.) And defence expenditures are just 3.7 per cent of the country's gross national product (R10 billion of R272 billion in 1990). Viewed another way, armed forces' spending was 15.2 per cent of the annual budget (figure for 1988/9).

In many ways the SADF is the product of a gestation period and sometimes rude infancy that parallels that of another highly professional 'first world' fighting force that shields a 'European' enclave carved out of an alien region and confronted almost continuously (and implacably) by 'third world' hostility: that is, of course, the Israeli Defence Forces (IDF). Like the IDF, the SADF's heritage is partly British, but with a healthy admixture of local custom and doctrine, and throughout its history it has had to combat a diversity of enemies in a wide variety of combat situations ranging from counter-terrorism to full-blown conventional war.

The SADF was founded in 1961 when the Republic of South Africa came into existence. At that time South Africa's armed forces, particularly the ground forces, were in a state of disarray arising from long-term neglect and underfunding. This was the product not only of nearly two decades of relative peace since the end of World War II but also of the absence of any real threat, either external or internal. Further, as a virtual auxiliary of the British armed forces (until 1961), South Africa's armed forces had been much affected by Britain's long retreat from its international commitments – a process that had begun in 1945. Thus, under Commonwealth defence arrangements, South Africa had been required to maintain a modern armoured division in fighting trim for possible deployment to the Middle East. To equip this division, beginning in 1952, South Africa purchased 200 Centurion main battle tanks (MBTs) from Britain. A few years later, in 1956, half these tanks were sold to Switzerland; at that time, they were deemed 'not required for South Africa's defence', essentially because Britain had abandoned its former Middle East commitments in the aftermath of the Suez Crisis.

The halcyon days of the SADF ended in 1975 with the South African intervention in Angola and the beginning of military operations, including cross-border operations, that over the years since have seen the SADF involved in a wide array of conflicts in the region in a variety of military roles, from the unconventional, such as counter-insurgency, to more conventional combined-arms operations, such as were carried out in Angola.

The SADF was organised in four service branches each under a chief: Army, Navy (SAN), Air Force (SAAF) and Medical Service (SAMS). Over them, the Chief of the Defence Staff reports to the Minister of Defence, a member of the President's Cabinet. The Minister of Defence is also responsible for the operations of Armscor, the state-run armaments industry. He is assisted by the defence staff.

The force structure included the Full-Time Force (FT), Citizen Force (CF) and Commandos. The FT was the relatively small active component of the armed forces. It included Permanent Force (PF) personnel, who are long-service professionals – generally officers, specialists and the regular infantry of the black battalions – and national servicemen (NSM), white conscripts performing their twelve-month active duty obligation.

The CF and Commandos were the armed forces' reserve components. CF personnel were ex-NSM serving out a twelve-year service commitment, which generally included about a month of military service each year (but no more than sixty days in any two-year period). Commandos were regionally based militia organisations, mostly light infantry, modelled on the Boer commandos of the late nineteenth century. Their organisational structure, weapons and missions were adapted to local conditions.

THE SOUTH AFRICAN ARMY

The Army emerged from the Angola war with enhanced prestige gained from its unequivocal, one-sided victories over MPLA and its Cuban and Soviet allies. By the end of the war it was quite apparent, as more than one observer noted, that the entire array of South Africa's enemies in the field could not defeat it militarily. However, the operations in Angola had revealed that the army had some serious problems that would have to be addressed in the future. Among these were: (1) cumbersome, multi-layered command, control and co-ordination structures that interfered with the smooth operational conduct of the war and permitted micro-management of combat units by senior officers who usurped tactical command functions; (2) inadequacy of the logistical support system; and (3) inadequacy or obsolescence of many weapons systems, particularly anti-tank and anti-aircraft means.

On the other hand, South African training, professionalism, and C^3I (command, control, communications and intelligence) and EW (electronic warfare) capabilities paid handsome dividends. And the use of certain advanced weapons systems, such as the G-5 gun-howitzer and modern anti-tank guided missiles (ATGMs), even in small numbers, more than made up for deficiencies in other areas.

Standard major weapons, by category, include the following.

AFVs

250	Olifant MBTs (main battle tanks)
1,500	Ratel IFVs (infantry fighting vehicles)
1,500	APCs (armoured personnel carriers)
1,600	armoured cars

The Olifant is a modernised, upgunned Centurion Mark V. Mounting a 105 mm gun, it is more than a match for any of the ageing Soviet-built tanks it might encounter in the region. Despite the international arms embargo (imposed in 1970 in reaction to South African defiance of the UN on the issue of South–West Africa), South Africa managed to rebuild its stock of Centurions by purchasing tanks from Jordan and India. The refitted South African Centurions were considered equivalent to similar Israeli and Swiss refits.

The versatile Ratel family of wheeled, 6×6 IFVs includes types suitable for a number of combat roles, including mounted infantry combat, fire support, anti-tank, command, control and co-ordination, electronic warfare and armoured recovery. The basic vehicle, the Ratel-20, was developed by Armscor and fielded in 1975 as South Africa's standard mechanised infantry combat vehicle. It is armed with two 7.6 mm machine guns and a 20 mm autocannon, has a three-man crew, and carries a nine-man infantry section. Variants are adapted to mount either a 60 mm mortar, 90 mm low-pressure gun or ZT-3 ATGMs.

Standard APCs include the mine-protected 4×4 Buffel, and the tough 4×4, mine-protected Casspir, a favourite of the police and counter-insurgency forces because of its mobility in bush, sand and other difficult terrain. The Casspir is being phased out in some units and replaced by the Wolf.

Reconnaissance functions and raiding are the province of the armoured car regiments, which are equipped primarily with the Eland, a South African version of the venerable French Panhard AML. The two basic types are the Eland-60, which mounts a 60 mm mortar, and the Eland-90, with a 90 mm low-pressure gun as its main armament. The Eland is being replaced by the advanced, eight-wheeled Rooikat, an agile but well-protected vehicle that mounts a 76 mm high-velocity gun and boasts a modern fire-control system.

Artillery

145	25-pounders (towed)
30	5.5-inch guns (towed)
75	G-2, G-4 155 mm gun-howitzers (towed)
40+	G-5 155 mm gun-howitzers (towed)
10+	G-6 155 mm gun-howitzers (self-propelled, SP)
120+	Valkiri, Bataleur 127 mm multiple rocket launchers (MRL; towed/SP)

Experience in Angola in late 1975 confirmed the obsolescence of South Africa's artillery arsenal, then consisting of World War II-vintage British 25-pounders and 5.5-inch guns, which were badly outranged by modern Soviet types. This led directly to the development of the G-5, a very advanced, long-range gun-howitzer. The self-propelled version of the G-5 is the G-6. The first operational deployment of these guns was in Angola in the 1987–8 fighting, and their performance was most impressive (decisive, some claimed). The guns are Armscor products, incorporating advanced technology developed by the controversial Gerald Bull's Space Technology Corporation and by Swedish metallurgists. With their 40-kilometre range, they are considered to be the world's finest artillery guns; many have been exported to Iraq and Iran. The G–2 (ex–British 4.5–inch gun) and G–4 155 mm guns are also elderly but considered interim equipments, bridging the gap between the phasing out of the older World War II–era materiel and the introduction of the G–5. In the Angola fighting, the G–4s backstopped the G–5s.

The Valkiri and its more modern successor, the Bataleur, are MRL systems copied from a Soviet BM–21 captured in Angola in 1975. The towed Valkiri 5 is a lightweight 12–tube version for use by airborne troops and light infantry; the Valkiri SP is a truck–mounted 24–tube version; and the Bataleur, introduced in 1990, is a truck–mounted 40–tube model, intended to replace the Valkiri SP.

Anti-tank and anti-aircraft South Africa's anti-tank capabilities include both guns and missiles. The weapons for the most part are dated (90 mm gun; SS–11 and ENTAC ATGMs), but adequate numbers of MILAN and the new, South African–developed ZT–3 ATGMs are now in service.

Anti-aircraft (AA) weaponry is a neglected area. AA weapons are primarily guns, mostly towed, including 20 mm, 35 mm, 35 mm Oerlikon, and 40 mm. The more modern systems are the 20 mm truck-mounted Ystervark and captured Soviet ZU–23–2 twin 23 mm SPAA. A modern SPAA gun is reportedly under development by Armscor. Surface-to-air missile (SAM) systems in service include mostly elderly types, like the Cactus, South Africa's version of the French Crotale SPAA and the Soviet Strela shoulder-launched heat-seeker, quantities of which were captured in Angola. In the most recent operations in Angola the AA contribution of UNITA, which had been equipped with the 'state of the art' USA shoulder-launched SAM, the Stinger, was vital.

Organisation for combat
On paper, the South African Army is organised into:
1   A variety of elite PF units, plus various related security forces units.
2   Two Citizen Force (CF) divisions, the 7th and 8th, plus the 44th Parachute Brigade, the 60th Mechanised Brigade, and supporting troops (divisional units, etc.).
3   Ten Territorial Force (TF) Commands and the Walvis Bay Military Area.

However, no South African division has taken the field since World War II, and in large-scale conventional combat South African forces have been task-organised in brigade-sized (or smaller), combined-arms combat teams. Further, all large-scale training exercises are conducted at brigade level.

In the Angola operations the combat teams were composed primarily of mechanised infantry. However, in some of the final operations, whether because they involved the assault of fortified zones or because there was a political motive to keep casualties to a minimum – or both – South Africa's version of 'tank heavy' attack formations were organised.

By Western standards, these were not tank-heavy combat formations, since the proportion of armoured battalions (South African squadrons) to infantry battalions was about 1:1.

THE SAAF

The SAAF is a modern, highly efficient air force that is powerful by regional standards. Its principal weakness is the relative obsolescence of virtually all its first-line equipment, composed of ageing French-built Mirage airframes, and the South African upgrade of the Mirage, called the Cheetah. These aircraft cannot match the MiGs of Angola's air force in many key performance categories, so the SAAF relies on the skill of its pilots and technical superiority in certain crucial areas, such as electronic warfare and air-to-air missiles.

A powerful component of the SAAF is the small but potent force of battlefield support helicopters, which in 1993 included an unknown number of high-speed, heavily armed Rooivalk combat helicopters. This aircraft is considered superior to the similar US Apache.

MPLA

The armed forces of the MPLA have had a checkered history. Numerically strong (some 150,000, including militia) and well equipped with ageing Soviet materiel, they are capable of generating enormous force power by regional standards, as they have shown on numerous occasions. But MPLA offensives against UNITA in 1975–6, 1985, 1986, 1987–8, and 1990–91 resulted in failure each time. And some of those failures were spectacular enough to gain worldwide attention. The MPLA's fighting men, many of whom are poorly trained adolescents, are not nearly a match for the South African soldier and compare poorly to UNITA's skilful light infantry. However, the MPLA attempts to compensate for this troop quality weakness by bringing to bear masses of materiel and firepower. It has come close to success several times, and some of its failures can be ascribed more to logistical breakdowns and lack of staying power than decisive defeat in the field.

The military arm of the MPLA is FAPLA (People's Armed Forces for the Liberation of Angola), but the acronym is usually associated with the ground forces, since the navy is small, and the air force is designated FAPA (Forcas Aeria Popular de Angola). FAPLA is organised administratively into ten military regions, some of which function as forward headquarters, and over seventy brigades, each of which numbers from 1,400 to 1,900 fighting men.

FAPLA brigades were organised like Soviet motorised rifle regiments and were provided with enough transport and combat vehicles to make them theoretically capable of sustained high-speed operations in conventional combat. Since this is not practical or attainable in the jungle of south-eastern Angola, FAPLA brigades differed from their Soviet counterparts by having a scaled-back armour component. Nevertheless, FAPLA has always enjoyed at least a numerical superiority in armour in all its operations.

FAPA is the most powerful air force in sub-Saharan Africa, mainly because of the large number of relatively advanced Soviet aircraft in its arsenal. With over 50 MiG-23s and 75 MiG-21s, FAPA has the potential to overwhelm numerically the SAAF with high-performance aircraft that match or exceed anything in the SADF's arsenal. However, FAPA's pilots, who showed skill in the last stages of the First War for Africa, still cannot match those of the SAAF man for man.

ANGOLAN OPPOSITION GROUPS

South African disengagement and Cuban withdrawal from Angola have magnified the military importance of the three armed opposition groups: UNITA, FNLA (National Front for the Liberation of Angola) and FLEC (Front for the Liberation of the Cabinda Enclave). Of the three, only UNITA is significant.

Formed in 1966 by the charismatic, pro-Western Savimbi, who is still its leader, UNITA emerged from the post-colonial turmoil as the MPLA's principal opponent. In the intervening years UNITA built a solid fighting reputation. By 1987 the group was considered Africa's best guerrilla fighting force. Based in south-eastern Angola, with its 'capital' at Jambo, UNITA fields approximately 30,000 regulars, armed and equipped with a variety of Western and captured Soviet materiel, and organised in 700-man battalions. Beginning in 1975, the SADF has supported or fought alongside UNITA on several occasions, most recently during 1987–8. It was during this latter period that SADF–UNITA combined operations were undertaken, with remarkable success, and UNITA battalions were taken in hand by the SADF for training in conventional warfare tactics and techniques.

In conventional operations UNITA forces fight as light infantry; they have a limited independent conventional capability. When integrated into an SADF combat team, UNITA elements are often deployed in front, or on the flanks, of the main force. They are invaluable in a number of roles: reconnaissance, screening, deception, ambush and feint attack. An important element in UNITA's arsenal is the US Stinger SAM, which helped limit the potentially decisive influence of FAPA's MiGs in the 1987–90 fighting.

NAMIBIA, SWAPO AND PLAN

Namibia is Africa's youngest nation, having achieved its independence from South Africa in 1990 after twenty-three years of warfare between Sam Nujoma's SWAPO (South-West African People's Organisation) insurgency and the South African government, which administered the territory.

Namibia is a physically forbidding, largely barren country that in 1884 was annexed by imperial Germany as German South-West Africa. The native Herreros were subdued by the Germans in a war during 1904–8. At the outbreak of World War I General Botha led troops of South Africa's Union Defence Force into Namibia and conquered it in a campaign that ended in July 1915 with German surrender.

In 1919 Namibia was designated a South African mandate by the League of Nations. The mandate was terminated by UN resolution in 1966, but South Africa rejected the resolution and continued to administer Namibia until 1990.

SWAPO, which draws its principal strength from the majority Ovambo tribe of northern Namibia, was founded in 1960 (although predecessor organisations date from 1957). Originally a political organisation, SWAPO soon began preparing for 'armed revolution' and conducted its first terror operations in 1965–6. SWAPO's military wing, the People's Liberation Army of Namibia (PLAN), was countered by the South African Police (SAP) and SADF units. At first, most South African counter-insurgency operations were carried out in Ovamboland, but the *coup d'état* in Lisbon in 1974 and subsequent Portuguese withdrawal from Africa transformed what had been essentially an 'internal' counter-terror campaign into a regional war, with SWAPO and FAPLA on one side and the SADF and UNITA on the other. The first South African cross-border ('external') operation into Angola was undertaken in May 1978, and several others, large and small, followed, until the end of the conflict in 1989.

Namibia's transition to independent self-government was achieved under UN auspices. SWAPO won Namibia's first election, in 1989, with 57 per cent of the vote (92 per cent of the Ovambo vote), and Sam Nujoma became the country's first president. PLAN, which retained its name, became the new country's defence force. It absorbed elements of the South-West Africa Territorial Force – its principal opponent in the days of the insurgency – but PLAN personnel filled all key positions and assignments in the new, amalgamated force.

PLAN's organisation and training had been as a guerrilla force, employing terror as its principal weapon and shunning conventional combat with the South African security forces. After independence, it made the transition to a conventional force structure, with conventional capabilities. The British assisted this process by providing training. However, with a strength of just 8,500 poorly equipped men, many of whom would be unreliable in an armed confrontation with the SADF, and few heavy weapons or combat air component, PLAN, by itself, was not an important factor militarily in the region.

Namibia has regarded South Africa as its chief enemy, although since independence relations between South Africa and Namibia have been cordial. Angola and FAPLA remained Namibia's allies, and Namibian contingency planning, based largely on the possibility of cross-border operations by the SADF, envisaged minimal conventional resistance by elements of PLAN (in order to gain sympathy worldwide), while much of the force dispersed and reverted to guerrilla warfare. PLAN and FAPLA have not formally co-ordinated military planning, but military relationships of the two revolutionary armed forces remained close.

THE SECOND WAR FOR AFRICA

The final, irretrievable breakdown of the on-again, off-again Lisbon Conference was accompanied by the usual heated rhetoric and chest-thumping by the opposing sides. Not surprisingly, and despite continued economic hardship throughout the affected region, military preparations were begun in earnest.

UNITA, FAPLA and the SADF were not unprepared; none had let its guard down since the events of 1987–91, though the intermittent cease-fires subsequently had permitted both FAPLA and the SADF to scale back, and the SADF had retired much of its obsolescent materiel as newer, more advanced equipment entered service.

The Great Powers, caught in the worldwide economic downturn and preoccupied with more pressing foreign policy crises, washed their hands of the latest African bickering, assuming, incorrectly as it turned out, that the regional antagonists were incapable of harming one another very much and for very long. At any rate, having done their worst to feed the flames for a couple of decades, and then done their best for a few years to put them out, they were content to prowl the sidelines, muttering impotently about what might have been.

A comparison of the military forces available to the belligerents is shown in Table 4.1.

'VITÓRIA': THE MPLA 'VICTORY OPERATION'

The MPLA was first off the mark in the new conflict, having evolved an operational plan that, for once, projected reasonable logistic support for mobile operations lasting more than two or three months. The controlling assumption was that, since UNITA's south-eastern Angola stronghold had been isolated (effectively) from SADF support by independent Namibia, it would be possible to overwhelm UNITA by a powerful, sustained offensive that adapted the Soviet concept of echeloned attack to African conditions.

It was vital to the plan that UNITA's isolation should be made as complete as possible. That meant blocking Western aid to UNITA from Zaire and South African aid or intervention from the air, from Namibia or from Botswana. Zaire was a problem, but none of the other possibilities was particularly practical under existing conditions. It was clear, furthermore, that if South Africa wanted to assist its ally, it would first have to establish operational preconditions for assistance, namely to occupy Namibian territory and establish forward bases from which to intervene again in Angola.

Luanda was not unaware of South Africa's predicament, and boldly planned to pre-empt the SADF in Namibia. The MPLA reasoned that South Africa, which on several occasions had violated the sovereignty of neighbouring states to achieve operational objectives, would not hesitate to violate Namibia's precarious sovereignty to come to the assistance of UNITA. After all, virtually everyone recognised that the elimination of UNITA would so upset the balance of power in the region that Pretoria might ultimately have to confront the prospect of fighting a decisive conventional battle for national existence in South Africa itself.

TABLE 4.1

COMPARISON OF COMBAT FORCES

ARMY	SADF/UNITA†	FAPLA/PLAN‡
Manpower	128,000	100,000
MBTs	320	500
IFVs	1,500	250
ACs	1,600	255
APCs	1,500	550
Artillery pieces*	300	550
MRLs	120	75
AIR FORCE		
Combat aircraft	320	190
Armed helicopters	18	28
AIR DEFENCE		
AAA guns	150	300
SAMs	74	160
NAVY		
Submarines	3	–
DDs/FFGs	–	–
Fast missile craft	9	6

Figures are approximate.

    * Including heavy mortars (= 120mm).

    † South African FT and NSM (61,000); UNITA 'regular' and 'semi-regular'. UNITA's conventional capabilities, particularly in heavy weapons, are minimal.

    ‡ FAPLA (91,500) includes actives, draftees and serving militia (ODP); PLAN's small active contingent has few modern heavy weapons.

Since the SADF presence in Namibia was limited by treaty to the military enclave of Walvis Bay, much removed from south-eastern Angola, a FAPLA pre-emptive attack into pro-SWAPO Ovamboland in northern Namibia would not only deny the SADF the forward bases it needed to intervene but would also isolate the battlefield in south-eastern Angola. It was in this strategic context that the MPLA's 'Victory Operation' was conceived.

In broad outline Victory envisaged simultaneous operations in the three 'traditional' Angolan theatres. In the Northern Theatre (actually east-central Angola), along the Benguela railway, FAPLA forces were to adopt an essentially defensive posture. But by aggressive patrolling and deception operations (Operation Profundo) they were to simulate offensive preparations in order to fix the UNITA forces in the region and prevent their transfer to the principal operational theatre to the south. Since FAPLA had in the past launched major offensives to clear the railway line, this sub-operation was expected to accomplish its purpose without over-burdening the logistical apparatus supporting the overall operation.

In the Eastern Theatre (actually south-eastern Angola), forces committed to Operation Pisador (Crusher) were charged with the final elimination of UNITA. The designated axis of advance was Cuito Cuanavale–Cunjamba–Mavinga–Jamba, as it had been many times in the past.

Operation Malho (Sledgehammer), mounted in the Western Theatre (along the Angola–Namibia frontier and in Ovamboland), envisaged a high-speed cross-border dash by a powerful mechanised force along the Namacunde–Ondangua–Grootfontein axis. The objective was to occupy Ovamboland in force and prevent the SADF utilising it as a base area to support UNITA. Grootfontein was the strategic key to Ovamboland.

Since Sledgehammer involved surprise and pre-emption, certain pre-operational conditions had to be established. First, the 'benevolent neutrality' or outright co-operation of PLAN had to be assured (although this was not considered an absolute, given PLAN's relative impotence). Second, all civilian and military airfields in the operational area had to be seized – not only to deny them to the SADF but also to secure them for use by the Angolan Air Force. To accomplish this, FAPLA planned to use its 500-strong 'special brigades' (commandos) in pre-operational cross-border raids to seize the airstrips at Rundu and Ondangua. In addition, an elite deep penetration team was formed to attack Grootfontein AFB (some 250 kilometres inside Namibia), which had been the SAAF's main airhead in the Angola interventions. This force, numbering just 112 men, was to be transported to its objective in Mi-8 and Mi-17 assault transport helicopters.

The operational planners had the vanguard of the Sledgehammer ground force entering Grootfontein (approximately 350 air kilometres from Namacunde) on D+1, to occupy and hold the town. Further, with MiG bases established at Ondangua and Rundu, and even at Grootfontein (if the aerodrome was secured with a minimum of destruction), Angolan air superiority in Ovamboland would be virtually assured, since the SAAF had nothing to match the FAPLA MiG-23s.

Having gained possession of Grootfontein the FAPLA Sledgehammer task force was to organise a defensive position in the rough triangle of roads connecting Tsumeb (north) with Grootfontein (south-east) and Otavi (south-west). With a good tar road leading back to Angola behind, a MiG CAP overhead, and absolutely flat, arid terrain all around, it was not thought that the SADF, however violently it reacted, would pose quite the threat it had in the past.

Combat forces earmarked for assignment to Victory's three sub-operations were:

1   Profundo: 5 brigades (6,000), plus 2 attached tank combat groups (300), Milse (1,000), and ODP (5,000); total 12,300.
2   Crusher: 15 brigades, including organic tank companies (150 T-54s and T-55s); total 28,500.
3   Sledgehammer: 10 brigades, including organic tank companies (100 T-62s), plus commandos; total approximately 20,000.

The total commitment to Victory was over 60,000 men, making it the most ambitious combat operation ever mounted in sub-Saharan Africa.

SADF PREPARATIONS AND PLANS

Well before the breakdown of the Lisbon Conference UNITA had warned Pretoria that the situation in south and south-eastern Angola had become serious. The MPLA build-up, coupled with markedly increased levels of military engineering activities in FAPLA-controlled areas, made it quite apparent that a large-scale military operation was imminent. UNITA was certain that it was targeted in Cuando Cubango, and informed the SADF that it expected to be on the receiving end of a two-pronged offensive, like that of 1987-8, sometime in late spring. UNITA, however, lacked an aerial reconnaissance capability, and so could not penetrate the MPLA's designs on Ovamboland.

Acting on UNITA's warnings, the SADF stepped up its intelligence activities, including clandestine operations in Namibia and Angola. Several weeks before Victory was launched, it had pieced together a fairly comprehensive picture of the FAPLA plan. However, some parts of the puzzle were overlooked, missed or misplaced: the carefully concealed mission of the 'special brigades' was not detected, and the size of the two offensive sub-operations was underestimated. But intelligence confirmation of the planned, massive FAPLA incursion into Namibia coinciding with the offensive against UNITA caused hours of worry at DHQ (Defence Headquarters), Pretoria, and within the Cabinet and SSC (State Security Council), as the politicians and top military staff considered the options.

In assessing the situation confronting them South Africa's leaders reasoned – not incorrectly as it turned out – that the decisive battles would be fought in Namibia, and that events there would largely determine the outcome of the fighting in south-eastern Angola. This, of course, was the obverse of the MPLA's reasoning.

Since Namibian independence in 1990 the SADF's Operations Staff Council (the joint service operational-tactical planning organ) had developed plans to deal with contingencies arising from Namibia's changed status. The possibility of a FAPLA incursion into Ovamboland to attempt to isolate UNITA in its enclave had been considered, and an operational plan, code-named Gemsbok, had been formulated to deal with it.

Like most SADF contingency plans, Gemsbok incorporated two of the basic elements of SADF doctrine: 'pro-active defence' and 'short, sharp war'. In brief, these doctrinal tenets required the SADF to pre-empt the enemy and, by the application of overwhelming force in a brief period, destroy it or convince it that to continue the conflict would not be worth the cost.

Gemsbok envisaged a decisive mechanised battle in the vicinity of Otjiwarongo, about 200 kilometres south-west of Grootfontein. The choice of this location recognised that FAPLA would have overrun the airstrips on the Angola–Namibia frontier, and probably Grootfontein too, before the SADF could muster the resources to oppose it. It was assumed, however, that Grootfontein was too far forward to be made operational for FAPA's jets.

Further, the SAAF, operating out of Windhoek and Walvis Bay, even Otjiwarongo itself, could provide close air support and fly top cover, contesting air superiority with FAPA's MiGs in a tactical environment that, if not ideal, was probably the best that could be hoped for under the circumstances. And, since Otjiwarongo was situated in a defile – west of the Waterberg, north of Mount Etjo, and east of the Franksfontein Range (all spurs or outliers of the Central Highlands) – movement toward it from the Grootfontein area would be channelled into rugged terrain that would favour the South Africans. Moreover, as a crossroad in a region with very few roads, Otjiwarongo was linked to both Windhoek and Walvis Bay, making it the most logical point for an SADF concentration.

Tactically, Gemsbok included defensive and offensive phases. The first, defensive, phase (Armadillo) was designed to absorb FAPLA's initial offensive blow, attrit the enemy's armour, halt its advance, and buy time for the build-up of the SADF counterattack forces, which would have to be brought forward from South Africa via Windhoek and Walvis Bay.

The second, offensive, phase – code-named Blackadder – envisaged a turning movement via Outjo–Okaukuejo–Namutoni to cut FAPLA's line of communications just east of the Etosha Pan and render its position in the Grootfontein region untenable.

SADF combat forces earmarked for Gemsbok included:

Serial 1:

1 2nd SA Infantry Battalion Group (Walvis Bay), including its organic tank squadron (13 Olifants); 1,000 men.
2 32nd Battalion (Pomfret, North Cape) (13 Ratel-AT-Z; 13 Ratel-90); 600 men.
3 4th Reconnaissance Regiment (Cape Town) (elite special forces); 500 men.
4 14th Parachute Battalion Group; 800 men.
5 60th Mechanised Brigade (53 Olifants); 2,300 men.
Strength of Serial 1: 5,200.

Serial 2:

1 82nd Mechanised Brigade (53 Olifants); 2,300 men.
2 49th Mechanised Brigade (53 Olifants); 2,300 men.
Strength of Serial 2: 4,600.

Units of Serial 1 were designated 'immediately deployable', that is, they could be at Otjiwarongo on D+1 or D+2, travelling overland from Walvis Bay or points in the northern Cape – or in the case of the reconnaissance commandos and paras, being transported to their destinations by aircraft. The formations of Serial 2 were to be assembled from 'on-call' CF units. These were to be mobilised and hurried into brigade forward assembly areas (FAAs) in Namibia as soon as they had completed assembly and organisation at their depots in South Africa. These formations were expected to be complete and at their FAAs within one week of their initial muster. In addition to the units designated for the Gemsbok operation, other CF units were elevated to 'on-call' status. The SADF's preparations were complete by late February 1994.

OUTBREAK OF WAR

At 0400 hours on 21 March 1994 (the fourth anniversary of Namibian independence) the Second War for Africa (as the South Africans styled it) began. Windhoek radio heralded the conflict by announcing that 'fraternal comrades [FAPLA] had entered Ovambo to guarantee Namibian sovereignty and prevent Boer interference with . . . [FAPLA's] final anti-bandit campaign in Cuando Cubango'. PLAN was urged to co-operate with FAPLA in the operation and 'resist Boer aggression to the limits of [its] capability' (South African transcription).

The effect of the broadcast on PLAN's rank and file might have been predicted. Units in contact (or imminent contact) with 'the Boers' dissolved; only those in Windhoek and points north and east maintained cohesion and followed SWAPO's outline plan for surviving the conflict. Units not at key airfields made haste to close on FAPLA's line of advance and come under FAPLA's 'protection'. Those at the three airfields simply awaited the arrival of FAPLA's commandos. That evening PLAN's effective fighting force numbered just 2,000 lightly equipped fighting men. All of them were diehard ex-SWAPO troops and officers and nearly all were either in Ovambo or close enough to get there in safety.

At midday Windhoek radio made its last announcement, described as a 'pre-recorded statement'. The strains of the Namibian national anthem, which had been playing incessantly all day, were interrupted by the voice of President Sam Nujoma, who announced that compelling circumstances required that the Namibian government 'should be removed to a place of safety', and that henceforth, 'until the conclusion of the present emergency, the government would be under the magnanimous protection of President Dos Santos of Angola'. As Nujoma signed off, the broadcast began to break up, indicating that SADF jamming had begun.

By 0500 hours the FAPLA commandos assigned to take Ondangua and Rundu airfields had completed their missions, which in effect consisted of accepting the keys from relieved SWAPO gatekeepers. The battalion or so of PLAN infantry in each place was told to return to its barracks, keep out of the way and await instructions. Most did, but a significant number decided 'their war' was over and set off on foot or in trucks for their home kraals.

At Grootfontein events took a rather different turn. The helicopters of the deep-penetration team touched down at 0530 hours after a tension-filled two-hour flight from N'Giva. As expected, there was no opposition; in fact, in obedience to orders, the local PLAN battalion was turned out on the tarmac in welcome. With some ceremony (attended apprehensively by a couple of platoons of the invaders, who were drawn up in line rather hastily), the base was handed over intact. In the operations building a dozen unreconstructed 'Boer' technicians were locked up so as not to embarrass anyone.

At 0600 hours precisely, as this comic-opera ceremony proceeded, four SAAF Buccaneers passed over the base at high speed just 200 metres above the airstrip, releasing CB-470 cluster bombs approximately 1,000 metres from the target. Each cluster bomb ejected forty 6-kg submunitions, which bounced on impact and then exploded, scything down the PLAN infantrymen and FAPLA commandos, who were quite unexpectedly caught in the open, on parade. Nearly 400 men were killed or maimed, including about 40 commandos. It was the greatest one-time loss that SWAPO had suffered since an eerily similar incident on 4 May 1978, when the SAAF had raided a SWAPO camp at Cassinga in southern Angola.

As the deep-penetration group's helicopters blazed amid this scene of carnage, a second flight of four Buccaneers overflew the airport, dropping cratering munitions that effectively destroyed the airport's immediate usefulness for fixed-wing aircraft. Then, as quickly as they had appeared, the Buccaneers were gone, returning to their base.

The SAAF's timing, certainly not intentional – the cluster bombs were meant to destroy or suppress PLAN's AAA capability – had been exquisite. Just ten minutes before the strike went in, commando Captain Jesus Barboza had waved off his MiG CAP, joking that he'd 'come to a war, but found a parade'. Barboza's mutilated remains lay among the dead.

Away to the north, at the Oshikango border post (everybody's favourite target during the days of the SWAPO insurgency), FAPLA's mighty invasion column passed the frontier in relative silence and good order. Everyone knew his role and his place in the grand scheme, which had been rehearsed often enough in the classroom, on the sand table and in TEWTs (tactical exercises without troops).

Still, there was a great deal of noise and traffic, both on the ground and in the air, and it is not surprising that, as came to light in retrospect, FAPLA's reconnaissance means missed entirely the shadowy presence and stealthy movements of the SADF's reconnaissance commandos, which hung about their flanks and rear. FAPLA's mission at this point involved rapid road-bound movement, and its writ did not extend too far from the tarmac ribbon leading to Grootfontein.

By the evening of 21 March FAPLA could congratulate itself on having initiated successfully a complex, large-scale military operation –

despite the disaster at Grootfontein (interpreted as a SWAPO failure with negligible implications for overall operational success). The main Sledge-hammer column had already penetrated to Osohama on the north-east periphery of the Etosha Pan, about 150 kilometres into Ovambo on the Oshikango–Grootfontein road. There had been no resistance, and it was expected that the column would close on Grootfontein the following morning.

Except for forward air controllers, FAPLA enforced strict radio silence in this first phase of Sledgehammer, so news of the disaster at Groot-fontein was largely concealed from the troops and morale remained sky-high. Meanwhile, in Cuando Cubango, FAPLA's Crusher offensive set off, gaining forty kilometres its first day, even though its advance had been hampered by thickly sown minefields and demolitions. Contacts with UNITA were disappointingly few, although FAPLA's combat engineers found some minefields covered by fire and called in MiGs and Mi-25s to disperse UNITA 'stay-behind teams' harassing the advance.

On the SADF side, D-Day of Gemsbok was remarkably uneventful. Apprised by reconnaissance commandos of the enemy's movements from its FAAs, elements of Serial 1 were moving into Namibia from Walvis Bay, Steinkopf and Plofadder even before radio Windhock's disingenuous 4 a.m. announcement. PLAN's border posts had been obliterated by Alouette III and Impala II ground attack helicopters, and subsequent resistance was negligible.

The van of the Walvis Bay column (2nd SA Infantry) had closed on Omararu by dusk and had scouts out toward Otjiwarongo, which the main body expected to gain on D+1. An armoured car platoon was pushed toward Okalundja, on the right-hand (eastern) fork toward Windhoek, but failed to uncover any SWAPO prepared to fight.

The southern columns, meanwhile, had advanced almost to Marien-thal, covering nearly 300 kilometres in wheeled APCs and IFVs on good roads (the Olifants were conveyed by tank transporters in both columns). If all went well, Windhoek would be entered on 22 March, before sunset. The 32nd Battalion's veteran 'buffalo soldiers' revelled in the enthusiastic welcome they received along the route.

Looking at the map, the SADF's planners realised that any PLAN troops foolish – or slow – enough to remain in Windhoek would be trapped on 22 March. They need not have concerned themselves: the events of D-Day had ended PLAN's four-year existence as a conventional force.

D-Day had witnessed a great deal of activity but, strangely, no air-to-air combat. Both sides had flown CAP for their motorised and/or mechanised columns, but neither had attempted to strike a hostile road column. Everyone recognised that this situation would not persist, and the SADF noted fleeting contact with high-speed photo-reconnaissance aircraft that broke away abruptly when approached.

DRAWING THE LINES

At daybreak on 22 March SADF Buccaneers revisited Grootfontein AFB. The attack followed the same pattern as that of the previous day: cluster bombs followed by cratering munitions. Casualties were few, since by that time the base was largely deserted, but the damage to the facilities and runways was severe. Though MiGs were in the area, the Cheetahs flying CAP for the raiders reported no contact.

The lead elements of the SADF's Walvis Bay column occupied Otjiwarongo at about the same time the BRDM-2s of FAPLA's 22nd Brigade (Sledgehammer's leading unit) rolled into Grootfontein, securing the town and sending patrols out to the south, east and west. Thick, dirty columns of smoke rose from Grootfontein AFB in the south, and knots of worn-out, dishevelled FAPLA commandos were gathered near the roadside.

Meanwhile, reconnaissance elements of FAPLA's 14th Brigade pushed into Otavi, west of Grootfontein, having turned right (southwest) at Tsumeb, while the 22nd Brigade proceeded to Grootfontein. As following units of the Sledgehammer column closed on Tsumeb, they were directed either to Grootfontein or Otavi and began to fill the great triangle of ground (Tsumeb–Grootfontein–Otavi) that had been designated for organisation as a defensive strongpoint.

The units at Otavi were just 150 kilometres from forward elements of the SADF in Otjiwarongo (as calculated from the previous day's intelligence data), and were reluctant to proceed further without tank and artillery support. Clearly visible in the distance to the south-west, along the line of the road to Otjiwarongo, SADF Bosbok light spotter aircraft circled lazily, taking in FAPLA's activity. Almost instinctively, the BRDMs scuttled for cover. In time, MiGs were vectored in and the Bosboks left. They were soon replaced by Seeker RPVs; Captain Eduardo Freitas, FAPLA's man on the spot, wished that his AD platoon had exhibited more march discipline and had taken its assigned place with the forward IFVs, but this was apparently not to be. The Seekers continued to buzz around overhead, like gigantic model airplanes, seemingly impervious to the nervous blizzard of small-arms fire directed at them. Freitas soon ordered a halt to what he regarded as an undisciplined waste of ammunition. His troops were not inexperienced, but the scrubby, sparse vegetation of the Ovambo savannah, occasionally relieved by barren granite hills, was not an environment they had trained to fight in and had undoubtedly contributed to their nervousness.

As Freitas pondered his next course of action, the SADF's Walvis Bay column began to concentrate in the vicinity of Otjiwarongo; occupying the airfield, and organising defensive positions in a shallow arc from Outjo in the north-west to Okawe in the north-east and the Waterberg in the east. The defensive perimeter was 110 kilometres long, a staggering distance for 1,800 men (2nd SAI Battalion Group and 14th Parachute Battalion Group) to cover, but the terrain was broken and bare, and the lines of approach were few, so the task was ambitious but not impossible. The troops of the column laid mines and looked southward for their comrades of the southern column.

The troops of the SADF's southern column entered Windhoek on schedule and occupied the airport, east of the city. PLAN diehards were encountered in small, ill-organised groups in and about Windhoek and were handled easily by 32nd Battalion combat teams.

On 23 March the southern column pressed on to Okahandja, north of Windhoek and on the direct route to Otjiwarongo. At Okahandja the column linked with the recce split from the Walvis Bay column. Resistance had been expected in this area but none was encountered. On the other hand, several dozen PLAN soldiers had been brought in as POWs. None had been taken in arms, and few were completely uniformed. The 32nd Battalion's reconnaissance teams fired on some PLAN APCs in the fields off the main road, but on inspection they were found to be abandoned and out of fuel.

From Okahandja the southern column drove on to Sukses, about 75 kilometres south of Otjiwarongo on the southern slope of the Waterberg massif. After sending patrols to the north-east, toward the southern flank of the Walvis Bay column's defensive perimeter, the column laagered.

As the southern column closed on the Waterberg, the troops of the Walvis Bay column continued their defensive preparations in the Otjiwarongo area. Tactical reconnaissance had now revealed that FAPLA was in great force to the north-east, but unexpectedly pusillanimous. Moreover, the FAPLA masses were observed digging in. The SADF, with some irony, now began to refer to FAPLA's defensive triangle as 'Stalingrad'. Patrols and reconnaissance teams were pushed forward with some impunity and, as in Angola, years before, some SADF observers were actually within enemy lines.

Of the ten FAPLA brigades committed to Sledgehammer, seven (14,000 men) were concentrated in Stalingrad. The remaining three (6,000) had been dropped along the road from Namacunde to Tsumeb, a distance of 300 kilometres, for security duty: they had, in effect, become operationally redundant 'line of communications troops'. This need not have been the case, but the brigades broke up into sub-units that bivouacked in and near the towns and larger kraals along the road and patrolled the tarmac between settled areas in APCs and jeeps. Under the circumstances, C^3I functions became largely decentralised, and important responsibilities were given to junior officers with little experience.

The tracks hemming the 4,800-square-kilometre Etosha Pan, a remarkable salt basin and game preserve east of Namutoni, were a particular concern for FAPLA's tactical planners, since they provided lines of approach to the Grootfontein road from the south and east, where the SADF was. FAPLA had pushed reconnaissance troops about twenty kilometres along each track but, not surprisingly, no trace of SADF troops had been found. In fact, the entire region was the province of special operations teams of the SADF's 4th Reconnaissance Regiment, which was engaged in one of its 'strategic missions'.

As the sun set on 23 March it was apparent that the war of movement had ended – at least temporarily. From Stalingrad in the north to the SADF's perimeter in the south, the lines were drawn in the sand. Both sides were prepared to defend their chosen ground, and both had good reason to await attack.

PRETORIA IMPROVISES

Every shred of intelligence data collected by the SADF in the days following indicated FAPLA's defensive scheme and Stalingrad's purpose. And as time passed, UNITA's situation in Cuando Cubango worsened. FAPLA's progress there was slow but inexorable. DHQ, Pretoria, would soon have to confront the possibility that Gemsbok would have to be modified to include offensive operations to eliminate Stalingrad. For the time being, however, the Armadillo sub-operation could proceed as planned, since the build-up of the Blackadder (formerly counterattack, now manoeuvre) force was not yet complete.

It was obvious to DHQ that Stalingrad could not be reduced by direct attack with the means available to Gemsbok. After some discussion, it was decided to mount an intensive effort to cut the strongpoint's vulnerable umbilical cord, and so force FAPLA either to leave Namibia or to come out of Stalingrad and engage the SADF in the open. The means available for this operation, code-named 'Python', were the 4th Reconnaissance regiment's special operations teams, already in position in Angola and Ovamboland along the FAPLA line of communications

(LOC), one flight of Cheetah Es, armed with laser-guided 'smart bombs' for deep interdiction missions, and a squadron of Buccaneers. Two flights of Cheetahs and one squadron of Mirage F1CZs were made available to fly escort for the bombing missions. In addition, elements of the SAAF's Rooivalk, Puma and Alouette battlefield support helicopter squadrons were allocated to the operation, though whether they would be used for interdiction or close support was dependent on the outcome of the initial, strategic phase.

The success of this phase, which was to merge into Blackadder, depended on the co-ordinated target-designation and elimination skills of teams that consisted of commandos on the ground with laser-designators and the Cheetah pilots in the air. Key bridges in Angola, particularly that over the Cunene River at Roçadas, were to be taken out by laser-guided bombs, as were the radars and C^3 facilities at Ondangua, the FAPA base that posed the greatest threat to the operation.

While these deep interdiction and attack missions proceeded, the Buccaneers were to interdict the Namacunde–Grootfontein road east of the Etosha Pan, in the Namutoni region. The launch of the air campaign against FAPLA's supply route was set for 0300 hours on 28 March (D+7).

The fighting in Namibia in the period between the end of the initial offensives and the start of the SAAF's air interdiction campaign had been confined largely to intermittent aerial combat in Ovambo. Interestingly, and unexpectedly, the SAAF had contended on equal terms with FAPA. Although the air combat had never been intense, or sustained, in a week of fighting FAPA had lost two MiG-23s and four other jets; the SADF had lost three Mirage F1CZs. The SADF attributed its relative success to the improved V3C Darter AAMs with which its fighters were armed. (These missiles, with 'all-aspect' intercept capabilities, had not been available in the 1987–8 Angolan fighting.) The early success of the SAAF eased some of DHQ's fears about the viability and sustainability of Python.

On 28 March the SAAF initiated Python. The first phase of the operation was strikingly successful: 'smart weapons' launched from Cheetahs destroyed the bridge at Roçadas and obliterated targets at Ondangua AFB, returning to base safely. Surprise and a modest stand-off capability had paid huge dividends. The Buccaneers, attacking the FAPLA LOC at dawn with bombs and rockets, achieved excellent results too, but at high cost. Two Buccaneers were lost to SAMs and crashed in the Etosha Pan; both aircrews were lost. However, damage to convoys and fighting vehicles along the road was extensive, and reconnaissance by Mirage R2Zs confirmed several large fires, secondary explosions and over 100 burnt-out vehicles along a ten-kilometre stretch of tarmac east of Namutoni. Since FAPLA had very little in the way of engineering equipment (or expertise), such bottlenecks were potentially very serious. Cheetahs flying escort for the raiders shot down a MiG-21, but lost one of their own to a MiG-23.

Python continued for five days until 1 April, when photo-reconnaissance revealed very little traffic along the road, and the SAAF began to switch to pounding the positions of the three FAPLA brigades strung out along the road on security duty. Concentrations of troops and vehicles belonging to these units had been identified by aerial reconnaissance, and were attacked by Buccaneers and Mirage fighter-bombers.

By 3 April the SAAF's losses in Python numbered five Buccaneers, seven Mirages, and two Cheetahs, a total of fourteen aircraft and a very disconcerting figure. Weighed against this, however, the SAAF had largely interdicted Stalingrad, which was running low on essentials in several supply categories, and had dispersed the three FAPLA brigades along the bomb-ravaged LOC. FAPA, flying mostly out of Rundu, had lost ten MiGs in aerial combat with Cheetahs, and several more had been destroyed or damaged in attacks against Otjiwarongo, which was heavily defended. MiG's flying out of Rundu (Ondangua had been abandoned) were limited in the amount of time they could 'loiter' over the battlefield because of the distance involved.

The SADF did not know it, but Luanda's top planners had begun to express 'serious reservations' about Sledgehammer. Further, several brigades had already been shifted from Crusher to the Roçadas region in Cunene for possible employment as a relief force.

Crusher had meanwhile taken Cunjamba, passed the Lomba river, and was approaching Mavinga, an unprecedented drive which represented the deepest FAPLA penetration of Savimbi's heartland. Progress had been relatively slow – though lightning-quick compared to previous FAPLA offensives in the region – and UNITA's troops had extracted a heavy toll as they fell back.

BATTLE OF NAMUTONI

In Ovambo the success of Python had made it possible to order SADF ground forces into action to carry out Blackadder under circumstances more congenial than expected when the plan was framed. Preceded by the 32nd Battalion, the 49th, 60th and 82nd Mechanised Brigades launched Blackadder on 3 April at 1800 hours, moving out at night toward the Etosha Pan via Outjo and Okaukuejo. The route was marked out by reconnaissance commandos, and the column moved in radio silence but with driving lights lit.

By dawn the column had split into two: one (western) column headed due north toward Ondangua, and one (eastern) column drove east on Namutoni. The western column, consisting of a mechanised battalion group of the 60th Brigade, had reached Okahakana by dawn, while the more powerful eastern column had entered Akomas.

The strenuous overnight march of 3–4 April had brought the Blackadder force to within 75 to 100 kilometres of the FAPLA LOC. At this point FAPLA had no knowledge of the SADF's turning movement, but the routine MiG morning reconnaissance from Rundu soon detected the SADF concentrations, and alarming reports of the SADF presence nearly astride the FAPLA LOC caused consternation in Luanda and Stalingrad.

Since (in view of Python's success) Luanda had been planning a withdrawal from Stalingrad to what was optimistically dubbed the 'Ovambo Line' – a new defensive hedgehog based on Ondangua – it was prepared to order the immediate abandonment of Stalingrad via Namutoni and Rundu. Five brigades (9,500 men and 50 T-62s) were to start for Namutoni and Ondangua on 5 April, while two brigades (3,800 men, 20 tanks) were to screen the rear of the larger column from the SADF force at Otjiwarongo and then slip away themselves to the northeast via a secondary road to Rundu. MiGs flying out of Rundu were to cover both columns, and the brigades diverted from Crusher were to move out of Angola to Ondangua, where they were to link with the Stalingrad column withdrawing north-west.

Luanda's latest scheme looked good on a map but ignored several basic realities. In the first place, the main Stalingrad column would have to fight its way out through the SADF force at Namutoni (see Map 4.2). The outcome of the battle would undoubtedly determine the outcome of the war and the future of southern Africa. However, both sides expected victory and looked forward to the imminent clash. Second, the units diverted from Cuando Cubango were nowhere near Roçadas yet and, therefore, were in no position to intervene in the decisive battle in Namibia. Third, the bridges in Cunene Province were still down, making any immediate relief of hard-hit Ondangua impossible. Finally, FAPLA, reduced to operating out of Rundu, was not capable of intervening decisively in the coming battle.

Combat actions on 4 April were limited to minor encounters between light forces of both sides in the Namutoni area. The 32nd Battalion initially reported contact with disorganised troops of a couple of FAPLA brigades. (These were easily driven off and were identified from POW reports as elements of the LOC security force.) Later, the buffalo soldiers engaged well-organised reconnaissance troops of the Stalingrad force and reported that the break-out attempt was imminent. Immediately, the main Blackadder force began to deploy for combat.

FAPLA's break-out attempt was made at dawn on 5 April, with three brigades attacking abreast in a north-westerly direction on a ten-kilometre front south-west of Namutoni. Two brigades moved a couple of kilometres behind as a second-echelon follow-on force. The FAPLA offensive was amply supported by artillery and by MiGs flying out of Rundu. The SADF task force in the vicinity of Namutoni defended a 25-kilometre-long semicircle that covered all the practicable southern approaches to Namutoni.

The Angolans, lacking adequate tactical reconnaissance, had hoped to turn the SADF position by swinging west of the main road and approaching Namutoni in overwhelming force from the south-west. The SADF position, however, was more extensive than the Angolan commander, Major General Joachim Soares, expected, and the powerful SADF artillery, utilising its long range to bring massed fire to bear on targets all along the front, pounded the attackers with intense concentrations unlike anything FAPLA had encountered before.

Under unremitting fire from the SADF artillery and then direct fire from tank guns and ATGMs, the FAPLA attack was stopped and then began to break up. In open and completely flat terrain, the attackers found no refuge from the SADF's fire. Soares committed his second echelon in a desperate attempt to sustain the attack, but the intensity of the defenders' fire was too great, and the attack of the second-echelon brigades foundered as well. FAPLA's combat air support was effective, but only briefly sustained, and the SAAF countered with a hard-hitting attack by fighter-bombers, followed by devastating low-level attacks by combat helicopters, including a flight of advanced Rooivalks, which administered the *coup de grâce* to FAPLA's T-62 force. Not a single FAPLA tank survived the combat – sub-Saharan Africa's greatest tank battle.

By mid-afternoon the combat was essentially ended, and the remnants of the FAPLA force had begun to disengage, attempting to withdraw to Stalingrad. The SADF followed at a distance, collecting prisoners and shooting up units that continued to resist. At Tsumeb toward dusk the remnants of Soares's column passed through Brigadier General Diego Amaral's fresh 54th Brigade, part of the two-brigade rearguard left in Stalingrad. Amaral was appalled by what he saw and knew immediately that it was the end. Confronting Soares, he asked for orders. Soares replied laconically: 'Request a truce; we've had a bad time of it and can't continue.' At 2000 hours Amaral met General

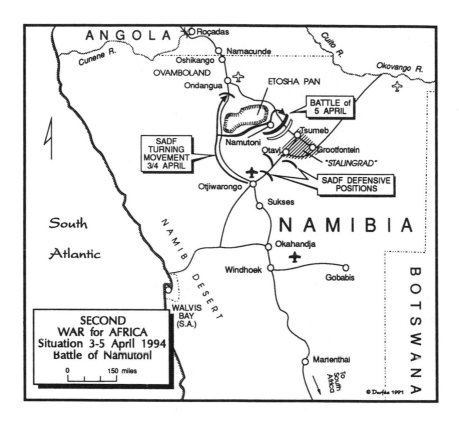

SECOND
WAR for AFRICA
Situation 3-5 April 1994
Battle of Namutoni

0   150 miles

Denys Vorder Breugge, architect of the SADF's tactical masterstroke, and requested a parley.

On 6 April at 0800 hours the battered remnant of Sledgehammer surrendered at discretion: 11,700 men and 20 tanks. The force that accepted FAPLA's surrender was outnumbered nearly two to one by its prisoners – testimony to the abiding significance of force quality in warfare.

DÉNOUEMENT

The remarkable victory of the SADF at Namutoni completely upset Luanda's plan to destroy UNITA. Dismayed by the crushing South African victory, which erased at one blow over 10 per cent of FAPLA's mobilised manpower, Luanda immediately called off operations against UNITA, and requested the Organisation of African Unity (OAU) to mediate its 'quarrel' with Pretoria. After a sham of 'negotiations', on

7 April the OAU announced that Angola's President Dos Santos, 'with the approbation' of Sam Nujoma and SWAPO, had agreed to an OAU-mediated cease-fire and resumption of the Lisbon Conference on the basis of status quo ante.

Pretoria rejected these terms and announced that it was prepared to move immediately on Rundu and Ondangua 'and beyond, if required by operational circumstances, in order to end for ever Marxist adventurism in southern Africa'. On 8 April the Blackadder force was reorganised into a 'flying column', consisting of two companies of the 32nd Battalion and a mechanised battalion group, and a 'heavy column', consisting of two and a half mechanised brigades, the remainder of the 32nd, and the 14th Parachute Battalion Group. The flying column was assigned the task of capturing Rundu, and the heavy column was ordered to move to Ondangua.

The SADF columns set out for their objectives on the afternoon of 8 April. A couple of hours into its march the flying column was attacked by MiGs and Su-22s flying out of Rundu. The attacking aircraft ran into the SAAF's CAP – Cheetahs at high and mid altitudes and Rooivalks at low altitude – and were turned away, losing two of ten aircraft (a Rooivalk downed a low-flying Su-22, earning the distinction of being the first SAAF combat helicopter to shoot down a high-performance, fixed-wing aircraft). The MiGs flying top cover knocked down a Cheetah before they used their superior speed to break off the engagement. Meanwhile, to the north-west, the heavy column moved on Ondangua impeded only by bomb craters and the wrecked hulks of FAPLA transport and fighting vehicles.

As the SADF columns rolled inexorably toward their destinations, Radio Luanda announced that President Dos Santos had ordered FAPLA forces to evacuate Namibia and 'regroup for the defence of the socialist homeland'. The announcement went on to state that Sam Nujoma had resigned the presidency of Namibia and SWAPO and that SWAPO's party central committee was prepared to enter into negotiations with South Africa.

On 9 April Pretoria announced that it was declaring a unilateral cease-fire in Ovambo and had agreed to the resumption of the Lisbon Conference provided Luanda agreed to certain preconditions. Broadly stated, these were:

1   The SADF would continue to occupy Ovamboland until a joint OAU–Arab League (Pretoria's nominee) peace-keeping force was formed to police the Angola–Namibia frontier.
2   Namibia's future status was to be negotiated separately, that is,

not linked to the FAPLA–UNITA negotiations.

3   FAPLA would immediately evacuate Cuando Cubango and Moxico provinces, ending the 'encirclement' of UNITA and, in effect, giving up the Benguela railway as hostage to bona fide participation in the Lisbon negotiations.

Luanda's leaders complained privately about Pretoria's 'extortionate terms', but accepted them nonetheless. There was no other practical course. With the belligerents, and the region, near economic collapse, the sighs of relief in the region and around the world were almost audible.

The world community, and the Great Powers particularly, had been preoccupied with the worldwide economic crisis and the great Russian Civil War, which overshadowed the side-show in southern Africa. Nonetheless, the statesmen of southern Africa were unanimously praised for having put down the sword.

Pretoria now found itself in a remarkably unexpected position. One battle and a few hundred casualties (see Table 4.2) had made it arbiter of the future of sub-Saharan Africa (in fact, South Africa had always been so, but it had taken a battle to illustrate the fact).

TABLE 4.2

HUMAN COST OF THE WAR

Nation/regime	Killed	Wounded	Total casualties
South Africa	69	268	337
UNITA	132	407	539
Angola (FAPLA)	576	1,648	2,224
Namibia (PLAN)	195	207	402

TNDM ADDENDUM: SECOND WAR FOR AFRICA

THE BATTLE OF NAMUTONI

Fought close to the ruins of the old imperial German fort and the rude village near by, Namutoni was the decisive battle of the Second War for Africa. It was in fact the only large-scale ground battle of the war.

Compared to other modern air–land battles, the forces engaged were small. The stakes, however, were high, and viewed in the regional context it was the greatest battle in the modern history of sub-Saharan Africa.

The SADF task force of General Vorder Breugge had deployed astride the Grootfontein–Ondangua highway to block the break-out attempt of General Soares's division-size FAPLA force. Vorder Breugge's force was superior in several categories, including troop quality, armour, combat air support and anti-tank weapons. It had the further advantage of surprise, since its presence on the FAPLA LOC had been detected just the day before.

General Soares's five brigades were similar to Soviet motorised rifle regiments, but were Angolan adaptations: organised, equipped and trained to fight in a jungle environment. They were strong in manpower, infantry weapons and artillery assets, but weak in armour. They had critical vulnerabilities that compromised their effectiveness in desert terrain, and these weaknesses were compounded by the relative technological backwardness of FAPLA (which was never fully apparent in the jungle environment of south-eastern Angola).

TNDM analysis showed that Soares's force could not hope to win at Namutoni. The battle was essentially a 'turkey shoot' for the SADF.

Table TNDM 4.1 summarises the battle statistics.

TNDM 4.1

TNDM STATISTICS: BATTLE OF NAMUTONI

SOUTH AFRICA	Strength	Losses	Daily losses (%)
Men	6,350	195	3.07
Armour	717	22	3.07
Artillery	68	1	1.47
ANGOLA			
Men	9,500	1,563	16.46
Armour	50	50	100.00
Artillery	140	10	7.14

CHAPTER FIVE

THE THIRD GULF WAR

BACKGROUND

On 28 February 1991 the Kuwait war (Operation Desert Storm–Desert Saber) ended with an armistice dictated to Iraq by the US-led United Nations coalition. In the aftermath of that armistice, it became evident that tensions in the region were unresolved. In light of the strategic importance of the region, and what has happened since, it is vital to understand the background of the Kuwait war and its aftermath.

The Kuwait war was not in fact the first Gulf war. That was the eight-year-long war between Iran and Iraq (1980–8). The economic dislocation caused by that earlier war, Iraq's expansion from a minor to a major regional military power, and the complicity of the West (and the other Gulf states) in supporting the regime of Saddam Hussein, all directly contributed to the decision by Iraq to invade Kuwait on 2 August 1990.

The aftermath of Operation Desert Storm in some ways exacerbated the situation in the region. The economic, social and political infra-structure of Iraq was thrown into disarray. Massive migrations by refu-gees from Iraq created new problems in Iran and in Turkey. In Kuwait the economic dislocation was on a greater scale than that in Iraq. In Saudi Arabia massive wartime expenditures resulted in a situation unique in that country's modern history, a cash-flow crisis. Jordan's attempt to maintain neutrality in Middle Eastern affairs had collapsed during the crisis under pressure from the pro-Iraqi Palestinian majority, and King Hussein had trouble in regaining lost stature. The general (but not universal) euphoria following the 'end' to the Kuwait war was replaced by a new realisation of the depth of regional problems.

A major result of the Kuwait war was further polarisation of the Arab nations in the region. It seemed certain that, if and when the immediate economic problems were solved, Saudi Arabia and Kuwait would amply reward the nations which supported them during the war. Debt-ridden Egypt, its economy moribund, was expected to benefit most from the largesse of the oil-rich Arab states. Other states, including Syria and Morocco, also expected to profit. However, the world oil glut, the shattered Kuwaiti economy, and the estimated $64 billion Saudi war debt, ensured that the rewards for loyalty would be years away.

Iraq, as instigator of the crisis, and Jordan, Yemen and the PLO, Iraq's principal supporters, all suffered in the aftermath of the war. No 'Marshall Plan' was discussed or even contemplated for Iraq. As a result, the economic devastation in Iraq remained unrepaired for years. In Kuwait antipathy toward the Palestinians for their collusion with Iraq resulted in arrests, deportations and murders. In Saudi Arabia the wholesale expulsion of Yemeni nationals was a consequence of Yemen's support of Iraq.

The refusal of the US to end the war decisively and to take direct action to destroy the regime of Saddam Hussein permitted that regime to suppress brutally the Kurdish and Shiite populations in Iraq. The migration of millions of refugees to sanctuary on the Turkish and Iranian frontiers, and the ensuing misery in the refugee camps, created an explosive situation. The idea of a Kurdish homeland was anathema to both Turkey and Iran, and neither nation had the desire or the ability to deal positively with the Kurdish problem. At the same time, the fantasy of a possible international 'Shiite Brotherhood' foundered on the reality of Arab–Persian enmity. Thus, in a few short weeks, a new stateless people emerged in a region already burdened with the problem of another stateless people, the Palestinians.

The failure of the UN coalition to carry the Kuwait war to a logical conclusion – apparent to a few at the time, and to many later – left the region in limbo. The UN established a nominal peace-keeping force, one capable of observing but without the power to maintain peace in the region. The Gulf Co-operation Council (GCC) partly funded a pan-Arab peace-keeping force (comprising GCC, Egyptian, Syrian and other Islamic contingents); however, it had neither the strength nor unity seriously to contest a challenge from either a renascent Iran or a renascent Iraq. The near-complete withdrawal of US forces was compelled by budget cuts within the US armed forces. The same budget cuts, of course, restricted the capability to bring US forces back to the region when or if it became necessary.

In sum, the Kuwait war – although it effectively ended Saddam Hussein's hopes of dominating the Middle East – resulted in the destruction of the Iraqi infrastructure, economic problems for Saudi Arabia and other GCC states, and two massive refugee problems. The final complicating factor in the region was the presence of Iran. Bordering Iraq on the east and comprising the northern shore of the Persian Gulf, Iran was nominally neutral during the Kuwait war. As a result, it was able to reap great benefits from the war. By seizing the 138 Iraqi aircraft flown to Iranian airfields during the war, Iran virtually doubled the effective size of its air force. Although Iran was engaged in a programme of economic reconstruction from the effects of the Iran–Iraq war, depressed oil prices slowed its recovery. It later became evident that the Iranian armed forces were also engaged in a reconstruction programme. International co-operation, particularly with the Commonwealth of Independent States (CIS), increased. Given the depressed state of the Russian economy and the excess of Russian military equipment due to unilateral and negotiated arms reductions, Iran was able to rebuild its weapons inventories through a quiet oil-for-arms exchange with the CIS. At the same time, and ominously, Iran continued to adhere to Islamic fundamentalism. Despite attempts at conciliation with the West, the militant Shiite regime remained a threat to all other Gulf nations.

The Iran–Iraq war had been the result of a confluence of events and suppositions remarkably similar to those that later characterised the Kuwait war. Saddam Hussein of Iraq sought to consolidate his seizure of power by engaging in a popular war against Iran. He believed (correctly in the case of the Iran–Iraq war) that the West would acquiesce in his aggrandisement. Saddam, furthermore, was right in calculating that the conservative Gulf states would, in large measure and if necessary, finance Iraq's war. The common threat to the conservative, Arabic, predominantly Sunni-Muslim states was seen to be the revolutionary, Persian, predominantly Shiite-Muslim state of Iran. However, Saddam's mistaken belief that political disarray in Iran (caused by the ongoing Islamic revolution) would assure a quick Iraqi victory resulted in an eight-year war of attrition.

The rivalry of Iran and Iraq did not cease, and was unaffected by the Kuwait war. Provocations continued, and both sides complained of border incursions after the end of the war. On 16 April 1991 Iran alleged that an Iraqi brigade had crossed the Iranian border in pursuit of Kurdish refugees. In return, Iraq claimed that Iranian border guards had earlier conducted a raid into Iraq, killing one Iraqi and temporarily holding captive seven others. More important, however, were Iraqi allegations that the Iranians had infiltrated Iraq in large force with the object of destroying Iranian refugee groups, based in the Basra area, that were opposed to the Islamic Republic of Iran. Over the next two years these incidents escalated to the point where the prospect of full-scale war between these two nations again threatened the entire Gulf region. This time, however, it was Iran that underestimated war-devastated Iraq.

THE FORCES

Because of the prior circumstances, the true war-making potential of the two major antagonists can only be estimated.

The human and materiel losses of the Iraqi Army in the Kuwait war were enormous. About 4,000 of 5,500 tanks and 2,500 of 3,500 artillery pieces in Iraq's pre-war inventory were lost. It is estimated that Iraqi personnel casualties were about 35,000 killed, about 65,000 wounded, 71,000 captured and 100,000 deserted. Losses incurred in suppressing the post-war insurrections in northern and southern Iraq were not serious. However, most if not all of the ethnic Kurdish units in the army (perhaps as many as twenty-two separate infantry brigades) dissolved. Elements of the several predominantly Shiite divisions that survived the Kuwait holocaust defected to rebels in the south following the war, only to be crushed by the still-intact remnants of the loyal and formidable (at least to the ill-prepared Shiite and Kurdish rebels) Republican Guards. In all, approximately 65 per cent of Iraq's pre-war army ceased to exist. Following the end of the Kuwait war the Republican Guards were partly reorganised, using equipment stripped from regular army units. The regular army, in turn, was partly re-equipped with materiel stripped from the remnants of the ethnic Kurdish and Shiite units that were disbanded following the Kuwait war.

The Iraqi Air Force suffered even greater attrition. Of some 689 pre-war combat aircraft available, approximately 250 were destroyed by coalition forces. An unknown number of additional aircraft were destroyed in hardened shelters. An additional 138 aircraft (the majority top-line, modern combat aircraft) fled to Iran, where they remained. It is estimated that fewer than 300 aircraft remained available, and many of these were non-operational due to lack of maintenance and spare parts. Following the war about twenty combat squadrons, with fewer than 225 aircraft, remained operational. The extensive Iraqi pre-war air defence system, shattered by repeated coalition attacks, no longer existed.

The Iraqi Navy, never a credible combat force, was essentially destroyed. Its losses during the Kuwait war included at least 30 of its 39 combat vessels. What remained were a few low-endurance coastal patrol boats.

Despite alarming news reports to the contrary, the UN embargo on arms to Iraq was effective for some time after the war, restricting the Iraqi capability to maintain or replace equipment. In the light of these considerations the post-war structure of the Iraqi armed forces at the end of 1993 was approximately as shown in Table 5.1.

TABLE 5.1

IRAQI ARMED FORCES

ARMY
REPUBLICAN GUARD FORCES COMMAND:
3 armoured/mechanised brigades
1 mechanised infantry division (the 'Baghdad' Division, Saddam's personal guard force, composed of three motorised and one mechanised infantry brigade)
4 motorised infantry divisions
REGULAR ARMY FORCES:
1 mechanised division
24 infantry divisions
8 reserve infantry divisions (cadre only, utilised for internal security duties)
1 airborne brigade
5 artillery brigades
AIR FORCE
11 fighter/ground attack squadrons
9 fighter squadrons

Iran, of course, had suffered heavy losses in its earlier war with Iraq. However, Iran did not suffer the destruction of its economic infrastructure, potentially the most devastating loss to Iraq in the Kuwait war. But the stagnation of world oil prices caused major economic hardship in Iran in the years following the Iran–Iraq war. Combined with the economic problems caused by relative diplomatic isolation, the loss of oil revenue severely curtailed Iran's ability to purchase arms and spare parts to replace and repair equipment lost in the Iran–Iraq war. It is now known, however, that Iranian oil and natural gas were exchanged with the CIS for finished goods that Iran needed. Much of the exchange was for the one excess item in the Russian economy: arms.

In the army the regulars probably manned most of the equipment requiring specialised skills: artillery, armour and air defence materiel. In general, the *Pasdaran* were highly motivated but lightly equipped. They acted as a shock force, emphasising light infantry tactics and night attacks.

Following the end of the Iran–Iraq war pilot training and operational serviceability remained a problem for the Iranian Air Force. However, support from the CIS slightly improved this situation. The seizure in 1991 of 138 Iraqi aircraft, most of which were modern Russian types, enhanced the Iranian Air Force's capability.

It is estimated that at the end of 1993 the structure of the rebuilt Iranian armed forces was approximately as shown in Table 5.2.

TABLE 5.2

IRANIAN ARMED FORCES

ARMY
REGULAR ARMY:

    4 mechanised divisions (equivalent to reinforced brigades)

    7 infantry divisions

    1 special forces division

    1 airborne brigade

    5 artillery brigades

REVOLUTIONARY GUARD CORPS (*PASDARAN*):

    4 armoured divisions (brigade-sized)

    24 infantry divisions

    3 marine infantry brigades

    many separate armoured, infantry, artillery, air defence and coastal defence battalions (many cadre only)

    500 light infantry battalions (*Basij*, 'Popular Mobilisation Army')

AIR FORCE

    8 fighter/ground attack squadrons

    4 fighter squadrons

NAVY (controls 3 marine infantry battalions)

A comparison of the military forces available to the belligerents is shown in Table 5.3.

By August 1991 most US combat forces had been withdrawn from the region. A Rapid-Reaction Brigade consisting of army special forces, airborne infantry, marines, and aviation assets remained on the northern Iraqi–Turkish border as a safeguard for the Kurds. US naval forces maintained a minor presence in the Persian Gulf, conducting mine-clearing and patrol operations off the Iraq–Kuwait coast. The US Air Force maintained a few transport elements in the region to conduct logistical support operations. The remaining forces deployed for Operation Desert Storm returned to the US or Europe or were disbanded. Major stocks of materiel and equipment were transferred to Saudi Arabia for use or storage. The remaining stocks were used to

TABLE 5.3

COMPARISON OF COMBAT FORCES

ARMY	Iran	Iraq
Manpower*	588,000	312,000
MBTs	1,300	1,450
IFVs	428	270
ACs	236†	488
APCs	1,140	2,230
Artillery pieces‡	4,350	1,278
MRLs	258	66
AIR FORCE		
Combat aircraft	230	225
Armed helicopters	100	60
AIR DEFENCE		
AAA guns	2,196	770
SAMs	222	196
NAVY		
DDs/FFGs	8	–
Fast missile patrol craft	29	9
Amphibious vessels	11	–

* Total mobilised strength. Approximately 323,000 Iranian and 204,000 Iraqi troops were eventually committed to battle before the end of the war.

† Includes 36 light tanks.

‡ Includes heavy mortars (120mm).

re-establish the Marine Corps pre-positioning squadrons at Diego Garcia in the Indian Ocean and on the US coasts.

European forces were also withdrawn, again except for those forces participating in security and relief operations in Kurdistan and Kuwait. The French contingent in Djibouti was the only other major European force in the region.

Thus, the major responsibility for regional security again devolved on the Gulf nations and their Arab allies. A Gulf peace-keeping force was established that was similar to the pan-Arab Corps deployed for the Kuwait war. This is shown in Table 5.4.

TABLE 5.4

GULF PEACE-KEEPING FORCES

GROUND FORCES

Saudi Arabia

    2 armoured brigades

    4 mechanised brigades

Egypt

    2 mechanised/armoured divisions

Syria

    1 armoured division (1 armoured, 1 mechanised and 1 artillery brigade)

Gulf Co-operation Council

    4 mechanised/armoured brigades

Equipment

    800 main battle tanks

    1,800 infantry fighting vehicles/armoured personnel carriers

    700 towed and self-propelled artillery pieces

AIR FORCES (primarily Saudi, with elements from the GCC)

    200 fighter and fighter/ground attack aircraft

BACKGROUND TO THE WAR

By the end of March 1991 the Kurdish and Shiite insurrections in Iraq had been brutally suppressed. Although badly shaken by their defeat by the allied coalition in Kuwait in February, and despite crippling losses in men, equipment and supplies, the Iraqi Republican Guards were more than capable of defeating the poorly armed rebels.

The aftermath of the insurrections left nearly two million Iraqi Kurds homeless, clustered in refugee camps in and near Turkey and Iran. Sporadic Kurdish guerrilla activity against the Iraqi army continued, and reprisals added to the number of refugees. International agencies provided some relief, but the burden that fell on Turkey and Iran strained already weak economies.

Attempts to oust Saddam Hussein failed; the pervasive Iraqi security system and Saddam's ability to thwart domestic opposition enabled him to maintain his hold on power. The Iraqi failure in the Kuwait war gave him an excuse to eliminate any threat to his regime from the military. The senior officer corps of the Iraqi regular army and air force were gutted by Saddam's reprisals. Some of these officers were able to flee the country, but most were imprisoned or executed. Senior air commanders and much of the Air Staff, held culpable for the success of the coalition air campaign, were particularly hard hit. Show trials of these officers were used as a vehicle to rehabilitate the reputation of Saddam with the Iraqi public and with the PLO and other Arab supporters. The method recalled post-World War I Weimar Germany, where it became 'common knowledge' that Imperial Germany had lost World War I because of the 'stab in the back' by communist and socialist traitors. In Iraq the 'stab in the back' was blamed on pro-Western members of the military and on the Kurds and Shiites. This propaganda ploy was willingly accepted by the Sunni–Muslim minority and by the PLO.

Saddam's control of Iraq was reasserted. Domestic support from the Sunni minority was restored, while the Shiite and Kurdish minorities remained disaffected. All dissent was punished by savage reprisals from the secret police and, where military action was required, from the Republican Guards.

In Iran economic recovery was threatened by the influx of refugees from Iraq. The ongoing struggle between secular and religious factions in the Iranian government limited the ability of international agencies to enter Iran and provide support to the relief operation. The religious extremists slowly regained ascendancy in the Iranian government as the refugee and economic situation worsened. The border incidents that followed the Kuwait war, and the cultural and religious differences that had sparked the earlier Iran–Iraq war, further added to the tension between the two nations. As the Iranian rearmament programme neared completion in late 1993, the mullah-dominated government secretly decided to resolve the situation by removing Saddam from power. An extensive propaganda campaign highlighting continued Iraqi oppression of the Shiites in Iraq, and the desecration of Shiite holy sites during the rebellion against Saddam, provided ample justification for Iran's increasing hostility to Iraq.

To achieve its aims, the Iranian government and the military high command made a number of assumptions as the basis for planning the projected campaign. The first, and most critical, was that the US (and, as a matter of course, the other Western allies) would not be able – or at least willing – to take action to prevent Iran from carrying out its plan. This was predicated on the belief that Saudi Arabia and the GCC would initially be unwilling to provide host-nation basing and support for the return of Western forces to the region. It was assumed that it would be politically unwise for Saudi Arabia and the GCC to turn again so soon to the US for support against another Muslim country. As in the case of the Iraqi threat in the Kuwait crisis, while Saudi Arabia and the GCC felt threatened by Iran, the resurgence of Saddam's power was seen by them as the greater threat.

The Iranian planners also assumed that they could make clear to the world and to Arab neighbours that the removal of Saddam and the protection of the oppressed Shiite and Kurdish minorities were the sole objects of Iran's action. They planned offensive military action primarily in the region north of the Euphrates River. Operations planned for southern Iraq were limited to the region around Basra and west, north-west and north of that city. The Iranians believed that the Saudis would see little threat to their border. They expected that Egypt would follow the Saudi lead, and that Syria would await any opportunity that presented itself.

The next major Iranian assumption was that Iraq would not receive major military support from other countries. The CIS, nominally Iraq's ally before the Kuwait war, would be diverted from supporting Iraq by Iran's economically attractive oil-for-arms trade agreement. Russian–Iranian co-operation was not only economically beneficial to the Russians, but also provided some domestic political benefit in the Shiite–Muslim minority regions of the CIS. Jordan was expected to remain neutral in the conflict between Iran and Iraq, as King Hussein continued his attempt to balance the Palestinian threat within his kingdom against the threat from Israel. The threat from Israel, itself preoccupied by the Intifada, was seen by the Iranian planners as minimal.

The Iranians also realised that these assumptions were transitory. Thus the Iranian campaign plan would have to lead to a swift victory, presenting a *fait accompli* to the rest of the world, and particularly to the other nations in the region. Essential to such a swift victory would be the element of surprise. This, of course, required that Iraq be unaware of Iranian preparations, a requirement that would preclude large-scale pre-war mobilisation and would limit the movement of forces prior to the war. Furthermore, the virtual destruction of Iraq's strategic reconnaissance capability in the Kuwait war could be expected to facilitate surprise. The backlash from the suppression of the Shiite majority in the south eliminated a major potential source of Iraqi intelligence, as Shiite opposition to the Iraqi regime grew. The purge of the Iraqi Air Force officer corps further reduced Iraq's minimal ability to gather and interpret aerial reconnaissance data. Iraq's isolation from the West ensured that Western intelligence – which would probably note Iran's preparations – would not reach the Iraqi military leadership.

Iran's plan provided for the use of Iranian special forces to set the stage for the war. They were to enter southern Iraq covertly to incite incidents between the Shiites and the Iraqi armed forces. At the same time Iran would encourage a new insurrection by Kurdish rebels in the north. They had secretly offered as an inducement the prospect of an autonomous Kurdish republic in northern Iraq, and provided supplies and equipment. If (as was possible given the past history of Iranian double dealing with the Kurds) insufficient numbers of Kurdish irregulars could be induced to co-operate, then Iranian special forces were to act in their place.

The provocations were expected to result in savage Iraqi reprisals. The mullahs had established a front group of Iraqi Shiite exiles in Iran, who would then call for Iranian protection and support.

Once insurrections were raging in northern and southern Iraq, the Iranians would attack. The Iranian plan capitalised on the Iranian advantage in manpower to strike Iraqi defences at a number of points simultaneously. The initial Iranian attack would employ infantry, armour and airborne and amphibious forces to overwhelm Iraqi forces in southern Iraq before the Republican Guards could move to blunt the assault. Once the initial objectives were reached, some of the Iranian forces were to revert to the tactical defensive to repulse the expected counterattack from the Republican Guards, while mechanised and armoured forces concentrated for a drive on Baghdad. The Iranian Air Force was to provide close air support for ground forces and was to establish air superiority over the battle area.

Three major axes of advance were planned.

1 *Abadan–Basra–An Nasiriyah* An assault crossing of the Shatt al Arab, west of Abadan, would be supported by an amphibious landing at Al Faw. An advance would then be made north-west to encircle Basra from the west, and to threaten the Euphrates River crossings at Al Qurnah, An Nasiriyah and As Samawah.

2 *Dezful–Al Kut–Baghdad* An attack west from the vicinity of Dezful–Ahvaz would seize the crossings of the Tigris River at Al Kut. An advance would then be made north-west, along the north bank of the Tigris towards Baghdad.

3 *Khosrovi–Khanaqin–Baghdad* A diversionary attack from Khosrovi south-west to Khanaqin would threaten Baghdad as well as Iraqi communications running north to the Kurdish oil fields near Kirkuk.

INFILTRATION BY IRANIAN SPECIAL FORCES

Iranian special forces teams began slipping into southern Iraq sometime in January 1994. (The exact date that operations began has not, to this date, been revealed by Iran; there is speculation by some that many of the Iranian teams had actually crossed into Iraq in the aftermath of the Kuwait war, and that, in the confusion following the war, they had been able to establish themselves as bona fide members of the Shiite community in Iran.) Terrorist actions against Iraqi garrison troops in the Shiite region began in mid-January. By late February terrorist activity was widespread, and the Iraqi response was increasingly brutal. It was also in February that the first small-scale special forces attacks on the Iraqi garrison in Kurdistan were made. The continued presence of US troops in Turkish Kurdistan muted the Iraqi response in the region. However, by early March international attention was again being focused on the brutality of Saddam's regime.

The growing tension in Iraq allowed Iran to complete its preparations in relative secrecy. All Iraqi intelligence resources were directed at eliminating the growing internal security threat. On 26 March 1994 a massive Iranian–organised protest march was held in Karbala. In response, Saddam deployed elements of the 8th Republican Guards Division and the 59th Infantry Division with orders to disperse the marchers. Early clashes between the marchers and the Guard quickly escalated into a full-scale riot; by the end of the day thousands of civilians had been killed or wounded.

Unfortunately for Saddam's regime, a videotape of the march – clearly showing Iraqi troops mowing down hundreds of Shiite men, women and children with machine gun and rifle fire – was filmed by Iranian agents and smuggled to Amman, Jordan. The tape was first broadcast by CNN on the evening of 27 March, along with pleas for help from the Shiite community in Iraq. Iran seized the opportunity. On 28 March the Iranian Parliament voted a condemnation of the act and issued an ultimatum: Iraq was given seventy-two hours to withdraw its troops from Karbala and other, ill-defined, Shiite 'sacred lands'.

Saddam and his advisers were evidently taken by surprise by the vehemence of the Iranian reaction, little suspecting that it was a long-planned pretext for an Iranian attack. Saddam made conciliatory overtures to Iran through the United Nations. However, at midnight on 30 March (twenty-four hours prior to the expiration of the ultimatum) the Iranian attack began. The Iraqis were ill-prepared for the attack, only twelve of Iraq's thirty divisions being in position on the frontier with Iran.

DIPLOMATIC ACTIVITY

Meanwhile, in London, several Iraqi opposition groups had met on 17 March to establish a new Iraqi Democratic Coalition (IDC). Nizar Hamdoon, former Deputy Foreign Minister of Iraq, and former Iraqi Ambassador to the US, was elected Chairman of the IDC, and was then unanimously elected 'Interim President of Iraq'. US Secretary of State Baker, who did not seem in the least surprised by this event, promptly invited Hamdoon to Washington for 'consultations'. During his highly publicised visit in the US (23–25 March), Hamdoon was taken to the White House by Secretary Baker to meet President Bush, and was escorted by the Assistant Secretary of State for Middle East Affairs on a tour of Capitol Hill, where he met key members of the Senate and House Foreign Affairs Committees. He then went to New York for a private meeting with the UN Secretary General (26 March). After the meeting neither the Secretary General nor Hamdoon would comment to the press about their meeting. As Hamdoon prepared to return to London, the news of the 'Karbala Massacre' erupted on world television. By 30 March, when the war broke out, Hamdoon had returned to the IDC's newly established headquarters in Paris.

DEPLOYMENT OF IRAQI AND IRANIAN FORCES

The sudden outbreak of war found much of the Iraqi Army deployed as an internal police force. The I Corps (Lieutenant General Mustafa Lafta) and the I Republican Guards Corps (Major General Hassan Safrawi), with more than a third of the army's striking force, were dispersed throughout central Iraq and Kurdistan. Similarly, the VI Corps (Lieutenant General Ali Abrash) and X Corps (Major General Omar Jamil) were scattered over western Iraq, garrisoning the Syria–Jordan frontier and the Shiite heartland around Karbala. Only the II Corps (Lieutenant General Haled Tourkmani) and elements of the V Corps (Major General Jibrael Chakkour), a total of twelve divisions, were in a position to oppose the initial Iranian assault.

Part of the II Corps was organised as a separate task force in the vicinity of Basra. The task force was commanded by Major General Abdul Sharba, who also was commander of the 4th 'Al Faw' Republican Guards Division, which division had been given two major missions. The first was to maintain order, by whatever means necessary, in the Basra area. The population, predominantly Shiite Muslims, had been brutally repressed by the Sunni Muslims of the Guard. With support

IRAN-IRAQ WAR
Initial Situation

0   100   km

100 miles

© Durfee 1991

from the Iranian special forces, guerrilla and terrorist activity had been widespread, leading to the dispersal of the Guard division as it attempted to cope with the situation. Thus, it was not prepared to fulfil its second mission, defence of the Iraq–Iran border in the area. Of the division's three motorised infantry brigades, one was dispersed in the Safwan–Az Zubayr–Umm Qasr sector; the second occupied defensive positions with a battalion at Al Faw and two battalions along the Shatt al Arab west of Abadan–Khorramshahr; and the third was at Basra, with two battalions on the east bank of the Shatt al Arab and the remaining battalion in the city. The 32nd Infantry Division was also deployed in the vicinity. The division occupied strongpoints along the Shatt al Arab, interspersed with the Republican Guard units. The Iraqi armour was deployed with the infantry division's tank battalion (forty tanks) scattered among the forward defensive positions, while the Guard's tank battalion (fifty tanks), the Guard's special forces battalion (in the Iraqi Army special forces units were actually mechanised infantry units having a stronger than normal complement of heavy weapons), and the infantry division's special forces battalion were in reserve at Basra.

The main body of the Iraqi II Corps was deployed with three infantry divisions (22nd, 23rd and 28th) abreast in the front line, roughly from Badrah to south of Al Amarah, a front of some 200 kilometres. A fourth infantry division (24th) defended the border from south of Al Amarah to a point east of Al Qurnah. Although this front was nearly seventy-five kilometres in length, it was well fortified and much of it was protected by marshes and the extensive water barriers created by Iraqi engineers in the first Iran–Iraq war. In reserve near Al Amarah was the 9th Mechanised Division.

The Iranians deployed three armies and two independent corps for the attack on Iraq. From south to north, along the Iran–Iraq frontier, these were the First Army (Lieutenant General Mahmood Paydarfar), the Second Army (Lieutenant General Ruhollah Banani), the Third Army (Lieutenant General Firuz Zabih), the VIII Corps (Major General Homa Katouzian) and the IX Corps (Major General Ali Fesharaki).

The Iranians intended to attack in echelon, from south to north, beginning with an amphibious assault on Al Faw Island at the mouth of the Shatt al Arab. The main attack was to be made west of Dezful, after Iraqi attention had been distracted by the attacks further to the south. The Iranian intention was to draw the Iraqi reserves to the area east of Al Amarah, weakening the position further north. The main attack, after penetrating the Iraqi defensive line on a narrow front (about thirty kilometres), was to advance generally westward along the east bank of the Tigris, to seize the river crossing at Al Kut.

The commander of the Iranian Army was General Ali Aghasi (a graduate of the US Command and General Staff College, 1972) who had gained extensive combat experience commanding, with distinction, first a division and then a corps in the earlier Iran–Iraq war. Aghasi had been relieved of his command in 1985 for advocating a negotiated peace with Iraq. He was under suspicion and in semi-retirement until 1988 when events in the war proved that he had been correct. Aghasi then received an appointment on the Iranian Armed Forces General Staff and was given the task of integrating the command structure of the regular army with that of the *Pasdaran*. Aghasi succeeded in eliminating much of the rivalry and suspicion that had existed between the two by setting up a system of officer exchanges between them. By 1991 it was common to find regular and *Pasdaran* officers interleaved at most echelons above battalion in both services. His efforts did not pass unrecognised: in late 1992 Aghasi was made chief military adviser to the team negotiating the oil-for-arms deal with the Soviet Union. In July 1993 Aghasi became Army Chief of Staff and was promoted to lieutenant general. As chief of staff, Aghasi directed the preparation of the contingency plan for a war with Iraq. In December 1993 he was promoted to full general and made Commander in Chief of the Army.

OUTBREAK OF WAR – ATTACK ON AL FAW

The Iranian attack opened on 30 March 1994 with an assault by the Amphibious Task Force (Brigadier General Amin Shaban) on Al Faw Island. The first wave, composed of three marine battalions, in hovercraft and amphibious assault vessels, landed at 2400 hours at the southern tip of Al Faw Island. Accompanying the marines was a *Pasdaran* armoured battalion with a total of 30 tanks. The marines were supported by naval gunfire from six naval vessels (three destroyers and three frigates) with 7 4.5-inch and 8 5-inch guns. Additional artillery support was provided by guns emplaced on the mainland, firing across the Shatt al Arab. The marines' objectives was to seize the town of Al Faw, with its docking facilities, and then drive north-west along the main road to Basra. Following the three regular marine battalions were three brigades of *Pasdaran* marines with 36 light tanks, transported in commercial roll-on-roll-off (RO-RO) vessels and other Iranian-flag bulk carriers. With this *Pasdaran* task force was an additional *Pasdaran* armoured battalion (30 tanks) and the marine brigades' three artillery battalions (54 guns).

The Iranian attack succeeded in isolating and destroying major portions of the Iraqi battalion that was on Al Faw Island. The marine landings bypassed the scattered Iraqi strongpoints and advanced rapidly to encircle the Iraqi positions west of Abadan.

OPERATIONS

AL FAW–BASRA

Simultaneous with the amphibious landings, the airborne brigade (three battalions with a total of about 1,500 men; Brigadier General Muhammad Rahman), escorted by three attack helicopter squadrons (27 helicopters), executed a heliborne assault to cut the Basra–Al Amarah road immediately south of Al Qurnah and in the vicinity of Az Zubayr. The airborne brigade established anti-armour ambushes on the roads north and west of Basra, and raided Iraqi command and communications facilities in the area.

The Iranian airborne assaults had mixed success. The landings near Az Zubayr suffered heavy losses as the Iraqis attempted to reinforce Basra with the brigade deployed south-west of the city. However, the Iranian battalion landing at Al Qurnah was able to seize the bridges north of Basra. A counterattack at Al Qurnah by the special forces battalion of the Iraqi 4th Republican Guards Division was repulsed by the airborne battalion and its supporting attack helicopters on the morning of 1 April. This airborne battalion linked up with the two divisions of the I Corps east of the Shatt al Arab, which had overwhelmed the isolated Iraqi battalions deployed on the east bank, at 2030 hours on 1 April.

The main assault crossing of the Shatt al Arab by the Iranian II Corps (Major General Fazhur Arasteh) followed these amphibious and heliborne assaults. The Special Forces Division attacked west from Abadan at 0300 hours. At the same time the 4th *Pasdaran* Infantry Division attacked west of Khorramshahr. The assault crossings of the Shatt al Arab were successful, although Iranian casualties were heavy. The strongpoints occupied by Guard units put up a fanatical resistance; those occupied by the war-weary conscripts of the infantry division, however, collapsed quickly.

The bridgehead was secured by dawn, and elements of the 1st *Pasdaran* Armoured Division (95 tanks) began crossing by ferry to support the attack. As bridges were completed, the remainder of the division crossed. At about 1100 hours the 1st *Pasdaran* Infantry Division was committed from the First Army reserve to reinforce the bridgehead.

The Iranian I Corps (Major General Reza Sarram) attacked at the same time as the II Corps. The 3rd *Pasdaran* Infantry Division and the 1st Infantry Division drove north-west from Khorramshahr to clear the Iraqi defence on the east bank of the Shatt al Arab. The isolated Iraqi battalions collapsed; again, only the Guard units put up a strong defence. By 2030 hours on 1 April advance elements of the corps had made contact with the airborne battalion at Al Qurnah.

After three days of intense combat, the Iraqi Guards division began retreating west from Basra on 2 April, harassed by Iranian attack helicopters and fighter-bombers. The two battalions defending on the east bank of the Shatt had been destroyed. Three more battalions on the west bank had been smashed, while a fourth suffered heavy losses covering the retreat; the division's special forces battalion had been wrecked at Al Qurnah. The Iraqi 32nd Infantry Division had virtually dissolved.

After a brief pause to reorganise, General Paydarfar directed that the First Army would pursue the retreating Iraqis. The II Corps with the 1st *Pasdaran* Armoured Division, the 1st *Pasdaran* Infantry Division, the 4th *Pasdaran* Infantry Division and the Special Forces Division advanced north-west towards An Nasiriyah. The I Corps with the 1st Infantry Division and the 2nd and 3rd *Pasdaran* Infantry Divisions advanced north and north-west from Al Qurnah towards Ash Shatrah and Al Amarah. The Airborne Task Force was attached to the II Corps, the Amphibious Task Force remained behind to mop up Iraqi remnants around Basra.

AL AMARAH–AL KUT

The initial Iranian attack in the central sector was made by the Second Army. The III Corps (Major General Shahram Ramazani), with the 5th and 6th *Pasdaran* Infantry Divisions and the 2nd *Pasdaran* Armoured Division (a total of 115 tanks), attacked Iraqi positions astride the Al Amarah–Ahvaz road at 2400 hours (simultaneous with the landings at Al Faw). The IV Corps (Major General Sepehr Chubin) followed one hour later (0100 hours), 20 kilometres to the north, with the 7th and 8th *Pasdaran* Infantry Divisions and the 3rd *Pasdaran* Armoured Division (an additional 115 tanks).

Four hours later (0500 hours), with Iraqi attention fixed to the south, the main attack by the Third Army began west of Dezful, 50 kilometres to the north. Three corps attacked abreast on a 45-kilometre front. From south to north these were the V Corps (Major General Shahrough Kazemzadeh), the VI Corps (Major General Amin Akhavi) and the VII Corps (Major General Fereidun Saikhal). Each corps consisted of a regular army mechanised division and two *Pasdaran* Infantry Divisions (115 tanks each), with a supporting artillery brigade. Three regular army infantry divisions, a regular army mechanised division, and a *Pasdaran* Armoured Division (270 tanks) were in army reserve.

The Iranian offensive had mixed success initially. The two southern attacks penetrated into the well-organised but thinly held Iraqi defensive positions, but at a heavy cost. However, elements of the Iraqi mechanised reserve at Al Amarah moved promptly to reinforce the front line.

Additional elements of the mechanised division were shifted further south, to deal with the Iranian heliborne landings at Al Qurnah. Thus, when the main Iranian attack began, the Iraqi reserve had been reduced to a single mechanised brigade.

The main Iranian attack quickly penetrated the positions of the Iraqi 22nd Infantry Division. The Iranians exploited their advantage vigorously, and the penetration developed into a breakthrough. As the Iraqi position crumbled under the massive onslaught, the Iranian reserves were committed and, seventy-two hours after the attack began, leading Iranian elements reached and seized the Al Kut–Al Amarah road at Ali al Gharbi.

By the evening of 2 April the Iraqi situation was critical. The 23rd and 28th Infantry Divisions opposing the Iranian Second Army, with the bulk of the 9th Mechanised Division, attempted to break contact and withdraw to Al Amarah and to the west bank of the Tigris. The battered Iranian divisions in this sector were at first unable to do more than harass this withdrawal. Further north, however, the Iraqi 22nd Infantry Division had been virtually destroyed, although scattered elements remained in isolated strongpoints, while other fragments were also attempting to withdraw south to Al Amarah. Iranian mechanised forces promptly began to advance on Al Kut, as planned, forcing the Iraqi 50th Infantry Division at Badrah to withdraw as well.

BADRAH

The Iranian VIII Corps made little progress against the Iraqi 50th Infantry Division defending the rugged terrain around Badrah. However, the success of the Iranian Third Army to the south threatened the Iraqi withdrawal route to Al Kut, forcing an Iraqi withdrawal. By the evening of 3 April the Iraqi 50th Infantry Division was on the outskirts of Al Kut, attempting desperately to delay the Iranian advance until reinforcements could arrive from northern Iraq.

KHANAQIN–MANDALI

The Iranian diversionary attack from Khosrani by the IX Corps met with minor success. The Iraqi 35th Infantry Division of the V Corps benefited from a well-constructed defensive position and rugged terrain, but the very ruggedness of the terrain facilitated the infiltration tactics favoured by the Iranians.

By the evening of 1 April the Iraqis began a slow withdrawal from the Khanaqin–Mandali sector as they endeavoured to prevent Iranian infantry columns from outflanking their positions. On the morning of

2 April additional elements of the Iraqi V Corps (the 38th Infantry Division and a reinforced brigade of the 39th Infantry Division) arrived from Mandali and were able to halt the Iranian advance.

IRAQI REACTION

The situation presented to the Iraqi high command at the end of three days was critical. Three major Iranian columns were advancing to the north-west in the Tigris–Euphrates valley. The Iraqi forces in eastern Iraq were in full retreat, and four of the twelve divisions in the region had been virtually destroyed. Additionally, four divisions of the Iraqi II Corps were threatened with encirclement east of Al Amarah.

In a major development, on 2 April Baghdad announced that Lieutenant General Maher Abdel Rashid had been appointed chief of staff of the Iraqi Army. Rashid was a gifted commander and a national hero in the first Iran–Iraq war who had objected to the preferential treatment given to the Republican Guard. He had been relieved of command in the summer of 1988 and had been placed under surveillance by the Iraqi internal security forces. The resurrection of Rashid was a measure of Saddam's assessment of the desperate situation. The sensible decisions made by the Iraqis in the critical days that followed, so unlike those made during the Kuwait war, showed the firm hand that Rashid quickly brought to the war.

Although Iraqi forces had begun moving from the north and west to reinforce the defence, it would be at least forty-eight hours before most of these units could intervene in the battle. The Iraqi high command (still nominally Saddam, but probably now, in fact, Rashid) decided to continue defending along the Al Kut–Al Hayy–An Nasiriyah–As Samawah line, while mobilising forces for a counteroffensive. Holding Al Kut, little more than 150 kilometres from Baghdad, was considered to be vitally important.

To stabilise this line, Rashid ordered several movements. The 'Baghdad' Republican Guards Division moved to Al Kut, joining the 50th Infantry Division formerly at Badrah. Remnants of the 9th Mechanised Division attempted to cover the retreat of the 23rd, 24th and 28th Infantry Divisions from Al Amarah to Al Hayy. The 8th 'Special Forces' Republican Guards Motorised Division and the 58th Infantry Division of the X Corps were moved from positions in southern Iraq to concentrate at An Nasiriyah and As Samawah, reinforcing the remnants of the 4th 'Al Faw' Guards Motorised Division retreating from Basra. Finally, a counterattack force was assembled west of Al Kut. This comprised the

I Republican Guards Corps with the 6th 'Nebuchadnezzar' and 7th 'Adnan' Republican Guards Motorised Divisions, and the 1st 'Hammurabi', 2nd 'Medina' and 3rd 'Tawakalna' Republican Guards Armoured Mechanised Brigades from northern Iraq and Kurdistan.

Unfortunately for the Iraqis, this sensible plan was overtaken by events at Ash Shatrah and Al Amarah. The three divisions of the Iranian I Corps advanced north and west from Al Qurnah, slowed by the marshy terrain, but virtually unopposed by the Iraqis. These divisions cut the Al Amarah–An Nasiriyah road on 6 April, a week after the Iranian offensive began. The evacuation of the four divisions of the Iraqi II Corps through Al Amarah, begun less than four days previously, had been hampered by persistent Iranian air attacks on the Tigris River bridges. With the northern road to Al Kut cut by the Iranian Third Army and the south-western road to An Nasiriyah cut by the Iranian I Corps, the bulk of the Iraqi II Corps was now trapped at Al Amarah.

At this time Iranian General Aghasi ordered the Third Army to a tactical defensive posture in anticipation of the expected Iraqi counterattack. However, the Iranian Second Army continued its offensive against the Iraqi forces surrounded at Al Amarah. Between 7 and 11 April the Iranians mounted attack after attack on the trapped Iraqi divisions. After four days of intense combat, the Iraqi remnants surrendered Al Amarah on 11 April. The Iranian Second Army then moved to reinforce the Iranian I Corps east of Ash Shatrah, which had continued to drive north to Al Hayy and west to As Samawah. The Iranian II Corps had also continued to advance, driving west in the Euphrates River valley and seizing the bridges west of An Nasiriyah on 7 April. These advances eventually rendered untenable the position of the Iraqi X Corps at An Nasiriyah and Ash Shatrah and also threatened the Iraqi position at Al Kut.

As a result of this Iranian success, a part of the Iraqi counterattack force assembled west of Al Kut was of necessity committed to defend at Al Kut and Al Hayy. This diversion delayed the Iraqi counteroffensive (originally planned for 6 April) until elements of the Iraqi VI Corps (the 52nd, 53rd, 54th and 55th Infantry Divisions), from the Syria–Jordan border, and the Iraqi I Corps (1st, 4th and 15th Infantry Divisions), from Kurdistan, could arrive. Both corps were delayed by motor transport shortages and by the terrible condition of the Iraqi road network (many of the roads in western Iraq had been heavily damaged during the allied 'Scud-busting' bombing campaign during the Kuwait war and were still unrepaired, while the roads in Kurdistan had been interdicted by Kurdish irregulars and Iranian special forces). The VI Corps finally took up positions between An Najaf and Al Kut on 8 and 9 April. On 10 April the I Corps was still en route from Kurdistan.

Local counterattacks by the Iraqi X Corps (elements of the 8th 'Special Forces' and remnants of the 4th 'Al Faw' Republican Guards divisions) were made from Al Hayy to Ash Shatrah on 8 and 9 April. However, the Iranians reacted by withdrawing the I Corps into the marshes of the An Nasiriyah–Al Amarah–Al Qurnah triangle. In the marsh the local Iraqi advantage in armour and mechanised forces was largely negated by the terrain and the stronger Iranian infantry and artillery. The frustrated Iraqis fell back north of Ash Shatrah.

Realising that there was little chance of success, General Rashid had decided to halt the planned counteroffensive at Al Kut, but was over-ruled by President Saddam. It was shortly after this that General Rashid surreptitiously contacted Hamdoon of the IDC and began cautious, secret manoeuvring to remove Saddam from power.

The Iraqi counteroffensive was finally under way on 10 April. The Iraqi I Republican Guards Corps (5th 'Baghdad', 6th 'Nebuchadnezzar' and 7th 'Adnan' Motorised Divisions and the 1st 'Hammurabi', 2nd 'Medina' and 3rd 'Tawakalna' Armoured/Mechanised Brigades) attacked east from Al Kut while the X Corps renewed the attack to the south. The Iraqi attack made little progress against the Iranian V and VI Corps of the Third Army and suffered heavy losses. On the morning of 11 April the Iranian VII Corps was committed to the battle, halting the Iraqi advance (see Map 5.2). By the evening of 11 April elements of the IV Corps of the Iranian Second Army, having completed the destruction of the Iraqi II Corps at Al Qurnah, arrived to reinforce the defence further. On 12 April the Iranian I Corps, west of the Tigris River, was reinforced by III Corps of the Second Army and began attacking north, driving the Iraqi X Corps towards Al Kut. On the evening of 12 April General Rashid, without consulting Saddam, ordered the Iraqi attack to halt, and the Republican Guards withdrew to a strong position on the Baghdad road west of Al Kut. The Iranians, who had also suffered heavy casual-ties, did not attempt to pursue.

By the morning of 13 April, two weeks after the war had begun, the Iraqis had solidified a strong defensive position running from Al Kut to An Najaf. Iranian General Aghasi was unwilling to renew the bloody war of attrition that had characterised the first Iran–Iraq war. Leaving the central front inactive, he ordered an advance by the VIII and IX Corps to threaten Iraqi Kurdistan and the left flank of the main Iraqi defences at Al Kut. At the same time the Iranian First Army, reinforced with the III Corps, was to continue to threaten the Iraqi right flank.

Thus, the immediate situation was, at least temporarily, a stalemate, with a slight advantage to the Iranians. Much of south-eastern Iraq was under Iranian control and heavy losses had been inflicted on the Iraqis. At

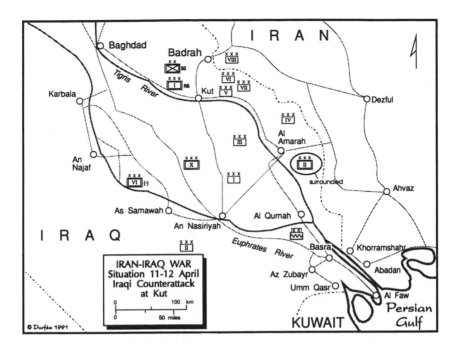

IRAN-IRAQ WAR
Situation 11-12 April
Iraqi Counterattack
at Kut

© Durfee 1991

this point, upheaval within Iraq and the international reaction to the conflict decided its outcome.

INTERNATIONAL REACTION

The initial international reaction to the war was ambivalent. Neither of the opponents had a high standing in the international community and opinion was divided regarding a desired outcome of the conflict. No international consensus on the war had been achieved before it became a stalemate. The UN Security Council had passed a series of resolutions demanding an Iranian withdrawal from Iraqi territory. However, little pressure was exerted by the US for a UN resolution on military action. Furthermore, the GCC did not initiate any military action to resolve the conflict: this would have required a consensus from the members and, without coercion from the US, no such consensus was forthcoming. Nor did the CIS take any lead in resolving the crisis. Economic conditions were too important for the Russian leadership to risk antagonising Iran. At the same time Iran, benefiting from its experience in the 'tanker' war and the US reaction to provocation in that case (which had resulted in destruction of Iranian naval vessels and militarised oil platforms), was careful to avoid provoking the US or any other neutral forces in the region.

Even if the UN, or the US independently, had resolved upon military action to end the war, it is hard to see what such action should have been, or how it could have had a decisive effect. The US Navy did bring carrier air power into the region within a few days. However, no more than two carriers (the *Eisenhower* and the *Theodore Roosevelt*) were available by 14 April, when the war was reaching a climax. The US 82nd Airborne Division reinforced the Rapid-Reaction Brigade based in Turkish Kurdistan, while elements of the I Marine Expeditionary Force and a number of fighter squadrons of the Ninth Tactical Air Force were deployed to protect Saudi Arabia and Kuwait, within the first week. However, in the case of the second Iran–Iraq war, unlike that of the Kuwait war, neither Saudi Arabia in particular nor the GCC in general perceived an immediate threat to the sovereignty of the Arab Gulf states. Therefore, they did not seek to have additional US forces deployed to the region.

However, the GCC did mobilise the pan-Arab peace-keeping force, which completed assembly in north-eastern Saudi Arabia and Kuwait on 15 April. The Arab states contributing to the peace-keeping force wisely refrained from provoking either Iran or Iraq. They realised that direct action against Iran without an overt and clear-cut provocation would have certainly sparked unrest within their own Shiite minorities. On the other hand, direct intervention with Iran against Iraq would have resulted in an immediate Iraqi military collapse, a result that was equally undesirable. Thus, the Saudi and GCC reaction was to watch and wait, while attempting to negotiate talks between the two contestants.

On 15 April the situation, which had appeared to be nearing a complete stalemate, suddenly changed. At Kirkuk in Iraqi Kurdistan, the withdrawal of Iraqi Army units to the south had allowed Kurdish insurgents to proclaim full sovereignty for their state. Renewed famine and civil disorder in the region caused the UN Secretary General, with full backing by the Security Council, to ask the US to move the 82nd Airborne and the Rapid-Reaction Force, with supporting UN forces, into Kirkuk. President Bush agreed and, by the evening of 15 April, the first units arrived at Kirkuk. The few remaining Iraqi units in the vicinity offered no resistance, fleeing rapidly to the south.

Meanwhile, General Rashid's emissary had contacted Hamdoon and assured him that the Iraqi Army was prepared to oust Saddam Hussein from power. On 17 April Hamdoon flew into Kirkuk on an Air France chartered aircraft. He was met by representatives of various Kurdish groups who pledged themselves to be willing to recognise Hamdoon's government in return for an assurance that the new Iraqi government would be organised as a federation of co-equal Kurdish, Sunni and Shiite states.

In Baghdad General Rashid moved quickly. The only major combat forces left in the capital were the 1st Airborne Brigade and Saddam's personal bodyguard, an infantry battalion from the 'Baghdad' Division. The airborne troops were regular army and had long disdained the pretensions of the 'elite' Republican Guards. They were also personally loyal to General Rashid, who had commanded the first airborne battalion formed in Iraq. In a spectacular operation, a heliborne company was dropped on to the presidential palace grounds, where it routed the Guards company on duty there. The remaining companies of the Republican Guards battalion then attempted to rescue Saddam, who was trapped in the palace. However, the companies were ambushed by the airborne troopers in the streets of Baghdad and were put to flight. Saddam attempted to escape from the palace in his armoured limousine but was killed.

Upon confirming Saddam's death, Rashid immediately called for a unilateral cease-fire and for UN protection for the new government of Hamdoon. The Iranian government promptly responded with a cease-fire order to its troops, bringing to a halt the heavy casualties sustained by both sides, as given in Table 5.5.

TABLE 5.5

HUMAN COST OF THE WAR

Nation	Killed	Wounded	Captured/missing in action	Total casualties
Iran	4,202	11,508	1,101	16,811
Iraq	6,146	18,439	8,620	33,205

The strong presence of the Arab peace-keeping force, now mobilised in Kuwait, and the recognition of Hamdoon's government by Saudi Arabia and the GCC, contributed to the Iranian decision. The recognition of Hamdoon as President of Iraq by the Kurds, by General Rashid and by the US greatly strengthened his hand when it came to dealing with Iran at the peace talks that began under UN auspices on 27 April.

INTERNATIONAL IMPLICATIONS

On 12 May a peace accord was signed between Iran and Iraq. Iran withdrew most of its forces from Iraq. Under UN mandate, the GCC peace-keeping force occupied southern Iraq along a line running west from Basra. Iran was allowed to maintain a police force in Basra, also under UN mandate, so as to guarantee Iranian navigation rights on the Shatt al Arab. The Republican Guards were disarmed and disbanded, with their arms and equipment going to the regular army.

On 1 June the US, Saudi Arabia and the GCC announced the creation of a new 'Marshall Plan' for the Gulf region. Economic assistance plans were placed, in effect to help re-establish the economic vitality of Iraq. At the same time negotiations were begun to provide similar economic assistance to Iran. Long-standing differences remained to be resolved, and negotiations are still being conducted. However, by mid-1994 the future for the region was brighter than it had been for the previous twenty years.

TNDM ADDENDUM: THE BATTLE OF AL KUT

On 10 April 1994 the Iraqi I Republican Guards Corps began a counter-attack in a desperate attempt to regain the initiative. The attack was made by three armoured/mechanised brigades (1st 'Hammurabi', 2nd 'Medina' and 3rd 'Tawalkalna' Republican Guards), two motorised infantry divisions (6th 'Nebuchadnezzar' and 7th 'Adnan' Republican Guards) and the 5th 'Baghdad' Republican Guard Mechanised Division (minus one infantry battalion). Supporting the attack was the 5th Artillery Brigade, five fighter-bomber squadrons, and two attack helicopter squadrons. The 50th Infantry Division (V Corps) was temporarily attached to the I Republican Guard Corps. It protected the left (northern) flank from the Iranian VIII Corps, which was slowly advancing from the vicinity of Badrah. Elements of the I Corps had been expected to have arrived from Kurdistan to reinforce the attack, but bad roads and attacks by Kurdish guerrillas and the Iranian Air Force, had slowed its movement to a crawl. Saddam Hussein, who had assumed direct command of the counterattack, refused to wait for the arrival of the I Corps and ordered the attack to go on as planned.

The defending Iranian Third Army had taken up hasty defence positions in the gently rolling, bare terrain east of Al Kut. The Iranian units deployed in this line were the V Corps (9th, 10th and 14th *Pasdaran* Infantry Divisions and 2nd Mechanised Division) and the VI Corps (11th, 12th and

13th *Pasdaran* Infantry Divisions and 3rd Mechanised Division). In support were three artillery brigades (3rd, 4th and 5th), five fighter/ground attack squadrons, and three attack helicopter squadrons. The VII Corps of Third Army was in reserve with three regular infantry divisions (2nd, 3rd and 4th) deployed in depth behind the V and VI Corps. The VII Corps also controlled two mechanised divisions (1st and 4th) and the 4th *Pasdaran* Armoured Division, which were the Third Army mobile reserve. The 3rd *Pasdaran* Armoured Division of the Second Army was expected to arrive from Al Amarah by the evening of 11 April to reinforce the defence further.

The Iraqi attack was at first successful, advancing nearly three and a half kilometres into the defences of the Iranian V and VI Corps. However, at dawn on 11 April the VII Corps, the Iranian mobile reserve, was committed and halted the Iranian attack. By the evening of 11 April the Iraqis had withdrawn under heavy pressure to their start-line.

Table TNDM 5.1 summarises the battle statistics.

TABLE TNDM 5.1

TNDM STATISTICS: BATTLE OF AL KUT

IRAQ	Strengths*	Losses	Daily losses (%)
Men	55,120	2,592	2.35
Armour†	1,048	388	18.51
Artillery‡	264	5	0.95
IRAN			
Men	91,000	2,788	1.53
Armour†	1,028	65	3.16
Artillery‡	582	5	0.43

* Total strength including reinforcements.

† Includes tanks, IFVs and armoured reconnaissance vehicles.

‡ Includes towed and SP guns and MRLS.

CHAPTER SIX

THE SECOND
KOREAN WAR

BACKGROUND

The division of Korea into two states, a result of US–Soviet suspicion and mistrust at the end of World War II, was made permanent as a result of the Korean War of 1950–3. The principal result of that conflict was to establish that neither Soviet-backed North Korea nor Western-supported South Korea possessed the resources (or was able to persuade its allies to supply the resources) required to unify the country. As a further consequence, the post-war demilitarised zone (DMZ) which separated the two states was flanked by two of the most heavily fortified borders on earth.

The government of North Korea – the Democratic People's Republic of Korea (DPRK) – was dominated by Kim Il Sung after the late 1940s. Kim had consistently pursued a policy of unremitting hostility toward South Korea, officially the Republic of Korea (ROK). Among other measures, North Korean agents sabotaged South Korean civilian aircraft, assassinated South Korean government officials, and instigated student unrest, while the North Korean armed forces committed numerous border violations and undertook other hostile actions along the DMZ. Successive South Korean governments made some peace overtures to the North, but Kim Il Sung's continuing campaign of harassment and provocation, coupled with remarkable intransigence, effectively stymied any moves toward peaceful settlement, and also provoked retaliation by South Korea.

In retrospect, the North Korean peace overtures during the period 1990–2 appear to have been either an extended ruse or a reflection of policy differences within Kim Il Sung's inner circle, perhaps resulting from an undisclosed illness of the 'Great Leader' himself. Regardless of the North Koreans' motives, the effect of their overtures was to lull the South Koreans into a false sense that relations with the North were

improving, and that the immediate risk of war had receded. The previously demonstrated ruthlessness of the North Koreans lends some
credence to the 'extended ruse' theory, but the death of most of the 'inner
circle' after the war ensures that this issue will remain unresolved.

Much of the reason for the great hostility between the rival Korean
regimes was that each desired to reunify Korea, but only on its own
terms. For Kim Il Sung and the North, this meant an authoritarian
communist government for the whole peninsula, complete with the
destruction of South Korea's capitalist economy. For South Korea, unification meant the end of communist rule in the North, and an end to
Chinese and Soviet influence as well. These conflicting goals and conditions for reunification were wholly incompatible. Unification was possible only if one regime subjugated the other militarily, or if one regime
suffered a complete collapse from within. The fundamentals of this
situation were recognised in both Seoul and Pyongyang, and when
coupled with the high levels of military preparedness on the peninsula
resulted in a potentially explosive environment. The threat of war in
Korea was never very far away.

HISTORY

Korea has since ancient times been strongly influenced by Chinese culture and social practices. Despite the close proximity of such a great
civilisation, however, Korea maintained its own cultural identity, and
existed as a unified state for most of the period since the mid to late
seventh century AD, when the Silla kingdom of south-east Korea
extended its authority over most of the country. Korea fell under Mongol domination after a long resistance (1231–61), but retained a large
degree of autonomy. Korea was later invaded by the Japanese ruler and
warlord Toyotomi Hideyoshi (1592–8), but the Japanese were unable to
gain a decisive victory over Korean forces and their Chinese allies and
withdrew after Hideyoshi's death. Korea was conquered by the Manchus
in a series of campaigns (1627–37), ending when the Koreans stopped
tribute payments to the Ming and began paying tribute to the Manchu
court, which continued when the Manchus became the Ch'ing dynasty
in 1644.

Korea's first contact with Europe came in the sixteenth and seventeenth centuries, first through Christian missionaries in China and then
through European merchants. The government regarded Christian
influence among the scholar–administrators as a grave threat, and persecuted them vigorously during the early to mid-nineteenth century, but

generally left Christian commoners alone. The power and influence of Japan, which grew rapidly after the Meiji Restoration of 1868, led to a Chinese–Japanese rivalry for influence in Korea in the 1880s and 1890s. The Korean government, riven by factionalism and hampered by a succession of young monarchs and accompanying regencies, was unable to play a significant role in this struggle. The Sino-Japanese War erupted because the Korean government asked for Chinese troops to help suppress the Tonghak Revolt (July 1894). Japan's overwhelming victory in that war effectively left Korea a Japanese protectorate. This status became official in December 1905, after Japan's victory in the Russo–Japanese War, and Korea was annexed outright by Japan in 1910.

Japanese rule in Korea was harsh and demanding. Widespread demonstrations and unrest in April–May 1919 led Japan to ease some of the most odious forms of control, but the Japanese still treated the Koreans poorly. The Korean economy was exploited to provide Japan with raw materials, rice and cheap labour. The Japanese imposed military rule in Korea in 1931, following their conquest of Manchuria, and many Koreans were conscripted into the Imperial Japanese armed forces, especially as labour and construction troops, while others were hauled off to Japan as farm and factory workers.

Unfortunately for Korea, Japan's surrender at the end of World War II and the end of Japanese rule did not restore peace to the peninsula. Soviet troops occupied Korea north of the thirty-eighth parallel, while US forces occupied the southern portion of the peninsula. Soviet forces, aided by local Communist cadres, set up a Communist regime which they installed in power as the Democratic People's Republic of Korea on 1 May 1948, under Kim Il Sung. The Soviets also created an army, in part manned by Korean veterans of the Chinese Communist Army who had been in Manchuria (also occupied by Soviet forces after the war). Korea south of the thirty-eighth parallel remained under US military government until – following UN-sponsored elections – Syngman Rhee was inaugurated as the first president of the Republic of Korea (15 August 1948). Although there was at first some traffic between North and South Korea, the increasingly totalitarian character of the North Korean government raised tensions.

The Republic of Korea, under increasing attack from northern-supported guerrillas and plagued by significant internal unrest (also in large part organised in the North), gradually built up an army with US assistance. However, by early summer 1950 this force – unprepared for war – contained fewer than 100,000 men, with little artillery, no tanks and no air force. In comparison, the North Korean People's Army

(NKPA) by that time consisted of some 130,000 well-trained personnel with about 150 tanks, 180 combat aircraft, and considerable artillery.

North Korean troops invaded South Korea on 25 June 1950, probably without the prior knowledge of the Soviet Union. The NKPA handily defeated the South Korean army and nearly conquered South Korea before hastily committed US forces halted them at the Pusan Perimeter in south-east Korea (August–September). The United Nations denounced the North Korea invasion and appointed US General Douglas MacArthur as commander of a United Nations army. In a counteroffensive, UN forces (largely US, but also including contingents from Britain, Turkey, France, Australia, Canada, and many others) drove north from the Pusan perimeter in coordination with a spectacular amphibious assault at Inchon outside Seoul (15 September). With the approval of the UN, General MacArthur continued his offensive north of the 38th parallel and nearly conquered North Korea.

The expectation of a UN victory, and of the consequent destruction of the Communist regime in North Korea, as well as concern about a permanent threat to Manchuria, triggered the intervention of the People's Republic of China. Massive Chinese forces moved across the Yalu River in November 1950, and drove UN forces back hundreds of kilometres in a series of offensives, capturing Seoul a second time (5 January 1951). UN forces finally halted this offensive, then mounted a counteroffensive in March. This was interrupted by a Communist counteroffensive in April. However, a renewed UN offensive in May and June left Seoul in UN hands (this time for good). The war dragged on in a two-year-long bloody and frustrating stalemate until an armistice was signed on 27 July 1953, after lengthy negotiations.

The end of the Korean War left the Republic of Korea and the Democratic People's Republic of Korea battered but substantially intact. An estimated 2 million Korean civilians were killed in three years of war, along with over 750,000 battlefield fatalities. During the war, as many as 2 million refugees left North Korea to escape the Communist regime. The material cost was also high, with much wartime damage to housing, road and rail lines, bridges and industrial plants. Both Korean governments afterward maintained close relations with their wartime benefactors, China and the Soviet Union for North Korea, the United States for South Korea. Both North and South Korea also had to recognise (very reluctantly, in the case of the North) that their more powerful allies would not support an effort to resume the war and to unify the peninsula by military force.

The Sino–Soviet rivalry which evolved in the late 1950s placed North Korea in an awkward position, trying to navigate a narrow 'middle ground' between its two allies without falling under the domination of either. This task was made still more difficult because, despite intense efforts toward economic autarky, the DPRK remained dependent on foreign sources for some types of machinery, aircraft, major naval vessels and other important items. Increasing liberalisation in the Soviet Union under Gorbachev cooled relations between Pyongyang and Moscow, and Kim Il Sung seemed determined to keep his country among the few remaining hard-line communist states.

At the beginning of the 1990s, North Korea was clearly losing ground in the peaceful competition between the two Koreas. Its population growth rate remained high, and as the growth rate of the South's increasingly wealthy population slowed, the North was gradually narrowing the demographic gap. If growth rates remained constant in both countries, North Korea's population level would have equalled that of South Korea around 2050, with about 90 million people in each country. There was some question whether the DPRK could adequately feed or house so many citizens, though. On the economic front, the situation was even bleaker for the DPRK. Its economy was stagnating and it failed to meet the goals of its major efforts to spur economic growth: the Six-Year (1971–7) and Seven-Year (1978–84) Plans.

At the same time the South Korean economy grew exponentially. Its 1988 gross national product, of US $150 billion, was over seven times as large as the North's estimated GNP of US $20 billion. Adjusting for the population difference, South Korea's economy was more than three times as productive as the North Korean economy. Further, South Korea enjoyed a significant and growing technological edge, and its 1989 military budget (US $9.88 billion) was more than twice as large as that in the North (US $4.15 billion).

North Korean officials were certainly aware of the growing disparity in the economic power of the two Koreas in the 1980s and early 1990s. China was occupied by its own development problems, and the Soviet Union was fading fast as a superpower, leaving North Korea to its own resources. There was some sentiment in Pyongyang for a rapprochement with the Seoul government, but the tentative feelers which both sides put out between late 1989 and early 1990s were burdened with the legacy of forty years of suspicion and hostility. After the US withdrew the last of its forces from South Korea in 1993, the North Korean government decided to take the risk of trying to unify the peninsula by force.

MILITARY POTENTIAL

NORTH KOREA

With a population of about 25 million in mid-1994, North Korea maintained standing armed forces totalling some 1.1 million, making it one of the most heavily armed states on Earth. There were also more than 600,000 well-trained and well-organised reserves. The armed forces were manned through compulsory military service, for terms ranging from three to ten years, depending on such considerations as branch and technical training. In addition to the regular forces, there was a Worker and Peasant Red Guard, 4 million strong, organised in provincial and local commands and units. All militia received some military training, but many units were unarmed.

The army was organised into seventeen corps, containing twenty-five divisions and eighty-two brigades, with twenty-six reserve infantry divisions manned by 500,000 reservists. The army operated about 3,500 tanks, 4,000 armoured personnel carriers (APCs), and nearly 1,000 other armoured fighting vehicles. There were also 2,500 towed and 3,300 self-propelled artillery pieces, 2,300 multiple rocket launchers (mostly truck-mounted), and some 11,000 mortars, along with extensive inventories of recoilless rifles, anti-tank and air defence guns, anti-tank missiles and other equipment.

The North Korean Navy numbered 41,000 officers and men, with another 40,000 reservists available. It operated 24 diesel-electric submarines (some of considerable age), 3 frigates, over 300 patrol craft (including 34 missile boats and 170 torpedo boats), 20 small minesweepers and two coastal defence regiments. Many of the smaller surface craft were built in North Korean shipyards, but the submarines were all from Chinese or Soviet sources, as were most of the missile systems employed on board combat vessels.

There were 70,000 officers and men in the North Korean Air Force, operating over 700 combat aircraft and about 60 combat helicopters. Most aircraft were either older Soviet models (MiG-21, Su-70) or Chinese versions of similar or even older aircraft (J-5, J-6, etc.). By 1992–3, however, there were 20 Su-25 ground attack jets, along with 48 MiG-23 and 30 MiG-29 fighters. The air force also operated a formidable air defence system, which included 72 SA-2, 32 SA-3 and 72 SA-5 surface-to-air missile launchers.

Many North Korean defence installations were heavily fortified, with important facilities built deep underground. This practice was the result of bitter experience gained during the Korean War, when UN air superiority plagued communist forces and caused heavy damage to

North Korean industrial and transport facilities. These precautions, and the density of North Korean air defences, made interdiction strikes inside North Korea costly and difficult in the event of war, although the superiority of the electronics available to South Korea offset the effect of North Korea's air defences. There were also reports (at least partially substantiated) of North Korean tunnels built to enable troops to approach, or even pass underneath, the DMZ while escaping detection. These activities were part of a continual programme of psychological pressure and physical testing by North Korean forces of the physical and moral preparation of South Korea's armed forces.

The North Korean nuclear weapons programme, which became an open secret in the early 1990s, had provided Kim Il-Sung with fewer than half-a-dozen fission bombs by late 1993. Although South Korea had no means of response, the North's military planners had no desire to devastate the country they wanted to conquer, and were also wary of the probable US response should they employ nuclear weapons.

SOUTH KOREA

The armed forces of the Republic of Korea numbered 750,000 officers and men, drawn from a population of over 44 million in mid-1994. Military service was compulsory for a term of thirty to thirty-six months. The active forces were backed by 4.5 million organised reserves. There was also a small coast guard and a 3.5 million-strong Civil Defence Corps.

The South Korean Army consisted of some 650,000 officers and men. These personnel manned four army and eight corps headquarters, with two mechanised and nineteen infantry divisions. There were also two independent infantry brigades and seven special forces brigades, two missile battalions with Honest John surface-to-surface missiles, two air defence artillery brigades, two surface-to-air (SAM) missile brigades and one aviation brigade. In the event of war, reservists manned a fourth army headquarters and another twenty-eight infantry divisions. Equipment included over 1,500 tanks, including 500 Type 88 (the South Korean version of the US M-1 Abrams, with a diesel engine replacing the Abrams' controversial turbine) and nearly 1,000 M-48A5, as well as 600 KIFV infantry combat vehicles (patterned on the US M-2/M-3 Bradley IFV), and 1,500 APCs. There were 4,000 towed and about 150 self-propelled artillery pieces, 140 Kooryong 130mm 36-tube rocket launchers, 5,300 mortars, 58 World War II-vintage self-propelled anti-tank guns, 600 air defence guns and about 600 SAMs. The army also operated nearly 100 attack and over 250 transport and utility helicopters.

The South Korean Navy contained 60,000 officers and men, including a 25,000-strong Marine Corps. The Navy operated 3 small inshore diesel-electric submarines, 9 destroyers, 25 frigates, 4 corvettes, 11 missile boats and 68 fast inshore patrol craft, 9 mine warfare vessels and 15 amphibious vessels with a total lift capacity of nearly 2,000 troops and over 150 armoured vehicles. The Naval Air Arm operated 35 anti-submarine helicopters (10 of them based aboard destroyers) and 24 S-2E maritime patrol aircraft. The Marine Corps was organised into two divisions and a brigade, plus support units, and was equipped with 50 M-48A5 tanks, 60 LVTP-7 amphibious tractors, artillery and truck-mounted Harpoon surface-to-surface missiles.

The South Korean Air Force, 40,000 strong, operated just under 470 combat aircraft. The most modern of these were 48 F-16C/D fighter/ground attack aircraft, and there were also over 200 F-5A and F-5E FGAs, and nearly 130 slightly older F-4D/E fighters. There were also counter-insurgency, reconnaissance, forward air control, search and rescue and transport units. The combat effectiveness of South Korean fighter planes was increased by their use of US-built AIM-7 Sparrow and the excellent AIM-9 Sidewinder air-to-air missiles.

South Korea depended on the US for most of its aircraft, and most of its larger naval vessels were also older US models. South Korea built its own tanks and infantry fighting vehicles (on US designs), as well as its own artillery, mortars and small patrol vessels. South Korea, recalling the bitter lessons of the summer of 1950, maintained its forces in a high state of readiness, generally well trained and well equipped.

One possible weakness in South Korean security was the legacy of several episodes of military rule: many civilians were deeply suspicious of the military leadership, which for its part tended to view political opponents as either dangerous radicals or communist dupes. This mutual suspicion was a significant handicap when war erupted, and North Korea would capitalise on the situation. The presence of North Korean-inspired agitators inside South Korea, and the consequent extensive South Korean intelligence network inside their own country, did little to ameliorate the political tensions between the military and elements of the civilian population.

OTHER POTENTIAL PARTICIPANTS

Several other nations might have been drawn into the conflict in Korea, because of historical ties or important national interests in the region. The most important of these were the US, the Russian Republic, the People's Republic of China and Japan.

THE UNITED STATES

The United States maintained troops in Korea after 1953, although the forces there were modest by the late 1980s, encompassing one infantry division and support troops (31,600 troops), and four air force tactical fighter squadrons with 84 aircraft and 12,000 personnel. Taking into account the end of the Cold War, and the smaller defence budgets of the 1990s, the US had to reduce its overseas commitments. The US presence in South Korea was more symbolic than material, and although the US reaffirmed its treaty obligations with the Republic of Korea the ground and air forces were withdrawn in 1992. This move followed the transfer to a Korean general of overall command of allied forces in Korea in early 1991. The departure of US troops in 1993 removed one cause of occasional strains in the US–Korean relationship.

Even with the withdrawal of US forces from South Korea itself, the US retained a significant military presence in the Far East, notably in Japan, where the US Air Force had about 120 combat aircraft. Japan also provided home-port facilities for 1 aircraft carrier, 8 surface combatants, 3 submarines and 3 amphibious ships. Moreover, a 23,000-man Marine Expeditionary Force (two brigades plus air units and support troops) was based on Okinawa in the Ryukyu Islands of southern Japan. The Seventh Fleet, usually stationed in the Sea of Japan and the East China Sea, had two carrier battle groups available, with a total of 116 strike and fighter aircraft, as well as significant amphibious assets.

THE RUSSIAN REPUBLIC

The Russian Republic, which included the Siberian and Maritime regions, shared a fifteen-kilometre border with North Korea. The Soviet Union had provided extensive material support to North Korean and Chinese forces during the Korean War. The changed political situation after mid-1991, and the limited Soviet role in 1950–3, indicated that the new Russian Republic would not be likely to take an active role in the event of renewed war. Depending on their internal political situation, and on their desire to appease (or antagonise) the US and South Korea, it was possible that the Russians would not even give North Korea materiel support. Nevertheless, the Russian military presence in the Far East was significant. There were five tank, thirty-two motorised rifle, two heavy machine gun artillery and three artillery divisions, plus an air assault brigade, in the Far East Theatre of Military Action (*Teatr Voennogo Deistviya*, or TVD). These forces included 8,500 tanks and over 10,000 artillery pieces and rocket launchers, about 1,100 helicopters and some 800 combat aircraft.

The Pacific Fleet, based at Vladivostok and on the Kamchatka peninsula, controlled 110 submarines and 70 major surface combatants,
including 2 *Kiev*-class aircraft carriers, 15 cruisers, 7 destroyers, and 45
frigates. Other forces assigned to the Fleet included 100 patrol craft,
over 100 mine warfare vessels, 21 amphibious ships and over 200 support and miscellaneous vessels. The Fleet also operated some 230 combat aircraft (including 26 Yak-38 V/STOL fighters aboard the carriers)
and 89 combat (primarily anti-submarine) helicopters, and controlled a
naval infantry division with one artillery, one tank and three infantry
regiments. Most of the ground forces were deployed with an eye
toward China, while the naval forces traditionally were deployed for
possible action against US and allied navies, although the new political
situation left them without a clear strategic purpose.

PEOPLE'S REPUBLIC OF CHINA

In view of China's close support of North Korea from November 1950
to the end of the Korean War, and the heavy cost in combat losses the
PLA bore during that struggle, China would closely monitor the progress of another war in the peninsula. However, awareness that the end
of the Communist regime in North Korea would not be likely to
threaten the regime in Beijing moderated the Chinese response, as did
adroit diplomacy by South Korea and her supporters. Moreover, the
Chinese government was displeased by the prospect of another war in
Korea. China was deeply concerned with its programme of internal
modernisation, and was also wary of the Russian Republic to its north.
Both those concerns affected its response to renewed war in Korea.

All of China's standing defence forces were referred to collectively as
the People's Liberation Army (PLA), and numbered over 3 million
officers and men, although force reductions were continuing to cut
costs. Many of China's best troops, with their most modern equipment, were deployed in Manchuria to guard that vital industrial region
against possible Russian attack.

In 1993, the PLA deployed ten tank, eighty infantry (four or five of
these mechanised) and five or six artillery divisions, plus numerous
support units. These forces operated nearly 8,000 tanks, at least 4,500
other armoured combat vehicles, 14,500 rocket launchers and large
quantities of other military equipment, including air defence and anti-
tank weapons, mortars and so on. The PLA Air Force, numbering
470,000 personnel, manned over 5,000 combat aircraft. The PLA Navy,
while primarily a coast defence force, had 4 nuclear and nearly 90
diesel-electric attack submarines, and its amphibious vessels could lift

6,250 combat troops and 374 armoured vehicles.

Most Chinese equipment was produced domestically on old Soviet designs, or more rarely on older Western patterns, and Chinese materiel was generally unsophisticated and sometimes crude. The Chinese were also inexperienced with the tempo and mechanised character of modern warfare, but their large materiel assets were a significant strength. Active intervention by Chinese forces would have dramatically changed the character of the Second Korean War. Such an eventuality was not really probable, however, and Chinese participation took the form of unenthusiastic support for North Korea through limited provision of supplies and logistical assistance.

JAPAN

Despite its powerful economy and large population (123 million people and a GNP of US$2,930 trillion in 1989), Japan was a military midget. It was constitutionally prohibited from spending more than 1 per cent of its GNP on defence, and although the government had grown clever at fudging the numbers to allow greater spending, a significant majority of the population supported a basically pacifist policy. For a nation which suffered as badly in World War II as did Japan, and which was the recipient of the only two nuclear weapons ever used in anger, this was an understandable reaction. However, the relative military weakness was not compatible with Japan's status as a regional (if not world) power. Certainly the outbreak of war in Korea gained Japan's immediate attention. A Communist victory there would have unquestionably had adverse effects in Japan, for there were growing economic ties between the Republic of Korea and its former colonial rulers.

Although Japan's armed forces were small, totalling less than 250,000 personnel, they were well trained and well equipped. Most of its neighbours looked with favour on Japan's military restrictions, reflecting on their unhappy experiences with Imperial troops in the first half of the twentieth century. And major effort to expand Japan's armed forces (properly the Ground, Maritime and Air Self-Defence Forces) would have met heavy political opposition in East Asia. Japan's army (Ground Self-Defence Force, or GSDF) contained 156,000 men in sixteen major combat formations (brigades and divisions), but did not see service abroad during the war. The 46,000-man navy (MSDF), with 14 diesel-electric submarines, 6 destroyers and 52 frigates, did see action, escorting merchant vessels into and out of the war zone. The Japanese air force (ASDF), 46,000 strong with its main strength lying in its 135 F-15 and 74 F-4E fighters, was best placed to play an active role in support of South Korea.

Japan had to balance any commitment of forces with potential risks and rewards. Japanese governments pursued an extremely cautious foreign policy after World War II, and a decision to commit forces to a conflict in Korea could not be taken lightly. Still, concrete actions in support of South Korea in its hour of need went far toward cancelling the bitterness many Koreans felt toward Japan for its harsh 35-year rule there.

THE CAUSES OF THE WAR

In 1993, the United States withdrew the 2nd Infantry Division and its supporting elements from South Korea. It made this move mainly in response to the need to reduce military expenditures (leading toward a reduction of the US Army from 750,000 personnel and eighteen divisions in 1990 to just under 500,000 personnel and twelve divisions in 1996). Recognition of the desire of the Korean people to exercise complete sovereignty over their national territory also contributed to this decision.

The United States felt some confidence taking this step for several reasons. First, the South Korean armed forces were capable, well armed and well trained. Their equipment was in many cases equal in sophistication and capability to that employed by US forces. Further, the presence of the US Seventh Fleet in the Sea of Japan and the East China Sea, and of substantial US forces in Japan and on Okinawa, provided some additional safeguards. Moreover, the US retained its close alliance with the Republic of Korea, continuing to nurture and strengthen ROK forces.

In May 1994, several months after the last US units left South Korea, student protests in favour of reunification broke out in Seoul and several other major South Korean cities. Student riots in South Korea were very nearly an annual spring event. Western observers occasionally quipped that tear gas was one of Seoul's most common springtime aromas. Although on some occasions under the military regime of the late 1970s and early 1980s they posed some threat to the government's stability, these riots were generally not a serious threat to either public order or national security. Bearing this in mind, however, the riots could not simply be dismissed as mere peaceful political protest. A portion of the annual unrest was produced by the activities of *agents provocateurs*, either smuggled into South Korea from the North, or encouraged (and sometimes paid) by Northern intelligence agents.

The riots which followed the withdrawal of US ground forces were particularly serious, however, as the more radical student protesters capitalised on the fact that there was no longer an external force preventing Korean reunification. Unlike previous years, where student ire had been directed against either specific government officials or against the ruling regime in general, these student rioters had a specific goal in mind: the 'peaceful unification' of the two Koreas. The government in Seoul, not surprisingly, viewed that eventuality with great misgivings, and directed the security forces to suppress the protests with more than their accustomed vigour. While police and army forces soon restored order in Seoul and other major cities after the unrest of late May and early June, South Korea's university campuses were still seething with unrest.

Against this backdrop, the leaders of the student protest movement organised a mass march to the DMZ, scheduled for 14 June, with the intent of crossing into North Korea and thus demonstrating the *de facto* unity of Korea. The success of this endeavour would have been a disaster for South Korea's government, and would have destroyed any justification for keeping the two Koreas separate. Republic of Korea security forces and army troops deployed to block the marchers about ten kilometres short of the DMZ, near the small city of Munsan and its bridge across the Imjin River. The marchers, numbering over 50,000, were more numerous than the ROK authorities had expected, and the security forces found themselves in a tense situation, with the added complication that some marchers were armed with gasoline bombs, hand-made smoke grenades, clubs and a few firearms.

Concerned by the unexpectedly large crowd of marchers, the local commanders of the security forces reacted violently to the arrival of the protesters. Gunfire from police and army troops, aimed over the heads of the crowd as its lead elements crossed the Imjin bridge, triggered the release of the protesters' homemade weapons, producing more confusion and some government casualties. The officers on the spot, now thoroughly unnerved, ordered the troops to open fire, and within seconds some 120 protesters were dead and 500 more injured, most of those among the few thousand who had crossed the bridge. The bulk of the crowd broke and fled, and in the ensuing panic several more people were killed, either trampled or shot by overzealous police and soldiers. Several dozen more were injured, and by the end of the day total casualties neared 1,000, with close to 200 dead.

Cries of outrage swiftly came in, not only from the United States and Europe, but also from many within South Korea. It took the better part of a week, until 20 June, to sort out what had happened, and several of the officers present were relieved, but by that time other events had taken

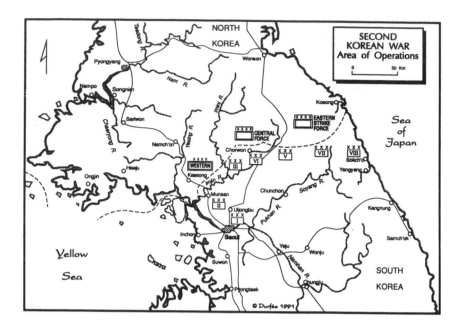

centre stage. Meanwhile, the most vociferous protests and most vigorous condemnations came from Pyongyang. The North Korean government seized the opportunity to denounce the ROK as a 'gang of bloodthirsty fascist murderers', and the ensuing propaganda onslaught from the North did little to ameliorate the crisis situation in the south. The 'Munsan Massacre' led to further strikes and protests in the South, including not only students but also common citizens, who were generally known for avoiding open political protest.

Under cover of this expanding crisis, the Democratic People's Republic of Korea began an unannounced military mobilisation four days after the incident at Munsan, on 18 June 1993. The mobilisation activity was soon picked up by US reconnaissance satellites, and the ROK government was immediately notified. This notification occurred about the same time that South Korea's own intelligence apparatus began noticing the activity, some three days into the mobilisation and one week after Munsan. The ROK government delayed its formal response for several days (21–3 June), trying to determine whether this was a serious threat of war or merely an effort to wrest concessions from the South through political pressure.

Six days after North Korea began mobilisation, South Korea announced that it was also mobilising, at the same time releasing solid documentation on North Korea's actions (23 June). The carefully prepared information release helped to rally public support behind the government. Although the actual mechanics of mobilisation in South Korea proceeded smoothly, the unsettled domestic political situation compelled the authorities there to retain two infantry divisions (5th, 14th), a corps headquarters (IV), and two special forces brigades (3rd and 7th) in rear-area security duties, reducing the strength along the DMZ from twenty-one divisions and eight corps (348,000 men) to nineteen divisions and seven corps (313,000 men).

PLANS AND DISPOSITIONS

Marshal Choe Gwang, Chief of Staff of the North Korean People's Army (NKPA), had given careful consideration to the development of a plan for conquering South Korea. Marshal Choe's plan capitalised on two major components of the situation: that the South Koreans would understandably expect the main thrust to come in the flat terrain along the west coast, close to Seoul and served by many transport routes; and that the South Koreans would be distracted by internal unrest.

To execute an unexpected offensive on the east coast, Marshal Choe set up the Eastern Strike Force headquarters, under Colonel General Paek Son San, at Wonsan. NKPA command assigned the III and V Mechanised Corps, containing the 1st Mechanised Division, plus four tank brigades and eight mechanised brigades, to the Strike Force as the main offensive element. Colonel General Paek's force would advance down the coast road through Sokch'o at least as far as Kangnung, to seize the eastern terminus of the Suwon-Samch'ok highway, and also capture the Kangnung airport. Supporting this effort would be General Yi Jong Ok's XIV Combined Arms Corps with three regular and two Type A reserve infantry divisions (which had completed mobilisation as part of the regular training cycle); seven brigades from the Special Purpose Corps, including commandos, Special Forces and amphibious troops; and 1st, 2nd, 5th and 8th (MRL) Army Artillery Brigades. General Paek's Eastern Strike Force included over 258,000 men, 1,100 tanks, 1,250 APCs, 742 guns and howitzers (72 85 mm, 424 122 mm, 108 130 mm, 90 152 mm and 48 180 mm) and 252 MRLs (126 122 mm, 72 200 mm, 36 240 mm).

As a massive diversion, the NKPA planned a large – but secondary – offensive near Seoul, and devoted to that effort the I Tank, II, IV and VI Mechanised, VIII through XII Combined Arms and XVI and XVII Artillery corps, with a total of ten tank and nineteen mechanised brigades, one motorised and fifteen regular infantry divisions, and the remaining four Army Artillery brigades. Three Type A and 12 Type B reserve divisions would join this effort when they completed mobilisation. The NKPA VII Infantry and XIII Combined Arms Corps covered the rugged central sectors, with four regular infantry divisions, plus one mechanised and one infantry brigade; one Type A and three Type B reserve divisions were slated as reinforcements for that area. General reserves included the XV Combined Arms Corps, with one regular and five Type B reserve infantry divisions, as well as one infantry, one tank and two motorised brigades. Table 6.1 shows the order of battle.

TABLE 6.1

NORTH KOREA: ORDER OF BATTLE

NORTH KOREAN FORCES: (MARSHAL CHOE GWANG)
EASTERN STRIKE FORCE: General Paek Son San

XIV Combined Arms Corps and III and V Mechanised Corps

1 motorised infantry division

4 tank and 8 mechanised brigades

3 regular infantry and 2 type-B reserve infantry divisions

7 brigades of the Special Purpose Corps

4 Army Artillery brigades

CENTRAL FORCE:

VII Infantry and XIII Combined Arms corps

4 infantry, 2 Type A and 3 Type B reserve infantry divisions

1 mechanised and 1 infantry brigade

WESTERN ARMY: Marshall O Yin Sok

1 Tank Corps; II, IV, and VI Mechanised Corps; VIII, IX, X, XI and XII Combined Arms Corps; XVI and XVII Artillery Corps

1 motorised infantry division

10 tank and 19 mechanised brigades

15 regular, 3 Type A and 12 Type B reserve infantry divisions

4 army artillery brigades

15 brigades of the Special Purpose Corps

GENERAL RESERVE

XV Combined Arms Corps

1 regular and 5 Type-B reserve infantry divisions

1 tank, 1 mechanised and 1 infantry brigade

South Korean defensive plans called for the bulk of their strength to be committed in the areas closest to Seoul. These forces included four Corps headquarters, with the 1st and 2nd Mechanised and 1st Marine Division under the I Corps around Seoul, and eleven infantry divisions under the II, III and VI corps along the DMZ. As already noted, the IV Corps with the 5th and 14th Divisions was on rear-area 'aid to the civil authority' duties, but the regular divisions were scheduled to be replaced by the 27th and 29th Reserve Divisions two weeks after mobilisation. Covering the rugged central sectors of the front were the V and VII Corps with four divisions and the 23rd Infantry Brigade. Lieutenant General Choi Song-Hoo's VIII Corps was deployed along the east coast, with the 17th and 21st Infantry Divisions, opposite the NKPA Eastern Strike Force. The units in the east contained 34,500 men, 100 tanks, 80 APCs, 198 howitzers (36 105 mm , 144 155 mm, 18 203 mm) and 18 MRLs; they were thus heavily outnumbered by the NKPA's Eastern Strike Force, but the narrow front reduced the odds significantly. General reserves, located south of Seoul, included the 2nd Marine Division and 22nd Infantry Brigade, while the 3rd Marine Brigade was at Pusan as an amphibious strike force. The reserve divisions (except for the 27th and 29th) were to be fed into the line as they completed mobilisation, but none of these was fully prepared for action on the twenty-fifth day after mobilisation (the nineteenth day for the ROK), when the NKPA struck. Table 6.2 sets out the South Korean order of battle, and Table 6.3 compares the ground force of the two protagonists.

TABLE 6.2

SOUTH KOREA: ORDER OF BATTLE

THIRD ARMY:
   VIII Corps (Lieutenant General Choi Song-Hoo), 2 infantry divisions
   V and VII Corps, 4 infantry divisions and 1 infantry brigade
FIRST AND SECOND ARMIES:
   I, II, III, and VI Corps:
   2 mechanised, 1 Marine and 11 infantry divisions
RESERVES:
   1 Marine brigade at Pusan
   1 Marine division and 1 infantry brigade, south of Seoul
REAR-AREA SECURITY:
   IV Corps, 2 infantry divisions and 2 Special Forces brigades

TABLE 6.3

COMPARISON OF COMBAT FORCES

ARMY	South Korea	North Korea
Manpower	720,000*	975,000
MBTs	1,700	3,255
IFVs	700	150
ACs	–	160
APCs	1,870	4,060
Artillery	3,930	7,650
MRLs	192	2,310
AIR FORCE		
Combat A/C	1,300†	716
Armed helicopters	185	75
AIR DEFENCE‡		
AAA guns	400	1,130
SAMs	282	72
NAVY§		
Submarines	26	24
DDs/FFGs	85	3
Fast missile craft	11	34

Strength figures reflect fully mobilised force levels, achieved about 5 August 1994 for both sides
* Includes US ground forces, 33,000 Army and Marines.
† Includes 470 Korean, 280 Japanese, 174 USN, 240 USAF and 138 USMC (552 US) combat aircraft.
‡ Figures do not include AA machine-guns, or hand-held and static SAMS.
§ Includes USN and Japanese MSDF vessels.

COMBAT

The NKPA opened its offensive on 14 July 1994, with massive artillery preparations. The NKPA Air Force also mounted a series of air strikes, mainly against ROK air bases and air defence installations, but suffered heavy losses from ROK air defences and from intercepting fighters, especially the F–16s, which completely outclassed anything in the NKPA arsenal except for a handful of MiG-29s. The NKPA's Chinese and older Soviet aircraft carried virtually no electronic countermeasures (ECM), and so were extremely vulnerable to South Korea's modern air defence missiles.

In the east, the full onslaught of General Paek's NKPA III and V Mechanised Corps struck Major General Lee Byung Yul's ROK 17th Division squarely. Although the NKPA advance was constrained by the narrow coastal road, their tanks and armoured personnel carriers swept through 17th Division's forward positions, taking full advantage of confusion spread in the ROK rear area by a handful of commando infiltration teams. Although tanks and TOW missiles took a heavy toll of the NKPA attackers, by the end of the first day the North Koreans had advanced six to ten kilometres into South Korea. They maintained their offensive drive through the night, and the gradual erosion of ROK antitank capabilities made the advance easier. By mid-afternoon of 15 July, Major General Lee's division had been compelled to fall back in much disorder.

In addition to the mechanised assault from the north, the 17th Division was also under heavy pressure from the NKPA's 6th and 9th Infantry Divisions of General Yi's XIV Combined Arms Corps (CAC), which were moving cross-country through the hills toward Sokch'o. That arm of the attack soon ran afoul of Major General Kang Seoung-Soo's ROK 21st Division, deployed west of Sokch'o and Yangyang, and their advance slowed to a mere crawl after 16 July. The next day, as the lead elements of the NKPA mechanised spearhead approached, Lieutenant General Choi's VIII Corps headquarters received permission to withdraw south of Yangyang. When intelligence reports about this reached

TABLE 6.4

HUMAN COST OF THE WAR

Nation	Killed	Wounded	Total casualties
North Korea	31,470	94,010	125,480
South Korea	13,120	51,730	64,850
United States	510	2,626	3,136
Japan	65	123	188

Note: Since Japanese participation in the Second Korean War was limited to air and naval actions, which have historically had a higher ratio of killed to wounded than that found in land combat, the MSDF and ASDF suffered an unusually high ratio of dead to wounded personnel. This factor also affected losses of the other participants, but their extensive ground forces largely conceal the statistical evidence of this effect.

Colonel General Paek, it seemed to him as if victory was nearly within his grasp. He had, however, reckoned without considering two major factors: the US Seventh Fleet and US–ROK–Japanese airpower.

By 15 July, Japanese ASDF and USAF F-15s were flying air superiority missions over South Korea, and additional US forces were hastening to support South Korea. The Japanese MSDF took over responsibility for shepherding convoys into South Korean ports, and within the first week of war accounted for three North Korean submarines. Aircraft from Seventh Fleet carriers struck at NKPA forces inside South Korea, and tangled repeatedly with North Korean aircraft, shooting down dozens. On 18 July, under cover of an air umbrella, the battleship USS *New Jersey* bombarded NKPA supply routes from Kosong south along the coast road, causing considerable damage and confusion.

The intervention of US and Japanese aircraft freed most of the South Korean Air Force's F-4s and F-5s for ground support, and the dense but primitive NKPA air defence guns presented a comparatively minor obstacle. NKPA losses to air attack mounted, and strikes against their logistical networks hurt still more. By 19 July, some units in Colonel General Paek's Eastern Strike Force were scrounging supplies from captured ROK stocks and damaged or destroyed North Korean vehicles. The NKPA Air Force, for its part, found attacking into South Korea a costly undertaking. Even if its aircraft avoided the F-15 and F-16 air-superiority aircraft, they then had to contend with ageing but effective Hawk SAMS, as well as Javelin and Stinger battlefield air defence missiles and the modern radar-aimed anti-aircraft guns employed by the South Koreans.

Meanwhile, the South Korean command was gradually recognising that the offensive in the west, despite its impressive force levels, was a secondary effort meant to divert their attention from the main attack in the east. Counterattacks by the South Korean 1st and 2nd Mechanised Divisions, whose Type-88 tanks and KIFV infantry fighting vehicles completely outclassed their North Korean counterparts, had halted and then shredded General Li Guk Ryol's NKPA I Armoured Corps in a vicious battle north-east of Munsan; by dusk of 20 July, Li's corps had lost 65 per cent of its tanks and nearly half of its APCs, and its battered remnants clung grimly to a few bridgeheads south of the Imjin River. Lieutenant General Pak Hong-Il's ROK VI Corps repulsed three separate assaults on Chorwon between 16 and 22 July, inflicting heavy losses on the attacking NKPA formations.

Taking stock of the situation, the South Koreans shifted a major portion of their air activities to the east coast, and hurried Major General

Roh Yung-Chung's 5th Division north from Kwangju (where it was replaced by the 27th Reserve Division and the 2nd Special Forces Brigade) toward Kangnung. Meanwhile Brigadier General Han Young Choul's 41st Reserve Division, which was based on the east coast, hastened its mobilisation and was brought under VIII Corps Command as it neared readiness. The ROK command assigned the hitherto-unblooded 3rd Attack Helicopter Battalion to the VIII Corps, and also readied the 3rd Marine Brigade for action. The 2nd Marine Division moved from general reserve to bolster the east flank of the VII Corps, threatened by the advance of the XIV Corp's infantry toward Yangyang.

Meanwhile Colonel General Paek's NKPA Eastern Strike Force, after a brief reorganisation, prepared to continue its attack south toward Kangnung, intending to renew the drive on 22 July. Allied aerial and satellite reconnaissance revealed indications of the planned attack, and the South Korean and US Air Forces struck hard at NKPA artillery concentrations shortly after midnight on 21 July and continuing into daylight. US-supplied cluster bombs and submunitions dispensers wreaked havoc among North Korean artillery, whose protecting air defence guns were hampered by the darkness and allied suppression tactics. Although few guns were lost, many crewmen were killed or wounded, soft-skinned support vehicles suffered heavily, communications were severely disrupted and much ammunition was destroyed.

Enough of the Eastern Strike Force's artillery survived to support the attack as planned, but the preparatory bombardment was anticlimactic and did little harm to the South Korean defenders. The NKPA's armour-mechanised column punched about six kilometres into ROK lines, but supporting attacks were stalled, and efforts to widen the breach were frustrated by the newly arrived attack helicopter battalion and allied battlefield air support. In fact, the renewed attack only got as far as it did because Major General Lee's battered 17th Division was reduced to less than 10,000 men and had lost all but 10 of its tanks. Moreover, the arrival of Major General Roh's 5th Division bolstered the defenders significantly, and some units of Brigadier General Han's 41st Reserve Division also got into action.

BATTLE OF YANGYANG

As the North Korean attack faltered and then stalled on 22 and 23 July, the South Koreans prepared a counterstroke to end the threat to the east coast. Major General Kang's 21st Division, which had suffered few losses, would attack east-north-east from its positions in the hills fifteen to twenty-five kilometres west of Sokch'o and Yangyang to cut the coast road somewhere near those two towns, and thus isolate the leading elements of III and V Mechanised Corps. Simultaneously, 5th and 17th Divisions, together with whatever portions of 41st Reserve Divisions were ready, would conduct holding attacks to distract the NKPA from 21 Division's efforts. Further, Brigadier General So Hak Rim's 3rd Marine Brigade would land just north-east of Yangyang and link up with 21st Division. Finally, 1st and 4th Special Forces Brigades would infiltrate the NKPA lines and wreak as much havoc and confusion in the rear as possible, and prevent the infantry divisions of the XIV Combined Arms Corps from assisting the mechanised forces.

The ROK attack began on 24 July with probes by 5th and 17th divisions, heavily supported by air attack. The naval presence off-shore, centred around the *New Jersey*, masked the assembly of amphibious forces and preparations for the landing. Major General Kang's 21st Division opened its offensive before dawn on 25 July, and advanced slowly. At the same time the first waves of the 3rd Marine Brigade came ashore, supported by the *New Jersey*'s guns and US naval aircraft. The simultaneous coordinated attacks unhinged the Eastern Strike Force's scanty and hasty defences, and the 21st Division linked up with Brigadier General So's Marines just outside Yangyang in the early afternoon of 26 July. While the 3rd Brigade turned to face south against the inevitable counterattack, the 21st Division wheeled to drive north up the coast road to liberate Sokch'o. Colonel General Paek's reaction to this counterattack was hampered by South Korean Special Forces activities as well as allied air strikes and Harpoon missile attacks on vital installations, some of them north of the DMZ.

The NKPA mechanised spearheads isolated south of Yangyang mounted a valiant but rather haphazard series of counterattacks which sometimes penetrated the Marine positions but failed to break through. By evening of 28 July, most of the North Korean tanks and other AFVs had run out of fuel, and what artillery remained to them (much had already been overrun with the fall of Yangyang) was nearly out of ammunition. Surrender was forbidden, so most unit commanders ordered their men to take what equipment they could and escape on foot after wrecking everything else. Many of the 40,000-odd North Koreans who tried to break out from the 'Yangyang Pocket' eventually made it back north of the DMZ, but nearly 10,000 were killed by ROK forces or died before they reached safety. Nearly 20,000 of the encircled troops were captured by the victorious VIII Corps, and most of these soldiers were stunned and demoralised by the sudden reversal of their fortune.

By 29 July, as the full impact of what had happened struck the NKPA command, General Yi's XIV Corps had re-established a solid line some twenty-five to thirty kilometres north of Sokch'o, but the Eastern Strike Force had lost over 80 per cent of its armoured vehicles and nearly 75 per cent of its artillery and MRLs, and close to 50 per cent of its original manpower was killed, wounded, or – like Colonel General Paek and many of his staff – missing in action.

SOUTH KOREAN COUNTEROFFENSIVE

In the meantime, the South Koreans were planning their next move. The situation along the lower Imjin and around Chorwon had effectively become stalemated. The NKPA either lacked the offensive capacity to break the Imjin line after the near destruction of I Armoured Corps, or was unwilling to suffer the unavoidably high casualties in men and equipment to crack the heavily fortified South Korean defences in those sectors. Although the defeat of the Eastern Strike Force and I Armoured Corps had significantly reduced the NKPA's offensive strength, the North Koreans retained impressive military power, and any major counteroffensive would find the South Koreans assuming the burdens of attack. Balancing this evaluation was clear evidence, gained from North Korean prisoners, that morale throughout the NKPA had suffered badly from news of the disaster of the battle for Yangyang. Moreover the 27th, 29th, and 41st Reserve Divisions were already mobilised and the other twenty would be ready for action within a few days, and so would significantly increase South Korean offensive capacity. Finally, additional US aircraft (including A-10 ground attack jets) had arrived in-theatre, along with the entire 2nd US Marine and 25th Light Infantry Divisions and additional US ground forces, including artillery, engineer and aviation units.

Between 30 July and 2 August the South Koreans replaced the seven regular divisions in the central and eastern sectors with nine reserve divisions under command of the Fourth Army and the VII and VIII Corps, concentrating thirty-five divisions (nineteen regular infantry, two mechanised, two Korean Marine and twelve reserve infantry divisions), plus four Special Forces Brigades under the First, Second and Third Armies and I, II, III, IV, V and VI Corps. The two US divisions and supporting troops operated under the II Marine Expeditionary Force (MEF) headquarters and were attached to the ROK First Army southwest of Munsan. These allied forces contained 568,000 men, nearly 1,500 tanks, 1,500 infantry fighting vehicles and APCs, 152 attack helicopters, over 3,000 howitzers and 165 MRLs. South Korean, US and Japanese aircraft dominated Korean skies, having achieved nearly complete air superiority. Most air strikes had been directed against troop concentrations and transport choke-points.

Against this force the NKPA deployed Marshal O Yun Sok's Western Army, with thirty-eight divisions (one motorised, sixteen regular and twenty-one reserve infantry) plus six tank and fifteen mechanised brigades, in nine corps (II, IV and VI Mechanised Corps; VIII, IX, X, XI and XII Combined Arms Corps and XVI Artillery Corps). These units contained close to 600,000 men, over 1,800 tanks, more than 2,000 APCs, some 3,400 guns and howitzers and 1,314 MRLs. The VII Infantry and XIII and XIV Combined Arms Corps were still in line on the eastern part of the front, and the XV Corps remained in reserve. The NKPA Air Force retained some 200 operational aircraft, but they were widely dispersed and communications problems made mounting a major air operation virtually impossible. The North Korean air defence system had also been badly damaged: most radars were either destroyed or inoperable, many gun and missile sites had been damaged, and communications and co-ordination were difficult.

The South Korean offensive north of the DMZ began early on 3 August with a series of massive air attacks. The main thrust came against the twenty-kilometre sector just north of the Munsan-Kaesong highway. Combat on that day was confused and often bitter as the attacking ROK troops eliminated the last NKPA bridgeheads south of the Imjin and laid their own bridges to cross the river. This struggle continued on 4 and 5 August as Lieutenant General Lee Tae-woo's ROK II Corps ground forward and approached the North Korean fortified zone behind the DMZ. Although the KNPA had slight numerical superiority in men and materiel, allied command of the air, coupled with superior communications and response time, created greater operational flexibility that more than offset the NKPA's strengths.

Lieutenant General Pak Hong-koo's III Corps breached the 'DMZ Line' in a three-day slugging match from 6 to 8 August, aided greatly by a series of carpet-bombing attacks by American B-52s and F-111s. (Two American B-2 'Stealth' bombers took part in one of these attacks, the first combat employment of these aircraft.) North Korean defensive efforts were hamstrung by allied command of the air, which often prevented NKPA division and corps commanders from controlling much more than a single brigade or regiment at a time. Lieutenant General Chun Doo-hak's ROK I Corps, with the 1st and 2nd Mechanised Divisions (among others) passed through the gap torn in the DMZ defences by Lee's II Corps between the evening of 8 August and midday on 10 August. They swung north-west and then west to reach the main highway from Munsan some fifteen kilometres north-west of Kaesong. Leading elements of the 2nd Mechanised Division reached the highway late on 12 August. This unit and those following, including the II MEF, nearly isolated the VIII and XI Combined Arms Corps along the coast and overran much of the XVI Artillery Corps.

Desperate to save something after a string of military reverses, the NKPA committed its last reserves to a counterattack. Personally directed by Marshal O, and comprising the VI Mechanised Corps and the over-size XV Combined Arms Corps previously held in reserve, the attack slammed into the eastward or right flank of General Chun's ROK I Corps on 14 August. Marshal O's troops made good initial progress toward Kaesong. For a time they nearly isolated the 2nd Mechanised Division, but their tank units suffered from TOW antitank missiles and ROK attack helicopters. Moreover, the commitment of the US 2nd Marine Division south of Kaesong threw the North Koreans back. Hammered by allied air attack, and with NKPA commanders increas-ingly out of touch with their subordinate units as the battle progressed, Marshal O's corps were driven back nearly to their starting position by 19 August.

THE END OF THE WAR

The five-day Battle of Kaesong (14–19 August) was the last 'throw of the dice' for the North Koreans. The failure of that attack, on top of the Eastern Strike Force disaster and the breaching of the DMZ line near Munsan, completed the disaffection of many NKPA officers. Frustrated with what they regarded as inept strategic leadership and inadequate consideration of risks and costs, a group of field-grade officers (mostly majors and lieutenant colonels) broke into the subterranean command post used by Kim Il Sung and his son Kim Jong Il, and shot both of them as well as Chief of Staff Marshal Choe. Most of the rebel officers were killed by loyal security guards in an ensuing firefight, and the military junta under Marshal O which took over control of the government had most of the survivors executed after pro forma trials.

Marshal O's new military government had to face two unsavoury facts. First, the Kims had thrust the country into a costly war and given it three serious military defeats. The NKPA had lost nearly half its tank force, much of its artillery, nearly three quarters of its combat planes and suffered heavy human casualties. Further, and in some ways more dam-aging, was the realisation that neither Russia nor China had come to aid them in their hour of need. Neither of those countries was willing to endanger their relations with the United States, nor were they willing to risk outright military involvement for a client-state whose leadership tended to ignore their counsel.

With the South Korean Army nearing Namch'on, the North Korean military junta took quick and sober stock of the situation, and proposed a cease-fire on 23 August. After hurried negotiations, a temporary cease-fire was concluded on 26 August and, despite some limited skirmishing, was made permanent on 2 September. Even as negotiators put the final touches on the military arrangements for the cease-fire, political leaders from North and South Korea had begun meeting to reach a permanent settlement. Over the next fourteen months, the Republic of Korea extended large levels of economic aid to North Korea to help sustain a transfer to a free-market economy and the production of consumer goods. The People's Democratic Republic opened its natural resources to exploitation by South Korean businessmen, and both countries sharply reduced their military forces.

Although there were several policy zig-zags by the government of North Korea as it struggled to chart its route through the perilous waters of democratisation and liberalisation, the end of the Second Korean War marked the end of the 'armed camp' on the peninsula. Although there were clearly major problems ahead, the two Korean republics were officially united as the Republic of Korea on 1 December 1995, almost fifteen months to the day after the final cease-fire was imposed. This arrangement ended one of the last geo-political remnants of the Cold War.

TNDM ADDENDUM: BATTLE OF YANGYANG

The stage for the Battle of Yangyang was set when stiffening South Korean resistance slowed and then halted the southward advance of General Paek's Eastern Strike Force on 22 and 23 July. The Eastern Strike Force was stretched in a long thin salient along the east coast, some seventy kilometres long and generally between twelve and twenty kilometres deep, widening considerably near the DMZ because of the effects of the XIV Combined Arms Corps' operations. Into this narrow area were squeezed most of Paek's offensive power, including nearly all his armour and artillery.

The South Koreans planned their attack to strike toward the town of Yangyang, where the inland arm would meet up with the 3rd Marine Brigade, which would land south of Sokch'o shortly after dawn on 25 July.

The Yangyang area was only weakly held by the NKPA. A battalion of the 36th Mechanised Brigade held the coast, and the rest of that brigade, along with the 34th Mechanised and 10th Tank brigades, lay around and inland of Yangyang. The local commanders had not been warned to expect an attack, and were in fact expecting orders to move south to reinforce Paek's armoured spearheads. The 36th Brigade's coastal battalion was overrun and virtually destroyed by the Marines but the brigade, caught off guard, otherwise took little part in the fighting on 25 July. Inland, the ROK 21st Division made only scant progress against the NKPA 36th Mechanised and 10th Tank Brigades, advancing less than a kilometre.

On 26 July the North Koreans had largely recovered from the surprise of the ROK offensive, but the success of the ROK 3rd Marine Brigade left their forces, especially the weakened 36th Mechanised Brigade, in an awkward position. Continued South Korean attacks led to the meeting of units from the 21st Division and the 3rd Marine Brigade outside Yangyang in mid-afternoon, and this success virtually sealed the fate of Paek's armoured spearheads around Kangnung.

TABLE TNDM 6.1

TNDM STATISTICS: BATTLE OF YANGYANG

NORTH KOREA (NKPA)	Strength	Losses	Daily losses (%)
Men	10,200	1,062	5.21
Armour	200	30	7.5
Artillery	54	1	0.93
SOUTH KOREA (ROK)			
Men	21,200	1,054	2.49
Armour	58	18	15.52
Artillery	162	0	0.00

CHAPTER SEVEN

THE
SANDINISTA WAR

Although the nations of Central America underwent major political changes between 1985 and 1991, significant potential for major conflict remained in the region. The basic political and social conflicts which had made the area a hotbed of guerrilla activity from 1978 to 1990 were still present, and were quite capable of flaring up once more. Renewed guerrilla war could in turn lead (as it nearly did in the 1980s) to regional conflict. Moreover, the location of the Panama Canal in the region and the proximity of Central America to the oilfields of Venezuela and Mexico, as well as the region's long-standing economic ties to the US, ensured that US policies and actions continued to interact with events in Central America.

THE SITUATION IN MID-1994

Central America consisted of seven nations between the Mexican and Colombian borders (see Map 7.1): Guatemala, Belize (formerly British Honduras), El Salvador, Honduras, Nicaragua, Costa Rica and Panama. Except for Belize, these nations shared a common Hispanic–American heritage. Their economies depended on agricultural exports, and industrial development had been limited. Further, with the partial exception of Nicaragua, their armed forces were relatively small and were equipped and organised mainly for internal counter-insurgency operations. The last regional inter-state conventional war in the area was the five-day 'Soccer War' between El Salvador and Honduras in June 1969.

In mid-1994 Panama was still recovering from the damage of the Noriega regime and the less favourable after-effects of the American intervention which deposed him in December 1989. This was the most recent conventional conflict in Central America. Since then the new, democratic regime in Panama had been coping with its many problems,

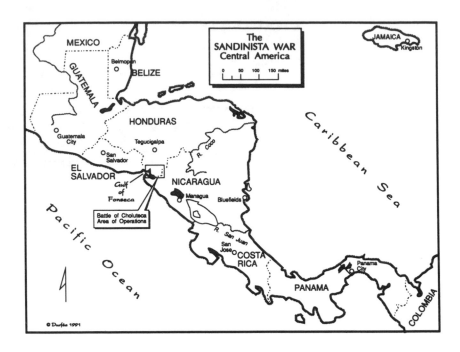

reorganising its armed forces to focus on internal security duties, while maintaining traditionally peaceful relations with nearby countries.

Early in 1990 Nicaragua underwent a major change of regime with the electoral defeat of the Sandinistas, the first instance where a Marxist, authoritarian government has surrendered power at the polls. However, the Sandinistas retained control of a well-organised grass-roots political machine which, although damaged by the adverse results of the election, was still a potent political force. Further, the Sandinistas remained in control of Nicaragua's armed forces, and in the administrative shake-up following the election the national intelligence services fell under military control, providing the Sandinista-dominated defence forces with a virtual monopoly of national security capabilities.

Guatemala's two-part presidential election ended in early January 1991 with the victory of Jorge Serrano Elias, a protégé of Efrain Rios Montt (and like him an evangelical Protestant). This introduced a new degree of uncertainty into Guatemalan, and hence Central American, politics. The guerrilla conflict in the countryside had declined in intensity, possibly because of the increasing strength of the government-backed popular militia. However, the continuing activities of right-wing terrorist death squads, coupled with security forces' excesses against demonstrations and protests, demonstrated that the fundamental conflicts were still very much alive.

In El Salvador the right-wing ARENA (Alianza Republica Nacionalista, or Republican Nationalist Alliance) party remained in firm political control, but the long conflict with the FMLN guerrillas in the countryside came to an end with the signing of a UN-sponsored peace treaty in Mexico City in January 1992. This agreement provided for the integration of the FMLN into El Salvador's political system, for the disarming of the guerrilla forces, and for a major reduction in the army's size. This remarkable achievement, due in part to the guerrilla offensive of fall 1990, and also sparked by the few guerrilla leaders who 'came down from the hills' and re-entered El Salvadoran political life, had ended the open conflict but left the nation's basic social and economic problems unresolved.

In contrast to the political instability and violence in most of the region, Honduras, Costa Rica and Belize remained relatively stable. The end of the anti-Sandinista Contra guerrilla campaign in June 1990, following the electoral defeat of the Sandinista regime, removed the official Contra presence from Honduras and thereby eased that nation's security problems. This followed closely on the inauguration of President Rafael Callejas, the first transition of power to an opposition party by election in Honduras since 1932. However, the Honduran Army continued to share with its neighbours many of the unsavoury characteristics of Central American military forces, including at least a potential for military interference in internal civilian politics.

Costa Rica underwent a general election in February 1990, in which the opposition gained power. The new government had to deal with major economic problems, but, with the end of the Contra insurgency in Nicaragua, was able to cope with these in what was – until August 1994 – a relatively peaceful regional environment.

HISTORICAL BACKGROUND

The general problems which traditionally faced the Central American nations were centred on issues of economic development and social progress. Since the arrival of Spanish settlers in the sixteenth and seventeenth centuries, the economies have usually depended on the employment of Indian workers or workers of mixed Indian–European descent (*mestizo*) for both agricultural production and for mining and other extractive industries. These workers were generally ill-educated, poorly paid, poorly housed and poorly fed, and usually had little hope or opportunity for advancement. Management positions, the professions, government and the armed forces were dominated by people of European descent or, in the case of Guatemala, where the population of European descent was unusually small, by mestizos and 'Europeanised' Indians.

The development of agricultural export-based economies in the early twentieth century, coupled with the advent of modern telecommunications and the resulting end of widespread isolation of rural communities in Central America, began the erosion of this traditional pattern of social organisation. In a few instances, land reform enabled some peasants (or campesinos) to become small-scale landholders, but the breakup of large estates was unpopular among both the local landowning classes and the foreign corporations and companies which owned plantations, usually for the production of export items like bananas. The realisation by the campesinos that they were being exploited as a cheap labour force to enrich others often led to frustration and anger. The general inability or unwillingness of the traditional local elites to admit the justice of reform often led to violent confrontation, and even revolt or revolution.

These essentially social and internal confrontations – such as the suppression of an agrarian reform movement, led by Farabundo Marti in El Salvador in the 1930s – were also affected by external political forces. Marxist and Communist beliefs and practices were the most active such forces. The recent European disillusionment with Marxist ideology and solutions had not yet affected Central or South America by 1994. The difficulties faced since 1990 by the Chamorro government in Nicaragua in its efforts to wean Nicaragua from Marxism illustrated the continuing appeal of revolutionary Marxism. The enthusiasm with which frustrated reformers embraced Marxist ideology may be readily appreciated when placed against the power and intransigence of the entrenched traditional power structures.

The continuing appeal of Communist ideology to the many unenfranchised and impoverished inhabitants of Central America, however, was not the whole story. Pre-dating the arrival of Marxist-inspired revolutionaries were the populist-nationalists of the early 1990s, such as César Augusto Sandino of Nicaragua. He was an ardent nationalist, and opposed the US and its allies within Nicaragua not because of Marxist antipathy to the great power of capitalism (he had little use for Marxists of any sort), but because he believed that US hegemony in Nicaragua, and in Central America generally, was harmful to the people and their society.

Sandino's distrust of the United States and its interests in Central America was passed on to the revolutionary organisation which appropriated his name, if not his ideals, the Frente Sandinista Liberacion

Nacional (FSLN), colloquially known as the Sandinistas. A significant portion of the Sandinista nationalist programme was epitomised by hostility to the US. This was often demonstrated publicly without regard for whether the demonstration would help or hurt Sandinista and Nicaraguan causes. This in part explained the Sandinistas' proclivity during the 1980s for taking deliberately provocative actions just after the US Congress had made some conciliatory move. The strong nationalist tradition in the FSLN ensured that, even with their loss of total control over the Nicaraguan economy and defence forces in 1990, they still retained a powerful and popular political card in their hand.

The widespread suspicion of American intentions and objectives in the region had a historical basis. First there was the *opéra-bouffe* affair of William Walker, a ne'er-do-well American soldier of fortune who twice invaded Nicaragua in 1856 and 1857, ruling there for a period of nearly a year (June 1856–May 1857). After his failure in Nicaragua, he tried again in Honduras in 1860. He again failed, and was executed by a Honduran firing squad (12 September 1860). The fact that Walker was a US citizen bothered Central American nationalists much less than the support, both overt and unofficial, which he received from the Pierce and Buchanan administrations in Washington.

The US again became involved in Nicaragua in the early 1900s, leading to extended US intervention (1912–25). These events were generally contemporaneous with US involvement in the Mexican Revolution (1912–20), the 'liberation' of Panama (1903), the occupations of Haiti (1915–33) and the Dominican Republic (1916–24), and intervention in Cuba (1906–9). Although the causes of these interventions have long since disappeared, many Central Americans have long memories of the actions and resentment is still high.

It is worth mentioning that neither the traditional elite nor the Marxist revolutionaries really have had the interests of the common people, especially the peasant farmers, at heart. To demonstrate this, one need only consider the methods of recruitment traditionally employed by both government and guerrilla military forces in the region. On paper, the armed forces of Guatemala, El Salvador, Honduras and Nicaragua were all manned through selective service. A certain portion of able-bodied males reaching a given age (usually eighteen or nineteen) were drafted into the army for a period of two to three years. In practice, this has occurred recently only in Nicaragua, where it was monumentally unpopular under the Sandinista regime and caused widespread passive resistance, and contributed in no small measure to bringing recruits to the ranks of the Contra guerrillas. The armies of El Salvador, Guatemala and Honduras relied on what amounted to press-gangs. Detachments of troops swept the towns and countryside, picking up any teenage boys or young men they happened to encounter and forcibly drafting them into the army. Those with influential or wealthy parents or relatives were usually rescued from such involuntary service, but poorer youths had little choice.

Similar practices provided the rank-and-file fighters of guerrilla forces, although their 'press gangs' necessarily operated on a smaller scale. This accounted for the curious phenomenon that in countries where the age of liability for military service is eighteen or nineteen, the average infantryman (or guerrilla) was usually two or three years younger. The youthful character of the Sandinista forces which drove Somoza out of Nicaragua in 1979 caused many Nicaraguans to refer to them as 'los muchachos' (the boys), but those Sandinista guerrillas were in fact older than most soldiers and guerrillas fighting in the region in the 1980s and early 1990s.

Finally, it is important to remember that – with a few relatively minor exceptions – the Central American nations had not fought each other. The skirmishing of the late 1980s between Nicaragua and Honduras was caused when Nicaraguan forces hotly pursued fleeing Contra guerrillas into Honduran territory, and the 'Soccer War' (24–28 June 1969) grew out of a long-festering border dispute, exacerbated by economic differences and an emotionally charged soccer rivalry. The first instance of formal conventional conflict between states in the region dates to 1885, when Guatemalan President Justo Rufino Barrios, allied with Honduras, made war against an alliance of Costa Rica, Nicaragua and El Salvador. This was an effort to unify Central America, and ended with Barrios' defeat and death at the Battle of Chalchuapa in El Salvador on 2 April 1885. The second interstate conflict was the Honduran–Nicaraguan War of February to December 1907, which ended when a Nicaraguan army occupied Tegucigalpa. The immediate cause was a set of border disputes, but the war also involved the successful effort by Nicaraguan Liberal strongman José Santos Zelaya to place his candidate, Miguel Davila, into office as president of Honduras.

The wars of 1885, 1907 and 1969 were anomalous, and each clearly represented an unusual condition of Central American international relations. Nonetheless, the potential for a regional war in Central America has ever been present. The imbalance of military power between Nicaragua on one hand and the other countries of the region on the other between 1980 and 1993 only strengthened the potential for war.

WAR-MAKING POTENTIAL

The defence forces of El Salvador, Honduras and Guatemala were organised along similar patterns. In each case the army was the dominant service, with the lion's share of equipment and manpower. The naval forces were little more than armed coastguards, but the air forces have usually possessed a few more or less modern combat aircraft, supported by helicopters (some armed), counter-insurgency aircraft and transport planes. The army equipment in each of these three countries was limited and generally light. What tanks they possessed dated from the 1940s or 1950s, and the rest of their armoured forces were composed of armoured cars and armoured personnel carriers, both of various nationalities and vintages. Their artillery consisted of towed 75 mm and 105 mm howitzers, with 82 mm, 107 mm and 120 mm mortars for infantry support. Their anti-tank weapons were older, generally US, rocket launchers and recoilless rifles, and their air defence weapons were 20 mm and 40 mm autocannon, some self-propelled, but without sophisticated radar or guidance systems.

Guatemala's army contained 41,000 officers and men, organised into three infantry brigades of two battalions each, thirty-six independent infantry battalions, five security battalions, two reserve counter-insurgency (COIN) battalions, and an engineer battalion. The army had 10 M-41A3 light tanks from the 1950s, 20 armoured cars and 34 armoured personnel carriers. There were also some 68 artillery pieces and 75 mortars. The air force contained 1,300 personnel, with 17 COIN aircraft (A-37B and PC-7) and 10 armed helicopters.

El Salvador's army was of similar size, totalling 40,000 personnel. It was organised into six infantry brigades comprising thirty-two infantry battalions, supported by a four-battalion artillery brigade, a two-battalion armoured cavalry regiment, an engineer battalion, five large (and US-trained) rapid-action counter-insurgency battalions, and a battalion each of airborne and air defence troops, both manned by the air force. The army had 5 World War II-era M-3A1 light tanks in store, 12 AML-90 armoured cars, some 96 APCs, 54 towed 105 mm howitzers and 360 mortars. The air force had 2,400 personnel; of its 8 Ourgon jet fighters, only one was generally operational, although most of the 28 COIN aircraft and 15 armed COIN helicopters were functioning.

Honduras' army, the smallest of the three, numbered only 15,000 personnel. It was organised into four brigades, comprising twelve infantry battalions and one cavalry regiment, with three artillery battalions, supported by an artillery regiment and one battalion each of special forces, engineers and air defence artillery. Major items of equipment were 12 British Scorpion light tanks, with 88 reconnaissance vehicles (mostly British), 24 105 mm and 4 M-198 155 mm howitzers, and 400 60 mm and 81 mm, 60 120 mm, and 30 Israeli Soltam 160 mm mortars. The 2,100-man air force operated 12 F-5 and 8 Super Mystere jet fighters, plus 13 A-37B Dragonfly ground attack aircraft and 39 helicopters.

The armed forces of Nicaragua contrasted sharply with those of Guatemala, Honduras and El Salvador. First they were larger, even with the reductions managed by the Chamorro government, totalling some 51,000 active duty personnel with over twice again that many trained and organised reserve and militia forces. Second, their officer corps was politically indoctrinated; all Sandinista officers were given extensive political training, and this was passed on to the rank and file, especially in the elite units. Third, and perhaps most important, the army was well equipped, with contributions from the USSR and Cuba, ostensibly for combat against an invasion by the United States.

The Nicaraguan Army totalled about 44,500 officers and men, divided among 18,500 long-service volunteer professionals, 10,500 conscripts, and 15,500 recalled reservists and militiamen. There was a total of 70,000 reserves, about 9,000 of them being on active duty, and 48,000 militia, with about 6,500 on active duty. The 29,000-man active army was organised into two armoured brigades, each of two tank and two mechanised infantry battalions; two motorised infantry brigades, each with three motorised infantry and one tank battalions; an artillery brigade with one rocket launcher group and three 152 mm howitzer groups; eight regional artillery groups, nine infantry battalions and three engineer battalions. Reserve forces were organised into twenty brigades containing one hundred and ten battalions. The militia contained eight brigades with thirty-four battalions, with twenty-four independent infantry and twelve COIN battalions, and twenty-three territorial defence companies.

This impressive array of units was equipped with 130 ageing T-54 and T-55 main battle tanks, 27 PT-76 amphibious light tanks, 102 BRDM-2 armoured cars, 19 BTR-60 and 120 BTR-152 APCs, 36 D-30 122 mm and 60 D-20 152 mm towed howitzers, and 35 BM-21 40-barrel truck-mounted 122 mm multiple rocket launchers. Additional firepower came from some 625 82 mm and 42 M-43 120 mm mortars. Anti-tank weapons included AT-3 Sagger missiles (12 of these on BRDM-2 armoured cars), 354 ZIS-2 World War II-vintage 57 mm guns, 84 ZIS-3 76 mm guns, and 24 M-1944 (BS-3) 100 mm guns. There were also at least 500 SA-7, SA-14 and SA-16 shoulder-launched (manpack) surface-to-air missiles. Most recently acquired were 40 ZSU-23-4 self-propelled anti-aircraft guns, with a four-unit battery assigned to each armoured or motorised brigade, and with several additional batteries available as army-level assets.

The Nicaraguan Navy comprised some 3,500 personnel, manning 22 patrol combatants (mostly older Soviet and Chinese fast inshore patrol craft), and 8 Soviet-built inshore minesweepers.

The Nicaraguan Air Force, in contrast to the army's equipment, possessed modest resources. It consisted of 3,000 officers and men. The COIN squadron operated 6 Cessna and 4 Italian light aircraft, and 6 Czech L-372C aircraft. There were also 7 Mi-25 Hind attack helicopters. Additional aircraft included 17 L-39C trainers, 6 An-26 and 2 Spanish C-212 Aviocar transport planes, 7 Mi-8 Hip and 30 Mi-17 medium transport helicopters, an assortment of 19 Soviet, Beechcraft and Cessna liaison planes, with 4 Mi-2 and 2 SA-316 liaison helicopters. In late 1992 and early 1993, the Nicaraguan Air Force took advantage of disarmament in Eastern Europe to acquire 24 MiG-21 fighters (in two squadrons) and 15 Su-7 ground attack aircraft (in one squadron). While clearly obsolescent if not obsolete, such jet combat aircraft represented a significant increase in air combat capability in the Central American environment.

POLITICAL DEVELOPMENTS LEADING TO WAR

The difficulties faced by the Chamorro government, and its inability to manage an effective economic development policy, contributed to a gradual decline in popular support during late 1991 and early 1992. This trend was exacerbated by some limited success by right-wing parties in parliamentary by-elections during the same period, increasing popular doubt that the new government could (or would) protect the hard-won and popular Sandinista social reforms. Several Sandinista-dominated labour unions and agricultural co-operatives staged large-scale demonstrations against the government in summer and autumn 1992, and with the security forces still controlled by the opposition, the government could do little to maintain order. Unrest spread, exacerbated by agitation (and some small-scale guerrilla activity) on the part of Contra veterans. Despite desperate government appeals for calm and patience, matters had reached a critical point by late November. On 4 December, the Sandinistas staged a bloodless coup, occupying government offices, temporarily dismissing the legislature and imposing martial law.

Since most of the disorder was a result of Sandinista activities, the new government was able to restore order within a few days. They took care to arrest no one (except for a few looters and a handful of former Contras rash enough to try and resist the coup by force), and guaranteed the preservation of civil rights, in an effort to soothe their understandably uneasy neighbours. Despite these assurances many Nicaraguans fled abroad, although former president Chamorro herself remained in Managua. The US expressed its concern over the disruption of the electoral process, and the UN Security Council voiced similar reservations, but no one took any action. As long as the Sandinistas held to their promises, and made no hostile moves against their neighbours, the US government expected little if any support from Latin America (or anywhere else) for open opposition to the new regime in Managua.

The Sandinista junta maintained a comparatively low profile for several months, but the FMLN uprising of February–March 1993 in El Salvador added a new complication to the situation. Although government forces were able to prevent the guerrilla forces from retaining any territory, the attacks in the city of San Salvador itself shook the government, and boosted the FMLN's prestige. In the wake of that qualified success, the FMLN appealed to the Sandinista junta for assistance, because the resurgent FMLN was able to secure new weapons and equipment only by capturing government materiel, or through risky small-scale smuggling operations through Honduras.

The Sandinista junta, especially the Ortega brothers, concluded that the FMLN had presented them with a golden opportunity to create the regional revolution in Central America which many of them desired. A Nicaraguan offensive into Honduras, with the twin goals of toppling the pro-US government there, and establishing a land supply link with the FMLN in El Salvador, would be the most direct way to achieve that goal. It was risky, but played upon definite Sandinista military strengths. Were such an attack successful it would demonstrate US weakness, and would be a triumph for the revolutionaries and for the struggle against US hegemony. If there was no American intervention, the defeat of their clients would be a serious blow. However, the clear military power of the US dampened their enthusiasm. It was one thing to defend Nicaragua against 'Yanqui' aggression; it was another matter entirely to invade a neighbouring country and thereby incur the wrath of the United States.

The Sandinistas agreed to aid the FMLN, but only if the international situation had drawn US attention – and US forces – elsewhere, and thereby limited the potential for major US intervention. Although the FMLN leadership was disappointed by the restrictions and the inevitable delay thus imposed, they understood the junta's reservations – having just been bested by superior firepower, much of it American-supplied – and agreed to create a contingency plan for another guerrilla offensive in El Salvador to coincide with the Sandinista offensive against Honduras.

MILITARY CONSIDERATIONS

The comparatively massive Nicaraguan mechanised and motorised forces (sixteen total battalions, with nearly 160 tanks and some 240 other armoured vehicles) gave the Nicaraguans a major capability for ground offensive operations. The Nicaraguans would not mount a major conventional offensive without maintaining a reserve, so they planned a main strike force to consist of two armoured brigades and one motorised brigade, all nine regular infantry battalions (organised in three brigades), two engineer battalions, the artillery brigade and four regional artillery groups, supported by four brigades of recalled reservists and militia. The second motorised brigade and remaining four artillery groups, along with most of the reserve and militia units, would be deployed within Nicaragua for internal security and defence duties, or along the rugged and less hospitable portions of the Nicaragua–Honduras frontier to distract Honduras' much smaller forces.

The main limiting factor in these considerations, from the Nicaraguan point of view, was the matter of logistics. Nicaragua possessed virtually no defence industry, and would have to stockpile ahead of time the resources needed for war. This was especially true for items like spare parts, heavy weapons ammunition and fuel, which were scarce enough in Nicaragua under peacetime conditions. Moreover, merely having the necessary resources inside the country was only half the struggle. Supplies had to be moved near the theatre of operations and then distributed to the troops. Necessary logistical preparations, coupled with the call-up of reservists and the large-scale deployment of forces to the border region, would telegraph Nicaraguan plans, unless these preparations were carried out over a long period. To try and conceal some of these preparations, they mounted a major concealment and camouflage effort, which was largely successful.

To help provide further cover for their preparations, and to provide a reasonable justification for some preparations which they made no effort to conceal, the Sandinistas provoked several small border clashes with the Hondurans. Ostensibly these were instances of Sandinista forces in 'hot pursuit' of small Contra forces, which had been operating inside Nicaragua. These clashes, and the continuing very real low-level Contra insurgency, provided the justification for improving roads along the Honduran border, increasing militia and reservist training, and moving six regular infantry battalions into the border area. These activities, in addition to contributing to the preparations themselves, also helped to conceal those preparations. The Sandinista commanders appreciated that surprise for the attackers would be a crucial, but at best fleeting, advantage.

Another major concern which faced Nicaraguan planners was the potential for US intervention. While major US ground forces would not be able to reach the theatre of operations for several days, the ready brigade of the 82nd Airborne Division could be deployed by air within two days, and US airpower would have an immediate effect on operations. Even one US aircraft carrier air wing would effectively triple the number of fighter and ground-attack aircraft available to the defenders. The main area of operations was within 1,600 kilometres of southern Florida, and within 1,800 kilometres of southern Texas. Additionally, the Gulf Coast from New Orleans to Tampa was less than 2,000 kilometres distant. This was within range of F-111s, and B-52G and B-52H aircraft could reach the battle area easily, even from bases in the northern states. A relatively modest allocation of combat aircraft would have a tremendous effect on the battlefield. Further, any logistical difficulties suffered by the Nicaraguans would be multiplied when their lines of supply and communications came under air attack.

To help offset US air power the Nicaraguans appealed to their Cuban allies. Although the Castro government had made some moves toward mutual conciliation with the United States, Cuba agreed to provide covert technical assistance to the Sandinistas. In addition to some technical troops, the Cubans provided 12 tracked SA-6 launchers and 24 SA-9 launchers, with re-loads for each system. These weapons were shipped from Cuba, then replaced with new units from former Soviet stocks long stored in Cuba. The weapons were partially disassembled before shipment to conceal the activity. The Cubans also openly replaced the old Nicaraguan SA-7s with newer SA-14s and SA-16s, and sent a few pilots and technical personnel to train Nicaraguan pilots and support staff for the newly acquired combat jets.

The covertly acquired SA-9s were joined with the publicly acquired ZSU-23-4 self-propelled AA guns in air defence units, with four of each system, to give the motorised and armoured brigades an air defence capability comparable with that of Soviet tank or motorised rifle regiments of the late 1970s or early 1980s. Two further groups of four SA-9s and ZSU-23-4s each were kept to provide air defence for two infantry brigades, but were retained under army control. The SA-6s, together with the remaining 16 ZSU-23-4s (for close-in defence), would provide air defence to the entire attacking force.

Sandinista military preparations were largely complete by early spring 1994. They then had only to wait for some crisis to distract the United States so that they could launch their invasion. The American intelligence community knew that the Sandinistas were planning something, but wasn't sure what it was. However, the American intelligence agencies alerted their Honduran allies, who began to erect some prepared defence around Choluteca, resurrecting measures they had taken ten years earlier. After late May, the Korean crisis occupied a high priority, and US vigilance and attention waned. This was just the opportunity for which the Sandinistas had been waiting.

GEOGRAPHY AND ENVIRONMENT

The Pacific lowlands of Honduras are the only area on the Honduran–Nicaraguan frontier where large mechanised forces can operate easily, as it is relatively flat and traversed by several good roads. The main road, part of the Pan-American Highway, leads south-west out of the Nicaraguan highlands through the town of Somoto and into the Honduran town of Choluteca, where it meets a secondary road coming north from Leon through Somotillo. From Choluteca, the main highway runs west-north-west to Nacamome, where the route splits. One branch heads north to Tegucigalpa, and the other west into eastern El Salvador and the port of La Union. These roads provide ready access to either Tegucigalpa and the highland core area of Honduras, or to eastern El Salvador. The only limiting condition is that the Choluteca plain contains some marshy areas along the Gulf of Fonseca, and several rivers traversing the plain from north to south are also significant, but scarcely insuperable, obstacles to military operations.

The Pacific coast of Central America has a tropical climate with consistently high temperatures year round. There is also a pronounced summer rainy season, with over three-quarters of the annual precipitation falling between May and October. Although mechanised movement would be somewhat impaired during the rainy season, both by mud and by high stream levels, the Sandinista command judged that the loss in mobility was an acceptable price to pay for cloud cover and bad weather, both of which would limit American airpower and hopefully would also slow the arrival of American ground forces.

THE WAR

The Sandinistas and FMLN had laid their plans in the expectation that they would have to move within a few days of making their decision to act, in order to take advantage of some fleeting American preoccupation with events in another part of the globe. As it happened, the crisis in Korea, and the ensuing Second Korean War (14 July–2 September 1994), arose over a period of weeks, and so gave the Sandinistas, and the FMLN in particular, time to prepare. On 24 July, eleven days after North Korea had launched its invasion of South Korea, the FMLN opened another major offensive in El Salvador.

Unlike previous FMLN operations, this one was undertaken in concert with external forces. The FMLN paid particular attention to airfields, bridges and the port of La Union on the north shore of the Gulf of Fonseca. The United States, preoccupied with the situation in Korea, gave little heed to events in Central America. Taking heart from American inattention, President Daniel Ortega Saavedra and the Sandinista junta decided to launch their offensive on 1 August 1994. Tables 7.1 and 7.2 show the order of battle and Table 7.3 compares the forces.

TABLE 7.1

NICARAGUA: ORDER OF BATTLE

NICARAGUAN FORCES: (Major General Luis Alvarez Peñon)
Main Force (Major General Luis Alvarez Peñon)
    1st Armoured Brigade
    3rd Motorised Brigade
    2nd Infantry Brigade
    3rd, 6th, 7th and 11th Reserve Brigades
    4th Militia Brigade
    Army Air Defence Group
    Artillery Brigade
San Marcos Column (Colonel Hector Ruiz)
    2nd Armoured Brigade
    3rd and 5th Infantry Brigades
    2nd Independent Air Defence Group
    2 artillery groups

The conflict began with three closely related Nicaraguan operations. The main column under Major General Luis Alvarez Peñon, with the 1st Armoured and the 3rd Motorised Brigades, attacked from Somotillo through El Triunfo toward Choluteca, swiftly brushing aside the Honduran National Police and Army border guard detachments and advancing rapidly along the highway. Colonel José Gonzalez Castro's 7th Reserve Brigade followed behind. The 2nd Armoured and 3rd Infantry Brigades, under Colonel Hector Ruiz, crossed the border near

TABLE 7.2

US AND ALLIED FORCES: ORDER OF BATTLE

HONDURAS: Brigadier General Manuel Diaz Ordoñez
  2nd Infantry Brigade (3 infantry, 1 artillery batallion, 1 armoured cavalry regiment)

EL SALVADOR: Brigadier General Jorgé Serrano Colón
  5th Infantry Brigade (2 infantry, 1 armoured cavalry, 1 artillery battalions)

UNITED STATES: Colonel Henry M. Talmadge, USA
  1st Brigade, 7th Light Infantry Division (2 infantry and 1 artillery battalions, 2 AH-64 troops)
Atlantic Fleet MEU **(Lieutenant Colonel Joseph Marino, USMC)** (1 reinforced infantry battalion)

TABLE 7.3

COMPARISON OF COMBAT FORCES

ARMY	Allies	Nicaraguans
Manpower	11,600	30,780
MBTs*	19	118
IFVs	6	–
ACs	90	42
APCs	61	76
Artillery pieces†	54	90
MRLs	–	30
AIR FORCE		
Combat aircraft	163	49
Armed helicopters	26	19
AIR DEFENCE		
AAA guns	34	36
SAMs‡	32	77

  Figures are approximate.
  * Includes PT-76 light tanks for Nicaraguans, and Scimitar and Scorpion light tanks for Hondurans.
  † Includes heavy mortars (120 mm).
  ‡ Includes manpack shoulder-launched weapons.

San Marcos de Cólon, following the secondary highway from Somoto, and also heading for Choluteca. Between these two thrusts, the 2nd and 5th Infantry Brigades crossed the frontier on a broader front, with the 11th Reserve Brigade following behind. On the northern flank of the Somoto attack, the 3rd Reserve Brigade crossed the border to provide flank and rear-area security for the northern mechanised column, and along the coast the 6th Reserve Brigade skirted the coastal marshes and aimed to pass south of El Triunfo before reaching the southern approaches to Choluteca. Finally, the 4th Militia Brigade remained in reserve just inside Nicaragua.

The invaders met no serious resistance until they encountered Lieutenant Colonel Alejandro Martinez's battalion of the 2nd Honduran Brigade, as the highway crossed the ridge west-north-west of El Triunfo. The quantity and quality of Lieutenant Colonel Martinez's anti-tank weapons were a rude shock to Major General Alvarez and his subordinates, but they pressed on despite losses and some confusion; few of them had any experience in mechanised operations above company level. The defenders were forced to fall back, as their flanks were soon threatened and they were wary of other approaching columns. The Honduran Air Force intervened as the Honduran battalion withdrew, but the SA-6s, SA-9s, ZSU-23-4s and hand-held SA-14s of the mechanised columns inflicted heavy losses on the attacking aircraft. By nightfall, the 1st Armoured and 3rd Mechanised Brigades had pushed some thirty kilometres into Honduras, and their supporting infantry was close behind on either flank.

Meanwhile, Colonel Ruiz's northern mechanised column, with the 2nd Armoured and 3rd Infantry Brigades, had a rougher time. The road through San Marcos de Cólon was difficult, and there was little room for manoeuvre off the road. Ruiz's progress was further hampered by a company of Honduran infantry, who had to be laboriously prised out of each successive delaying position. By day's end the 2nd Armoured and 3rd Infantry Brigades had advanced barely ten kilometres, but the Hondurans had been driven off by infantry of Colonel Hernandez's 2nd Brigade advancing cross-country over forested mountains.

The Sandinista troops continued to probe during the night, and determined that the Hondurans had broken contact and pulled back toward Choluteca. Under cover of darkness, the Sandinistas resupplied their advance units and evacuated wounded and injured personnel. At dawn on 2 August, they resumed their advance and pressed on toward Choluteca. The converging roads compelled an anticipated redeployment to avoid congestion. Colonel Hernandez's infantry brigade crossed the San Marcos road to circle around Choluteca from the north, and advanced down the east bank of the Choluteca River, but only reached the river by nightfall. Meanwhile, the 5th Infantry Brigade crossed the El Triunfo road to approach Choluteca from the south, and kept pace with the El Triunfo column as it neared Choluteca. Colonel Ruiz's column on the San Marcos road (2nd Armoured and 3rd Infantry Brigades) was still behind schedule, and as night fell on 2 August it was descending from the highlands some twenty kilometres north-east of Choluteca.

Although the second day generally was as successful as the first, the Sandinistas gained some ominous indications of US intervention. One ground attack mission by A-10 Warthogs, escorted by F-16s, destroyed or crippled 5 tanks and 3 APCs along the El Triunfo road, and the much-vaunted shoulder-launched SA-14s and SA-16s were not very effective against US tactics and countermeasures. Two attacking aircraft, however, fell to the heavier SA-9s, and attacks later in the day were less effective as the pilots worked to avoid the SAMs. However, the high command in Managua had intelligence that the USS *Forrestal* carrier battle-group would arrive offshore within twenty-four hours, that a brigade of the 7th Light Infantry Division was arriving by air in Tegucigalpa during the late afternoon, and that the Atlantic Fleet's Marine Expeditionary Unit (MEU) was transitting the Panama Canal. Unknown to the Sandinista or FMLN command, Brigadier General Jorge Serrano Colón's 5th Brigade of the El Salvadoran army was preparing to move on Choluteca, with the Armoured Cavalry Regiment in the lead.

August 3 began less satisfactorily for the Sandinistas, as a pre-dawn strike by US FB-111 fighter-bombers, attacking from high altitude to avoid SA-6 fire, severely damaged the air defence radar complex at Masaya, near Managua. The temporary loss of Masaya, which was out of action for over a week, gravely weakened the Nicaraguan Air Force. Numerous strategic sites inside Nicaragua were subject to US air attack in ensuing days, mostly by aircraft from the *Forrestal*. Equally damaging was the conventional air attack delivered against the San Marcos road column at first light by B-52s, again flying at high altitude to avoid SAMs. The tank battalions of Colonel Ruiz's column were badly shaken up, and many soft-skinned vehicles were damaged or destroyed, and over two dozen tanks and APCs were lost. This delayed the column for nearly a day. The side-effects of this air strike postponed the first attack on Choluteca until early afternoon on 3 August.

The Sandinistas committed most of five brigades to the assault on Choluteca: 1st Armoured, 3rd Motorised, 2nd and 5th Infantry, and three battalions of Colonel Gonzalez's 7th Reserve. Their air force had suffered heavy losses, and so was able to manage only six Su-7 sorties early in the afternoon. The defenders included most of Brigadier General Manuel Diaz Ordoñez's 2nd Honduran brigade, less about two companies (losses and detachments); one battalion of the 1st Brigade, US 7th Light Infantry Division (the others were still en route), with a battery of 6 M-102 105 mm howitzers and two attack helicopter troops with 14 AH-64 Apaches and 8 OH-58 Kiowas. Lieutenant Colonel Joseph Marino's MEU, which had begun landing at La Union just after dawn on 3 August, was slowed by FMLN attacks and its lead elements had just crossed into Honduras that evening.

Despite modest ground forces, the US–allied forces had extensive air support, including 8 AV-8B Harriers and 4 Marine AH-1W helicopters, 12 F/A-18As from the *Forrestal*, and 10 A-10s, 10 FB-111s, and extensive fighter cover from F-16s and F-15s. It was the air support that won the day. Even with their impressive air defence capability, the Sandinista attackers were hard-pressed to protect their ground forces from air attack. The A-10s, flying so low they nearly brushed the treetops in order to avoid detection by the SAMs, accounted for more than 20 tanks and armoured vehicles. Still, despite countermeasures, tactics and undisputed pilot skill, the US lost 2 aircraft and 3 helicopters in the afternoon's battle.

The Sandinistas, their command structure battered by aerial bombardment, and unused to the stresses and strains of high-intensity mechanised combat, gained a few precarious toeholds in the outskirts of Choluteca, but only at considerable cost. By nightfall, they had control of nearly half the city, and Major General Alvarez and his unit commanders believed they had nearly broken the defenders. However, their tank and AFV forces had suffered heavily, and the continuing presence of US aircraft through the night hampered their efforts to regroup their battered, weary and shaken units and recover their damaged equipment. To add to their woes, by early evening the leading elements of Brigadier General Serrano's 5th El Salvadoran Infantry Brigade and the attached Armoured Cavalry Regiment began to arrive, hastening up the road from La Union through Nacaome: one of the armoured cavalry battalions, two infantry battalions and an artillery battalion. Lieutenant Colonel Marino's Marines had also finally got free of the morass around La Union and were also nearing the battlefield, close on the heels of 5th El Salvadoran Brigade.

Dawn on 4 August found the Sandinistas – now on the defensive – under attack by growing numbers of allied troops. The Marines, weary but eager for action, attacked from the west, with an infantry battalion supported by a battery of towed 155 mm howitzers and a platoon of 5

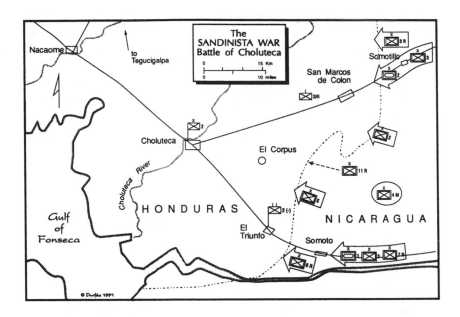

M-1 tanks. Two battalions of Colonel Henry M. Talmadge's 1st Brigade, 7th Division, struck against the northern shoulder of the battle-line, and more troops of the 1st Brigade were arriving, funnelled by air through Tegucigalpa. The Sandinista armoured forces, although still capable of action, were suffering from fatigue, and over half of their air defence systems were out of action. Further, their infantry forces were fatigued and weakened by losses. Shortly after midday a combined counterattack, with Marine and El Salvadoran forces striking from the west and Talmadge's 7th Division troops attacking from the north, slammed into the Sandinista forces in Choluteca. Reeling from the onslaught and hammered by air attacks, the Sandinistas were driven back several kilometres in considerable disorder. Although they were still some forty to fifty kilometres inside Honduras, the tide of battle had clearly turned against them.

CEASE-FIRE

By mid-morning of 5 August, the government of Nicaragua agreed to accept a cease-fire under the terms of the joint OAS–UN resolution and to withdraw its troops from Honduras. The Sandinista regime had suffered a serious reverse. The war had been undertaken without gaining public support, and many Nicaraguans, even those usually faithful to the revolution, thought attacking a neighbouring country was dangerous and ill-advised as a matter of principle, and that it was foolhardy because of the near-certainty of US intervention. Demonstrations in Managua between 6 and 14 August compelled President Ortega and the junta to resign, and a provisional government took office, promising elections within six months.

The crisis had ended, except for the necessary business of cleaning up. Nicaragua had lost much of its offensive punch: its air force was virtually destroyed, as were over 40 per cent of its tanks and AFVs, along with much of the artillery. Perhaps more serious, nearly 60 per cent of the air defence systems were destroyed or disabled, and the few remaining SAM launchers had only a few missiles each available for use.

ASSESSMENT

As the Duke of Wellington said after the Battle of Waterloo, 'This was a damned close-run thing.' A delay of US intervention by as little as twelve hours, or a few more hits on the attacking aircraft, would have been disastrous for the Hondurans. Brigadier General Diaz's 2nd Brigade would have been wholly incapable of holding Choluteca alone against a determined Sandinista assault. It is worth remembering, when considering this campaign and its results, that the forces of the Nicaraguan regular army (without counting any reserve or militia units) attacking into the Choluteca plain outnumbered the *entire* Honduran army by nearly two to one; the 2nd Brigade, with the armoured cavalry regiment, was outnumbered by about four to one overall. It is also worth remembering that the Nicaraguan Army had considerable combat experience in actions up to battalion level, and many of its officers, NCOs and enlisted men were veterans. This experience applied not only to the regular army, but also to both the militia and the reserves.

Yet in retrospect it is difficult to see what the Sandinistas expected to gain from their invasion of Honduras. Even had there been no US intervention, and even if the invasion had been successful, the survival of the Sandinista dictatorship depended upon public support. Even had the Sandinistas gained a victory, and then installed sympathetic regimes in Honduras and El Salvador, there was no guarantee that such a regional political arrangement would be any more satisfactory to the people of Nicaragua than was the prewar situation.

Moreover, regardless whether the Nicaraguan invasion succeeded or was defeated, the basic social and economic problems in the region would remain. The Chamorro government, despite earnest efforts and considerable support from the US, had been unable to restore the Nicaraguan economy to real working order in 1990–2. Similarly, the socioeconomic ills affecting Guatemala, Honduras and El Salvador were bound to continue. The Sandinista débâcle did not cause the collapse of either the FMLN in El Salvador or the URNG guerrilla coalition in Guatemala, although both were weakened. Neither has the Sandinista defeat apparently encouraged these other guerrilla groups to enter the political process, and work with the government to bring peace and prosperity.

Sad to say, the defeat of the Sandinista Nicaraguan invasion of Honduras did not really change the situation in Central America, although the long-term removal of the FSLN from Nicaraguan politics was certainly welcomed in the US. The problems could not, and cannot, be solved by so swift and simple a method as war.

Table 7.4 set out the human cost of the war.

TABLE 7.4

HUMAN COST OF THE WAR

Nation	Killed	Wounded	Total casualties
Honduras	96	301	397
US	52	232	284
El Salvador	28	85	113
Nicaragua	373	918	1,291

The comparatively low incidence of killed to wounded for US forces was attributable largely to the widespread use of lightweight modern body armour by US personnel. The higher proportion of Nicaraguan battle deaths in relation to total casualties was due to losses suffered during aerial bombardment, which has historically inflicted a high rate of fatalities, and to inefficient medical support.

TNDM ADDENDUM: THE BATTLE OF CHOLUTECA

The battle of Choluteca, the only major battle of the war, involved three main actions. The first of these was the Nicaraguan assault on 3 August. The assaulting forces, commanded by Major General Alvarez, included the 1st Armoured and 3rd Motorised Brigade, the 2nd and 5th Infantry Brigades, and three of the five battalions of the 7th Reserve Brigade. Supporting this effort was the Artillery Brigade and most of the Army Air Defence Group. The Nicaraguan attack began just before dawn, but despite their great superiority in tanks and artillery they made little headway. By afternoon they had secured only a few toeholds on the outskirts of Choluteca, and had suffered heavy casualties, including over 40 armoured vehicles. The defenders, including the remainder of the 2nd Honduran Brigade and the lead battalion of 1st Brigade, 7th US Light Infantry Division, had easily contained the attackers, supported by A-10s, Marine AV-8Bs, and Navy F/A-18s from the USS *Forrestal.*

Another factor contributing to the Nicaraguan repulse was the damage inflicted on Colonel Ruiz's column on the San Marcos Road by the pre-dawn B-52 attack. The 2nd Armoured and 3rd Infantry Brigades between them lost some eight tanks, twelve other armoured vehicles, six artillery pieces, nearly two dozen soft-skinned vehicles and about 250 personnel casualties. It took Ruiz and his subordinates most of the daylight hours to sort out the confusion, reorganise and resume the advance. This delay proved crucial, and prevented Alvarez from renewing his attack the following day (4 August).

The arrival of the rest of the 1st Brigade, 7th Division, along with Lieutenant Colonel Marino's Atlantic Fleet MEU and elements of Brigadier General Serrano's 5th El Salvadoran Infantry Brigade, allowed the allied commanders to take the initiative. Colonel Talmadge slipped one of his battalions across the San Marcos Road, backed up by one of Serrano's infantry battalions and a troop of AH-64s. This force effectively blocked Ruiz's battered column from coming to the relief of Alvarez, although the US infantrymen were hard pressed on several occasions during the day.

Meanwhile, with the marines striking from the south and the remainder of Talmadge's brigade attacking from the west, the allied troops drove the Nicaraguans back nearly a kilometre. Again, the allied success was ensured by US air support and the combat power of Army and Marine attack helicopters, but the Marines' LAVs and M-1 tanks also were a significant factor. The two wings of the allied attack each advanced about two kilometres, driving the Nicaraguans out of their toeholds in Choluteca. By the evening of 4 August, Alvarez and Ruiz concluded that they could make no headway against the allied forces in front of Choluteca, and on the morning of 5 August Alvarez began to withdraw his forces.

TABLE TNDM 7.1

TNDM STATISTICS: BATTLE OF CHOLUTECA

NICARAGUA	Strength	Losses	Daily losses (%)
Men	11,600	861	3.71
Armour	93	39	20.97
Artillery	84	1	0.59
Fixed-wing aircraft*	6	0	0.00
US/ALLIED			
Men	8,700	524	3.01†
Armour	116	50	26.38
Artillery	52	0	0.00
Helicopters	26	5	9.62
Fixed-wing aircraft	31	2	3.23

* One day only.

† About one-third of the allied losses in men and about half the armour losses occurred on the first day, when the allied total strength was 4,050 men and about 60 armoured vehicles. Thus the allied casualty rate on the first day was about 4.5 per cent, and the tank loss rate about 24.4 per cent.

CHAPTER EIGHT

THE WAR FOR TRANSYLVANIA

The departure of Soviet military forces, and hence of most Soviet power and influence, from East-Central Europe in 1990–1 removed the region's great peace-keeping force of the post-World War II period. The ethnic, national and religious rivalries that have long dominated the history of Eastern Europe, especially in the Balkans, did not disappear but were merely masked during the period of Soviet hegemony. As independence – along with internal rivalries – returned to Eastern Europe, it was often remarked that, as European statesmen and diplomats of the late nineteenth and early twentieth centuries were fond of saying, the Balkan region had again become 'the powder keg of Europe'. Hopes that creation of democratic institutions in East-Central European countries would impart stability and reduce the chances that revolution or resurgent nationalism would lead to armed conflict, were only partly realised.

BACKGROUND

East-Central Europe includes Poland, Hungary, Czechoslovakia, Romania, Yugoslavia, Albania, Bulgaria and Greece. However, although Greece lies within the area geographically, it has strong political and economic ties with Western Europe and suffers from few of the ethnic divisions which plague its northern neighbours. By 1993 just over 86 million people lived within the boundaries of the six nations lying between Greece and Poland, divided among over a dozen major (and many smaller) ethnic groups, including Bulgarians, Turks, Czechs, Slovaks, Germans, Hungarians, Albanians, Macedonians, Romanians, Serbs, Croats, Bosnians, Slovenes and Montenegrins. The distribution of ethnic groups was (and is) uneven. For instance, although Albania's population was 98 per cent Albanian (most of the remainder were Greek), over a third of all Albanians lived in Yugoslavia. Likewise, while

96.6 per cent of Hungary's people were ethnic Hungarians, and the remainder mostly Germans and Slovaks, some 1.9 million ethnic Hungarians, known as *Szeklers* – some 20 per cent of all ethnic Hungarians – lived in Romania. These sample figures were not merely statistics, they reflected serious and dangerous problems. The revolution which toppled Nicolae Ceausescu's dictatorship in Romania was sparked when security forces killed an ethnic Hungarian priest in Timisoara (or Temesvar), a centre of the *Szekler* community in Romania.

While Hungary and Albania contained largely homogeneous populations, with fewer than 4 per cent belonging to minority ethnic groups, this was a rarity in the region. Almost 15 per cent of Bulgaria's nearly 9 million people were non-Bulgarians, mostly Turks (765,000) with smaller numbers of Gypsies and Macedonians (whom the Bulgarian government believed were really Bulgarians). About 12 per cent of Romania's 23.6 million people were members of ethnic minorities; the largest group was the 1.9 million Hungarians, but there were 930,000 Bulgarians, Germans, Turks and others.

Czechoslovakia's ethnic composition was even more diverse. Nearly two out of three of its 15.8 million citizens were ethnic Czechs (9.86 million), and almost another third (just under 5 million) were Slovaks. But although only one Czechoslovak citizen in twenty was neither a Czech nor a Slovak, there were about 600,000 Hungarians, 80,000 Poles, 50,000 Germans and again as many Ukrainians and Russians, plus about 60,000 others.

Two major historical events were responsible for the modern ethnic and demographic structure of the Balkans. The first was the Slavic westward migration from the fifth to ninth centuries AD, which brought the Slavs from their original homeland in modern Russia west and south into what is now Czechoslovakia, Poland and the Balkans. Pre-Slavic populations survived in Romania, Greece and Albania, and in scattered pockets elsewhere. Soon after their arrival in western and southern Europe, the Slavs were divided by religion into two groups. The Poles, Czechs, Slovaks, Slovenes and Croats became Catholic; they also adopted the Latin alphabet and were generally orientated toward Germany and Western Europe. The other Slavs, notably the Bulgarians and Serbs, as well as the Russians, followed the Greek Orthodox Church, fell under Byzantine cultural influence and adopted the Cyrillic alphabet.

This division between Catholic–Latin Slavs and Orthodox–Cyrillic Slavs was intensified by the second great historical development: the Ottoman Turkish conquest of the Balkans between 1350 and 1560. Greece, Bulgaria, Albania and most of Yugoslavia were conquered by the Ottomans. Romania also fell under Ottoman suzerainty, but the

Turkish hold there was less secure than elsewhere in the Balkans. The Turks also overran most of Hungary between 1525 and 1560, but were driven out by the Habsburgs in the late 1600s and early 1700s. The liberation of the rest of the Balkans from Ottoman Turkish rule did not occur until the nineteenth and twentieth centuries. During the centuries of Ottoman rule, some Slavs adopted Islam, and there are large communities of Muslims in Bosnia, Bulgaria and especially Albania. Further, as a matter of military security, the Turks settled colonies of farmer-soldiers in their Balkan realms, especially in northern Bulgaria and south-eastern Romania, where their descendants still identify themselves as Turks.

The legacy of Turkish domination was deep and lasting. Turkish rule in the Balkans began to ebb only after the Napoleonic Wars, Serbia winning autonomy in 1817 and Greece full independence a few years later, in 1832. The process was not completed until after European Turkey had been reduced to its present dimensions following the Second Balkan War in 1913. The centuries of Turkish domination had left most of the Balkans with no tradition of autonomy, with atrophied political and judicial institutions, and with considerable residual hostility toward the Turks, coupled with friendship toward whatever European nation had championed their cause in the process of gaining independence.

The conflict between Romania and Hungary is newer than the centuries-old rivalry between Serb and Croat in nearby Yugoslavia. Indeed, during their common struggle against the Turks, Hungary often provided aid to the princes of Wallachia (between the Danube and the Carpathians) and Moldavia (between the Carpathians and the River Prut). Such assistance, however, was often interrupted by disputes and conflict among the anti-Turkish rulers. The Hungarians were the first people of East-Central Europe to win freedom from Turkish rule. This was mainly the result of Austrian Habsburg military victories over the Turks in the late seventeenth and early eighteenth centuries, which added Hungary, Transylvania, Slovenia and most of Croatia to the Habsburg domains.

Romania, largely comprising the principalities of Wallachia and Moldavia, gained autonomy from the Ottomans in 1829. The principalities were allowed to unite in 1859 as part of the settlement of the Crimean War. Romania gained complete independence in 1878, and became a kingdom in 1881, following the Russo–Turkish War of 1877–8. The seeds of Romanian–Hungarian hostility grew during the late nineteenth and early twentieth centuries, as Hungarian treatment of the Romanian population of Transylvania was repressive and sometimes harsh. Despite this issue, Romania long retained friendly relations with Austria–

Hungary and Germany. However, heavy Allied pressure brought Romania into World War I on the Allied side in late August 1916. But then Central Powers forces, under German leadership, promptly inflicted a crushing defeat on Romania. Only Russian support allowed the Romanians to retain a foothold in Moldavia and to resist capitulation until the Great October Revolution (in November 1917) took Russia out of the war. Romania then had no choice but to accept harsh peace terms from the Central Powers (May 1918). However, it was delivered from those terms by the Allied victory six months later.

The defeat of Austria–Hungary allowed Romania to achieve its long-term goal of gaining Transylvania, viewed by many Romanians as the cradle of their national culture. The region had been the core homeland of the Dacian kingdom – conquered by the Roman Emperor Trajan (101–6) – which many Romanians held to be their predecessor. Not surprisingly, Hungary objected to the loss of Transylvania, not least because of the substantial Hungarian population living there. The Hungarian communist regime of Bela Kun twice resorted to military measures to restore Hungarian rule in Transylvania, but the ragged Hungarian forces were soundly beaten both times (March–May and July–August 1919). Romanian forces occupied Budapest (August to November 1919) but withdrew under Allied pressure, accepting the boundary established by the Treaties of Saint-Germain (1919) and the Trianon (1920).

Hungary resented the loss of Transylvania, and that is why the alliance with Germany which developed in the late 1930s enjoyed considerable popular support. As a result of the Russo–German non-aggression pact of September 1939, Romania was compelled to accept Soviet annexation of Bessarabia (the region between the Prut and Dniester rivers, gained in 1918), and later lost the north-eastern half of Transylvania to Germany's Hungarian ally. (This latter area would witness the bulk of the combat in the Transylvanian war of 1993.) Although Romania and Hungary avoided armed conflict during this period, this did not hold true for the later stages of World War II. After the coup of 23 August 1944, which deposed General Ion Antonescu and brought Romania into the war as a Soviet ally, Romanian troops fought under Soviet command against German and Hungarian forces in Hungary.

Hungary's long association with the Axis resulted in comparatively harsh peace terms at the end of World War II. The Treaty of Paris (February 1947) provided for restoration of the Trianon frontiers and limited the size of Hungarian armed forces. The treaty also left Hungary with Soviet occupation forces and $300 million in reparations.

The Hungarian–Romanian conflict, which lay hidden under Soviet domination for over forty years, again came into the open in the late 1980s. Hungary's communist regime, perhaps mindful of the unsuccessful 1956 revolution, had begun small-scale economic reform in the late 1960s and early 1970s. By the mid-1980s, Hungary's economy was the most free in East-Central Europe. Although consumer goods were in short supply and prices were high, their quality and availability were better than anywhere else in the Eastern Bloc. In fact, the economy of Hungary (like those of Czechoslovakia and Poland) experienced significant growth after 1991–2. Economic reforms were followed by political liberalisation, in 1989–90. Although the Hungarian Socialist Workers' Party abandoned its communist ideology in favour of democratic socialism in late 1989, it was unable to retain power in the April–May 1990 general elections, and a centre-right government took office that May.

As these internal reforms were progressing, the Hungarian people and government grew increasingly concerned with the situation in neighbouring Romania. President Ceausescu's massive rural resettlement programme of the late 1980s strained Romanian–Hungarian relations. Ceausescu's programme involved the destruction of old rural towns and villages, and the transfer of their inhabitants to new, specially built rural centres. This process met particular resistance from the *Szekler* (Hungarian) population of Transylvania, where many regarded it as an attempt to destroy their sense of community. Many Romanians of Hungarian descent fled to Hungary, as did much of the remaining German community in Romania, and the Hungarian government submitted formal complaints before several international forums. In August 1988 Hungarian Prime Minister Károly Grösz met Ceausescu at Arad in Romania, but this effort to resolve the conflict was unsuccessful.

The violent and bloody revolution which toppled the Ceausescu regime in late December 1989 ended the immediate conflict over treatment of the Hungarian minority in Romania. There were some signs of continuing Romanian hostility toward the *Szekler* population in Transylvania, as demonstrated by the large-scale riot in Tirgu Mures in March 1990, but there was no official Romanian policy directed against the Hungarian minority in Romania. Nevertheless, the subsequent failure to create a multi-party republican government in Romania placed much of the revolution's achievement in jeopardy. Subsequent renewed repression of the *Szeklers* fanned the glowing embers of Hungarian–Romanian hostility.

WAR-MAKING POTENTIAL OF HUNGARY

Like most of its neighbours, Hungary industrialised only in the late nineteenth and early twentieth centuries, some sixty years after the process had begun in Western Europe. By the early 1990s Hungary had developed a substantial industrial base. Its comparatively long recent exposure to elements of free enterprise had also made its industries relatively efficient. Further separating the Hungarian industrial sector from those of its neighbours was its unusual emphasis on consumer goods, including textiles, food processing and paper products. Other important industrial activities included the chemical and engineering industrial base. Hungary's domestic petroleum production, which provided some 23 per cent of domestic consumption in the late 1980s, proved particularly important in wartime.

Hungary did not produce any major weapons systems, but did build its own river patrol craft as well as its own armoured personnel carriers, the PSZH D-944, based on the Soviet BRDM reconnaissance vehicle. With the disappearance of the Warsaw Pact in 1990, Hungary's armed forces were no longer under any obligation to obtain weapons from the Eastern Bloc, and began to purchase equipment from other sources, including Austria, France and the US.

In mid-1993 Hungary's armed forces totalled 94,000 officers and men, including 50,500 conscripts, who served for eighteen months. The army contained 74,000 active duty personnel, with 125,000 reservists to man active units fully. It was organised into three corps, each with one tank brigade, four motorised rifle brigades and one artillery brigade, along with reconnaissance, air defence and engineer units. There was a fourth tank brigade at army level, plus a Scud and FROG-7 missile brigade, a fourth artillery brigade, an anti-tank brigade, a SAM-4 air defence battalion and an airborne battalion. Most units were 'Category B', manned at 50–75 per cent strength, and were brought to war establishment by reservists. The army also controlled the Danube flotilla, with six armed patrol vessels and several dozen small craft.

Most of the army's equipment was still of Soviet manufacture. As older weapons needed replacement, and especially as Hungary's fleet of over 1,200 T-54 and T-55M tanks reached obsolescence in the early 1990s, Hungary turned to Western European and American suppliers for new systems. The Hungarians, partly on the basis of their demonstrated economic achievements, won an agreement for licensed production of the French AMX-40 main battle tank, armed with a 120 mm gun and comparable or superior in strike power to the Soviet T-72.

The air force contained 22,000 officers and men, including 8,000 conscripts, with 9,400 reservists available. Its main strength consisted of 28 F-5 E/F, 24 F-16 A/B, and 10 MiG-23MF jet combat aircraft. The air force's 35 Mi-8 and Mi-17 transport helicopters could move over 800 combat troops in one lift, and there were three attack helicopter squadrons, with 12 Mi-8Fs and 40 Mi-24Ds.

WAR-MAKING POTENTIAL OF ROMANIA

Romania had emerged from World War II with a modest industrial base, which expanded greatly under the communist regime after 1947. The domestic oil industry, centred at Ploiesti and along the Black Sea coast, produced 34 per cent of the crude oil and 54 per cent of the natural gas consumed in Romania. Other important industries included metallurgy and machine-building, chemical production, and food and textile processing.

The traditional 'smokestack' industries enabled Ceausescu's Romania to create a significant defence industrial base. This development, which grew in part out of Ceausescu's desire to limit Soviet and Warsaw Pact influence, was aided by Western investment and licensed production agreements with some Western European industrial firms. Romania produced most of its own tanks, armoured vehicles and artillery, usually based on older Soviet designs; these included the TR-80 (a T-55 variant), TAB-77 (based on the BTR-70), TABC-79 and TAB-71. Romania also built most of its own naval vessels, ranging in size from patrol craft to destroyers. The Romanian aerospace enterprise CIAR built the Orao jet trainer/light strike fighter jointly with Yugoslavia's SOKO aircraft works, and a licensing agreement with Aerospatiale of France permitted construction of modified versions of the Alouette III and Puma helicopters (as the IAR-316 and IAR-330) by Romanian factories. CIAR also produced a few entirely Romanian light utility and training aircraft.

Romania's armed forces were organised along patterns similar to those of its former Warsaw Pact allies. There were 163,000 total active duty personnel in the armed forces, including 107,500 conscripts serving for a period of twelve months in the army and air force, or for two years in the navy. The army contained 126,600 officers and men, organised into four army areas. There were two tank and eight motorised rifle divisions, of which one tank and one motorised rifle division were at or near full strength (Category A), the other tank and three more motorised rifle divisions at 50–75 per cent strength (Category B), and the remaining four divisions were Category C units, at about 25 per cent of full strength. The partly manned units were brought to war establishment by 178,000 army reservists, but readying them for combat took several weeks for the Category B units and as long as three or four months for the Category C divisions.

In addition to the ten divisions, the army also contained three mountain brigades, two artillery regiments, a five-regiment anti-tank brigade, two Scud missile brigades, four airborne regiments and extensive air defence units, including four anti-aircraft brigades and three SA-6 mobile SAM regiments. The army was reasonably well equipped, but much of the equipment was ageing or obsolete. The army's 2,800 tanks included over 1,000 World War II-vintage T-34s and 414 cumbersome TR-580s (modified versions of the 1950s-vintage Soviet T-10 heavy tank), as well as 757 T-55, 30 T-72 and 556 TR-80 models. There were over 400 World War II-era assault guns, including 326 SU-76s and 84 SU-100s, as well as a few Su-152s. There were 127 MLI-84 infantry fighting vehicles, based on the Soviet BMP-1, and nearly 2,600 APCs, including 156 TAB-77 (based on the BTR-70), 387 TABC-79 and 1,912 TAB-71 (based on the BTR-60PB) models as well as small numbers of MTLBs, BTR-60s, and BTR-50s.

The artillery inventory was extensive, but much of the equipment dated back to World War II, and there were even pre-1939 Czech pieces in the inventory. There was only a handful of self-propelled guns, but over 500 multiple rocket launchers, all of local manufacture. The mortar inventory was also large, including 50 160 mm and 12 240 mm pieces, as well as hundreds of 120 mm and 82 mm pieces. There were 32 FROG-7 and 18 Scud missile launchers. Anti-tank weapons were extensive but older, including some 400 AT-1 Snapper and AT-3 Sagger missiles, and 300 57 mm, 85 mm and T-12 100 mm guns. Air defence weapons included 400 30 mm, 37 mm, 57 mm, 85 mm and 100 mm guns as well as 140 SA-6 launchers and numerous shoulder-launched SA-7 missiles.

The navy numbered 9,000 officers and men, backed by 6,000 reserves. The major bases were at Mangalia and Constanta, with smaller riverine bases at Braila, Giugiu, Sulina and Tulcea on the lower Danube. Major naval vessels included 1 old Soviet *Kilo*-class diesel-electric submarine, 1 destroyer, 4 frigates and 3 Soviet *Poti*-class corvettes. Smaller combatants included 6 *Osa*-class missile boats, 42 torpedo boats, 40 mine warfare vessels, and 33 patrol craft, 21 of them on riverine duties, as well as 10 support and special-purpose vessels. The navy also operated a 2,000-man coast defence force, which controlled ten coast artillery batteries and eight anti-aircraft batteries, and operated one regiment of naval infantry on mobilisation.

The air force included 28,000 officers and men, and would add 19,500 reservists on mobilisation. This force operated 370 combat aircraft, including 60 MiG-17 and 50 IAR-93 Orao fighter-ground attack planes, with 45 MiG-23 and 185 MiG-21 fighters. There was a 37-plane transport regiment, and over 180 light utility and transport helicopters capable of moving up to 1,700 troops in one lift. There were also 165 trainers, including 15 IAR-93 and 15 MiG-21 armed trainers available for combat operations. Air defence also came under air force responsibility, and included some twenty sites with 135 SA-2 missile launchers. Tables 8.1 and 8.2 list the battle order of the two protagonists, and Table 8.3 compares their forces.

TABLE 8.1

HUNGARY: ORDER OF BATTLE

HUNGARIAN ARMY: (General Ferenc Gyulai)
Army assets
    2nd Tank Brigade, Artillery Brigade, Air Defence Brigade, Anti-Tank Brigade, Air
    Mobile Battalion
I Corps (General Imre Esterhazy)
    1st Tank Brigade; 8th, 11th, 18th and 21st Motorised Rifle Brigades; Artillery Brigade,
    reconnaissance and air defence battalions
II Corps (Lieutenant General Peter Nyers)
    9th Tank Brigade; 15th, 19th, 51st and 59th Motorised Rifle Brigades; Artillery
    Brigade, reconnaissance and air defence battalions
III Corps (Lieutenant Läszlö Kärolyi)
    4th Tank Brigade; 17th, 47th, 71st and 74th Motorised Rifle Brigades; Artillery
    Brigade, reconnaissance and air defence battalions
Hungarian Air Force (Lieutenant General Istvan Berend)

OUTBREAK OF THE TRANSYLVANIAN WAR

The failure of democratic government in Romania led, in early summer 1992, to the installation of an authoritarian nationalist regime, with some communist overtones, under National Salvation Front leader Ion Iliescu. Romanian national identity was strong, as Romanians regard themselves as an island of Western European civilisation in a sea of Slavs. This national identity led to a popular campaign directed against Romania's ethnic minorities, beginning in the last months of 1992. By the end of the year the Hungarian government, particularly sensitive to Romanian

TABLE 8.2

ROMANIA: ORDER OF BATTLE

ROMANIAN ARMED FORCES: (General Anastase Stanculescu)
Army assets
  22nd, 23rd and 24th Mountain Regiments; 25th and 27th Airborne Brigades; 15th and
  17th Artillery Brigades; 31st and 33rd Anti-Aircraft Artillery Brigades; 30th, 32nd and
  34th SAM Brigades
4th Tank Division (Lieutenant General Ion Tanasie)
6th Tank Division (Lieutenant General Victor Maniu)
7th Motorised Rifle Division (Lieutenant General Petre Radulescu)
9th Motorised Rifle Division (Lieutenant General Radu Caposu)
17th Motorised Rifle Division (Major General Ion Corneliescu)
18th Motorised Rifle Division (Major General Vasile Tufescu)
Third Army (General Titel Mihailescu)
  4th and 6th Tank, and 7th and 18th Motorised Rifle Divisions
Air Force (Lieutenant General Ionel Campeanu)

TABLE 8.3

COMPARISON OF COMBAT FORCES

ARMY	Hungary	Romania*
Manpower	68,500	107,600
MBTs	1,116	1,688
IFVs	600	140
ACs	242	170
APCs	1,650	2,200
SP artillery	174	0
Towed artillery	612	882
MRLs	72	252
AIR FORCE		
Combat aircraft	85	340
Helicopters	52	64
AIR DEFENCE		
AAA guns	96	216
SAMs†	106	120

  Figures are approximate.
 * Romanian figures do not include the four unengaged Category C motorised rifle divisions,
   which were not ready for combat by 1 October.
 † These figures do not include missile launchers in static positions, nor do they reflect
   SA-7/SA-14 manpack missiles.

treatment of the *Szeklers*, faced a popular clamour for intervention, as the Romanian repression of Hungarians in Transylvania grew more intense. Earnest entreaties by Hungarian Prime Minister Jozsef Antall and President Arpad Goncz in spring 1993 produced no change in Romanian behaviour.

Given a Romanian pogrom against the *Szeklers*, which also affected the few remaining Transylvanian Germans, the stage was set for war. Ultra-nationalist Romanians supported chauvinistic policies, which over the course of months were transformed into government-sanctioned persecution of the *Szekler* minority. Hungary threatened armed action if the repression were not reduced, and President Iliescu, angrily protesting 'interference in internal Romanian affairs', called the bluff. Hungarian Prime Minister Antall accordingly ordered the mobilisation of military reserves on 20 August 1993, and Romania followed suit the next day. The Hungarian General Staff, which had been planning for such a war for years, expected that its troops would be ready for operations by 14 August. The Romanian high command, whose four Category C motorised rifle divisions would not be ready for action until the first week of November at the earliest, hoped to postpone – or at least prolong – the war at least long enough for them to enter combat.

The Hungarians, well aware of the Romanian situation, made great efforts to begin an offensive as soon as possible. They concentrated on mobilising the I and II Corps before the III Corps was fully ready, gambling that the absence of the III Corps would be offset by the surprise gained by striking a few days early.

On 25 September General Ferenc Gyulai, Chief of the Hungarian General Staff, decided that his army would start its offensive on 1 October. This was three days earlier than originally planned, and some units would not be ready. But Gyulai believed this would be offset by the benefit of a surprise offensive. Through intense effort, the Hungarians completed the mobilisation and training of all of the I and II Corps, all the army-level units, and the 4th Tank and 17th Motorised Rifle Brigades of the III Corps by 30 September. The General Staff expected the rest of III Corps to be ready within a week, by 7 October.

OPENING OPERATIONS (1–6 OCTOBER)

The Hungarians opened their offensive before dawn on 1 October, with air strikes against Romanian Air Force fields and air defence installations in western Transylvania. Calculating that with just 85 strike aircraft and combat-capable trainers they could not mount effective attacks against all the Romanian airfields, they chose to strike at those closest to their border, hoping to reduce rather than to eliminate Romania's larger air force. Following the air strikes, the I Corps, led by General Imre Ester-hazy (with the 2nd Tank Brigade, and two reserve artillery and two anti-tank battalions), crossed the frontier in north-eastern Hungary (see Map 8.1). Further south, opposite Oradea, the 9th Tank Brigade with the 15th and 51st Motorised Rifle Brigades of Lieutenant General Peter Nyers's II Corps also struck across the frontier, while the rest of that corps followed behind the lead elements and behind the I Corps. Finally, the 4th Tank and 17th Motorised Rifle Brigades (of Lieutenant General Läszlö Kärolyi's III Corps) crossed the frontier moving toward Arad.

The Hungarian troops quickly crushed or bypassed Romanian frontier guards, and swept deep into Romania. By the evening of 1 October, all the major attacking columns were engaging Romanian Army forces. The two Hungarian III Corps brigades in the south encountered the forward elements of the Romanian 9th Motorised Rifle Division, under Lieutenant General Radu Caposu; further north the bulk of the II Corps ran into Major General Ion Corneliescu's Romanian 17th Motorised Rifle Division, while I Corps units swarming around Satu Mare and hastening up the Somesul valley nearly swamped Lieutenant General Petre Radule-scu's Romanian 7th Motorised Rifle Division and slammed headlong into the bulk of the 4th Tank Division, under Lieutenant General Ion Tanasie. The Romanians had been caught off guard, and their sluggish response cost them heavily as surprised units abandoned positions and equipment, and the Hungarian advance spread disorganisation and confusion throughout 1 October.

By mid-morning on 2 October, Romanian commanders had a clearer picture of the situation and began to react. In the south, Caposu's 9th Division halted the Hungarian advance on Arad, although its lead mech-anised regiment had been mauled in the opening actions. Kärolyi pre-pared a formal assault as he brought up the corps artillery and support units. At Oradea Corneliescu's 17th Division was unable to organise an effective defence, and superior Hungarian weapons (2S1 self-propelled guns and BMP infantry combat vehicles in particular) enabled the three Hungarian brigades to drive the Romanian division some twelve kilo-metres east toward Cluj on 2–3 October. In the north the Romanian 7th Division was hard pressed by the Hungarian 1st Tank and 8th Motorised Rifle Brigades, and although forced away from Satu Mare the division gave ground grudgingly.

Late on 2 October Romanian Lieutenant General Tanasie's 4th Tank Division seized an opportunity for a counterattack, and ploughed into the Hungarian 11th and 18th Motorised Rifle Brigades. The startled

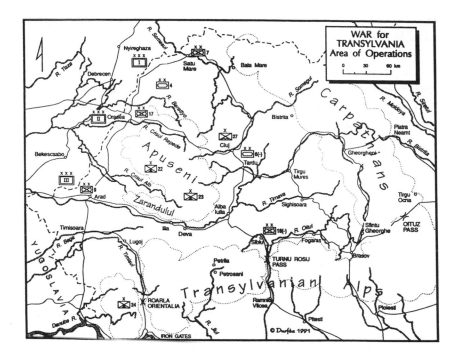

Hungarians were roughly handled at first, but soon halted the Romanian drive. Reacting swiftly on the night of 2–3 October, Major General Reszo Kälman's Hungarian 2nd Tank Brigade, with the 21st and 51st Motorised Rifle Brigades (from the II Corps), converged to strike back. Supported by a squadron of Mi-24D attack helicopters, on 3 and 4 October they severely damaged Tanasie's 4th Tank Division. Unpleasantly surprised by superior Hungarian weapons and leadership, the 4th Tank Division recoiled with heavy losses.

By the night of 5–6 October it was clear to the Romanian Chief of Staff, General Anastase Stănculescu, that the Romanian Army had lost the 'Battle for the Frontier'. Corneliescu's 17th Division had virtually ceased to exist as a combat formation, and while the 9th Motorised Rifle Division was holding around Arad, the northern wing of the forces along the frontier (the 4th Tank and 7th Motorised Rifle Divisions) were falling back toward Dej and Baia Mare. The only bright spot for the Romanians was their air force: though damaged by Hungarian attacks in the first days of the war, Romanian aircraft were able to establish tentative air superiority, and attack Hungarian supply lines and combat units with some effect.

The Hungarians had several reasons for optimism. They had captured both Satu Mare and Oradea, and some units had advanced up to sixty kilometres into Romania. They had routed one division and roughly handled two more, although their southern thrust had been stalled close to the frontier. Only the 11th and 18th Brigades had taken significant losses (about 15 per cent of their combat strength each), but they were regrouping south of Satu Mare. The outnumbered Hungarian Air Force was, however, increasingly compelled to concentrate on counter-air missions, leaving only eighteen ageing MiG-21 trainers for ground attack missions. On the other hand, Hungarian quality of aircraft and pilots, especially the F-16s, made up for much of the numerical disadvantage.

THE HUNGARIANS PRESS ON (7–15 OCTOBER)

General Stănculescu began to shift Romanian forces to prepare for an expected decisive battle around Cluj and Tirgu Mures. He ordered the 23rd Mountain Brigade to move into the western Zarandulul Hills to back up the 9th Division, and moved the 22nd Mountain Brigade north toward the Crisul Repede Valley to threaten the southern flank of Nyer's II Corps. Meanwhile, as the feared *Szekler* uprising in south-eastern Transylvania had not materialised, the Romanian 18th Motorised Rifle and 6th Tank Divisions called in their detached regiments and concentrated in the upper Muresul valley around Tardu. The 4th Tank and 7th Motorised Rifle Divisions were retreating toward Tardu as well. The Romanians hoped that the resulting four-division force, newly designated the Third Army and placed under the command of General Titel Mihailescu, would be able to halt the invaders and throw them back. The Romanians realised that their Category C divisions could not possibly be ready before the clash around Tardu, forecast for 14 October.

The Hungarians continued their advance as the Romanians adjusted their deployments, between 6 and 11 October. Tanasie's 4th Tank Division made a stand at the bend of the Somesul River north-east of Dej on 8 and 9 October, but expected support by the 7th and 17th Motorised Rifle Divisions did not materialise. Radulescu's 7th Motorised Rifle Division had been closely pursued, and had suffered heavy losses in the frontier battles, and the 17th Division continued its disorderly retreat. The 4th Tank Division grudgingly gave ground. By 12 October the northern wing of Esterhazy's I Corps (the 1st Tank with the 8th and 21st Motorised Rifle Brigades) had reached the Somesul near Dej, having advanced some 105 kilometres in eleven days. The lead Hungarian units also encountered improvised Romanian attack helicopters (armed IAR-316Bs) based at Cluj, but many of these fell to SA-9 missiles and

ZSU-23-4 guns. Hungarian helicopters had to contend with relatively unsophisticated Romanian air defences, but entered battle only when the Hungarian Air Force could keep Romanian jets away.

In the south, carefully prepared attacks by the Hungarian 4th Tank and 17th Motorised Rifle Brigades on 3 –5 October failed to dislodge the Romanian 9th Division, but did add to the casualty lists for Károlyi's III Corps. The rest of the Hungarian III Corps' motorised rifle brigades were finally ready on 8 October, and the renewed attack on 9 October left Caposu's Romanian 9th Motorised Rifle Division facing encirclement when its southern flank was threatened. The division withdrew westward up the Muresul valley, slowing the main Hungarian advance to a relative crawl.

On a brighter note for the Hungarians, on 11 October Major General Bela Hanäk's 74th Motorised Rifle Brigade and the III Corps reconnaissance battalion (Lieutenant Colonel Peter Spira) entered Timisoara, abandoned by the Romanians. The capture of this city, with its substantial Hungarian population, gave a significant boost both to Hungarian morale, and to their propaganda efforts. Hanäk's brigade passed through Lugoj on 13 October and approached the Ilia–Deva area almost unopposed, thus compelling Caposu's 9th Division to withdraw further (14–15 October) to cover the same area. This advance brought Károlyi's III Hungarian Corps within striking distance of Alba Iulia and entry into the Transylvanian plateau through the Muresul valley.

General Mihailescu's Third Army assembled around the Cluj–Tardu–Tirgu Mures position between 13 and 15 October. In addition to the unblooded 27th Airborne Brigade at Cluj itself, with remnants of the attack helicopter units, the 6th Tank and 18th Motorised Rifle Divisions were also nearly full strength. The 17th Division, harried unmercifully for nearly two weeks as it straggled east along the Crisul Repede, was reduced to about 40 per cent of its former strength, with only some 80 tanks and 120 APCs remaining. In the estimation of its commander, Corneliescu, it was no longer fit for operations. Tanasie's 4th Tank Division was better off, with about 70 per cent of its original strength and equipment, but Radulescu's 7th Motorised Rifle Division had also suffered, down to about 60 per cent of its original strength of seventeen battalions – seven tank and ten infantry. Hungarian forces were in better condition, averaging about 75–80 per cent of authorised strength, but the 8th and 11th Brigades in the I Corps had suffered severely, and in each of these brigades the two tank battalions were at no more than 50 per cent strength.

THE BATTLE FOR GILAU BRIDGE (16–21 OCTOBER)

By 15 October it was apparent to Hungarian Chief of Staff General Gyulai that his troops had not damaged the Romanian Army as much as he had expected. He therefore resorted to a risky air mobile assault to break the Romanian line. The chosen point of attack was the road bridge across the Somesul Cald at the small town of Gilau, about twenty kilometres west of Cluj; the Romanians had not destroyed the bridge because that would sever their only overland communications with the remnants of the 17th Division. Gyulai decided to use his air mobile battalion (Lieutenant Colonel Miklös Ranki) to seize the bridge, and to have the 51st and 59th Motorised Rifle Brigades cross the Somesul Cald a few hours later, with Kälman's 2nd Tank Brigade following close behind. These forces would then sweep on to Tardu, unhinging the whole Romanian left flank and threatening Alba Iulia.

The operation did not proceed as planned. General Stänculescu, aware of both the importance of the Gilau bridge and the weakness of the 17th Division, had reinforced that unit with a tank regiment from Lieutenant General Victor Maniu's 6th Tank Division, and had deployed an airborne battalion from the 27th Brigade to hold the bridge itself. The Hungarians launched their attack just before dawn on 16 October with a heavy artillery barrage. The helicopter approach to the bridge went smoothly, covered by the air force's remaining fighters, and with support from Mi-24D and Mi-8F helicopter gunships, Ranki's paratroopers soon seized the bridge and its approaches. Meanwhile, the two motorised rifle brigades smashed into the Romanian front, but found the defences denser and more resolutely manned than expected. They were unable to break clear until early evening, and then only with the help of Kälman's 2nd Tank Brigade. Once again, the relative invulnerability of Hungarian self-propelled artillery to Romanian counter-battery fire gave the Hungarians a crucial edge. In the meantime, Ranki's airborne troops at the bridge held on grimly, and repelled both an unco-ordinated tank attack and assaults by infantry from the Romanian 27th Airborne Brigade with IAR-316B helicopter support. The Hungarian airborne troops suffered heavy losses, however.

The Hungarian main body, still disorganised from the day's battle, nevertheless pushed on into the night, and reached the bridge just after midnight on 17 October. By this time Ranki's battalion had less than 400 able-bodied men left, and was effectively ruined as a combat force. So far, however, the Hungarian gambit had paid off: they had taken the bridge intact and were poised to strike at the Romanians' left rear. The Romanians, whose command and control operations had not improved with the stress of campaigning, responded in energetic but unco-ordinated fashion. Leaving the uncommitted battalions of the 27th Airborne Brigade to cover the front, Maniu swung his division to strike at the Hungarian bridgehead, but his main attack did not begin until early afternoon on 17 October.

The Hungarians had meanwhile brought forward reinforcements, including a battalion of the Army Anti-tank Brigade. As the bulk of Maniu's 6th Tank Division hammered at them from the east, its detached tank regiment, supported by elements of the 17th Division, struck the western flank of the bridgehead, coming down both banks of the Somesul Cald. The units of the Romanian 17th Division, battered and weary as they were, struck with particular desperation; the division would be cut off unless they could reopen the road. Despite mounting casualties and repeated air attacks, the Hungarians held on. Their SAM units, running low on missiles, were replenished in a daring helicopter resupply run, covered by F-16 fighters. They prevented Romanian MiG and Orao fighters from pressing their attacks too closely, and the anti-tank battalion's guns and missiles – replenished at the same time – accounted for many Romanian tanks and APCs.

The battle of Gilau Bridge raged for nearly three days, but in the end Maniu had to admit his troops could not destroy the bridgehead. On the morning of 20 October the Romanian 6th Tank Division broke contact and retired toward Tardu. At Romanian Third Army headquarters, General Mihailescu radioed orders to the 5,000-odd survivors of the 17th Division to destroy any heavy equipment they could not save and retreat south-west into the Apuseni Hills. One major reason for the Romanian retreat was that patrols of the Hungarian 8th Motorised Rifle Brigade had discovered that only airborne troops were in the Romanian line north-east of Cluj. The 8th Motorised Rifle Brigade's attacks there, coupled with other attacks by the rest of the I Corps against the Romanian 4th Tank and 7th Motorised Rifle Divisions south of Dej and Bistrita, had drawn off Romanian resources.

FINAL OPERATIONS (22–29 OCTOBER)

Units from Lieutenant General Nyers's Hungarian II Corps entered Cluj on 22 October and, with the help of poorly organised but enthusiastic *Szekler* partisans, drove out the Romanian rearguard. At the same time, the Hungarian 9th Tank and 19th Motorised Rifle Brigades turned south toward Tardu. The news that Hungarian troops had secured Cluj and were at the outskirts of Tardu reached Mihailescu of the Romanian Third Army (his headquarters now at Sighisoara) just as he learned that the 9th Division had abandoned Deva and was withdrawing in disorder towards Alba Iulia (morning of 23 October). Although Major General Vasile Tufescu's 18th Motorised Rifle Division hastened south to help the 9th Division, the roundabout route it had to use (the best roads had been cut by the Hungarians) meant that Tufescu's lead units did not reach Alba Iulia before the 9th Division arrived (25 October).

Lieutenant General Caposu's Romanian 9th Division was now in near-complete disorder. This, coupled with the need to cover the road to Sibiu and defend Alba Iulia against threats from the north and south, meant that Romanians faced the likelihood of the loss of most of Transylvania. They still held almost all the Zarandulul and Apuseni Hills, and all the country south and east of a rough line from the upper Muresul through Tardu to Alba Iulia to Sibiu. But their forces were battered and worn, and only the 18th Division was substantially intact.

On the Hungarian side, Károlyi's III Corps had suffered little. The II Corps was also in good condition, although the brigades involved in the battle for Gilau Bridge had taken significant losses. The I Corps had detached the 11th Motorised Rifle Brigade for rear-area duties, but had transferred its tank battalion to the 8th Brigade, so that most of its troops were in the same condition as the III Corps units.

Faced with this gloomy situation, and after considerable, heated internal debate, President Iliescu accepted a UN cease-fire proposal and offered to open peace negotiations on 26 October 1993. Although some Hungarians, notably Károlyi of the III Corps (who wanted to capture Alba Iulia), argued that the war should continue, Prime Minister Antall's government and General Gyulai considered that they had won a signal victory. They had humbled the Romanian Army, liberated about half of the *Szekler*-inhabited area of Transylvania, and had suffered relatively light losses for their efforts. Scattered fighting flickered along the front until 28 October, when Hungarian and Romanian representatives signed the cease-fire agreement at Cimpia Turzii, just east of Tardu, at 1100 hours on 29 October. The war had lasted twenty-nine days, and its cost in human terms is shown in Table 8.4.

INTERNATIONAL REPERCUSSIONS

Most European governments had been appalled by the outbreak of the Transylvanian war. Western Europe generally had admired the Hungarians for their early, enthusiastic and generally successful conversion to capitalist democracy in the 1980s. On the other hand, many Western

TABLE 8.4

HUMAN COST OF THE WAR

Nation	Killed	Wounded	Total casualties
Hungary	2,038	8,153	10,191
Romania	3,541	11,891	15,432

Europeans, notably in France and Italy, considered the Romanians a sister nationality, recalling Romanian artists and writers of the 1920s and 1930s, before the advent of World War II and the rise of the communists. Few nations had any interest in reopening the question of frontiers, and even fewer wished to face the problems of ethnic integration in national societies which had little or no tradition of cultural plurality.

Considering Romania's unsavoury national chauvinism, and the success of Hungary's aggressive military operations, no other government was ready to lend Romania any concrete aid. Since only those two countries were involved in the conflict, the international community, especially the embassies in Bucharest, performed a valuable service by helping to arrange the negotiations which ended the fighting.

While there had been little international involvement in the war itself prior to the cease-fire negotiations, the post-war settlement was another matter entirely. Granting Hungary possession of any districts of Romania with a Hungarian or *Szekler* majority population would set a dangerous precedent, especially concerning the Hungarians living in the Vojvodina district of Yugoslavia. Since 1967, and the aftermath of the Six-Day Arab–Israeli War, the international community had generally accepted the principles of the UN Charter and abjured warfare for conquest, even to deliver an oppressed national minority. Furthermore, a major change in international frontiers would upset the entire situation in East-Central Europe, which had proved frail enough with the departure of Soviet troops in 1989–91. On the other hand, the European Community and the UN Security Council could scarcely ignore the demonstrated chauvinistic nationalism of Romania, and were in agreement that something had to be done to relieve the conditions of the *Szekler* population in Transylvania.

The negotiations for the final peace settlement dragged on for over a year, and many European diplomats grew thoroughly disgusted with both sides. The eventual Treaty of Prague restored the pre-war frontiers and set up three quasi-autonomous districts within Transylvania. The districts had their own police, courts, schools and civil administration, but Romania retained sovereign rights of taxation and the responsibility for defence. Special passports for residents of these *Szekler* districts proved a later problem, since many Romanians outside Transylvania wanted them so they could travel abroad more easily. There were near-riots in several Romanian cities over government efforts to restrict passport issue before that situation was resolved.

The compromise settlement, as is so often the case, left both countries unhappy and unsatisfied. Romania had to accept a real diminution of its sovereignty, while Hungary had to accept continued Romanian control of Transylvania. On the other hand, Romania lost no territory to another country, and the rights of the *Szeklers*, over which the conflict had begun in the first place, were protected. In all, the peace settlement showed good promise of preventing a recurrence of the situation and the internal conflicts which had led to the war in the first place, while adhering to fundamental precepts of the UN Charter regarding the inadmissibility of military conquest.

TNDM ADDENDUM: THE BATTLE OF GILAU BRIDGE

At about 1.30 p.m. on 17 October 1993, the Hungarian bridgehead of Gilau Bridge came under attack by the Romanian 6th Tank Division and elements of the 17th Motorised Rifle Division, commanded by Lieutenant General Victor Maniu. The Romanian forces numbered just over 17,000 men, with 480 tanks and other armoured fighting vehicles, 180 artillery pieces and 27 helicopters. The bridgehead, which had been captured by Lieutenant Colonel Ranki's paratroopers on 16 October, was held by Major General Reszö Kálman's 2nd Tank Brigade (loaned from the army for the operation), together with 51st and 59th Motorised Rifle Brigades of Lieutenant General Peter Nyers's II Corps, supported by elements of II Corps' Artillery Brigade and Air Defence Battalion, and two battalions of the Army Anti-tank Brigade. Hungarian forces included 10,700 troops, with 419 tanks, 114 artillery pieces and 7 helicopters. The Romanian Air Force had disputed air superiority.

Maniu's Romanian attackers struck the bridgehead from three sides, but because of the confusion present among the units of the 17th Motorised Rifle Division they were unable to co-ordinate their attacks effectively. Nyers, who had taken command of the bridgehead forces personally because of the seriousness of the situation, was able to shift his scant reserves to blunt successive thrusts by Romanians from the afternoon of 17 October to mid-morning the next day. Maniu halted his attacks temporarily, and for a few hours relative calm descended on the field as both sides regrouped. The Romanians mounted a second series of attacks beginning in mid-afternoon, but these were also repelled. Hungarian air defence units, which played a crucial role in keeping the Romanian Air Force from intervening in the battle, were resupplied by a dramatic helicopter mission during the climax of the battle, just after dusk on 18 October. By late morning on 19 October, the units of the Romanian 17th Division were no longer capable of action, and Maniu began to disengage his battered forces in mid-afternoon. The battle had been costly for both sides, as shown in Table TNDM 8.1.

TNDM 8.1

TNDM STATISTICS: BATTLE OF GILAU BRIDGE

HUNGARY	Strength	Losses	Daily losses (%)
Men	10,700	1,086	5.07
Armour	419	153	18.26
Artillery	114	3	1.32
Helicopters	7	2	14.29
ROMANIA			
Men	17,050	1,552	4.55
Armour	481	253	26.30
Artillery	180	4	1.11
Helicopters	27	6	11.11

CHAPTER NINE

EGYPT'S WAR WITH LIBYA AND SUDAN

BACKGROUND

Relations between Libya and Egypt were tumultuous over more than two decades after Muammar Qaddafi rose to power in Libya in 1969. Qaddafi's virulent brand of socialistic-Islamic fundamentalist government clashed frequently with the more moderate and pragmatic socialistic-secular government of Egypt. Although technically allied with each other against Israel during the Arab–Israeli Wars of 1948, 1956, 1967, and 1973, four years after the end of the 1973 October War Libyan–Egyptian relations had soured to such a point that full-scale armed conflict broke out. Although the Libyan–Egyptian border war of 1977 lasted less than a week, Egyptian forces conclusively demonstrated their superiority over the poorly led Libyans.

The Camp David Accords of September 1978, which ended the state of war between Egypt and Israel, resulted in renewed tensions, not only between Egypt and Libya but also between Egypt and the entire Arab world. Animosity between the two countries was exacerbated by the widely held belief that Libya was implicated in the assassination of Egyptian President Anwar Sadat in October 1981. In more recent years, tensions were further increased by Libyan complicity in the destabilisation of the governments of Chad and the Sudan. The US bombing of Libya in 1986 (retaliation for Libyan terrorist activity against Americans in Europe) did not affect Libya's relations with Egypt, but was received with quiet approval by most Egyptians.

Despite this, it had appeared in the years prior to 1992 that tensions between the two countries had relaxed. Falling oil prices reduced the income produced by Libya's sole major export. As a result, Qaddafi was forced to seek foreign investment in an effort to maintain Libyan economic stability. To make his regime more palatable to foreigners, Qaddafi of necessity reduced his high-profile support for terrorist organisations. By 1989 his efforts to improve Libya's international standing had resulted in a near normalisation of relations with Egypt.

However, subsequent events in the Middle East interacted to worsen those relations and eventually led to open warfare. A major factor was the Kuwait war of 1991. Egypt's steadfast support of the US and conservative Saudi Arabia put her at odds with Libya's *de facto* support of Iraq. The worsening situation in Iraq caused by UN-approved sanctions was used by Libya as a means to paint Egypt as a participant in a blatant aggression against an outnumbered Arabic neighbour. The economic rewards that Egypt received from Saudi Arabia further allowed Libya to portray the Egyptian government as a 'mercenary lackey' of the Saudi kingdom. Libya also exploited the Arab world's perception of Egypt acquiescing in the continued Israeli occupation of the West Bank and the Golan Heights. These factors also placed a proportion of the Egyptian populace at odds with their government, a situation that the opportunistic Qaddafi exploited.

A propaganda campaign to discredit Egypt's newly regained stature in the Arab world would probably have been insufficient, in and of itself, to spark a conflict between the countries. However, Qaddafi had a well-known predilection for meddling in the affairs of other Arab and North African nations. The disasters suffered by Libyan 'volunteers' in the Chad civil war were a direct result of this meddlesome tendency. Furthermore, the continued presence of Egypt's best-trained and -equipped army units in Saudi Arabia was too great a temptation for Qaddafi. The absence of these units from Egypt seemed to him a 'window of opportunity' for the Libyan Army possibly to succeed in a campaign against the otherwise superior Egyptian armed forces. Libya's close ties with Sudan and improved relations with Chad provided allies in Qaddafi's attempt to unseat the Egyptian government.

Egypt continued to support Saudi Arabia, the acknowledged leader of the conservative Sunni-Muslim Arab community. This undoubtedly fuelled anti-government feelings of radical pro-Palestinians among leftist elements within Egyptian society. Further unrest developed in the fundamentalist Islamic factions of Egypt. The Islamic fundamentalists had exhibited a long-standing antipathy toward the secular Egyptian government. Both these dissident factions were already receiving covert support from Libya.

THE FORCES

The best units of the Egyptian Army, and the most modern equipment, were deployed to Saudi Arabia as Egypt's contribution to Operation Desert Shield. A major portion of these forces remained in Saudi Arabia after the war as part of a pan-Arab peace-keeping force. These forces were fully subsidised by the Saudi government, a strong inducement for the financially straitened Egyptian government to keep the forces there.

The forces remaining in Egypt were generally in a low state of readiness, and much of their obsolete Soviet equipment was in storage and of doubtful serviceability. The units in Egypt had no more than 30–40 per cent of their heavy equipment (tanks, APCs/IFVs, artillery) operational and, even when fully mobilised, many were less than 90 per cent of full strength.

The Egyptian Air Force did not deploy major elements other than helicopters to Saudi Arabia. As equipment modernisation continued, the readiness of the air force was substantially higher than that of the ground forces. In the event of war, the air force was likely to be the initial line of defence for Egypt. The Air Defence Command was substantial and well organised. Although the missile battalions were largely equipped with obsolescent Soviet systems (SA-2, SA-3 and SA-6) of doubtful effectiveness, some missile batteries were equipped with modern, effective systems: HAWK and Crotale.

The structure of the Egyptian armed forces in late 1993 was as shown in Table 9.1.

The Libyan Army had had little experience in large-unit combat. The border clash with Egypt in 1977 and the Libyan involvement with Chad in the 1980s had revealed many shortcomings of the Libyan armed forces. Command and control, co-ordination, tactics and logistical expertise were all lacking. In theory, Libya had sufficient battalion-size units to field an additional ten mechanised infantry divisions. However, the Libyan officer corps was unable to provide personnel qualified to staff additional divisions. Furthermore, even if all reservists were recalled, there would have been insufficient personnel and equipment to support such an expansion. For these reasons, in early 1993 the Libyan Army utilised the personnel and equipment of cadre-strength battalions to form ten separate mechanised infantry brigades.

Operational readiness in the Libyan Air Force was low. Support personnel and pilots from North Korea, Syria and Pakistan provided what little capability the air force possessed. The performance of the Air Defence Command in the brief combat operation against the US was very poor.

TABLE 9.1

EGYPTIAN ARMED FORCES

ARMY

4 armoured divisions (1 in Saudi Arabia)
8 mechanised infantry divisions (1 in Saudi Arabia)
2 armoured brigades (1 Presidential Guard)
4 mechanised infantry brigades
3 infantry brigades
2 air mobile infantry brigades
1 parachute brigade (in Saudi Arabia)
14 artillery brigades (2 in Saudi Arabia)
7 commando groups (3 in Saudi Arabia)

AIR FORCE

8 fighter/ground attack squadrons
16 fighter squadrons
4 attack helicopter squadrons
11 transport helicopter squadrons

AIR DEFENCE FORCE

100 air defence artillery battalions
125 air defence missile battalions
24 air defence missile batteries

NAVY

10 submarines
4 guided missile frigates
21 guided missile boats
18 patrol boats
3 amphibious ships

The structure of the Libyan armed forces in late 1993 was as shown in Table 9.2.

Only minor Sudanese forces were available to take offensive action against Egypt. Their forces had never conducted operations against a conventional enemy. Their entire previous combat experience had been in less than completely successful counter-insurgency operations.

The Sudanese armed forces committed to the war were as shown in Table 9.3.

A comparison of the military forces available to the belligerents is shown in Table 9.4.

TABLE 9.2

LIBYAN ARMED FORCES

ARMY

1 armoured division

2 mechanised infantry divisions

1 Revolutionary Guard Corps (mechanised brigade)

1 Pan-African Legion (mechanised brigade)

1 National Guard mechanised brigade

7 separate mechanised infantry brigades

3 separate light mechanised brigades

5 artillery 'groups' formed from:

   38 armoured battalions (cadre only)

   54 mechanised infantry battalions (cadre only)

   41 artillery battalions (cadre only)

7 parachute battalions

5 commando battalions

3 air defence missile brigades

2 air defence artillery battalions

AIR FORCE

7 fighter/ground attack squadrons

9 fighter squadrons

4 attack helicopter squadrons

7 transport helicopter squadrons

11 air defence brigades

NAVY

6 submarines

3 guided missile frigates

7 guided missile corvettes

24 guided missile boats

23 patrol boats

5 amphibious ships

2 amphibious craft

TABLE 9.3

SUDANESE ARMED FORCES

ARMY

2 armoured brigades
1 mechanised brigade
1 artillery regiment
1 air defence artillery battalion

AIR FORCE

1 fighter/ground attack squadron
1 fighter squadron

TABLE 9.4

COMPARISON OF COMBAT FORCES

ARMY	Libya/Sudan	Egypt
Manpower	142,000	320,000*
MBTs	2,495	3,190
IFVs	480	430
APCs	1,775	2,785
ACs	670	300
Artillery pieces†	1,450	1,750
MRLs	656	300
AIR FORCE		
Combat aircraft	516‡	411
Armed helicopters	45	74
AIR DEFENCE		
AAA guns	624	3,605
SAMs	180	858
NAVY		
Submarines	6	10
DDs/FFGs	3	4
Fast missile patrol craft	54	39
Amphibious vessels	7	3

* When fully mobilised. About 180,000 men were mobilised and committed.
† Including heavy mortars (120 mm).
‡ Many of questionable serviceability.

BACKGROUND TO THE WAR

The government of Egypt expected that support of Saudi Arabia during the Kuwait war would be rewarded by a massive Saudi economic assistance programme for the ailing Egyptian economy. Unfortunately, the cost of that war, combined with depressed oil prices, forced a Saudi financial retrenchment. Despite Egyptian threats to withdraw its contingent from the Gulf peace-keeping force, the expected Saudi aid was delayed, causing increased economic hardship in Egypt. Faced with huge deficits, in March 1993 the government enacted austerity measures, including sharp cuts in food subsidies for the poor. As the Egyptian economic depression deepened, protests against government policy increased. The Islamic fundamentalist movement placed the blame for the problems on government secularism, claiming that the tenets of Islam had been violated by the failure to provide support for the poor. Anti-Israeli and anti-US feelings were exploited by the fundamentalists and the Palestinian minority in Egypt, who claimed that the economic troubles were part of a US–Zionist plot to weaken Arab states.

Under the direction of Qaddafi, Libyan contacts within the PLO and fundamentalist groups provided support and direction for the protests. As these increased in size and fervour the Egyptian government retaliated with mass arrests of opposition leaders and with the banning of large-scale demonstrations. In response to the government crackdown, terrorist factions began a campaign of violence directed against minor officials, police and government supporters.

As violence and unrest mounted, the Libyan armed forces were directed by Qaddafi in April 1993 to prepare plans for a possible attack on Egypt in support of an expected anti-government revolt. Libyan intelligence estimated that significant portions of the Egyptian armed forces had been rendered ineffective, either through disaffection or by being deployed as part of the peace-keeping force in the Gulf.

Also in April, Qaddafi began to apply strong diplomatic pressure on the Sudanese government in an effort to bring that country into an alliance against Egypt. He first threatened to cut oil shipments to the Sudan. Later, Qaddafi threatened the withdrawal of the strong Libyan 'volunteer' army contingents that were aiding the Sudanese against the opposition Sudanese People's Liberation Army. In late June the Sudanese government caved in and entered into a secret military alliance with Libya.

On 2 July the plan was presented to Qaddafi by Colonel Saeed Ali, the Libyan Armed Forces Chief of Staff. After directing that a few changes be made, Qaddafi approved the plan and directed that 14 October 1993 would be D-Day. The final plan was approved by Qaddafi on 7 July.

An essential ingredient of the Libyan plan was the destruction of the effectiveness of the Egyptian Air Force. For two reasons this mission could not be assigned to the Libyan Air Force. First was its low operational readiness and its inexperience in low-level precision bombing, the type of attack necessary to carry out such an operation. Second was the large number of foreign personnel in critical positions in the Libyan Air Force. The Libyan high command believed that these men could not be entrusted with prior knowledge of the operation. Furthermore, it was anticipated that US early-warning aircraft would detect an air attack and would alert the Egyptians. For these reasons the mission to destroy the Egyptian Air Force was given to Libyan special forces, operating in concert with terrorist organisations and Egyptian rebels.

A second mission for the Libyan special forces was the decapitation of the Egyptian command and control structure by the assassination of key government and military officials and the destruction of command, control and communications facilities. A final task, assigned to four parachute battalions, was the sabotage of road and rail lines running west and south from Alexandria and the Nile Delta. The preparation and execution of these tasks were deemed to be absolutely necessary before conventional operations could begin.

A cadre from three commando battalions, composed primarily of PLO members resident in Libya, were to enter Egypt several months before the start of operations. They were to contact the Egyptian resistance elements, to establish safe houses, and accumulate weapons. Once this clandestine infrastructure was created, the remaining personnel of these three battalions would secretly enter Egypt, shortly before operations began. The commandos were split into assault teams of fifteen to twenty men each and assassination and sabotage teams of three to five men each. In total, over 100 targets were to be attacked simultaneously when operations began.

A further requirement for success was a rapid and complete breakthrough of the Egyptian border defences in the early hours of the attack. The paucity of good hard-surfaced roads that follow an east–west axis was seen to be a problem. It was anticipated that the best route into Egypt, the coastal road, would be strongly defended. For these reasons, it was planned that Libyan forces would advance in two main columns. One column would attack east from Capuzzo, breaking through the Egyptian defences at Salum and engaging the Egyptian reserves at Sidi Barrani and Matruh.

The second column, to the south, would execute a turning movement, advancing east from Sidi Umar to the Siwa-Matruh road, then turning north-west and north to the coast so as to take the Egyptian defences from the flank and rear. A number of small, lightly equipped columns were to seize Siwa and then were to traverse the tracks of the Qattara Depression. These columns had the important mission of out-flanking and, if possible, capturing the critical bottleneck at El Alamein on the coast. Three parachute battalions, with the bulk of the helicopter transport available, would support the movement through the Qattara Depression. As a contingency, two commando battalions, reinforced with thirty tanks, were held ready to take advantage of the confusion resulting from the commando attacks to make an amphibious landing east of El Alamein to reinforce the attack and to cut communications along the coast road. It was expected that command, control and morale problems in the Egyptian Navy, resulting from the commando attacks, would negate Egyptian naval superiority.

The alliance with Sudan made possible a secondary attack into south-ern Egypt. The Sudanese, with Libyan elements attached, were to advance in two columns. The first, predominantly Libyan, was to attack north from Lake Nuba along the Nile Valley toward Aswan, El Kharga and Luxor. The second, entirely Sudanese, was to advance north along the Red Sea coastal road. It was hoped that these attacks would divert Egyptian reserves and possibly block the return of the divisions from Saudi Arabia.

It was emphasised that speed would be critical to the success of the operation. The confusion and disarray created by the special forces' operations were expected to have their greatest effect on Egyptian capa-bilities in the first three to five days of the operation. It was furthermore anticipated that Egyptian Army units withdrawn from Saudi Arabia would not be able to intervene effectively for less than a month after the operation began.

THE WAR

The complex Libyan plan ran into difficulties from the outset. The infiltration of commando forces into Egypt began in late July and early August. The infiltration was only partly successful, nearly half of the commandos being intercepted by Egyptian security forces while attempting to enter the country or soon afterwards. When the Libyan command realised that the covert operations were in danger of com-promise, it was decided to accelerate the attack plan. The commandos, with their PLO allies, were ordered to begin operations two weeks early, on 1 October 1993. As a result many of the attacks miscarried. Few of the

Egyptian airfields were successfully attacked, while only a handful of the key government and military personnel targeted were killed.

However, a number of the attacks were successful. Among the most critical were: the Egyptian Air Force Headquarters, destroyed by a massive truck bomb; 62 aircraft, including 14 F-16 A/C, 8 Mirage 5Es, 10 F-4Es, 12 J-6s and 5 MiG-21s, were destroyed or damaged at airfields in the Nile Delta by infiltrators with rocket-propelled grenades; the assassination of General Zayyard Al Tabari, Chief of Staff of the Egyptian Army, and General Faoud Mohamad, Commander of the Egyptian Third Army at Cairo; and the wounding of Egyptian President Hosni Mubarek. However, the most serious was the loss of two of the four division commanders in the delta (Major General Talal of the 2nd Armoured Division and Major General Kalil of the 6th Mechanised Division) and several key members of the division staffs in the Delta, killed by infiltrators while en route to their headquarters.

The Egyptian mobilisation was ordered to begin on 29 September, forty-eight hours prior to the planned start of the Libyan attack, after interrogation of captured infiltrators partly revealed Libyan intentions. When the Libyan attack began on 1 October, the Egyptian units on the border had completed deployment to their defensive positions. Egyptian forces in the Delta, hampered by the loss of key command personnel and low readiness, moved more slowly. Not one of the four divisions in the Delta was able to complete mobilisation in less than a week. However, the Presidential Guard Armoured Brigade, always maintained at a high state of readiness, began moving to reinforce the border within twenty-four hours and was in the vicinity of El Alamein when the attack began. The two air mobile brigades, also highly ready elite units, were dispersed to reinforce security at air bases, military and government command centres, mobilisation sites and other key facilities. These well-trained troops played a key role in repelling further attacks by Libyan commandos.

INITIAL AIR OPERATIONS

The Egyptian Air Force was seriously hampered by the destruction of Air Force Headquarters. However, a number of wing commanders showed commendable initiative, ordering their squadrons to execute a series of pre-planned strikes (totalling 82 aircraft) at the major Libyan air bases at Bardia, Darnah and Tubruq on the morning of 1 October. Although poorly co-ordinated, the strikes inflicted some damage (1 MiG-23BN, 2 Su-20s and 1 Mirage 5 were destroyed on the ground), while escorting fighters shot down 12 Libyan interceptors (2 MiG-21s, 9 MiG-23s and 1 Mirage F-1ED). Egyptian losses were 1 F-4E and 2 F-16Cs.

Libyan air operations were initially directed to support the advancing ground forces; however, a number of strikes were made on air bases in the Delta and on a number of the Nile bridges. A total of 47 aircraft were launched on these strikes; 14 (3 Su-24s, 6 Su-20s and 5 MiG-23s) were lost, all to Egyptian interceptors. Egyptian losses were minor (1 Mirage 5E, 1 F-16A and 1 Ch J-7), although one Nile bridge suffered major damage, and was closed to traffic for seventy-two hours.

In the following week Libyan air attacks on targets in the Nile Delta continued. However, as Libyan losses to Egyptian air defences rose, the strength of the attacks waned. Cross-river traffic on the Nile was never fully halted; neither were operations from Egyptian air bases. The ineffectiveness of the raids confirmed the inability of the Libyan Air Force to perform deep strike missions. By the end of the first week of the offensive, the weakened Libyan Air Force was forced to cease operations over the Nile Delta. From then until the war ended, Libyan air missions were primarily for air defence, although sporadic ground support missions continued to be flown with marginal success. Total air losses for the first week (including losses on the ground and in close air support missions) were 83 aircraft for Libya, 97 for Egypt.

GROUND OPERATIONS

The Libyan attack began at 0400 hours on 1 October 1993, with a massive artillery bombardment of Egyptian positions along the border. During this bombardment, elements of the Libyan 1st and 2nd Parachute Infantry Battalions made a heliborne assault near Buq Buq, in an attempt to cut off the forward brigade of the Egyptian 4th Mechanised Division in its positions along the frontier at Sidi Omar, Salum and Capuzzo. A similar assault was made by the Libyan 3rd Parachute Infantry Battalion to cut the Siwa–Matruh road.

The initial Libyan attacks were generally successful, although the inexperience of the headquarters of the hastily organised mechanised brigades in the first echelon caused some problems. The 1st and 2nd Mechanised Brigades quickly overran an Egyptian battalion at Sidi Omar and advanced towards Bir El Rabia, followed by the 1st Mechanised Division. The 3rd Mechanised Brigade encountered heavy resistance, however, as it advanced south from Bardia toward Salum. The leading element of the brigade (a reinforced tank company) became mired in the strong Egyptian defensive position in the coastal defile east of Halfaya Pass. The Libyans were then encircled and annihilated by the defending Egyptian battalion. An attempt by the main body of the brigade to break through to the surrounded advance guard was repelled with heavy casualties. By the evening, the situation on the coast was fluid; the Egyptian battalion had withdrawn into a strong position centred on Halfaya Pass, covering the Bardia–Salum coastal road as well as the Capuzzo–Bardia road. The remainder of the Egyptian 4th Mechanised Division was in a hasty defence, running from Buq Buq (where the Libyan 1st Parachute Infantry Battalion was maintaining a tenuous hold on the coast road against strong Egyptian counterattacks) to Bir El Rabia. The 3rd Egyptian Armoured Division had completed assembly at Matruh and was prepared to execute a counterattack on Sidi Omar, Salum or on the Libyan forces advancing from Sidi Umar. Map 9.1 shows the theatre of these operations.

At Siwa the Egyptian position was more precarious. The Libyan 3rd Parachute Infantry Battalion's landing zone covered two alternative battery firing positions for the artillery battalion of the Egyptian 1st Mechanised Brigade. Both batteries attempted to occupy the position later in the day and were destroyed. Sheer bad luck (the Libyans had no prior knowledge of the battery positions) had eliminated two-thirds of the Egyptian artillery support. As a consequence the Egyptian brigade commander decided to withdraw north-east to Bir El Basur. This withdrawal was completed with little difficulty by evening on 2 October. The Libyan National Guard Mechanised Brigade and the 1st Light Mechanised Brigade followed in pursuit while the 2nd and 3rd Light Mechanised Brigades moved east toward the Qattara Depression as planned.

On 2 October the Libyan Second Army continued to advance, reaching Bir El Qatrani while reconnaissance elements encountered parts of the Egyptian 3rd Armoured Division on the Siwa–Matruh road near Abar El Kanayis. As the seriousness of this thrust became clear to the Egyptian command, the 3rd Armoured Division deployed to defend Matruh. A welcome reinforcement was the Presidential Guard Armoured Brigade, which arrived at Matruh from El Alamein at 1.00 p.m.

Meanwhile, at Halfaya Pass the Egyptian situation brightened somewhat as the battalion there continued to hold against repeated Libyan attacks. The Libyan 1st Mechanised Brigade was diverted to reinforce the badly battered 3rd Mechanised Brigade, and attempted to assault Halfaya from the west. The result was a Libyan disaster. Long-range fire from dug-in Egyptian tanks and TOW anti-tank missiles shredded the

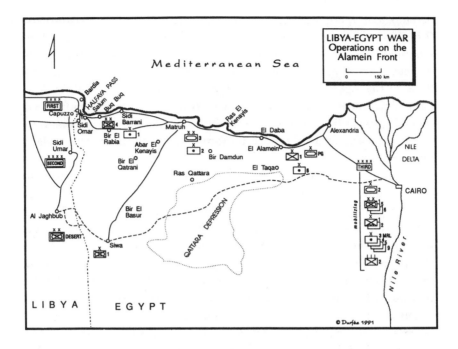

armoured battalion of the 3rd Mechanised Brigade. All 41 tanks in the Libyan brigade were knocked out; most were irreparably damaged. One infantry battalion was dispersed with severe losses by Egyptian artillery fire and air strikes directed from the position in Halfaya.

The Egyptian position improved further when the 4th Mechanised Division broke through Libyan airborne troops at Buq Buq and re-established contact with the Halfaya defenders. Badly needed supplies of ammunition and food were forwarded to the position while numerous casualties were evacuated. However, an attack on the 4th Mechanised Division by the Libyan 1st Mechanised Division and 2nd Mechanised Brigade in the evening again severed the road near Buq Buq, leaving the defenders of Halfaya isolated once more.

Further south on 3 October the Egyptian situation remained serious. The commander of the 1st Mechanised Brigade, realising that the Libyan Second Army had cut the retreat route to Matruh, decided to defend instead at Bir El Basur. The Libyans attacked with the National Guard Mechanised Brigade and the 1st Light Mechanised Brigade. The Egyptians inflicted heavy casualties on the Libyans, but were hampered by lack of artillery support. The misfortunes of the 1st Mechanised Brigade were compounded when Libyan radio-intercept units triangulated the position of the Egyptian main command post. Two battalions of multiple rocket launchers (36 BM-21 and RM-70 launchers) fired into the target area. Many key staff personnel were killed or wounded, and most of the brigade's command and communications vehicles were destroyed or damaged. As a consequence, all communications to the Egyptian Second Army at Matruh were temporarily lost. Co-ordination with the Egyptian Air Force broke down, and for six critical hours (1.00–7.00 p.m., 3 October), no air support missions were flown. By evening the Egyptian position had begun to crumble under a relentless Libyan artillery barrage.

International pressure against the Libyan aggression also began to develop during the day. An emergency session of the UN Security Council called for an end to hostilities and for the withdrawal of Libyan forces from Egypt. Qaddafi, believing that the Egyptian defence was about to collapse, ignored the Security Council resolution.

Also on 3 October, the Libyans began a co-ordinated attack to break through to Matruh. The 2nd Mechanised Division, with the 1st Armoured Division in reserve, attacked north-east astride the Siwa Matruh road. To the west, the 4th and 5th Mechanised Brigades attacked north-east to Bir Atiya. The 6th Mechanised Brigade reinforced the 1st Mechanised Division, which attacked north to Sidi Barrani. The 1st, 2nd and 3rd Mechanised Brigades made holding attacks on Halfaya Pass.

The Egyptian 4th Mechanised Division finally began to collapse under this assault. It had been weakened by two days of unremitting artillery fire. Of its seven infantry battalions, the better part of two were in the Halfaya position. One had been overrun and destroyed on the first day, the remaining four now had a combined strength of less than three battalions. The armoured strength of the division was also depleted. Twenty-five of the division's 100 operational tanks were in Halfaya. The Libyan 6th Mechanised Brigade, attacking before dawn (3.00 a.m.), struck the seam between the Egyptian 3rd Armoured and 4th Mechanised Divisions at Bir El Rabia and drove deep into the Egyptian defences, reaching the coast road east of Sidi Barrani at 3.00 p.m. on 3 October and then turning east. The Libyan 1st Mechanised Division, attacking further to the west, expanded this breach and forced the defending Egyptians west into Sidi Barrani. By 7.00 p.m. on 3 October, the Egyptian 4th Mechanised Division was desperately attempting to hold on to the eastern outskirts of Sidi Barrani.

Until the left flank of the Egyptian 4th Mechanised Division collapsed, the 3rd Armoured Division had contained the attacks of the Second Army, inflicting heavy casualties on the Libyans. A counter-attack by the Presidential Guard Armoured Brigade had shattered the Libyan 4th and 5th Mechanised Brigades, driven them in panic back toward Bir el Qatrani, and threatened the eastern flank of the Second Army. However, the worsening Egyptian situation to the west had in turn exposed the rear of the Presidential Guards to attack by the Libyan 6th Mechanised Brigade. The Guard was forced to withdraw to Matruh, grudgingly giving ground to cover the retreat of the 3rd Armoured Division. By nightfall the Egyptians occupied a new position running from Matruh south-east to Bir Damdum.

By the end of 3 October the Egyptian situation, which had initially appeared to be improving, had taken a very serious turn. The 4th Mechanised Division (except one brigade which had managed to escape the encirclement and join the 3rd Armoured Division) was holding tenuously at Halfaya and Sidi Barrani, but was isolated. The 1st Mechanised Brigade was being overrun at Bir El Basur. The remnants of the Egyptian Second Army were attempting to form a new line east of Matruh. Only a trickle of reinforcements had begun to arrive from the slowly mobilizing units in the Nile Delta. However, the Libyan Army had also taken severe losses. Nevertheless, Libyan columns had advanced deep into the Qattara Depression, reaching a point due south of Ras Qattara.

On the Sudan front, events had moved more slowly. The Libyan and Sudanese columns had crossed the border on 1 October, encountering only sporadic resistance by border guards. Serious resistance was not met until 3 October, when the Sudanese column on the coast road encountered elements of the Egyptian 4th Mechanised Brigade south of Marsa Alam (see Map 9.2). The outnumbered Egyptians conducted a skilful delaying action, seeking only to gain time for the mobilisation of reserves in the Upper Nile region. A brigade-size task force of the 8th Mechanised Division, all that could be hastily mobilised from the division, performed a similar mission against the Nile Task Force advancing toward Aswan along the eastern shore of Lake Nasser. By the end of 3 October the slow advance had brought the Libyan–Sudanese forces about halfway (100 kilometres) to their objectives: Marsa Alam and Aswan.

On 4 October the Libyans on the northern front attempted to exploit their successes of the previous day. The 1st, 2nd and 3rd Mechanised Brigades, aided by a heliborne assault by the 1st and 2nd Parachute Infantry Battalions, executed a converging attack on Halfaya Pass. A concentrated barrage by all available artillery of the Libyan First Army (almost 400 guns and MRLs) supported the attack. The battered Halfaya defence finally gave way, and at 1.00 p.m. the last Egyptian remnants surrendered.

In the four-day battle for Halfaya Libyan casualties had been heavy. In

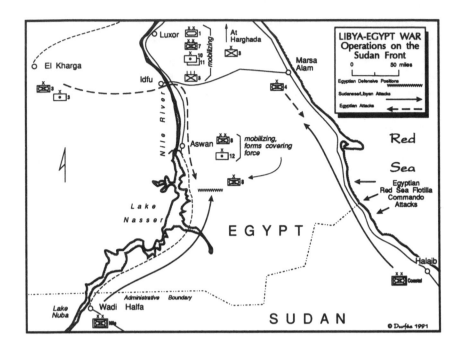

the three mechanised brigades principally involved, 1,200 out of 11,500 men had been killed, wounded or were missing, while 89 out of 123 tanks were damaged, destroyed or had broken down. The rudimentary Libyan logistical capability prevented most of the damaged and broken-down tanks from being repaired. The three brigades were regrouped as a division-size task force under command of the 2nd Mechanised Brigade.

At Sidi Barrani the rump of the Egyptian 4th Mechanised Division made a desperate break-out attempt. The division massed on the south-west edge of the defensive perimeter and smashed through a brigade of the Libyan 1st Mechanised Division. The Egyptians then raced south, cutting through to Bir El Rabia, and raising havoc among rear echelon personnel of the Libyan First Army. The rampaging 4th Mechanised Division finally ground to a halt when its carefully hoarded supplies of fuel gave out. The last gasp of the Egyptian division was a fitting end to a brief saga which had seen them surprised and badly hurt on the first day, only to recover and maul one-third of the Libyan forces deployed against the Egyptian Second Army.

The fourth day also saw the end of the beleaguered Egyptian 1st Mechanised Brigade. With its command decapitated in the destruction of brigade headquarters, the individual units of the brigade had continued a disjointed fight until they were overwhelmed. Fragments of the brigade managed to escape to Ras Qattara and link up with the 3rd Armoured Division, south-west of Bir Dandum.

Fortunately for the Egyptians, the wild 'death ride' of the 4th Mechanised Division completely dislocated Libyan plans to attack at Matruh and bought time for the Egyptians to reorganise their defences. Significantly, the first major reinforcement from the Third Army in the Nile Delta, a mechanised brigade of the 1st Mechanised Division, arrived at El Daba that evening.

On 5 October the Libyan Second Army began to probe the Matruh defensive position, while the First Army reorganised and hunted down the last remnants of the 4th Mechanised Division. Also on this day, Egyptian air activity began to increase, as the Egyptian Air Force started to recover from the damage inflicted by the surprise Libyan commando attacks. Until this time Egyptian air action had been concentrated on Libyan air bases and air defences. As a result, Libyan airfields had been heavily cratered, Libyan radar sites badly damaged, and many of the Libyan air defence missile batteries were either damaged, destroyed or out of missiles. Complicating the Libyan position was the declaration by the CIS that all arms shipments to Libya (including a large number of air defence missiles that were en route at this time) had been suspended indefinitely. With Libyan air defences steadily eroding, the Egyptians decided to concentrate their air efforts on close air support and on severing the Libyan supply lines.

That evening the UN confirmed the unilateral arms embargo declared by the CIS by enacting a resolution calling for a full military and economic embargo of Libya. The US began airlifting ammunition and critical spare parts to Egypt. Again Qaddafi decided to ignore the international pressure, ordering the Libyan forces to make an all-out effort to break the Egyptian defences.

On 6 October the Libyans began a massive attack in an effort to break through the Matruh defence line. The Libyan First Army (minus the task force composed of the 1st, 2nd and 3rd Mechanised Brigades, plus the 6th Mechanised Brigade of the Second Army) attacked eastward along the coast road. The Libyan Second Army attacked north-east and east from Bir Damdum toward El Daba and El Alamein. The National Guard and 1st Light Mechanised Brigades moved up from Bir El Basur as reserve for the Second Army, along with the battered 4th and 5th Mechanised Brigades.

In the Qattara Depression the 2nd and 3rd Light Mechanised Brigades prepared to seize the commanding height of El Taqa on Hunter's Plateau south of El Alamein. The 3rd, 4th and 5th Parachute Infantry Battalions were to utilise all available transport helicopters in an air assault to support this attack. It was planned that once El Taqa was in Libyan control, the Desert Force would proceed to roll up the Egyptian defences from south to north.

Meanwhile, at Libyan high command headquarters near Capuzzo, Qaddafi had been eagerly following satellite news reports of events in Egypt. The Libyan leader was awaiting the first signs of an Egyptian internal collapse. On the morning of 6 October international news reported that the US Sixth Fleet was standing off Port Said, evacuating embassy dependants and non-essential personnel. More significantly for Qaddafi, unconfirmed reports stated that units of the Egyptian Navy at Alexandria had mutinied. Qaddafi leaped to the conclusion that the long-expected revolt had begun and that the now unprotected Egyptian coast was exposed to the preplanned Libyan amphibious assault. Accordingly, Qaddafi ordered that the landing be made on the evening of 6 October, to cut the coast road east of El Alamein. This hasty decision by Qaddafi was to have disastrous results for the Libyan Navy.

Unfortunately for the Libyan amphibious force, the extent of the unrest in the Egyptian Navy had been wildly exaggerated by the news media. The crews of one Egyptian missile boat and a training ship had briefly refused to follow orders in the wake of the surprise Libyan commando attacks on 1 October. However, when the extent of the Libyan aggression became apparent, most of the unrest had subsided. Furthermore, despite being occupied with the evacuation of US nationals from Egypt, the US Sixth Fleet had not ignored the Libyan Navy. Aircraft from the Sixth Fleet in the Mediterranean had pinpointed the location and movement of the Libyan amphibious group. By order of President Bush, this information was quietly transmitted to the Egyptians. As a consequence, the Libyan flotilla was surprised off Ras El Kenayis by a co-ordinated attack by the Egyptian Air Force and Navy. Initial attacks were made by Egyptian Air Force fighter-bombers using French-made AM-39 Exocet and AS-30 Laser guided missiles. A total of seven of the twenty-three Libyan vessels were hit. One Libyan frigate was hit by four missiles and sank within minutes; the other vessels were all heavily damaged, many in danger of sinking. A few minutes after the air attack ended, the Egyptian Navy entered the fray. Eight missile boats accompanied by six anti-ship missile-equipped helicopters had utilised the coastal radar clutter to slip west behind the Libyans and attack them from the rear. All six of the now stationary damaged Libyan ships were hit again, and four sank. In addition, seven undamaged vessels were also hit, three of which sank immediately. In the confusion, one Libyan missile boat mistakenly engaged a Libyan LST at close range, hitting her with three missiles. The LST sank at once. When the Egyptians turned away, the Libyan survivors decided to return to base. There were no Egyptian casualties.

Meanwhile, south of El Alamein, the Egyptians were also holding their own. The initial Libyan infantry assault seized the crest of El Taqa, but an Egyptian counterattack pushed them back. The main Libyan mechanised attack further to the east, directed at Alam Halfa Ridge, was stopped by Egyptian tanks and anti-tank missiles in prepared positions on the ridge, which systematically destroyed the lightly armoured Libyan vehicles. With the superb observation point provided by El Taqa in Egyptian hands, the strong Libyan artillery was ineffective. Conversely, with good observation, the outnumbered Egyptian guns fired with great effect.

Meanwhile, further to the west on 6 October, the Libyan main attack succeeded in slowly pushing back the Egyptian defenders near Matruh, although at a heavy cost. The Egyptian armoured forces continued to defeat the Libyans in tank versus tank duels. However, the Libyan artillery superiority forced the Egyptians to adopt a delaying posture, trading time and space to keep their casualties low. By nightfall the Egyptians had withdrawn from Matruh, which had been demolished by Libyan shellfire. News of the Libyan attack on the El Alamein position forced the commander of the Libyan Second Army to withdraw to prevent encirclement. By dawn on 7 October the Egyptian 3rd Armoured Division, and attached units, was west of El Daba, conducting a stubborn delaying action against continuous Libyan attacks.

On 7 October the Libyans made a final desperate effort to recover the momentum of their attack (see Map 9.3). The 1st Armoured Division with the armoured brigades of the 1st and 2nd Mechanised Divisions attached, a total of over 300 tanks, massed on a narrow sector west of Ruweisat Ridge to break through the Egyptian position. The artillery of the 1st Armoured Division was reinforced with two artillery groups; a total of 390 artillery guns and MRLs were in support. The 2nd Mechanised Division (–) the National Guard Mechanised Brigade, the 1st Light Mechanised Brigade and an artillery group (about 100 tanks and 324 artillery guns and MRLs) were to support the Desert Force in a renewed attack on El Taqa. The 1st Mechanised Division (–), 6th Mechanised Brigade and an artillery group (about 100 tanks and 294 artillery guns and MRLs) were to conduct secondary holding attacks along the coast. The 1st, 2nd, 3rd, 4th and 5th Mechanised Brigades, hardest hit in the fighting of the past week, remained in reserve.

Unknown to the Libyans (now strategically blinded since Egyptian air superiority prevented Libyan reconnaissance aircraft from approaching the front), however, the remainder of the Egyptian 1st Mechanised

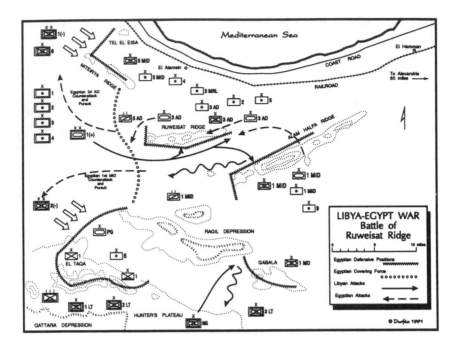

LIBYA-EGYPT WAR
Battle of
Ruweisat Ridge

Egyptian Defensive Positions
Egyptian Covering Force
Libyan Attacks
Egyptian Attacks

© Durfha 1991

Division had arrived during the night and was taking up positions alongside the 3rd Armoured Division. Other Egyptian reinforcements included four artillery brigades from the Delta (3rd MRL, 4th, 5th and 9th), and a mechanised infantry and artillery brigade of the 5th Mechanised Division. The remainder of the 5th Mechanised Division was expected to become available during the day. Furthermore, the 1st and 2nd Air Mobile Infantry Brigades, their security duties in the Delta taken over by reservists, were air-lifted in to bolster the defence of El Taqa. These reinforcements brought Egyptian strength to about 500 tanks and 500 artillery guns and MRLs. Thus, the Egyptians had achieved near parity in armoured forces. Although the Egyptians were still outmatched in numbers of artillery guns, the observation post on El Taqa decisively increased the relative effectiveness of the Egyptian artillery.

The final Libyan attack started with a deceptive success. The Libyan artillery preparation scoured the desert landscape in an impressive display of sound and fury. Shortly before dawn (5.45 a.m.), Libyan infantry advanced to seize the Egyptian outpost line, with little opposition. At 8.00 a.m. the massive Libyan armoured phalanx began its advance and quickly penetrated deep into the Egyptian position south of Ruweisat Ridge. But at 9.30 a.m. the Libyan situation abruptly changed. The Egyptian artillery, nearly silent up to that point, opened devastatingly accurate counter-battery fire on the Libyan artillery positions. Adjusted from El Taqa, the Egyptian artillery (particularly the highly accurate long-ranged Soviet 130 mm guns) smashed many of the Libyan batteries. The Egyptian Air Force, also attacking targets identified by observation, added to the destruction. At the same time the advancing Libyan armour was brought under fire from Egyptian ground- and helicopter-launched anti-tank missiles on Ruweisat Ridge. Using tactics developed against the Israelis in the 1973 Ramadan war, Egyptian anti-tank teams had dug in on the southern slope of the ridge and, further south, on the western extremity of Alam Halfa Ridge. The result was a gigantic anti-armour ambush as massive volleys of missiles were fired in co-ordinated attacks against the Libyan tanks. The Libyan armour was nearly helpless. Its artillery support vanished as the Libyan batteries attempted to displace to avoid the relentless Egyptian counter-battery fire. The supporting Libyan infantry was also hit hard by the seemingly omnipresent Egyptian artillery and went to ground.

On the coast road the badly battered Libyan 1st Mechanised Division opposed by a reinforced brigade from the Egyptian 5th Mechanised Division, made no progress. In the south the renewed assault on El Taqa inched forward against the Egyptian 1st Infantry and 1st and 2nd Air Mobile Brigades, which had been reinforced with the Presidential Guard Armoured Brigade and a mechanised infantry brigade from 1st Mechanised Division. Despite heavy casualties, the Egyptians finally halted the attack well short of the vital crest.

As night approached the Egyptians counterattacked with three armoured brigades (two from the 3rd Armoured Division and one from the 1st Mechanised Division), driving west along the southern slope of Ruweisat Ridge into the left flank of the Libyan Second Army. The surviving Libyan armoured vehicles, silhouetted by the setting sun, were systematically destroyed by the longer-ranged guns of the Egyptian's US-made M-60 tanks. After nightfall the thermal sighting systems of the Egyptian tanks remained effective and the destruction continued. The Egyptian counterattack swiftly gained momentum as the Libyan division began to dissolve. The Egyptian 3rd Armoured Division overran most of the surviving artillery of the Libyan Second Army. Then the division turned northward, driving into the flank of the Libyan First Army, routing it. The Egyptian 1st Mechanised Division drove westward into the flank of the Libyan 2nd Mechanised Division, forcing it to withdraw.

Dawn on 8 October revealed the full extent of the devastation wrought upon the Libyan Second Army. Over 200 wrecked or abandoned tanks and at least as many other vehicles were scattered over the plain south of Ruweisat Ridge. The remnants of the Libyan First and

Second Armies, as well as the Desert Force, were withdrawing to the west, harassed by the Egyptian Air Force and pursued warily by the Egyptian 1st and the now fully deployed 5th Mechanised Divisions. The Egyptian 3rd Armoured Division, exhausted by a week of intensive combat, halted west of El Alamein after completing the rout of the Libyan First Army.

Meanwhile, far to the south, on the Sudan front, events continued to move at a snail's pace as logistical problems, the terrain and skilful Egyptian delaying actions held the Libyan–Sudanese advance to a crawl. As the war reached a climax in the north on 7 October, Libyan forces approached the outskirts of Aswan, while the Sudanese neared Marsa Alam. The Egyptian Air Force, although concentrating on the critical battles in the north, had applied sufficient strength on this front to force the overextended Sudanese Air Force on to the defensive.

The Egyptian 8th Mechanised Division had completed mobilisation at Aswan and had been reinforced by the 3rd Mechanised and 8th Artillery Brigades from El Kharga. This reinforcement had brought the division's strength to over 200 tanks and 160 artillery guns and MRLs. The Libyans discovered that their superiority in artillery was not a factor, given the increasing strength of the Egyptian Air Force. An inconclusive skirmish during the day south of the Aswan High Dam ended when the Libyans broke off the action having learned the extent of the disaster at El Alamein. On the following day the Libyans began a withdrawal to the Sudanese border.

On the coast the Egyptian 4th Mechanised Brigade had been reinforced by the 1st Parachute Brigade, airlifted from Saudi Arabia, and the armoured and artillery battalions of the 3rd Infantry Brigade from Harghada. In addition, the Egyptian Navy Red Sea Flotilla supported operations of the 3rd Commando Regiment against the vulnerable Sudanese supply line on the coast road. When the Libyans, who were inland, withdrew, the Sudanese followed.

The next six days were relatively quiet as Egyptian forces harassed the retreating Libyans and Sudanese on both fronts. By the end of the second week of the war, the Egyptians had completed the mobilisation and redeployment of most of their army. The revitalised Egyptian Second Army in the Western Desert consisted of two tactical groupings. The first group consisted of the 2nd Armoured Division, 1st and 5th Mechanised Divisions and four artillery brigades. The second group included the 3rd Armoured Division (with the Presidential Guard Armoured Brigade attached), 6th Mechanised Division, 1st and 2nd Air Mobile Brigades, 2nd Commando Regiment and two artillery brigades. Battlefield salvage and repair had replaced most of the losses in the 3rd

Armoured Division and Presidential Guard, bringing total Egyptian strength to nearly 1,200 tanks and over 600 artillery guns and MRLs. The demoralised Libyans attempted a stand at Sidi Barrani. They could muster fewer than 300 tanks, and less than 600 guns and MRLs. Libyan logistics were a shambles. Fuel, ammunition, food and water were all in short supply.

The Egyptian riposte was swift and deadly, reminiscent of O'Conner's offensive against the Italians in the same area in 1940. Within twenty-four hours the Libyan defence collapsed, and almost 25,000 Libyans were encircled and captured near Sidi Barrani. The war was now virtually over. It remained only for the Egyptians to decide whether or not to continue operations into Libya in an effort to unseat Qaddafi. The human cost of the war is given in Table 9.5.

TABLE 9.5

HUMAN COST OF THE WAR

Nation	Killed	Wounded	Captured/missing in action	Total casualties
Libya	3,280	9,830	25,000 (est.)	38,110
Sudan	110	342	27	479
Egypt	1,798	5,393	8,000 (est.)	16,191

The Egyptian victory at Sidi Barrani coincided with renewed efforts by the UN Security Council to end the fighting. With the disastrous turn of events in the desert, Libya was quick to agree to a cease-fire. Despite heavy pressure within the US administration to allow the Egyptians to unseat Qaddafi, the US President made a personal appeal to President Mubarek of Egypt (who had recovered from the wound he suffered in the abortive assassination attempt) to end the fighting. On 16 October, fifteen days after the start of the war, the cease-fire took effect. A UN observer force was quickly put in place, policing a demilitarised zone along the Libyan side of the Egypt–Libya border.

For Egypt, victory in the war brought no respite from economic disaster. Although the Egyptian armed forces had remained loyal to the government, fundamentalist religious groups and secular reformers remained adamantly opposed to the regime. The vast expenditures of the war (only partly made up by military shipments from the US) added to the existing national debt, and resulted in a near collapse of the already shaky Egyptian economy. Fortunately the US intervened before the economic chaos could spark a political revolt. A US- and Saudi-sponsored 'Marshall Plan' was created to provide economic aid to Egypt. Further relief came from the UN, which negotiated an exchange of Libyan oil to Egypt as partial reparation for the war.

In Libya the Egyptian adventure was the last straw. Within days bloody fighting erupted between pro- and anti-Qaddafi factions. As the situation deteriorated, Qaddafi prepared to flee the country. However, en route to the airport he was seized by rebels and summarily executed on 18 October. From then until 25 October bloody fighting erupted between various Libyan factions. Finally, on 26 October the UN intervened. A UN peace-keeping force, formed from the French Rapid Action Force, Italian Marines and British Commandos, landed at Bardia, Tobruq and Benghazi. They were quickly joined by elements of the Tunisian and Algerian armies, which moved overland to occupy Tripoli. By 1 November Libya had been placed under UN trusteeship, a part of its oil revenue going to help support Egypt.

INTERNATIONAL IMPLICATIONS

During the war a massive US airlift brought critical supplies of military materiel to Egypt. The prestige gained by the US in the Middle East for its commanding role in the Kuwait war was enhanced by the outcome of the Libya–Egypt war and its aftermath. Surprisingly, it was the CIS that initiated the arms embargo that helped cripple Libyan logistics. This decisive move partly restored the reputation of the CIS in the region.

TNDM ADDENDUM: BATTLE OF RUWEISAT RIDGE

Ruweisat, fought on the same bare, rocky terrain that witnessed the World War II battles of Alam Halfa and El Alamein almost exactly fifty years earlier, represented the last desperate attempt of the Libyan Army to defeat Egyptian forces in the Alamein sector. The battle was fought in two phases, over twenty-four hours. The Libyans massed a heavily reinforced armoured division on a narrow front and attempted to break through the defensive positions of elements of the Egyptian 3rd Armoured and 1st Mechanised Divisions. Attacking an hour before dawn, for four hours the Libyans, despite Egyptian air superiority, were able to penetrate deep into the Egyptian position south of Ruweisat Ridge.

Suddenly and unexpectedly the Libyans found themselves ambushed by carefully prepared anti-tank positions on the southern slope of the ridge. A series of massive artillery concentrations, directed from observation posts on high ground at El Taqa, added to the confusion of the attackers, while Libyan artillery was silenced by effective Egyptian counter-battery fire and renewed attacks by the Egyptian Air Force.

Shortly after noon the Egyptians were reinforced by reserve elements of the 3rd Armoured and 1st Mechanised Divisions. The Egyptians counterattacked, and by early evening the badly shaken Libyans had been pushed back to their starting positions. The Egyptians continued their attack, and in the night fighting their technological advantages, particularly night vision equipment, paid handsome dividends. By dawn on 8 October the Libyans were in disorganised flight. The Libyan Second Army was effectively destroyed as a fighting force.

The battle statistics are summarised in Table TNDM 9.1.

TABLE TNDM 9.1

TNDM STATISTICS: BATTLE OF RUWEISAT RIDGE

EGYPT	Strength	Losses	Daily losses (%)
Men	33,825	903	2.67
Armour	586	83	14.16
Artillery	333	3	0.90
LIBYA			
Men	29,974	1,022	3.41
Armour	552	139	25.18
Artillery	359	12	3.34

CHAPTER TEN

THE SINO–RUSSIAN CONFLICT

BACKGROUND

During the last half of the twentieth century, north–eastern and central Asia have been dominated by two great powers: the People's Republic of China and the Union of Soviet Socialist Republics. Although these two nations were close allies during the Korean War (1950–3), their alliance ebbed in the late 1950s. Indeed, Chinese and Soviet forces clashed several times on the Sino–Soviet border in Manchuria between 1965 and 1972, producing some expectation in the West that a war between the two powers was imminent. Moreover, Chinese perception of the Soviets as a threat led them to seek closer ties with the United States, Europe and Japan, beginning in the early 1970s.

Geopolitical considerations had much to do with the Soviet–Chinese rivalry. For their part, the Soviets were acutely aware that resource-rich but infrastructure- and population-poor Siberia was the nearest region to the teeming population of China, and Russian historical experience with foreign invaders served to increase their concerns over long-term security in the Far East. At the same time, China's major industrial region, the Beijing–Harbin corridor, lay within relatively easy striking distance of the Soviet Union.

Compounding these geographical concerns were issues of ideological rivalry between Moscow and Beijing. These were further complicated in the later 1980s and early 1990s by Gorbachev's reform efforts and Deng Xiaoping's adherence to 'traditional' Maoist economic doctrine and the primacy of the Chinese Communist Party. A clear difference between the two states' attitudes toward dissent was shown by Gorbachev's acceptance of the East European revolutions of fall 1989 and Deng's bloody crackdown directed against the pro-democracy Tienanmen

Square demonstrations of May and June that same year.

These conflicts and rivalries applied to an even greater degree following the dissolution of the Soviet Union during the latter half of 1991. After that time, the Chinese faced not one rival but several, most of them committed to capitalism, and with their nationalist aspirations no longer bound by their ties to Moscow.

The rivalry between China and Russia – or the Soviet Union – was not new, and, considering the size and inherent ambitions of these two neighbours, might even have been inevitable. The Romanov tsars of Russia pursued a vigorously expansionist policy in the Far East and Central Asia beginning in the late seventeenth century, and these efforts inevitably led to difficult relations and eventual conflict with China. In those days China was governed by the Manchu or Ch'ing dynasty, which had completed its conquest of China from the native Ming dynasty in 1644. Although early Russian expansion lay outside China's traditional sphere of interest, the activities of the two empires collided in the late 1600s. The Ch'ing court, hoping to use the Russians as a check on the Mongols, concluded the Treaty of Nerchinsk with Russia in 1689.

Unhappily for the Ch'ing, the Russians did not stay contained in Siberia. As the Ch'ing dynasty weakened and its armies were increasingly outmatched by European forces, the Russians pressed into Chinese-dominated areas. By 1858–60 they had gained most of Central Asia, the 'Maritime Province' east of the Ussuri River (including the valuable port of Vladivostok) and Sakhalin Island. So great was Russian influence in northern China that when the Russians built their Trans-Siberian Railroad, the main track to Vladivostok ran through the middle of Manchuria.

Although the Russo–Japanese War of 1904–5 at least temporarily replaced Russia's influence with that of Japan, there was no renaissance of Chinese sovereignty. Indeed, only the end of World War II, and the Soviet Union's successful effort to drive Japan from north-east Asia, marked the beginning of China's restoration as master of its own territory. The Sino-Soviet frontier followed the border defined in 1858–60, when the Russians extorted territorial gains as compensation for their role as mediators between China and the Anglo–French allies in the Second Opium War. Perhaps understandably, the Chinese government did not see these borders as either inviolable or permanent, and desired either compensation or boundary adjustment as recompense for the wrong done China in the late nineteenth century.

The Chinese Revolution of 10 October 1911 (the 'Double Tenth' – tenth day of the tenth month), and the Russian revolutions of March and November 1917, marked major changes in relations between the two states. As part of their effort to gain international friends during the 1920s, the new Soviet regime in Moscow established close ties with the nationalist Kuomintang (KMT) regime in southern China, headed by Chiang Kai-shek. The Soviets lent the KMT crucial support during the early stages of Chiang's Northern Expedition (1926–8), sending not only weapons and technical experts but also political organisers. Chiang, suspicious of Soviet motives, later moved to block or destroy Soviet influence. In the wake of failed uprisings by Communist and left-wing KMT activists in several south–central Chinese cities in the spring and summer of 1927, Soviet advisers were expelled from KMT-controlled areas.

The defeat of the 1927 insurrections did not end Soviet influence in China, for they retained close ties with the Chinese Communist Party (CCP). Several Soviet advisers accompanied Mao Zedong's forces during segments of the 'Long March', although Chiang's defeat of the CCP's urban strategy in 1934–5 discredited the policy advocated by the Soviets. There was comparatively little contact between the CCP and Moscow during most of Mao's Yenan period (1936–47), but after the Japanese surrender in September 1945 the Soviets began to funnel large quantities of material support to the CCP, who were preparing for a final armed showdown with Chiang's KMT forces. Superior CCP strategy and leadership, coupled with Russian support and growing popular disenchantment with the KMT, helped secure the Communist conquest of China during the Civil War of 1946–9.

China remained a close ally of the Soviet Union until the late 1950s, and – with Moscow's encouragement – committed large ground forces to Korea in the autumn of 1950 to forestall a complete UN victory. While most of the military personnel in North Korea were Chinese, the bulk of the equipment and weapons used by them was furnished by the Soviets, just as the US supplied its South Korean and UN allies. Internal political and economic differences between the Soviet Union and China, however, led to cooler relations in the late 1950s, and increasingly strident mutual criticism.

Much of the rift between China and the Soviet Union had its basis in Communist ideology, or more precisely in differing interpretations of that ideology. The Soviets followed the traditional interpretation of Marxist doctrine, which held that the real proletariat (working class), and hence the proper leaders of Communist society, were industrial or factory workers. In an industrial nation this made some sense, but since China's industrial base was so small, and its agricultural sector so large, Mao created a divergent interpretation. Since his early organisational efforts in the countryside in the early 1930s, he had chosen to build on the peasantry as the Marxist proletariat, reasoning that they were the real working class in China and that there were too few industrial workers to provide an adequate base for a revolutionary movement.

Not surprisingly, Mao's modifications to traditional Marxist revolutionary doctrine attracted immense criticism from Communist theorists, especially those of the established Communist parties of Europe and the Soviet Union. His ideas attracted some followers, however, in Asia, Africa and Latin America, where socio-economic structures were still essentially agricultural. This rancorous dispute, marked by mutual accusations of ideological heresy and 'revisionism', was a standoff. It did, however, serve to split the Communist world by driving a wedge between the two great Communist powers.

Another factor which adversely affected the Sino-Soviet alliance was China's interpretation of its relationship with outsiders in general, and in particular with Europe, the United States and Japan during the nineteenth and early twentieth centuries. Before the Double Tenth revolution, the office in the Imperial government bureaucracy responsible for dealing with foreigners was called the 'Ministry for Barbarian Affairs'. The Chinese have always considered themselves superior to *da bidzes* – large-nosed foreigners. This attitude was not changed by their encounter with technologically superior Europeans in the nineteenth century; this merely enraged them and made them very suspicious of foreign influences. This suspicion frequently manifested itself in unusual or idiosyncratic policies, but was nonetheless a significant factor in China's relations with the outside world.

The Soviets exercised considerable influence within China during the 1950s, as the sole source of foreign technical expertise and modern military hardware. The Soviets, however, were not congenial allies; this unhappy fact of life hampered Soviet relations with other nations throughout the seventy-four years of the Soviet regime's existence. Soviet arrogance, or at least ignorance of local concerns, coupled with China's perception of its dependence on the Soviets, also contributed to Mao's efforts to distance himself and his government from the Soviet Union. The much-touted 'opening' of China to the West in the early 1970s was a continuation of these efforts, by balancing the Soviets against the United States.

China's entry into the 'community of nations', and its near-simultaneous entry into the UN, marked its arrival as a major power. The death of Chairman Mao in 1975 held some promise for an end to ideologically driven excesses, but was only partly fulfilled in the subsequent decade and a half. China opened to the West strictly on its own terms, and while travel to, and trade with, the People's Republic was no longer remarkable, much of China's internal policy reflected the unhappy legacy of Mao's Cultural Revolution and Communist authoritarianism.

A vivid demonstration of this occurred in the spring of 1989, during the heyday of the Tienanmen Square pro-democracy protests. President Gorbachev, attending the long-planned Sino–Soviet summit in Beijing (15–18 May), was acclaimed by many demonstrators as a hero of democracy for his efforts toward reform and liberalisation in the Soviet Union. But the continuation of the demonstrations during his visit, despite low-key reports from the government, was seen by the Communist establishment as an unpardonable affront, enforcing on it an unacceptable 'loss of face'. It was this incident, more than any other, that triggered the harsh and bloody suppression of the demonstrators on 3–4 June. The 'incident' also indicated the difference in attitude toward public protest between the Soviet and Chinese governments. As the Soviet Union moved toward a free-market economy and a Western-style republican form of government, the gulf between China and the Soviet Union grew. Changes in Chinese policy were gradual and uneven, as the regime struggled to balance the power of the 'doctrinaire' and 'technocratic' interest groups.

For their part, the Soviets became increasingly unconcerned with issues of Communist doctrine. They were concerned, however, with China's military power and political influence. Growing Chinese influence and arms sales in the Middle East and Persian Gulf regions, coupled with Chinese support for the *mujaheddin* in Afghanistan and the prospect of prolonged political unrest in India after the death of Rajiv Gandhi, caused considerable concern among Soviet policy-makers. The People's Liberation Army (or PLA, the official name of the Chinese armed forces) had for several years been engaged in a major modernisation effort. This effort clearly included not only hardware but also plans, tactics and operational doctrine. A more modern PLA, containing several armoured and mechanised infantry divisions, improved air defence capabilities, more self-propelled artillery, and a more modern air force, posed a significantly greater threat to Soviet security in Central Asia and the Far East.

China's foreign policy, aside from some propagandistic bombast, was generally modest and practical, and was unquestionably affected by the domestic developments in both the Soviet Union and China. China's interests in Africa and the Middle East continued, and, given limited Soviet capacity to play the role of patron for 'radical' Arab nations like Syria and Iraq, expanded. The prospect of a militarily more powerful but domestically repressive China, with great influence in the Middle East, was not a pleasing vision for the Soviet Union, nor, for that matter, for the US, Europe or Japan.

WAR-MAKING POTENTIAL OF CHINA

No one in the late twentieth century was likely to underestimate the military capacity of the People's Republic of China, the most populous nation on Earth. China had over 1.1 billion inhabitants, more than three times as many as the Soviet Union's 290 million, and was geographically the third largest country in the world (much of the area of the two largest – the USSR and Canada – was Arctic wilderness). China's size and geography contributed significantly to its security situation. China's extensive western territories in Central Asia provided, among other things, a useful buffer zone for the population and economic centres in eastern and central China. On the other hand, the important industrial region of Manchuria, containing some of China's most crucial armaments factories, both threatened and were threatened by the nearby Trans-Siberian Railway and Vladivostok. Because of Manchuria's industrial importance, China was certain to commit major forces to defend that region in the event of a Soviet attack. These forces automatically posed a threat to the Russian Republic's Maritime Province and the narrow overland link to central Russia.

China's military–industrial complex was extensive, but much of its product was simple and unsophisticated, and industrial production was modest, even by Soviet standards. The Chinese were certainly capable of designing effective weapons systems and military equipment, but against the demands for modernisation in the rest of the overextended economy, production levels of newer and better military material were very low throughout the 1980s. Per capita production of crude steel totalled 53.8 kilograms in 1988, against 562 kilograms in the Soviet Union, 403.3 in the US, and 802.3 in Japan during the same year. Figures for electrical energy production, possibly a better measure of industrial capacity in the modern era, showed an even greater disparity. China produced 443.5 kWh per capita in 1988, while the Soviet Union managed 5,879.3, Japan 5,692.7 and the energy-rich United States 10,804 kWh. China, however, managed to feed its growing population, unlike the Soviet Union, which has not been self-sufficient in agriculture since the late 1920s, shortly after the Communists replaced the Tsar.

The Chinese were acutely aware of their industrial weakness, and consequent military material weakness. This dictated their basic defence strategy of 'protracted struggle', which was influenced by their long military history – most recently their experience in the long civil war against the Kuomintang – and coloured by Chairman Mao's ideology. This doctrine was based on known Chinese strengths, namely the size of the country and its population, and was designed to limit or reduce any potential enemy's materiel superiority by tying him down in a long-term combined conventional and guerrilla struggle on the Chinese mainland.

However, even though modern China retained much of the organisation apparatus to wage such a war, including the militia organisation and the decentralised defence command structures, the government and leadership of the People's Republic came to realise that this would not be enough to win a modern war. The mass infantry army required for the 'protracted popular struggle' strategy would not prove useful if China were attacked by an opponent both numerous and technologically advanced, like the Soviet Union.

Consequently, the PLA in the early 1990s was in transition. The ground forces were experimenting with several new weapons systems and combat organisations, while the air and naval forces were absorbing sophisticated modern aircraft, ships and missiles. These efforts were related to the continuing deliberate shrinkage of the PLA since the mid-1980s. Personnel levels declined from a high of about 5 million to barely 3 million, and some hundred and twenty ground force divisions were reduced to just over ninety. Despite advances, however, the Chinese PLA was still a far from modern military force. Most PLA combat planes were patterned on Soviet designs from the late 1950s and early 1960s, like MiG-19s and MiG-21s. Similarly, the PLA's tanks were largely patterned after the venerable Soviet T-54, and little of the army's artillery was self-propelled.

By the mid-1990s, the PLA contained a total of 2,820,000 officers and men, organised into four branches: the PLA Strategic Rocket Forces (SRF), with 80,000 personnel; the PLA Army with just over 2,000,000, the PLA Navy with 260,000, and the PLA Air Force with 460,000. The active forces contained some 1.35 million conscripts, 79.6 per cent in the army, and were supported by a trained reserve component of 1.2 million, also undergoing a major reorganisation. The SRF controlled 12 ICBMs and 60 IRBMs, all with nuclear warheads, organised into 6 missile armies. (A Chinese army, like its Soviet counterpart, was roughly the equivalent of a corps in Western military forces.)

The PLA land forces, which contained the lion's share of PLA manpower, were organised into seven Military Regions. These regions contained a total of twenty-eight Military Districts and three Garrison Commands (Shanghai, Beijing and Tianjin). The main combat units of the army were eighty infantry divisions (including six mechanised and nine 'motorised') and ten tank divisions. Supporting these were four field artillery and three air defence divisions, fifty independent engineer regiments, several dozen independent artillery and air defence regiments, and two helicopter aviation battalions. These forces were organised into twenty-four Group Armies, each of three to five combat divisions and supporting units. The PLA Air Force also included a corps of three airborne divisions, an independent airborne division and support troops, all of which fell under army command and operational control.

Army weapons inventories included between 7,500 and 8,000 main battle tanks, 2,000 light tanks, and over 3,000 infantry fighting vehicles and armoured personnel carriers. Artillery included several hundred self-propelled guns, plus 14,500 towed guns and howitzers and 3,400 multiple rocket launchers. Heavy infantry weapons included several thousand mortars, as well as numerous anti-tank weapons (rocket launchers, recoilless rifles, guided missiles). Air defence artillery units contained some 15,000 anti-aircraft (AAA) pieces, with a large inventory of obsolescent air defence missiles such as the manpack HN-5/HN-5A family, patterned after the old Soviet SA-7, and the twin self-propelled HQ-61, patterned on the Soviet SA-6.

PLA naval forces operated 4 nuclear and 88 diesel-electric attack submarines, 18 destroyers, 37 frigates and 52 minesweepers. Smaller combat vessels included 215 missile boats, 160 torpedo boats and about 540 patrol craft. China's amphibious fleet of 16 LSTs and 42 LSMs, with over 400 landing craft, could move 6,250 troops and 374 armoured vehicles in one lift. The navy also included 28 tankers, 1 small-craft tender and 5 submarine tenders, 36 transports, 35 survey and research vessels and 25 ocean-going tugs.

The PLA Navy also controlled the 27,000-man Coastal Defence Force, equipped with guns and surface-to-surface anti-ship missiles, a 6,000-man Naval Infantry (Marine) Force, and a 25,000-man Naval Air Force. This latter organisation controlled 150 bombers, 50 fighter/ground attack aircraft, 600 fighters, a few maritime patrol planes, and about 60 anti-submarine helicopters, as well as some 60 light transport, utility, and training aircraft.

The PLA Air Force, which controlled air defence, strategic strike and ground support elements, operated over 5,000 combat aircraft. These included 120 H-6 medium bombers (patterned on the Tu-16) and 350 H-5 light bombers (patterned on the Il-28). China had relatively few modern combat aircraft, all built on Western models from the early 1980s: 90 Q-7 (AV-8A Harrier) fighter/ground attack planes, with 135 J-9 (simplified Tornado F-2) and 90 F-10 (modified Mirage 2000) fighters. Older aircraft included 500 Q-5 fighter/ground attack planes, some 4,000 jet fighters, 300 reconnaissance planes, 600 transports and 400 helicopters. Air defence units controlled over 16,000 35 mm, 57 mm, 85 mm and 100 mm AAA guns, along with HQ-61 and HQ-2/-2A/-2J (SAM-2 pattern) surface-to-air missiles.

In general, PLA forces were large and competently led and trained. Neither officers nor enlisted men, however, were familiar with the conditions of modern warfare. More serious were the related weaknesses in terms of defence and operational doctrine for major conventional war, and the lack of sufficient modern weapons and equipment. The most serious equipment shortcomings were in main battle tanks, infantry fighting vehicles, self-propelled artillery, battlefield air defence weapons and modern combat aircraft. These problems seriously inhibited the PLA's capacities.

WAR-MAKING POTENTIAL OF RUSSIA

The armed forces of the Soviet Union had also undergone several major changes, mostly as a result of Gorbachev's reforms and the associated withdrawal from Eastern Europe. All of the forces, especially the army and the tactical air force (frontal aviation) had had their strength reduced significantly since the mid-1980s. The armed forces also faced major funding reductions as the governments of the successor republics struggled to convert to a free market economic system and make their industries more productive and efficient. In an effort to raise badly needed foreign capital, the Soviets had begun to sell off much of their older equipment, and after the collapse of the USSR several of the republics continued this practice. Such moves dovetailed with plans to reconfigure the army's reserve system. The new forces of the republics, almost of necessity, adopted more defence-oriented strategies to replace the out-moded (and unrealistic) offensive strategies developed between 1950 and the mid-1980s.

Although Gorbachev's early reforms, and the growth of democratic expression among Soviet workers (such as the coal-miner strikes of summer 1990 and spring 1991), had revealed glaring weaknesses in the Soviet economy, the new republics, especially Yeltsin's Russian Republic, retained a large industrial base. Traditionally, the Soviets had relied on large numbers of relatively unsophisticated weapons, while their newer and more complex systems were produced in more modest numbers. This was particularly true for modern aircraft like the Tu-160 Blackjack bomber and MiG-29 and MiG-31 fighters, and modern naval vessels like the *Typhoon* ballistic missile submarine, the *Akula* and *Oscar* attack subs, *Slava*-class missile cruisers, and *Sovremennyy*-class destroyers. Faced with the inescapable consequence of the high cost of advanced weapons production, the Soviets had to accept lower force levels.

Agreement in the summer of 1991 with the United States in completing the protracted Strategic Arms Reduction Talks (START) resulted in lowered nuclear force levels and costs. Improved Soviet–US relations, and relatively cordial relations between the US and most of the republics, coupled with lowered nuclear force levels, also encouraged the republics to reduce their extensive air defence (VPVO) forces when the Soviet Union disappeared in December 1991.

A large share of the former Soviet armed forces had fallen to the Russian Republic, which inherited more than half the Army and Air Forces, and about two-thirds of the Navy. There were five major branches: the Strategic Rocket Forces (SRF), which operated land-based ICBMs; the Army (which included extensive helicopter forces); the Air Defence Troops (VPVO), embracing both fighter aircraft and SAM units; the Air Force, which handled air operations in support of the Army, and any air operations not under VPVO or SRF control; and the Navy, which also controlled naval aviation and naval infantry assets. The Russian Army, with about 520,000 personnel, was the largest of these branches. The SRF contained 30,000, the Air Defence Troops 80,000 and the Air Forces 110,000, while the Navy and its subordinate forces contained 200,000 personnel. The Ministry of Defence directly controlled some 220,000 personnel involved in electronic warfare, logistical, training and civil defence duties. Further, there were 70,000 railway and construction troops, and the 65,000-strong KGB and 60,000-strong MVD (Internal Security Ministry), responsible for frontier security and rear-area security tasks, were earmarked to perform extensive military-related duties in the event of war.

Like the Chinese, the Russians had retained some obsolescent or obsolete equipment, but their newest and best material matched first-line US and Western European systems, or came very close. As the numerical strength of the Army declined, the quality of its equipment rose as older systems were sold or discarded, and the proportion of newer equipment increased in relation to total inventories.

As of early 1995, the Russian Army was organised into eight Military Districts (MD). These organisations contained twelve tank, thirty-six motorised rifle, two airborne and four artillery divisions. There were also three heavy artillery brigades, three air assault brigades and numerous regiments and battalions of engineers, artillery and air defence forces assigned to fronts and armies. The 11,000-strong *Spetsnaz* special force was organised in five brigades and two regiments, and there were at least twelve attack helicopter regiments with 60 armed helicopters each.

Soviet divisions fell into one of three categories of manning and readiness. Category A divisions were at 75 per cent manpower strength or better, with complete equipment sets, and were considered combat-ready; most of these units were deployed in the Far East or in western

Russia. Category B units were at 50–75 per cent manpower with generally complete equipment, and would be ready to move in three days (although complete combat readiness might take as long as one or two months). Category B was considered normal peacetime establishment. Many Russian units were at Category C, with 20–50 per cent of personnel, and older equipment. These forces needed at least a week to absorb reservists, and sixty to ninety days to complete retraining and become combat-ready. Under the old Soviet system, there were a handful of Category D or 'mobilisation-only' units, with a caretaker cadre of perhaps 5 per cent of active strength. These units, including one tank and three motorised rifle divisions, were essentially equipment stockpiles, and would take four to six months to reach operational readiness. The Russian Republic had abandoned this readiness category, but several republics (including Ukraine) had retained them.

The Russian Army contained considerable equipment holdings, including nearly 10,000 modern main battle tanks, 2,000 reconnaissance vehicles, some 15,500 infantry fighting vehicles and over 14,000 APCs. There were about 13,000 artillery pieces, including some 2,000 multiple rocket launchers. Many of the 6,000 towed units were elderly, although nearly all the 7,000 self-propelled pieces were fairly modern. There were also over 3,000 heavy mortars of 120 mm to 240 mm calibre. Anti-tank weapons included numerous guided missiles and about 1,000 anti-tank guns (most of the latter obsolescent at best), and air defence systems included over 3,000 anti-aircraft guns including the modern ZSU-23-4 23 mm guns and 2S6 with a twin 30 mm gun and SA-19 missiles, and nearly 1,500 mobile air defence missile launchers. Finally there were some 2,000 helicopters, including over 1,000 Mi-8, Mi-24 and Mi-28 attack helicopters, some 800 transport helicopters, and about 200 more with electronic warfare and general purpose/liaison functions.

The air defence troops (VPVO) contained 80,000 personnel, operating over 700 fighter/interceptor aircraft, and some 200 SAM sites with nearly 1,400 launchers. The Russians had used the armaments reductions of the early 1990s to discard all of their old SA-1, SA-2 and SA-3 systems. The air force was in a similar situation, with some 100,000 personnel and over 1,400 modern combat aircraft. The older materiel had been sold or discarded.

The Soviet Navy declined in strength during the disarmament of the early 1990s and division among the republics had not helped either. However, it retained a major role in Russian defence policy. The Russians chose to retain nearly all of their more modern surface ships and submarines, discarding most of their older coastal forces, destroyers and small cruisers. Again, with the dramatic drawdown of forces in Eastern

Europe and the European portions of the Soviet Union, naval reductions came most readily in the Northern, Baltic and Black Sea Fleets (some of which formed the core of the Ukrainian Fleet), not in the Far East Fleet, which was based around Vladivostok and on the Kamchatka peninsula.

The Kirghiz, Tadzhik and Turkmen Republics in Central Asia retained relatively small active military forces, amounting to the equivalent of one or two motorised rifle divisions, with a few hundred tanks and 50 to 65 helicopters, and small air forces of 50 to 80 aircraft. The Kazakh Republics, with a population of about 18 million by early 1995, and the Uzbek Republic, with 21.7 million people, had more significant military establishments. The Kazakh Army contained one tank and three motorised rifle divisions, along with a small combined-arms corps (effectively a motorised rifle division reinforced with two tank regiments), a heavy artillery brigade and an airmobile brigade. The Kazakh Air Force, which combined the functions of the old Soviet Air Force and Air Defence Force, mustered 250 combat aircraft. The Uzbek Army mustered two tank and five motorised rifle divisions, along with an artillery brigade, an airmobile brigade, and a parachute regiment, and its Air Forces (the Uzbeks retained the old Soviet organisation) contained 365 combat aircraft.

POLITICAL DEVELOPMENTS LEADING TO WAR

As recently as the late 1980s the state of relations between China and the Soviet Union, while containing the seeds of possible confrontation and conflict, seemed scarcely to suggest a war in the immediate future. The military modernisation programme which the Chinese carried out between 1991 and 1995 redressed the balance considerably, but not to as great a degree as the Chinese hoped. In retrospect it is also clear that the PLA command was not as ready for war as the Chinese civilian leadership believed, and this had serious consequences for China.

The PLA was not really capable of facing the Russian Army on anything like equal terms until the mid-1990s. The PLA's ground component was still primarily an infantry force, and much of its equipment was based on thirty-year-old designs. Its communications and transport resources were limited and relatively primitive, and doctrinal and operational capacity to resist a modern air-ground offensive was outdated. The PLA possessed the designs for more modern equipment, and had been experimenting with a variety of new doctrines, tactics and combat organisations since the late 1970s in a sustained but fairly low-key effort to improve its conventional ground combat capability.

By the early 1990s, however, the PLA had embarked on a real programme of modernisation. Its military capacities, especially on the ground, improved significantly between 1991 and 1995. Increased production of modern main battle tanks, infantry fighting vehicles, armoured personnel carriers and self-propelled artillery was begun to equip its ten armoured and six mechanised infantry divisions. Nine other divisions received enough tanks, armoured vehicles and modern artillery to increase their combat capabilities significantly, and were officially designated as 'motorised' formations.

Substantial numbers of modern fighter and fighter/ground attack aircraft were emerging from aircraft production lines. These aircraft were Chinese-produced versions of Western combat aircraft, the originals of which had been purchased in the late 1980s and early 1990s. Chinese ground forces also received better battlefield air defence resources, including modern self-propelled automatic cannon and anti-air missile systems.

The new successor-republics to the Soviet Union, for their part, had not ignored this expansion of Chinese military capabilities. Their inevitable reaction had been partly subsumed in a general reorientation of ex-Soviet military power, away from the traditional orientation toward Western Europe, and toward deployments and postures directed toward Central Asia, the Persian Gulf and the Far East. Further, while the combined armies of the Commonwealth amounted to only one hundred and seven divisions, as opposed to the 1989–90 Soviet Army total of two hundred and ten divisions, Russian force levels in the Far East remained substantial: a total of thirty-six of their fifty-five divisions were deployed in the Siberian, Transbaykal and Far Eastern MDs by late 1994.

The international political situation was changing in the early 1990s. The new republics' need to concentrate on internal reconstruction led them to give short shrift to erstwhile Soviet clients in South Asia and the Middle East. The Chinese, on the other hand, continued to maintain client-state relationships with countries hostile to former Soviet clients.

The assassination of Rajiv Gandhi in the late spring of 1991 at one stroke halted India's climb toward regional military power, and also cost the Soviets one of their best anti-China cards. The time India needed to create a new national political consensus after the end of the long Nehru–Gandhi Congress regime gave China a 'window of opportunity' in the 1990s. Pragmatic Chinese foreign policy endeavoured at once to take advantage of this situation, at least in terms of the Chinese alliance with Pakistan. The Kuwait war also provided China with a similar opening in the Middle East. The Chinese had already taken some steps to increase their clout in the Persian Gulf region through missile sales to Saudi

Arabia, and sales of naval vessels and jet fighters to Egypt. China also lent extensive technical and material assistance to Algeria's nuclear weapons programme, yet another indication of China's intentions in the region. Expansion of Chinese influence in the Middle East did not ease Russian concerns over the long-term security situation in that region.

Expansion of Chinese influence caused the Russians concern in other areas. One such area was Mongolia. China had historically regarded Mongolia as part of its sphere of influence, and that was indeed the case until about 1920. Mongolia had the second oldest communist government in the world, younger only than that of the Soviet Union. With the withdrawal of most Soviet troops from Mongolia, and the peaceful end of the communist monopoly of power there in the early 1990s, the road was open for expanded Chinese influence. Moreover, the Chinese were used to dealing with their own Mongolians in their province of Inner Mongolia. A similar situation existed in North Korea, which has trodden a careful line between the two communist powers since the late 1950s. Even the Russian Republic, generally recognised as a major power, was both unable and unwilling to block increased Chinese influence in North Korea, although the North Koreans were reluctant to encourage this.

The states of the Commonwealth were already deeply wary of China's teeming millions coupled with that country's considerable technical potential. The Russian Republic was also concerned about China's close proximity to the valuable mineral resources of underpopulated Siberia. Increasing Chinese influence among the Central Asian republics concerned policy makers there and in Moscow. By 1994, China appeared also to be rendering covert support for opposition movements among several Central Asian nationalities, many of whom had close ethnic relatives in western China. This presented the Russian leadership with the deeply disturbing prospect of either a hostile Central Asia or a series of wars to retain and support friendly regimes there. There had already been many manifestations of unrest there in the late 1980s and early 1990s. As a result of this situation the Russian Republic moved to co-operate closely with the Kazakh Republic and the smaller Tadzhik and Kirghiz republics, in the mountains south-east of the Kazakh Republic. The Uzbek Republic was unwilling to commit to the alliance wholeheartedly, but allowed allied forces to traverse its territory and lent some minor logistical support. The Turkmen Republic was preoccupied by internal dissent (some of this Chinese-sponsored), and was also suspicious of Russian military overtures, so opted not to co-operate. The Russian and Kazakh governments together made several warnings to the Chinese, and backed these up by raising their military preparedness, and shifting military forces eastward, toward China.

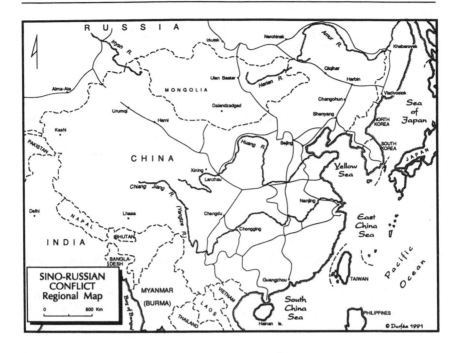

Even in the face of direct and indirect Russian warnings, China made no effort to modify those policy initiatives that aroused Russian and Kazakh concerns. Beijing apparently calculated either that the Russians and their allies would not risk military action or that the PLA would be able to deal effectively with any offensive by Russia and its allies. Faced with Chinese intransigence, by early spring 1995 Russian, Kazakh, Tadzhik and Kirghiz leaders saw little choice other than military action. The Kremlin and Alma-Ata calculated that they had little to lose, but possibly a great deal to gain, from a conventional war against China.

Together, the two larger states persuaded the Kirghiz and Tadzhik governments to co-operate. Russian political and military planners, consulting with their counterparts in the Tadzhik, Kazakh and Kirghiz republics, saw an offensive by forces from all four republics into China as a classic 'limited war', intended not to destroy the People's Republic of China as a political entity, but to demonstrate to Beijing that the Commonwealth, or at least Russia and Kazakhstan, would not tolerate an expansionist-irredentist China, and had the power to enforce its intolerance. The objective was to damage and humble China, but not destroy it. Thus the Russians and their allies did not plan to employ either nuclear weapons or chemical agents, which they considered weapons of total war. They had, however, no such reservations on employing sophisticated conventional weapons.

THE MONGOLIAN 'INCIDENT'

The spark for the actual outbreak of hostilities was provided by an *opéra-bouffe* effort of China-based Mongolian nationalists to invade the Mongolian Republic and depose the newly democratic, and still pro-Russian, government in Ulaan Baatar. The invaders, who travelled by truck and numbered perhaps 2,500 men equipped with light infantry weapons, crossed the frontier on 19 July 1995. They had hoped to spark a general uprising, but the Mongolian citizenry was in no mood to change regimes, and only a few dozen local volunteers flocked to the banner of the 'Free Mongolian Army'. The Mongolian government mobilised its two Category B motorised rifle divisions, and sent the 2nd Division to intercept the invaders. In a series of running fights south-west of Dalandzadgad between 21 and 23 July, the invading force was dispersed or destroyed.

The Mongolian Army had handily defeated the threat with few casualties, but the Russians were understandably outraged. China denied any official involvement, and later investigations suggested that – while the 'Free Mongolians' enjoyed some moral support – they received virtually no physical backing through official government channels. Despite Chinese protestations of innocence, on 28 July Russian President Boris Yeltsin presented a harsh ultimatum to the Chinese ambassador to Moscow, demanding several reversals of Chinese policy. Unwilling to be humiliated, and failing to read Russo-Kazakh determination properly, Chairman Zhang Li-de's government refused the ultimatum. When the date and time specified had passed, just after midnight Moscow time on 2 August, war began. Tables 10.1 and 10.2 list the battle order of the Russian alliance and China respectively, and Table 10.3 compares the ground forces.

OUTBREAK OF WAR

The dust had not settled from the comic-opera clash at Dalandzadgad before the Russian military machines in the Far East moved into action. Divisions and armies concentrated from their dispersed peacetime locations as far away as Moscow, gathering at points along the Soviet frontier. The Chinese, who had considerable warning of Russian and Kazakh activities, apparently believed the moves were merely threats to put pressure on Beijing. In fact, they were the preparatory activities for the invasion of northern China.

The Russians pulled forces from seven of their eight Military Districts:

TABLE 10.1

RUSSIA AND KAZAKHSTAN: ORDER OF BATTLE

TUKESTAN FRONT

First Kazakh Army: General Abulhassan Karzametov

    1 tank and 4 motorised rifle divisions (1 Russian, 1 Tadzhik-Kirgiz); 1 airmobile and 1 artillery brigades

    1 independent (Russian) motorised rifle division

Tenth Army (General Pyotr A. Rumantsev)

    4 motorised rifle and 1 artillery division

Mongolian Army Provisional Corps (Lieutenant General Dumaagyin Ochirban)

    2 motorised rifle divisions

TRANSBAYKAL FRONT: Colonel General Dmitri S. Egorov

Ninth Army (General Andrei D. Zaikov)

    1 tank and 3 motorised rifle divisions

Eleventh Army (General Mikhail V. Romanov)

    4 motorised rifle divisions

Twelfth Army (General Lavrenti K. Bakatin)

    1 tank, 3 motorised rifle and 1 artillery divisions

FAR EAST FRONT: Marshal Pavel I. Cherkorin

Fifth Guards Tank Army (General Konstantin I. Malenkov)

    3 tank and 1 motorised rifle divisions

Eighth Guards Army (Lieutenent General Ilya M. Maslyukov)

    1 tank and 3 motorised rifle divisions

Third Army (General Kyril K. Platov)

    1 tank and 3 motorised rifle divisions

Fourteenth Army (General Sergei S. Slobov)

    4 motorised rifle divisions

Seventeenth Army (General Georgi P. Bolgansky)

    4 motorised rifle divisions

Airborne/Airmobile Forces

    1 airborne (*desant*) division; 2 airmobile brigades

Special Task Force (Lieutenant General Maxim G. Gerasimov)

    2 motorised rifle divisions

SUMMARY

    1 tank army, 9 armies, 1 Mongolian corps, 1 task force: 8 tank, 37 motorised rifle, 1 airborne divisions; 3 artillery divisions, 3 airmobile brigades and 1 artillery brigade 8,040 MBTs, 749,300 men

TABLE 10.2

CHINA: ORDER OF BATTLE

LANZHOU (WESTERN) MILITARY REGION
5 Border Guard divisions

Eleventh Group Army (General Qing Jiyun)
1 tank, 1 mechanised, and 2 motorised divisions

Fourteenth Group Army (General Pu Yilin)
1 motorised and 3 infantry divisions

BEIJING MILITARY REGION
1 artillery division
3 Border Guard divisions

Ninth Group Army Lieutenant General Yao Jihua)
3 infantry divisions

Twenty-Seventh Group Army (General Hao Jiang)
3 infantry divisions

Fifteenth Group Army (Lieutenant General Li Shangkung)
1 airborne and 2 infantry divisions

Sixteenth Group Army (General Wu De)
1 tank and 3 infantry divisions

Twenty-first Group Army (General Wang Zemin)
1 tank and 3 infantry divisions

Thirtieth Group Army (General Wu Liang)
1 tank and 3 infantry divisions

SHENYANG (NORTH-EAST) MILITARY REGION: Marshal Zao Qichen
1 artillery division
7 Border Defence divisions

First Armoured Group Army (General Yang Zhen)
2 tank and 2 mechanised divisions

Fifth (Mountain) Group Army (General Tang Qihua)
4 infantry divisions

Twenty-third Group Army (General Deng Xeqian)
1 tank, 1 mechanised and 2 motorised divisions

Twenty-fourth Group Army (General Tian Jiwei)
1 mechanised, 1 motorised and 2 infantry divisions

Thirty-fifth Group Army (General Beng Dili)
1 tank, 1 motorised and 2 infantry divisions

SUMMARY
Thirteen Group Armies
8 tank, 5 mechanised, 7 motorised, 1 airborne, 30 infantry, 2 artillery and 15 Border Defence divisions
6,180 MBTs and 829,000 men

TABLE 10.3

COMPARISON OF GROUND FORCES

ARMY	Russian	Mongol	Kazakh	Tadzhik-Kirgiz	Chinese
Personnel	669,700	17,700	49,100	13,800	829,000
MBTs	6,875	350	660	155	6,978*
IFVs	12,490	250	1,127	310	708
ACs	1,690	70	130	45	–
APCs	11,572	200	686	332	4,716
Artillery	8,157	175	536	144	4,068
MRLs	1,296	70	72	24	1,506
AIR FORCE					
Combat A/C	1,355	28	180	45	1,980
Armed helicopters	710	10	100	20	30
AIR DEFENCE					
AAA guns†	820	60	74	18	1,152
SAMs	1,680	–	150	38	240

Figures are approximate.
* Chinese MBT figure includes 798 Type-62 and Type-63 light tanks
† The Soviet SA-19/2S6 combined gun/SAM system is listed here as an AA gun; the Russians employed a total of 172 of them, and the Kazakhs had 12 in their 1st Tank Division.

only the Fourth Combined-Arms Army in the St Petersburg MD remained intact, and the Second Guards Tank Army was retained around Moscow as a strategic reserve. The Kazakhs contributed one combined-arms army, which contained one Russian division from Siberia, and a combined Tadzhik–Kirghiz division. Russian forces were deployed in Siberia (a four-division army and one independent motorised rifle division), Transbaykal (three armies, one from the North Caucasus MD), and Far East (one tank army from the Volga–Urals MD, four combined-arms armies with one from the Moscow MD and another from Volga–Urals, one two-division Special Task Force, plus an airborne division and two airmobile brigades). The remainder of the small Kirghiz and Tadzhik armies planned to make a few small-scale attacks to keep the Chinese guessing, and pledged their infrastructure to help the Kazakhs and Russians.

The First Kazakh Army (General Abulhassan Karzametov) would attack eastward toward Urumqi, with the independent division from the Siberian MD advancing southward through west-central Mongolia in support. The Siberian Tenth Army (General Pyotr A. Rumantsev) would push south into Mongolia and join forces with the two-division Mongolian 'corps' at Dalandzadgad. From the Transbaykal MD, the Ninth Army (General Andrei D. Zaikov) would follow the rail line from Irkutsk through Ulaan Baatar toward Beijing, while the Twelfth Army (General Lavrenti K. Bakatin) would advance toward Qiqihar in north-western Manchuria, and Eleventh Army (General Mikhail V. Romanov) remained available in reserve to support either operation. Further west, the Fifth Guards Tank Army (Colonel General Konstantin I. Malenkov) of the Far Eastern MD would lead the drive on Harbin from Blagovesh-chensk with the Eighth Guards Army (Lieutenant General Ilya Mas-lyukov) in support. The Third (General Kyril K. Platov) and Fourteenth (General Sergei S. Slobov) armies would head south from Birobidzhan–Khabarovsk up the Sungari River, and the Seventeenth Army (General Georgi P. Bolgansky) and the Special Task Force (Lieutenant General Maxim G. Gerasimov) would attack toward Mudanjiang and Jixi from the Del'nerchensk area.

The Russo–Kazakh plan depended on three main factors for success. First, they had a clear material advantage in armoured vehicles and in artillery, not only in numerical terms but also qualitatively. Second, the Russians and their allies expected their air forces (790 fighter and 900 fighter/ground attack aircraft) to gain complete control of the air. They planned to use their air power both for direct combat support and on deep strike/interdiction missions. Finally, the Russo–Kazakhs expected that their attack helicopters and anti-tank weapons would deal with China's significant armoured forces, while their airborne and airmobile forces would sidestep Chinese blocking positions, and thus facilitate the advance of their main armoured and mechanised efforts.

For their part, although they had not expected hostilities actually to begin, the Chinese had a well-developed and simple contingency plan. Over half of their forces were concentrated in Manchuria, including the 'experimental' First Armoured Group Army, intended for use as a counterattack force. Fifteen Chinese Border Guard divisions were deployed along the frontiers, most of them well dug-in. If it came to war, the Chinese hoped to punish the Russians enough to compel them to suspend operations. The Chinese considered that they did not have to gain a battlefield victory; merely avoiding defeat and forcing the Russians and their allies to choose between a cease-fire and a war of attrition would give them eventual success, regardless of the Russian choice.

The opening move of the war was a series of predawn Russian and Kazakh air strikes against Chinese airfields and air defence installations on 2 August. Many of the attacking aircraft were the formidable Su-24s, and they caused considerable damage to Chinese installations. They also caught many PLA aircraft on the ground, destroying or damaging several hundred. At first light, Russian and Kazakh ground forces began to move.

THE OPENING PHASE IN THE WEST (2–25 AUGUST)

General Karzametov's First Kazakh Army, staging from Alma-Ata and Ayaguz, advanced in three columns. On the right, the Kazakh 2nd Motorised Rifle Division and the 8th Airmobile Brigade advanced down the highway toward Yining, with its valuable airfield. The central column, with the Kazakh 1st Tank and the Tadzhik–Kirghiz Motorised Rifle divisions, headed south-west down the rail line from Aktogay on the shortest route to Urumqi. The northern column, consisting of the 32nd (Siberian) and Kazakh 4th Motorised Rifle Divisions, crossed the frontier at Bakhty (about 100 kilometres north of the central column), and pushed south-east to threaten Karamay. The 38th Motorised Rifle Division, also from the Siberian MD, covered the northern flank of the Tenth Army, advancing on the roads north of the Tarabatay Mountains to approach Urumqi from the north.

These forces quickly disposed of the three Chinese Border Guard divisions, and by the end of 3 August the southern column had secured Yining. At dawn on 4 August, Karzametov sprang an operational surprise by moving the 8th Airmobile Brigade, with its accompanying attack helicopter regiments, through a narrow valley north-east of Yining to seize Jinghe on the incomplete rail line from Urumqi. This move unbalanced the defensive preparations of General Qing Jiyun's Chinese Eleventh Group Army, and compelled its three divisions facing the Soviets (the 33rd Motorised Division was still at Urumqi) to fall back hastily. Despite their withdrawal, General Qing's 7th Tank and 22nd Mechanised divisions were severely damaged by Soviet armour and attack helicopters, although one adventurous Soviet tank battalion was ambushed by a regiment of the 22nd Mechanised Division, and suffered grievous losses. Further north, the 38th Motorised Rifle Division encountered little opposition, and advanced swiftly.

By 8 August, the First Kazakh Army and the 38th Motorised Rifle Division were less than twenty kilometres outside of Urumqi, and the Eleventh Group Army's outnumbered divisions were battered and worn. After a two-day pause, on 10 August the Kazakhs opened the assault against Urumqi. The fighting raged for over a week, with local

Chinese militia forces giving a particularly good account of themselves. The Kazakhs suffered heavy losses in tanks and armoured vehicles, but by nightfall on 18 August they had secured most of Urumqi. On the 20th General Karzametov temporarily halted further offensive operations, having achieved his initial objective by occupying the entire Dzungar Basin as well as Urumqi and its environs.

Meanwhile, General Pyotr Rumantsev's Tenth Army conducted an extensive road march on several routes through western Mongolia to reach the Mongolian corps around Dalandzadgad in south-central Mongolia. Rumantsev's lead unit, the 31st Motorised Rifle Division, did not reach the area until 11 August, and the remainder of the Tenth Army trailed in over the next three days, having covered an average of 1,500 kilometres per unit. Wear and tear on the army's vehicles and equipment had been considerable, and it was not ready for operations until 19 August. This delay, which Karzametov and Transbaykal Front commander Colonel General Dmitri S. Egorov had only partially anticipated, allowed the Chinese 42nd Infantry Division of General Pu Yilin's Fourteenth Group Army to move west and reinforce the hard-pressed Eleventh Group Army, and gave more time for General Hao Jiang's Twenty-seventh Group Army in western Inner Mongolia to prepare for action.

General Zaikov's Russian Ninth Army hastened down the highway/rail line from Lake Baykal through Ulaan Baatar south into northern China. His army's lead troops, the 22nd Motorised Rifle Division, were already in Mongolia on D-Day (2 August), and the comparatively short route (900 kilometres) the army had to follow brought them into combat with the 17th and 49th PLA Border Defence Divisions on 8 August. Zaikov's initial attacks made good progress and virtually destroyed the two Border Guard divisions, but the swift response of the Sixteenth and Twenty-first Group Armies (Generals Wu De and Wang Zemin) on 14 to 16 August halted the Soviet advance less than fifty kilometres inside China. Russian probes on 19 August met stiff Chinese resistance, in part because the altitude of the battlefield (over 1,000 metres above sea level) limited the Russian Mi-8 assault helicopters (whose out-of-ground-effect hovering ceiling was only 800 metres). Nonetheless, the PLA units suffered considerable losses. Recognising that the Ninth Army might face heavy opposition, Colonel General Egorov had began to move General Mikhail Romanov's Eleventh Army from its assembly area south of Chita toward the battle area through northeastern Mongolia on 6 August. This approach march was some 1,400 kilometres long, and consequently Romanov's army was not in place and ready for action until 17 August.

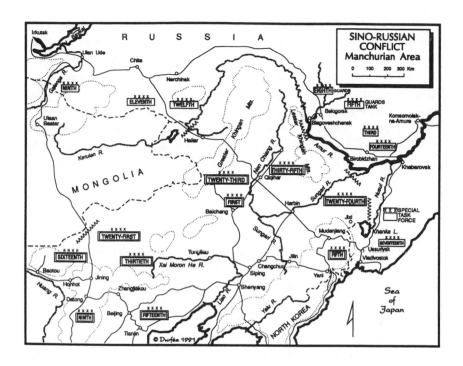

THE OPENING PHASE IN THE EAST

Further east, the remainder of Transbaykal Front – General Lavrenti Bakatin's Twelfth Army and the 7th Artillery Division, headed through northwestern Manchuria toward Hailar along the old, pre-1905, Trans-Siberian Railroad line. As had happened in Dzungaria and Inner Mongolia, Bakatin and the Twelfth Army made short work of the Chinese Border Guard divisions, aided by gently rolling terrain which facilitated mechanised operations. Moreover, the Twelfth Army's route lay over lower ground than that of the Ninth Army, and Bakatin's attack helicopters turned the Chinese retreat into a rout. Lead elements of the Twelfth Army reached Hailar on 6 August, and had crossed the crest of the Greater Khingar range on 11 August. Soon after, the 9th Tank and 33rd Motorised Rifle Divisions (comprising Bakatin's first echelon) encountered advance forces of General Deng Xeqian's Twenty-third Group Army, whose main strength lay west of Qiqihar. The series of meeting engagements which followed, spread over six days and several thousand square kilometres of ground, were a great mechanized mêlée. When the dust had settled on 19 August, Deng's Twenty-third Group Army had halted Bakatin's drive some 150 kilometres north-west of Qiqihar.

Deng's achievement was fleeting, however, because the other PLA forces in Manchuria were reeling from the hammer-blows of Marshal Pavel I. Cherkorin's Russian Far East Front. Colonel General Malenkov's Fifth Guards Tank and Lieutenant General Maslyukov's Eighth Guards Armies threw bridgeheads across the Amur on 2 and 3 August, and by evening on 5 August had smashed through the 19th and 37th Border Guard Divisions astride the Harbin highway. The eight Russian divisions quickly pushed through the Lesser Khingar mountains. On 11 August, Nenjiang fell to the 11th Guards and 17th Guards Motorised Rifle Divisions of the Eighth Guards Army, after a sharp fight with the 38th Division of the Chinese Thirty-fifth Group Army. Most of the attention of the Fifth Guards Tank and Eighth Guards Armies was focused on the Thirty-fifth Group Army (General Beng Dili) in front of them, especially its 10th Tank and 35th (Motorised) Divisions.

The PLA troops fought well, but superior Russian mobility and firepower gradually compelled them to give ground southward in a week of heavy combat (12–19 August). Marshal Zou Qichen, commander of the PLA's North-east Military Region, decided to commit his major reserve, the First Armoured Group Army under General Yang Zhen, on 19 August. Yang moved the First Armoured Group Army north from its assembly area west of Harbin to strike at the western flank of the Russian advance. The two Russian armies, forewarned by aerial reconnaissance, were ready when the attack came; Malenkov met Yang's attack with a counter-stroke of his own from the north. The battle raged for four days over the partly wooded hills and valleys about 150 kilometres north-west of Harbin, around the small cities of Kedong and Baiquan. Despite the battlefield's proximity to PLA airfields around Harbin and Qiqihar, Russian aircraft quickly gained control of the skies and provided crucial assistance to the hard-pressed Russian Army units. The initial PLA tank-mechanised attacks on 20 August were stalled, and from 21 to 23 August the First Armoured was hammered by Russian tanks and artillery, Mi-24E and Mi-8F attacks, and Su-24 and Su-25 strikes. Many Chinese tanks and armoured vehicles fell victim to Russian anti-tank missiles.

The Chinese attacks faltered, and the pressure on the northern flank of the First Armoured Group Army grew. Early on 24 August heavy losses compelled General Yang to break off the battle. The Fifth Guards Tank Army had suffered relatively light losses, although the 17th Motorised Rifle Division could only muster 100 tanks and nine battalion-equivalents of infantry on 25 August. However, the two Chinese Group Armies (Yang's First Armoured, and Beng Dili's Thirty-fifth) had suffered severe damage, and were operating at considerably reduced strength. Only Soviet wariness, and the timely arrival of LTG Yao Jihua's Chinese Ninth Group Army from the Beijing Military Region on 25–26 August prevented a collapse of the entire Harbin sector. The Battle of Kedong-Baiquan, as it was later known, also served to unhinge the position of General Deng's Twenty-third Group Army north-west of Qiqihar, since its northern flank and rear were now threatened by the victorious Russian forces, north-west of Qiqihar.

At the same time as the Fifth Guards Tank and the Eighth Guards Armies crossed the Amur around Blagoveshchensk, the Third and Fourteenth Armies crossed the Amur further east around the mouth of the Sungari River. Their main crossing was covered in part by an air assault by a regiment from the 102nd Guards Airborne Division. Although it took the two armies three days to completely drive off the Chinese 21st and 41st Border Guard divisions, the Russians faced greater problems from the terrain and the limited road net (there were only two 'good' roads, one on either bank of the Sungari, and both of them single-lane and only intermittently gravelled). This region was defended by General Tian Jiwei's Twenty-fourth Group Army. Able to advance only on single-division fronts after 7 August, General Platov (Third Army) and General Slobov (Fourteenth Army) relied on a series of battalion-sized paradrops by the 102nd Guards Airborne Division and heli-borne 'leap-frog' movements by the 86th Airmobile Brigade to pry the Chinese from their positions. The lightly equipped airborne and airmobile units suffered severely in these intense operations, but with their aid Platov and Slobov drove into the higher and more open country around Tonghe, northeast of Harbin, by 26 August. By that time only Platov's Third Army was still fully committed in the Sungari valley, as the 45th and 60th Motorised Rifle Divisions of Slobov's Fourteenth Army had pushed south of the river to secure the flank and try to make contact with Lieutenant General Gerasimov's Special Task Force.

General Bolgansky's Seventeenth Army and Gerasimov's Special Task Force operated on a semi-independent basis, as their lines of operation were separated from the other four armies of Marshal Cherkorin's Far East Front by some 300 kilometres. Gerasimov's Task Force crossed the Ussuri (Nusul) River early on 2 August, and drove along the road toward Jixi. The 55th PLA Border Guard Division at Hulin caused them some problems on 4 and 5 August, but an envelopment by the 50th (Far East) Airmobile Brigade on 6 August ended PLA resistance there. Gerasimov's drive west ran into heavy resistance from the Chinese 15th Division in the hills in front of Jixi, and his offensive was stalled there from 9 to 17 August.

Further south, Bolgansky's Seventeenth Army attacked straight into the hills toward Mudanjiang, which was defended by the Fifth (Mountain) Group Army of General Tang Qihua. Bolgansky's offensive was hampered by the narrow approach route and the rough terrain, which the PLA forces exploited, bitterly contesting every ridge line. As the Seventeenth Army had made scant progress by 8 August, General Bolgansky pulled the 50th Airmobile Brigade south to help his main effort, thereby ensuring a virtual halt to Gerasimov's effort. With the aid of that unit's attached attack helicopters, the Seventeenth Army gradually ground its way westward through the stubborn Chinese defenders to Suifenhe (11 August). After nearly two weeks of heavy going, the 51st Motorised Rifle Division finally crossed the Muling River (23–24 August), less than fifty kilometres short of Mudanjiang. By that date, though, events to the north-west had provoked a major change in the military situation in Manchuria.

THE SECOND PHASE IN THE WEST
(25 AUGUST–15 SEPTEMBER)

In the Dzungar Basin in far north-west China, Karzametov's First Kazakh Army and the attached 38th Division halted and regrouped for several days before resuming operations on 27 August. Leaving the 38th Motorised Rifle Division to hold Urumqi and environs, Karzametov drove east on the highway along the northern slopes of the Bogda Shan. His immediate objective was the city of Hami, headquarters of General Pu's Fourteenth Group Army. Once more, the altitude limited the combat utility of the Kazakhs' Soviet-built helicopters. Moreover, by this time Karzametov's units were over 1,200 kilometres from their main supply depots and support facilities at Ayaguz, and most regiments were at less than three-quarters strength.

Faced with mounting casualties and dogged Chinese resistance, the First Kazakh Army advanced slowly. However, the advance was facilitated when the fresh 47th Motorised Rifle Division, detached from Rumantsev's Tenth Army, drove south from Bayan-Ondor in Mongolia toward Hami. The city fell after two days of fighting (10–11 September). By that time, even the 47th Division was at the end of its logistical tether, and Karzametov ordered the First Kazakh Army to suspend operations. He detached several regiments to conduct security sweeps in the Dzungar Basin, where partisan (or bandit) activity was complicating Russian administration and straining the increasingly frayed and ragged lines of supply and communications.

Meanwhile, General Rumantsev's Tenth Army and the Mongolian

'Corps' had finally opened their offensive on 19 August. The Russian 28th, 31st and 35th Divisions and the 1st and 2nd Mongolian Divisions crossed the frontier near the railhead of Ejin Qi, in Chinese Inner Mongolia, about 400 kilometres south-west of Dalandzadgad. The advancing Russian troops and their Mongolian allies made good initial progress, capturing Ejin Qi on 21 August and advancing some 80 kilometres into China by the 25th. The Russians were faced by five divisions: the 28th, 29th (Motorised) and 43rd of Pu's Fourteenth Group Army and the 27th and 31st Divisions from Jiang's Twenty-seventh Group Army to the east. Although the PLA units were outgunned, they fought tenaciously and caused the Russians considerable casualties, especially in lighter armoured vehicles. By 31 August the Tenth Army had ground forward over 200 kilometres, but flank and rear security had absorbed the attention of three of the five available divisions. With offensive operations in the hands of only the 31st and 35th Motorised Rifle Divisions, Rumantsev decided that he could make no further progress without additional forces. He halted the advance on 2 September.

The Russian Ninth Army's drive on Beijing, supported by the Eleventh Army, resumed on 20 August. These two armies, commanded as a 'task front' by Ninth Army's General Zaikov, were more than a match for the defending Sixteenth and Twenty-first Group Armies, which had barely 1,100 tanks (mostly Type-69s) against nearly 1,300 more modern Russian tanks (T-80s, T-72s and T-64s) and some 750 BMP-3s with 100 mm smoothbore guns. As the two defending PLA armies reeled under the Russian blows on 22–26 August, the Beijing Military Region command released General Yu Liang's Thirtieth Group Army, which moved north-west from its assembly area north of Beijing.

On 28 August, Zaikov shifted his front's axis of advance slightly eastward to avoid the hill country north of Jining. The redirected Russian advance slammed headlong into Yu's arriving Thirtieth Group Army, and a confused battle raged in the open country north-east of Zhangjiakou and west of the upper Xai River for five crucial days. Romanov's Eleventh Army, the main Russian force involved, maintained a slight upper hand because of its superior mobility, greater communications capacity and faster response time, and because of the awesome firepower of the now-dwindling Russian helicopter forces, down to some 25 Mi-8Fs and nearly 30 Mi-24Es. Although each of the three PLA armies involved in these operations contained a tank division, their infantry divisions (nine of the twelve divisions present) were all unmounted infantry, and they suffered heavily in the open country from Russian mechanised and armoured forces. The Russians took Zhangjiakou on 3 September, and the next day the weakened Twenty-first and Thirtieth Armies were compelled to withdraw into the hills north of Beijing, where they took up entrenched positions dug by hurriedly mobilised militia from the capital.

The Russians made several strong probes of this position between 6 and 9 September. Heavy PLA artillery concentrations, and the realisation that a breakthrough would cost dearly, convinced Zaikov that further offensive operations would not be worth the additional casualties. A regiment of the 16th Guards Motorised Rifle Division (Eleventh Army) made a great show of capturing a three-kilometre stretch of the Great Wall on 7 September, a scene widely carried in Commonwealth and Western media over the next several days.

The PLA situation on the Beijing front was more precarious than the Russians realised, largely because nearly all Chinese reserves were committed. Only one army had been moved into north-east China from the interior; Lieutenant General Hu Wing's small Eighth Group Army from the Jinan Military Region, with the 3rd Tank and 6th and 16th Infantry Divisions. This force joined General Yao's Ninth Group Army in the Shenyang-Changchun corridor. Only General Li Shangkung's Fifteenth Group Army remained in reserve around Beijing and Tianjin.

THE SECOND PHASE IN THE EAST
(25 AUGUST–15 SEPTEMBER)

The defeat of General Beng's Thirty-fifth Group Army north-east of Qiqihar (10–17 August), and the ensuing defeat of General Yang's counterattack with the First Armoured Group Army (20–24 August), had compelled Deng's Twenty-third Group Army to fall back on Baicheng to avoid encirclement. Qiqihar fell to the Russian 17th Guards Motorised Rifle Division (Eighth Guards Army) on 26 August, while Malenkov's Fifth Guards Tank Army swept through the relatively open country between Qiqihar and Harbin, intent on seizing the lower Nen River crossings and then smashing into the north-eastern flank of the Chinese Twenty-third Group Army. The 38th and 40th Infantry Divisions of Thirty-fifth Group Army were badly cut up in the ensuing free-for-all, and by 29 August had virtually ceased to exist as organised units. The more mobile and more heavily equipped 10th Tank and 35th Motorised Divisions fared only slightly better, and were divisions in name only by the time they reached comparative safety in the Sungari bend south-west of Harbin on 29–30 August.

Faced with the better part of three Russian armies, comprising four tank and six motorised rifle divisions, General Deng's hard-fighting (and still cohesive) Twenty-third Group Army was compelled to fall back from its Baicheng positions on 31 August and 1 September, and he withdrew south along the rail line toward Changchun and Siping. Although the battered state of the Manchurian transport net posed staggering problems for the Russian Twelfth Army's overworked logisticians, they managed to keep enough supplies flowing to the army's divisions to maintain a close pursuit of the Twenty-third Group Army.

Meanwhile, Maslyukov's Eighth Guards Army (less the 15th Guards and 17th Guards Motorised Rifle Divisions) had closed in on the northwestern front of Harbin's defences (28–31 August), at the same time as the Third and Fourteenth Armies, under General Platov's operational control, closed in on Harbin from north-east and east. The PLA defenders included some scattered remnants from the First Armoured Group Army, nearly all of General Tian's Twenty-fourth Group Army (which had survived the Sungari River campaign in fairly good condition), and the 7th Artillery Division. Unfortunately for General Tian's defensive efforts, most of the 7th Division's numerous artillery pieces and rocket launchers were towed, and both weapons and crews suffered heavily from Russian air and helicopter attacks during the eight-day battle for Harbin.

The Russians initially made only minor progress, but a full-scale air assault by 102nd Guards Airborne Division on 3 September captured the Sungari River bridges north of Changchun. Although that operation was attended by all the confusion common to airborne landings, the 7th Guards Tank Division reached the 102nd's airhead around midday on the 4th. This left General Tian's forces surrounded in Harbin, although the two Guards divisions had to repel determined but uncoordinated counterattacks on 6 and 7 September, mounted by forces from General Hu's Eighth and General Yao's Ninth Group Armies coming north from Changchun. The pounding which Harbin and its defenders underwent during the entire battle took its toll, and with large portions of the city reduced to rubble the Russians had fought their way to the city centre on 9 September, effectively ending the battle. Some units from Tian's Twenty-fourth Group Army escaped to the east and south and, avoiding portions of the Fourteenth Army, eventually reached the comparative safety of the hill country between Jilin and Mudanjiang (10–15 September).

As the Battle for Harbin raged, and the redoubtable Chinese Twenty-third Group Army was gradually herded southward by Bakatin's Twelfth Army, further east Bolgansky's Seventeenth Army and Gerasimov's accompanying Task Force neared Mudanjiang. Beginning on 31 August, they were assisted by operations of the 45th and 60th Divisions from Slobov's Fourteenth Army, although the 60th was recalled to take part in the Battle for Harbin on 4 September. Gerasimov's forces captured Jixi on 5 September, the same day that the Seventeenth Army reached the outskirts of Mudanjiang. With Harbin surrounded, and with Mudanjiang under determined Russian attack from the east, General Tang was ordered to disengage his Fifth (Mountain) Group Army from the Mudanjiang area and fall back on the area between Yani and Jilin on 7 September. Mudanjiang fell next day. That same day Gerasimov's 37th Division – on the extreme right of the Russian advance – finally met the 45th Divison of the Fourteenth Army at Linkou, some 70 kilometres west of Jixi. General Bolgansky left Gerasimov's troops to hold the communications lines open and try to suppress or contain the guerrillas active north of Jixi, while he reorganised the Seventeenth Army.

SOBER REASSESSMENTS

These developments left the Chinese forces in Manchuria in a situation that was close to desperate. By 10 September the PLA had failed to win any notable military successes, and had been able to halt only the Russian advance on Beijing. Further, the Twenty-fourth and Thirty-fifth Group Armies had been nearly destroyed, while the First Armoured Group Army had been badly mauled. The Fifth (Mountain) and Twenty-third Group Armies were in relatively good condition, but were far apart, and the Twenty-third Group Army would soon face the combined onslaught of the Twelfth, Eighth Guards and Fifth Guards Tank Armies. Even the most optimistic PLA commanders were under no illusions about how *that* battle would turn out.

The combined Eight and Ninth Group Armies around Shenyang and Changchun were also in an unenviable situation. Although their forces were nearly fresh, the cities they had been sent to defend had suffered heavily from weeks of Soviet air attacks directed against arms factories, military bases and transport facilities. Further, any determined battle for the two cities would lead to even greater destruction, not to mention heavy civilian casualties. The PLA commanders in Manchuria generally shared the opinion that, while their forces could keep fighting for several more weeks, they were no longer capable of repelling the Soviet invasion.

Another issue also concerned the PLA leadership. Although they had abandoned most of the tenets of the old Maoist doctrine of 'protracted peoples' war', they had planned to make extensive use of militia forces to handle rear-area security and garrison duties. Several PLA commanders had reported that militia units were refusing to answer the call-out, while other units had deserted. The problem was especially acute in the cities, and the general reluctance of the militia had contributed to the comparatively swift and easy Russian capture of Harbin. A few PLA commanders suspected (correctly, as post-war investigations showed) that the bloody Tienanmen Square crackdown in 1989, and ensuing similar smaller-scale crackdowns in the early 1990s, had alienated much of the Chinese populace from the government, and had severely tarnished the image of the PLA. Few Chinese were willing to die for a regime which they strongly believed had betrayed them. With all these considerations in mind, the PLA leadership, including Marshal Zou, began pressing the Politburo to open negotiations with the Soviets.

The Russians, meanwhile, had modified their own plans. The experience of the battle for Harbin had dramatically reduced their enthusiasm for urban fighting. Marshal Cherkorin decided that the most productive course of action would be to isolate the remaining PLA regular forces in Manchuria. To accomplish this, he proposed that Malenkov attack down the Baicheng–Siping railway, and then send the Fifth Guards Tank Army south across the Xai River and reach the coast south-west of Shenyang and west of the Liaotung Peninsula. This operation would not only isolate the sixteen PLA Divisions remaining in Manchuria, but would also threaten Beijing and Tianjin from the north-east. Only Deng's Twenty-third Group Army was in any position to oppose Soviet plans and, with Girenko's improvised 'Task Front', comprising the Twelfth, Eighth Guards and Fifth Guards Tank Armies (thirteen divisions in all) ranged against it, that army would be unable to resist for very long.

On 12 and 13 September, while the Russians prepared for the next phase of their operations, the Chinese leadership in Beijing gradually realised that they had grievously miscalculated, and that the only way to control the damage was to accept a cease-fire. As a group of PLA commanders pointed out to the more stubborn members of the Politburo in a memorable meeting on 12 September, the fact that few of the guerrilla units set up in Manchuria were obeying orders was not an auspicious sign. It would do no good to retreat into the interior of China, snapped Lieutenant General Wang Ziakung, Director of Operations, if the guerrilla forces raised from the militia followed their own orders and 'behaved like bandits'.

Diplomats from the UN, especially from the other three uninvolved permanent Security Council members (Britain, France and the US) seized the opportunity afforded by the lull in combat to appeal to both sides for a cease-fire. Opinion was divided among Russian military leaders in Moscow. Some were reluctant to agree to an early cease-fire, hoping to delay it for a week or more and so allow them to undertake the offensive across the Xai River in order to separate the Manchurian forces from the rest of China. Cooler heads in Moscow and most Kazakh leaders in Alma-Ata, though, recognised that the advantages of a more decisive victory over China were not worth further casualties and the loss of good relations with the 'Western' powers. Further, the principal Russian and Kazakh objective of inflicting a bruising but limited defeat on China had been achieved. With last-minute haggling over battle lines and positions, and prisoner exchanges, the combatants agreed to suspend major offensive operations on 14 September, but the cease-fire did not take effect until 20 September.

POLITICAL RAMIFICATIONS OF THE WAR

The principal result of the Sino–Russian War was drastic reduction of Chinese influence in the Middle East and Africa. Several of China's more recent allies swiftly came to the conclusion that China had pushed too hard too fast, and quickly drew away from their alliances. Among China's more steadfast friends, the major lesson was the clear demonstration of China's relative military weakness, and the comparatively poor showing made by Chinese weaponry against Russian equipment. In some respects, the war did more for the new Russian Armaments Combine than had been anticipated, and the Combine had to scramble to fill new orders.

On a slightly longer-term basis, the ensuing peace agreement (the Treaties of Shenyang and Vladivostok, signed in September 1996 and January 1997) helped to stabilise the balance of power in north-eastern Asia. The Russians gained favourable resolution of several long-simmering and minor border disputes, but more important the Chinese were compelled to relinquish their long and dearly held claims to large areas of southern Siberia and most of Mongolia based on the eighteenth-century holdings of the Ch'ing dynasty. Surprisingly the Chinese abstained, without exercising their veto, in UN Security Council Resolution 144 of 1995, which demanded that all members of the UN forswear any historically based claims upon the territory of any other nation. In a memorable speech in the Security Council, the Chinese representative agreed that such claims were blatantly imperialistic and quite out of place on the eve of the twenty-first century.

Another important result for the Russians and the Kazakhs was that the West began to reconsider whether the new republics were as feeble as popular wisdom considered them, and that the Commonwealth might not be a paper tiger after all. Clearly, the full benefits of market reforms and economic restructuring had not come to pass, but it was equally clear that Russia, and the new Commonwealth, were forces to be reckoned with in international politics. Many Western news reports spoke favourably of Russian Army treatment of Chinese civilians and of their respect for private property, traits not notably present in the last major campaigns of that army, in Eastern Europe in 1945 and in Afghanistan between 1980 and 1989.

The effects of the war within China were manifold. First, the defeat destroyed the results of most of China's foreign policy successes over the previous decade. The Chinese also realised that, at least for the time being, they would be unable to play either a 'Russian' card against the US and Europe, or the US–European card against the Russians. In their hour of need the Chinese found themselves alone, with even their Mongolian kin arrayed against them. Further, the revelations of Chinese military weakness exposed the PLA to numerous political attacks for having promised much and delivered virtually nothing, and for having betrayed the nation and the revolution. The PLA's defence, that its distasteful activities in suppressing domestic political unrest had robbed it of popular support, won few friends within the government but at least indicated that there was plenty of blame to go around. Popular demonstrations against both the government and the PLA in the months after the war were generally not suppressed, although police forces (but no military units) were used to maintain civil order.

The long-term effects of the defeat on the Chinese government were more difficult to assess. The regime had taken a great gamble and lost. Not only had recent gains been sacrificed, but considerable damage had been wrought both on the nation's armed forces and on its industrial base. The factory districts of Shenyang and Changchun were badly damaged, while that of Harbin was virtually destroyed. The costs of rebuilding were great, and this reconstruction would take time and technical expertise, neither of which would be available for other efforts.

For China, Russia and the Kazakh Republic, the post-war era has entailed a reassessment of their policies. China could not continue to view the rest of the world as both inferior and suspect, and has had to accept that it is merely one nation (albeit an important and potentially powerful one) among many. On the other hand, the Russians have realised that they would have to reach some long-term accommodation with China; they simply could not start a punitive war every time China began to exercise influence beyond its frontiers. While an alliance was too much to hope for, and was unrealistic without more shared national interests, China and Russia would have to reach some sort of permanent relationship which would allow each state to deal with the other on a more or less equal basis. That realization provided real hope that the mayhem and destruction of the war (the human cost of which is given in Table 10.4) might actually have produced a positive result.

TABLE 10.4

HUMAN COST OF THE WAR

Nation	Killed	Wounded	Total casualties
Russia/Kazakhstan	22,829	91,318	114,147
China	43,809	121,426	165,235

The higher rate of Chinese fatalities in combat was due to a combination of Soviet air superiority and more sophisticated weapons, and less efficient PLA medical services.

TNDM ADDENDUM: BATTLE OF KEDONG–BAIQUAN

The Chinese commander of I Armoured Group Army, General Yang Zhen, launched his counteroffensive on the morning of 20 August 1995. His army, comprising the 1st and 2nd Tank Divisions and the 3rd and 6th Mechanised Divisions, had planned to strike north against the flank of the Soviet Far East Front's V Guards Tank Army. Unfortunately for the Chinese, the Russians had been forewarned by satellite reconnaissance, and had hastily planned a counterattack of their own.

Initially, General Yang's armoured forces made good progress against Russian screening forces, but during the night of 20/21 August the leading elements of I Armoured Group Army ran into increasing Russian resistance. General Yang modified his plan and reoriented his forces in the early hours of 21 August, and prepared to renew his attack at first light. By that time the bulk of Colonel General Konstantin I. Girenko's V Guards Army had moved into position, and the Russian divisions attacked in the early morning of 21 August, driving the PLA troops from their hastily prepared positions. During most of 22 August, the I Armoured Group Army fought a series of delaying actions, but by 23rd August heavy losses compelled the Chinese to withdraw, and Girenko's troops began their pursuit. Wary of going too far too fast, Girenko (with the approval of Marshal Cherkorin) allowed General Yang's battered formations to break contact late in the day on 24 August. By this time Russian units had advanced an average of over thirty-two kilometres. The battle had lasted almost five days, including three days of intense combat, and had virtually wrecked the once-proud I Armoured Group Army.

TABLE TNDM 10.1

STATISTICS: KEDONG-BAIQUAN

CHINESE	Strength	Losses	Daily losses (%)
Men	50,400	3,880	2.57
Armour	1,091	326	9.96
Artillery	324	11	1.13
SOVIET			
Men	49,850	1,542	1.03
Armour	2,565	152	1.98
Artillery	687	9	0.44
Helicopters	70	6	2.86

Glossary

Air superiority Preponderance in air strength of one combat force over the opposing force such that the weaker force cannot interfere prohibitively with the other's conduct of air, ground or sea operations. Although air superiority provides one side with general domination of the airspace over surface combat operations, it does not mean total denial of air operations by the weaker side.

Air supremacy That degree of air superiority wherein the opposing air force is incapable of effective interference with ground, sea or air operations.

All-aspect intercept capability The capability of certain advanced, late generation air-to-air missiles (AAMs), like the South African Kukri, to acquire and home in on a target from any angle of attack and with greater discrimination than available to earlier AAMs.

Army In the US Army, an army is a unit comprising two or more army corps (see **Corps**) and support units. In the Russian Army, the Chinese People's Liberation Army (PLA) and forces patterned on their model, an army comprises three to five divisions and is roughly analogous to a large US or Western European corps.

Basij Iranian 'Popular Mobilisation Army' volunteers. A paramilitary branch of the Iranian armed forces, controlled by the *pasdaran* (see **Pasdaran**). Mostly youths, *basij* are equipped only with small arms, and are virtually 'cannon fodder', utilised in human wave assaults or to clear minefields.

Bomblet See **Cluster munitions.**

Carpet bombing A tactic of aerial bombardment pioneered by the US during World War II, in which large numbers of bombers cover the target area, and any enemy units within it, with a 'carpet' of bombs.

CEV See **Relative combat effectiveness value.**

Cluster bomb See **Cluster munitions.**

Cluster munitions A class of weapons that utilise large numbers of smaller munitions ('bomblets' or submunitions), distributed over a wide area, to attack dispersed targets. The submunitions may be high-explosive, anti-tank or anti-personnel mines, or a combination of the three. The dispenser is usually a simple canister which may be delivered in a bomb (which can be a smart weapon, see **Smart bomb**), an artillery shell, a rocket, a missile (see **Cruise missile**) or a reloadable container mounted on an aircraft.

Collateral damage Damage to non-military structures and facilities resulting from a strike on a nearby military target. Also, euphemism for civilian casualties resulting from military operations.

Combat air patrol (CAP) An air patrol over an area or force for the purpose of intercepting and attacking hostile aircraft before they are able to reach their objective.

Combat effectiveness value See **Relative combat effectiveness value.**

Combined arms A term referring to the concept of integrating the efforts of armour, infantry, artillery and air support in co-ordinated operations directed by a single tactical or operational commander. This concept is common to most modern mechanised armies, including the Soviet.

Confrontation states Those hostile Arab states having a frontier with Israel; currently Lebanon, Syria and Jordan. Egypt was a confrontation state before making peace with Israel in 1979.

Corps In the US and Western European armies, a tactical unit composed of two or more divisions and usually commanded by a lieutenant general. A large Western corps is similar in size to a Soviet or PLA army. In the modern Hungarian Army, a corps comprises five combat brigades, an artillery brigade, and air defence and reconnaissance battalions.

Counter-battery fire (or mission) Fire directed against enemy artillery positions, intended to destroy or neutralise enemy artillery weapons.

Cratering munition Any munition (usually a bomb) designed specifically to make craters on a runway or other surface in order to deny its use to the enemy.

Cruise missile A surface-to-surface missile, designed to fly at low altitudes along a programmed route to a specific target. Cruise missiles are utilised to attack deep targets (see **Deep Strike**) where either the nature of the target's location or the strength of enemy defences makes attack by conventional aircraft impractical.

Deep strike A type of air attack directed against enemy lines of communication, logistical support, transport routes and rear-area facilities deep in enemy-held territory. Also, deep-penetration attack or raid.

Electronic warfare (EW) The military employment of electronics to prevent or reduce an enemy's effective use of radiated electromagnetic energy (generally thought of in terms of communication and detection), and to ensure one's own effective use of radiated electromagnetic energy.

Fighter An aircraft designed to engage and destroy enemy aircraft.

Fighter/ground attack (FGA) An aircraft designed for a dual role as a fighter (see **Fighter**) and for attack of ground targets.

Flip-bombing See **Toss bombing.**

Forward air controller (FAC) Anyone responsible for directing aircraft to targets by radio in an operation involving close air support.

Front In Soviet army usage, a front comprises two or more armies, usually with a geographical designation (e.g. Far East Front). A front is roughly analogous to a US Army Group.

Human factors Those considerations affecting warfare that are essentially dependent upon, or the result of, human behaviour, such as morale, fear, suppression or surprise.

Improved conventional munition (ICM) See **Cluster munitions.**

Interdiction Air or artillery attacks intended to destroy, prevent or hinder enemy supply, communications and movement.

Intifada An uprising of the Palestinian population of the West Bank and Gaza Strip against Israeli occupying forces and particularly against Israeli policies opposing an independent Palestinian Arab state.

KGB Komitet Gosudarslvennoi Bezopasnosti, or Committee of State Security. This is the internal and external intelligence, counter-intelligence, espionage and covert action agency of the Soviet Union, combining in one organisation the functions of the Central Intelligence Agency (CIA) and Federal Bureau of Investigation (FBI) in the US.

Laser designator A ground-based or airborne target 'designator' that focuses a thin beam of low-power laser energy on a target, turning it into an energy emitter that laser-guided weapons can home in on.

Laser-guided Refers to the guidance system of 'smart bombs' and other weapons that home in on laser energy, whether 'beam-riders' or those that home in on sources of laser radiation.

Light infantry Infantry with a minimum of heavy equipment and few heavy motor vehicles, intended to possess great strategic mobility. Light infantry is also intended for operations in difficult terrain unsuitable for 'heavy' mechanised or motorised forces.

Likud This is one of the two principal political parties in Israel, a union (*likud*) of several smaller right-wing parties, adamantly opposed to seeking peace with the Arabs by compromise or by territorial or other concessions.

Line(s) of communications (LOC) The route or routes connecting forces in the field with their bases and sources of supply and reinforcement.

Logistics The activities necessary to support a force in the field, including but not limited to supply, medical care and the construction and operation of facilities.

Mechanised forces Military units which are carried entirely in tracked or wheeled vehicles, generally capable of movement over almost all terrain. Armoured units are a type of mechanised force.

MEF (marine expeditionary force) A USMC air-ground task force generally consisting of a marine division and its associated air wing. An MEF may handle larger or smaller forces, as necessary.

Military district (MD) In the Soviet Union, the military district is the basic peacetime territorial military administrative unit. Units assigned to a military district would form two or more armies in the event of mobilisation. In China, military regions perform a similar role.

Militia In the Soviet Union, militia refers to the paramilitary civil police force. In most other countries, however, militia forces are part-time units, activated only for periodic training or in times of emergency.

Minelet See **Cluster munitions.**

Motorised forces Military units which move by wheeled motor vehicle. Such forces, when mounted, are generally limited largely to movement by road.

Motorised rifle (see also **Mechanised forces**) The Soviet term for mechanised infantry, in wide use in Eastern Europe as well.

Palestine Liberation Organisation (PLO) A loose federation of anti-Israeli Palestinian refugees, seeking by any and all means (primarily force of arms through various forms of terrorism, as well as by diplomatic pressure) to end Israeli control over the West Bank and Gaza Strip and (ultimately) to bring about the overthrow of the Israeli state, so as to establish Palestinian Arab control over the region known, prior to 1948, as Palestine.

Pasdaran (properly *pasdaran inqilab*). The Iranian revolutionary guard corps, a semi-irregular branch of the Iranian armed forces, directly responsible to the ruling Islamic Revolutionary Council. The *pasdaran* includes lightly equipped ground, naval, and air forces and controls the *basij* (see **Basij**).

Paramilitary (force or organisation) A force or group that is distinct from a country's standing professional forces, but resembling them in such aspects as organisation, equipment, training or mission.

Patriot A surface-to-air (SAM) missile system, produced by the Raytheon Company and the Martin Marietta Corporation that is the centrepiece of US theatre air and tactical ballistic missile defence. The Patriot system demonstrated a very high rate of success in intercepting and destroying Scuds fired by Iraq against Israel and Saudi Arabia in the Kuwait (or Gulf) war of January and February 1991.

Peace-keeping force A military force established by international agreement to maintain peace in a contested area.

PLO See **Palestine Liberation Organisation.**

Posture. Describes the offensive or defensive deployment, preparation, mission and intent for combat operations of armed forces. Offensive postures include deliberate attack, hasty attack and pursuit. Attacks may be a main effort, a secondary effort or a holding action. Defensive postures include fortified defence, prepared defence, hasty defence, delay and withdrawal. A counterattack is an attack mounted by a defender designed either as a riposte to disrupt an enemy attack or to seize the initiative from the enemy.

Pre-emptive attack (or strike) An attack initiated on the basis of evidence that an enemy attack is imminent. Thus, through surprise, the initiative may be seized from the enemy.

PW (POW) report Intelligence information gathered by interrogation of prisoners of war.

Ramadan An Islamic holy month of fasting, abstinence and self-denial. It is the ninth month of the Islamic year. During the month Muslims must abstain from food, drink and sexual intercourse from dawn to dusk.

Recce Slang, originally British, for reconnaissance, reconnaissance mission; pronounced 'rekky'.

Relative combat effectiveness value A value representing the quantified per capita capability of one military force to operate effectively against another force. A value of 1.0 means that the two forces have equal capability. A value less than one means an inferior capability with respect to the opposing force; a value greater than one represents a superior capability with respect to the opponent.

Remotely piloted vehicle (RPV) An unmanned aircraft that is utilised for reconnaissance or electronic warfare (EW) missions.

Roll on-roll off vessel (RO-RO) A ship designed to allow vehicles to drive into and out of the hold without specialised cargo handling devices.

Smart bomb An aircraft-delivered munition or bomb fitted with a guidance mechanism (and, sometimes, propulsion mechanism) that enable it to hit targets with a high degree of accuracy. Guidance may be based on radar, laser, infra-red sensors, TV or other means. A smart bomb may be a specially designed munition (as in the US stand-off attack missile (SLAM)) or a conventional bomb (an iron or 'dumb' bomb) fitted with a guidance package, and sometimes a propulsion package (as in the US Paveway guided bombs). See **Stand-off air attack** and **Cruise missile.**

Soviet Guards Units of the Soviet army honoured for battlefield performance during World War II. During that war the title conferred advantages of equipment and supply, but contemporary Guards units are indistinguishable from non-Guards units.

Special (operations) forces (SOF) Any military force trained for unusual or unconventional operations, for example US Army Special Forces, British SAS, US Navy SEALs, etc.

Stand-off air attack A form of aerial attack of ground targets that utilise 'smart' weaponry (see **Smart bomb** and **Cruise missile**) to allow the attacking aircraft to stay out of range of land- or air-based defence systems.

Strategic mission A military mission that carries out or fulfils a strategic purpose, such as long-range strikes against vital targets by strategic air forces or special forces.

Submunitions See **Cluster munitions.**

Tactical Numerical Deterministic Model A computerised simulation (or model, or representation) of combat developed by Colonel T N Dupuy, USA, Ret. It is based upon the Quantified Judgment Method, which is described in his book, *Numbers, Predictions, and War* (New York, 1979).

Task force A grouping of units under one commander, usually formed for the purpose of carrying out a specific operation or mission. This usually is a temporary grouping, but can be permanent, and applies to ground, naval or air forces.

Task group In the navy, applies to a component of a naval task force. May be applied to land forces as a synonym for a task force.

Theatre of operations/theatre of war A geographical area within which military operations occur. A war may involve multiple theatres of operations, as did World War II. If there is only one theatre, that zone may also be called the theatre of war.

TNDM See **Tactical Numerical Deterministic Model.**

Toss-bombing A method of bombing in which an aircraft flies on a line toward the target and pulls up in a vertical plane, releasing the bomb at an angle that will compensate for the effect of gravity drop on the bomb.

TVD (Teatr Voennogo Deistviya) A Russian military term meaning 'theatre of strategic military action'. A TVD comprises one or more military districts (usually two or three), and includes coastal waters and airspace as well as dry ground. In Russian military parlance, a TVD is 'a space where the different strategic groupings of the armed forces, to include ground, air and naval components, deploy and conduct military action to achieve the objective of the war'.

West Bank That portion of pre-1948 Palestine, west of the Jordan River, that remained under the military control of Transjordan (later Jordan) at the end of the Israeli War of Independence (1948–9). It was conquered and occupied by Israeli forces in the Six-Day War of 1967.

The Tactical Numerical Deterministic Model; A Tool for Analysis of, and Planning for Military Combat Options

BACKGROUND

The analyses of some of the discrete military events described in this book were made possible by use of the TNDM, a computer-assisted, mathematical model of combat. The origins of the TNDM go back to 1965, when I was working on a research study for the US Army which had for its purpose an evaluation of trends in the lethality of weapons over history. I developed a concept of measuring this in terms of their ability to inflict casualties, or to do other damage, over a period of time. The result was a methodology for calculating the Operational Lethality Index (OLI) of any weapon, at any time in history. The characteristics considered were accuracy, reliability, number of human targets rendered casualties for each 'strike' of a weapon, the range at which it could do damage, and the density of the target array. For 'mobile fighting machines,' like tanks or aircraft or warships, which combine one or more direct-fire weapons with mobility and protection, consideration was given to factors representing the speed of the machine, its range or radius of operation and its ability to survive when hit by hostile weapons. The calculations in applying these considerations and characteristics of a given weapon produced a numerical 'proving ground' value representing the number of casualties the weapon could inflict in one hour under ideal circumstances.

The next step in the development of a model of combat was the derivation of the Quantified Judgment Method, which used historical experience to consider all the factors affecting the actual ability of all the weapons in a military force to inflict damage upon an opponent on a battlefield. Among the many physical variables affecting the effectiveness of weapons – and forces equipped with weapons – were such obvious factors as terrain, weather, and season, as well as more complex but nevertheless important factors as mobility and vulnerability. Values, or methods for calculating values, for these factors were obtained by detailed analysis of sixty World War II battles which took place in Italy in 1943–4. These values were tested and confirmed (or in a few instances, slightly modified) by applying them to battle data for about 150 additional battles or engagements, mostly from other theatres of World War II, but including fifteen battles from World War I and about sixty from the 1967 and 1973 Arab-Israeli wars, plus two from the Napoleonic Wars and two from the American Civil War.

One thing which became very evident in this process of quantitative historical analysis was the overwhelming importance of human factors. But what also became evident is that – despite the vagaries of human nature and behaviour – values representing human factors fell into clear patterns. One need only look at the application of actuarial analysis to insurance and to medicine to realise that this is typical of human nature and human behaviour in all fields of endeavour and activity and under any and all circumstances. When human beings are involved, there will always be exceptions to the patterns; for instance, the survival of some people to ages of more than 100 years. But the patterns are clear.

Since my colleagues and I were dealing with a large number of examples – initially 60, later more than 200 – our analysis was actuarial. Others, like American military historian Theodore Ayrault Dodge about a century ago, have flirted with this concept of patterns in battles and warfare. But, prior to the development of the Quantified Judgment Method, no one had attempted to do this systematically and scientifically.

The first human factor I was about to quantify was that of surprise. Next, and possibly most important, was that of relative combat effectiveness. It is evident from the most cursory look at history that some armies and some generals have performed better than others, regardless of circumstances. Our detailed analyses of the first sixty battles in Italy forced us (reluctantly, I must say) to the conclusion that the Germans were consistently better than the Allies (British and Americans), by a margin of about 20 per cent. This meant that, on average, the quantified predictions of battle outcomes could be matched by quantified results, only if a factor of 1.2 was applied to the Germans. Yet we also discovered that one or two American divisions performed as well as some of the best German divisions; further analysis revealed that this was a reflection of leadership qualities. On the Eastern Front, the relative combat effectiveness value (CEV) of German superiority over Soviets averaged an amazing 2.5 from 1941 to 1943, and was still about 1.8 at the end of the war. In other words, given comparable equipment, 100 Germans were on average the equivalent of about 120 American and British soldiers, and about 250 Soviet soldiers. This does not mean that the Germans were stronger, smarter, braver or more highly motivated than their Allied opponents; they were simply more professional.★

Similarly, we discovered an average Israeli CEV superiority of 2.0 over Arab opponents in the Arab-Israeli wars. Thus, on average, 100 Israeli soldiers in those wars were the equivalent of about 200 Arab soldiers. The differences among the Arabs – in clear patterns – was also interesting. The Jordanians were the best, having a CEV with respect to the Israelis of about 0.6 (in other words, the Israeli CEV was about 1.6 with respect to the Jordanians). The Jordanian CEV relationship to the other Arab forces was as follows: Egyptians, 1.15; Syrians, 1.3; Iraqis, 1.8. Again, we do not believe that the Israelis were smarter, stronger, braver or more highly motivated than the Arabs, or that the Jordanians are a kind of 'super-Arab.' It is simply that through a combination of cultural and professional phenomena the Israelis have proven themselves able to utilise their forces more effectively than have their opponents, and that the Jordanians are evidently professionally superior to the other Arab forces.

That is the background of the methodology employed to assess the outcomes of the hypothetical battles in the speculative wars in this book. At the end of each chapter there is a TNDM Addendum, in which the results of one or more TNDM 'runs' of one battle (and in one case, two battles) are presented in summary form. The inputs for each 'run' reflect the forces and weapons available to each side in the

---

★This discovery prompted me to write a book – *A Genius for War; The German Army and General Staff, 1807–1945* (Englewood Cliffs, NJ, 1977) – to explain both how this phenomenon of superior German military professionalism developed, and why it did not in any way substantiate Hitler's concept of a 'master race.'

battle (or one phase of the battle), and all circumstances affecting the battle, such as terrain, weather, season and the like. When required by the narrative, or otherwise reasonably reflective of the situation, at least two behavioural variables are expressly considered: surprise and relative combat effectiveness. In the hypothetical battles of Shaykh Miskin and Dimona in Chapter 1, we have entered relative combat effectiveness values (CEVs) of 2.0 for the Israelis. On the basis of less thorough assessment of previous fighting in Angola and Southwest Africa, we have given a similar CEV value to the South Africans in Chapter 4.

DESCRIPTION

The Tactical Numerical Deterministic Model (TNDM) is an empirically based combat model derived from historical research. The model emerged from a collaborative effort by Colonel T N Dupuy, USA, Ret. (noted military historian, military theorist and designer of historically based combat models), and Dr James G. Taylor (respected author of works concerning modern Lanchester-type models) in developing a new differential-equation attrition methodology based on historical data. By a mathematical process similar to the Lanchester Equations, the TNDM attrition methodology provides results consistent with those that occurred in historical engagements.

The TNDM is briefly described by its title: It is essentially a *tactical* battle model, although it can be used for planning and analyses of both operational and strategic campaigns. It is *numerical*, with quantified inputs leading to quantified outputs through a set of mathematical relationships. It is *deterministic*, in that any given set of inputs will always yield the same outputs. (While it may be argued whether combat is essentially deterministic or essentially stochastic, a forecast must be deterministic, whether arrived at by a stochastic or a deterministic process.)

The TNDM is a computer-assisted mathematical simulation of air and land combat. The TNDM was developed from and validated by actual results of previous (historical) combat. The circumstances and results of more than 250 historical combat engagements have been reduced to numerical inputs and outputs, linked by a series of computations. Most of these engagements were division-level encounters in World War II and the 1967 and 1973 Arab-Israeli wars. All inputs, assumptions and relationships are open and explicit. (There is no 'black box'.) Consideration is given to *all* significant variable factors affecting combat outcomes. The human or behavioural factors of combat (so-called 'intangibles') are considered and represented in the model, to reflect their effects upon battle outcomes in actual combat. Both direct and indirect effects of air support of ground operations are represented realistically.

The TNDM is directly based on the most comprehensive research currently available concerning fundamental dependencies among identifiable combat variables. Models not based on this unique historical research are unable to reflect faithfully such significant dependencies and are likely at best to represent environmental, behavioural and operational variations in an *ad hoc* fashion. On the other hand, the TNDM allows realistic parametric variations in attrition with respect to theoretically more than 2,000 different environmental situations.

The TNDM is a quick-response, inexpensive tactical model suitable for planning and analysing a variety of combat situations, ranging from a small-unit, low-intensity combat engagement to conventional multi-day division, corps or army battles. Tactical decisions at the chosen level of aggregation are entered by the user. Tactical decisions at lower levels of aggregation are embedded within the model. Because of its ability to reflect actual combat outcomes at different levels of aggregation, the TNDM is, in effect, a self-contained hierarchical model.

The TNDM attrition module can also be substituted for the attrition module of an existing model based upon a heterogeneous Lanchester-type methodology. Since the TNDM methodology is historically based, it is more scientifically justified than any methodology not consistent with historical experience. It has also been validated using historical engagements.

TNDM inputs include the following: numbers of personnel, lethality effects of all weapons, numbers of armoured vehicles, other vehicles and aircraft; the battlefield effects of environmental factors such as terrain, weather and season upon combat outcomes; the operational effects of defensive posture, mobility, vulnerability, fatigue and surprise. Different levels of tactical competence of troops and leaders may be entered as combat effectiveness values. Logistical inputs are possible also for certain circumstances.

TNDM outputs are as follows: mission accomplishment (success or failure); movement (attacker's advance rate); personnel casualties and materiel losses, and recovery rates of damaged materiel items.

The TNDM has relatively few inputs and fast operating time. It is programmed to operate on a microcomputer. It is intended to facilitate analysis of combat operations of actual and proposed forces, units and weapons.

The TNDM was developed using Turbo-Pascal and has been tested extensively in the United States and abroad. The software is modular and can easily be integrated into the architecture of existing time-step and event-step combat simulations. The software can be applied in a variety of ways across a broad spectrum of combat model architectures depending on analytical requirements: force-balance investigations, force-on-force evaluations, and as a ground combat 'underlay' for designing or evaluating new combat systems/technologies.

Modern Weapons on the Modern Battlefield

An understanding of the nature, capabilities and limitations of the weapons of modern warfare will help the reader to understand the events described in this book. This brief description is intended to facilitate that understanding, but it is not intended to be (nor can it be, given space limitations) a comprehensive list of the weapons systems used by the major combatants.

Armoured fighting vehicles (AFVs) are armoured mobile fighting machines. AFVs include light and main battle tanks (MBTs), armoured cars (ACs), and armoured reconnaissance vehicles (ARVs).

Light tanks are utilised generally for battlefield reconnaissance and are usually lightly armoured and armed, typically with guns of around 75 mm calibre. In many armies light tanks have been replaced by lighter, and less expensive, armoured cars and other wheeled or tracked reconnaissance vehicles.

MBTs are the heavy striking power of modern mechanised armies. They are normally heavily armoured and armed (with guns of 105 mm calibre or greater). MBTs utilize fire, shock and manoeuvre to defeat the enemy.

All AFV designs in general, and tank designs in particular, are a compromise between mobility, protection and firepower. The mobility of an AFV is limited by its weight, which is a function of the amount of armour (protection), the size of its gun (firepower) and its power-train (engine and transmission). Armour may be enhanced by the use of various new materials such as ceramic composites, like Chobham armour, and high-density depleted uranium meshes (currently found only in the US-built M1A2 Abrams MBT). AFV engines are generally diesels, although gas turbines are used in a few types.

An item of major importance (and a large part of the expense) for modern AFVs is the fire-control system. It is widely accepted that modern anti-tank projectiles and missiles can successfully damage or destroy even the most heavily armoured MBT, if they can hit it. Thus, to be effective, an AFV must be able to find and successfully hit targets on the battlefield. Modern fire-control systems allow this to be done while the AFV is manoeuvring at high speed, over rough terrain and in poor visibility. Sensors gauge the distance to the target, wind speed, ambient temperature, curvature of the barrel, cant of the vehicle, and a host of other factors to ensure that the round fired hits the target.

Typical MBTs include the US Abrams and M-60A3, the Soviet T-72, the British Chieftain, the German Leopard and the French AMX-30. Typical light AFVs include ACs such as the Soviet BRDM-2 and the South African Rooikat, and the British Scorpion light tank.

Armoured personnel carriers (APCs) and infantry fighting vehicles (IFVs) are the primary transports for infantry on the battlefield. Both types of vehicles are lightly armoured, normally carry a light gun and, sometimes, an anti-tank guided missile. The APC is intended for transport only, with the infantry disembarking to fight. The IFV (which can be considered to be a type of AFV) is designed to allow the infantry to fire while they remain 'mounted' in the vehicle. Neither the APC nor the IFV is a tank. The allocation of space and weight to provide a crew compartment in the vehicle precludes the carrying of sufficient armour to protect the vehicle from anything other than small-calibre projectiles and shell fragments.

Typical APCs include the US M-113, the British FV-432, the Egyptian Fahd and the Soviet BTR series. Typical IFVs include the US M-2 Bradley, the Soviet BMP, the French AMX-10, the South African Ratel, the German Marder and the British MICV-80 Warrior.

Anti-tank (AT) weapons are designed to engage and defeat AFVs in general and MBTs in particular. It is generally accepted that the best anti-tank weapon is another tank, but it is neither practical nor desirable for an army to disperse its tank strength about the battlefield to support nontank units. Instead, lighter and (usually) less expensive weapons systems have been designed for the sole purpose of defeating opposing tanks.

The two major types of anti-tank projectiles are kinetic energy (armour-piercing, or AP) and high explosive anti-tank (HEAT) rounds. Kinetic energy rounds rely on the energy generated by the mass and velocity of the projectile to pierce the target's armour. The velocities required mean that this type of round can be effectively fired only from high-muzzle-velocity guns. (Although some progress has been made in producing missile systems of comparable high-velocity performance.) HEAT rounds depend on the energy produced by a plasma jet (the so-called Munro Effect, formed by the explosion of a shaped charge in the warhead) to 'burn' through armour. Since the effect is produced by the explosion of the warhead, there is no need to accelerate the projectile to the velocities required for kinetic energy rounds. This means that a HEAT round can be fired effectively by any low-velocity gun, missile or rocket system. However, low-velocity weapons often miss rapidly moving targets at long ranges. Moreover, the development of simple counters to HEAT warheads (spaced armour, Chobham armour and reactive armour) has markedly reduced the capability of all anti-tank systems that rely on them.

Anti-tank weapons originally were simple, towed, high-muzzle-velocity guns—in essence tank guns without the tank. Towed guns still exist, the most common type being the lightweight, low-muzzle-velocity recoilless rifle.

The most common anti-tank systems are the anti-tank guided missile (ATGM) and its companion, the anti-tank rocket launcher (ATRL). An ATGM utilises a launcher (either portable or mounted on a vehicle) to fire a missile that is controlled in flight to give a theoretically high probability of hitting the target. Control systems for ATGMs may utilise radio, wire, or laser beams for guidance. The simpler ATRL, almost always a portable weapon, dispenses with the sophisticated guidance systems and as a consequence has a lower probability of hitting. All ATGMs and known ATRLs use HEAT warheads.

Typical anti-tank guns include the US M-40 recoilless rifle and the Soviet D-44 gun. ATGMs include the US TOW and Dragon, the Soviet AT-3 Sagger, the British Swingfire and the Franco–German Milan and HOT. ATRLs include the US LAW and the Swedish AT-4 Carl Gustav.

Infantry weapons include all portable small arms, such as pistols, rifles and machine guns. Another important infantry weapon is the mortar: a simple smooth-bore or rifled tube, usually mounted on a heavy baseplate and bipod, which is designed to fire high-explosive shells at very high trajectories over relatively short ranges. Mortars may be as small as 51 mm calibre or as large as 240 mm. In the larger calibres mortars effectively become artillery pieces, and some armies treat them as such.

Artillery weapons include the conventional howitzer and gun, as well as so-called gun-howitzer systems, multiple rocket launchers (MRLs) and surface-to-surface missile systems (SSMs). Artillery systems may be either towed or self-propelled (SP).

The primary task of artillery is to provide fire support for the direct-fire arms: armour and infantry. Normally, artillery fires indirectly at the target, that is, the target is not visible to the person who aims the gun. To perform this task with accuracy, the precise location of the firer, the target and the observer directing the fire must be known. Ordinarily, this is done by using survey techniques, determining the location of the various points on a map by reference to a common geographical point. Modern satellite positioning systems have eliminated the need for a fixed geographical referant, greatly simplifying the process.

Conventional systems fire a shell, with either a high trajectory, as in a low-muzzle-velocity howitzer, or with a relatively flat trajectory, as in a high-muzzle-velocity gun. MRLs and SSMs fire rockets. An MRL fires a large number of rockets in a salvo at a single target area. An SSM fires a single, large warhead against a target area. Projectiles and warheads for all artillery systems may be conventional high explosive, improved conventional munitions (ICM), chemical or biological agents, or nuclear.

Typical conventional artillery systems include the US M-109 SP 155 mm howitzer, the Soviet 2S1 SP 122 mm howitzer, the South African G-5 towed SP 155 mm gun-howitzer, the Soviet M-46 towed 130 mm gun and the Italian–German–British FH-70 towed 155 mm gun-howitzer. Typical MRLs include the Soviet BM-21, the US MLRS and the Chinese Type 63. Typical SSMs include the Soviet Scud-B, the US Lance and the French Pluton.

Air defence (AD) systems protect ground forces and installations from air attack. The system may consist of guns, surface-to-air missiles (SAMs), or both. AD guns, also known as air defence artillery (ADA) or anti-aircraft artillery (AAA), are generally found in calibres from about 12.7 mm up to 57 mm. Larger gun systems are still occasionally found (up to 130 mm in calibre), but have generally been replaced by modern SAM systems. Most small-calibre gun systems are relatively short-ranged (typically one to three kilometres) and are deployed to defend specific points. SAM systems fire a missile that may be guided by radar, by infra-red or optically (or a combination of the three). SAM systems can be very long-ranged (slant ranges of up to 40 kilometres are not uncommon) and may thus be deployed to defend large areas. As with artillery and anti-tank systems, AD weapons may be either towed or self-propelled. AD systems can degrade the effectiveness of air attacks, but they cannot by themselves defeat a powerful, co-ordinated air attack.

Typical AD guns include the US M-163 SP 20 mm Vulcan, the Soviet ZSU-23-4 SP 23 mm and ZU-23-2 towed 23 mm, and the German RH-202 towed 20 mm and Gepard SP 35 mm. Typical SAMs include the US Patriot, the Soviet SA-7, and SA-14 portables and the French Crotale.

Aircraft provide support for operations by the direct attack of enemy ground forces, or close air support (CAS), by interdicting communications and supply routes, by attacking the economic and industrial base of the enemy and by opposing enemy aerial operations (counter-air).

Aircraft may be either fixed-wing (aeroplanes) or rotary-wing (helicopters). Aircraft armament may include guns, bombs, rockets and guided missiles. The capabilities of aircraft are defined by the ordnance they are able to carry, as well as by their range, speed, manoeuvrability and the sophistication of their electronics systems.

In general, fixed-wing aircraft can carry heavier loads, and have greater range and speed than rotary-wing aircraft. However, rotary-wing aircraft can operate from more spartan facilities that are closer to the battlefield and, with their slower attack speeds, generally can deliver ordnance with greater accuracy than can fixed-wing aircraft. They can also avoid observation, and seek protection, by hovering below such masks as trees, hills and buildings. As a result, rotary-wing aircraft (attack helicopters) have largely supplanted fixed-wing aircraft in the battlefield CAS role.

Typical fixed-wing aircraft include the German-British-Italian Tornado, the US F-15, the Soviet Mig-23 and the South African Cheetah. Typical rotary-wing aircraft include the US AH-64 Apache, the Soviet Mi-24 Hind and the South African Rooivalk.

Electronic warfare (EW) is a rubric that covers a great number of activities on the modern battlefield. Aspects of EW include:

1   Electronic surveillance measures (ESMs) to track and identify the emission 'signatures' of threat electronic devices. Various ground-, air- and sea-based stations utilise receivers, recorders, signal processors and foreign-language interpreters to monitor threat electronics systems.

Sensors identify the presence of an object, its location, direction and speed of movement, and what it is. Radar and sonar, as well as infra-red detectors and magnetic anomaly detectors (MADs), are examples of devices used as detection sensors. Sensors may be land-, sea- or air-based.

2   Electronic control devices (ECDs) bring automation to the modern battlefield. They process data from many signal sources. The airborne warning and control (AWACs) aircraft, also known as airborne early warning (AEW) aircraft, used by many nations, process data from radar and other sensors and then transmit information to friendly aircraft to give optimum solutions for the interception of enemy aircraft. AWACs also control the traffic flow of friendly aircraft over the battlefield.

3   Electronic counter-measures (ECMs) are used to deceive or disrupt enemy electronic devices. ECMs can be as simple as dropping chaff (strips of radar-reflective foil) to create a false radar return. A more sophisticated ECM operation is jamming — broadcasting on the same frequency as the enemy so as to block the transmission of the enemy's signal. Specialised ECM aircraft such as the US EF-111 Electric Fox and F-4G Wild Weasel are common in modern aerial operations.

4   Electronic counter-counter-measures (ECCMs) are used to defeat enemy ECMs. High-powered signals can 'burn' through jamming. Another technique uses ECDs to shift automatically through different frequencies to defeat jamming. Most ECM aircraft also have an ECCM capability, as do many AWACs aircraft.

5   Electronic deception measures (EDMs) utilise decoy transmitters and false transmissions to decoy enemy electronic systems.

6   Stealth technology makes use of various high-technology materials and devices to defeat enemy sensors. Stealth aircraft are designed with minimal radar cross-section, and infra-red emission dampers to minimise detection of engine heat, and operate under conditions of minimal electronic signal output to prevent detection by enemy ESM systems.